The PreTest/McGra
the house officer and
vade mecums for use a
a concise review of p
clinical findings, outlines the approach to diagnosis and the steps involved in patient management. The text features current bibliographic references dealing with aspects of disease processes, clinical evaluation, and treatment that are beyond the scope of these manuals. Generalists also may find this series helpful in supplying readily accessible, clinically oriented information for use in daily practice.

NOTICE

Medicine is an ever-changing science. As new research and clinical experience broaden our knowledge, changes in treatment and drug therapy are required. The editors and the publisher of this work have made every effort to ensure that the drug dosage schedules herein are accurate and in accord with the standards accepted at the time of publication. Readers are advised, however, to check the product information sheet included in the package of each drug they plan to administer to be certain that changes have not been made in the recommended dose or in the contraindications for administration. This recommendation is of particular importance in regard to new or infrequently used drugs.

MANUAL OF CLINICAL PULMONARY MEDICINE

Lawrence G. Miller, M.D.
Clinical Fellow in Medicine
Massachusetts General Hospital
Boston, Massachusetts

Homayoun Kazemi, M.D.
Professor of Medicine
Harvard Medical School
Chief, Pulmonary Unit
Massachusetts General Hospital
Boston, Massachusetts

McGraw-Hill Book Company
Health Professions Division
PreTest Series

New York   St. Louis   San Francisco
Auckland   Bogotá   Guatemala   Hamburg
Johannesburg   Lisbon   London   Madrid
Mexico   Montreal   New Delhi   Panama
Paris   São Paulo   Singapore   Sydney
Tokyo   Toronto

Library of Congress Cataloging in Publication Data

Miller, Lawrence G.
   Manual of clinical pulmonary medicine.

   (PreTest McGraw-Hill manuals of clinical medicine)
   Bibliography: p.
   Includes index.
   1. Lungs—Diseases—Handbooks, manuals, etc.
I. Kazemi, Homayoun. II. Title. III. Series.
[DNLM: 1. Lung diseases. 2. Lung diseases—Physiopathology. 3. Respiratory tract diseases. WF 600 M648m]
RC756.M55   1982   616.2'4   82-12715

ISBN 0-07-042167-6

Editor: *John H. Gilchrist*
Project Editor: *Sylvia E. Hines*
Editorial Assistant: *Donna Altieri*
Production: *Rosemary J. Pascale, Judith M. Raccio*
Printer: *Hull Printing Company*

Copyright © 1983 by McGraw-Hill, Inc. All rights reserved. Printed in the United States of America. Except as permitted under the Copyright Act of 1976, no part of this publication may be reproduced or distributed in any form or by any means, or stored in a data base or retrieval system, without the prior written permission of the publisher.

1 2 3 4 5 6 7 8 9 HUHU 8 7 6 5 4 3 2

For Phyllis and Katheryne

Contents

	Preface	ix
1	Respiratory Physiology	1
2	Pulmonary Function Tests	33
3	Asthma	43
4	Chronic Airways Obstruction	63
5	Respiratory Failure	89
6	Adult Respiratory Distress Syndrome	111
7	Oxygen Therapy	127
8	Pneumonia	137
9	Pulmonary Disease in the Immunocompromised Patient	165
10	Mycobacterial and Fungal Diseases	185
11	Interstitial Lung Disease	213
12	Lung Neoplasms	247
13	Thromboembolic Disease	273
14	Preoperative Evaluation and Postoperative Management	293
15	Disorders of Respiratory Control	303
16	Pleural Diseases	317
	Abbreviations	339
	Index	345

Preface

Objectives

This book is designed as a brief text of clinical pulmonary medicine, in which we have attempted to achieve a balance of discussion, specific clinical recommendations, and references. What we have not written is a textbook of physiology, a comprehensive text, or a compilation of references; however, we have incorporated aspects of each of these approaches.

Physiology serves as the basis for our discussion. Each chapter includes a brief presentation of pathophysiology and its effects on lung function. We have chosen for discussion topics of greatest clinical interest and applicability, as, due to space limitations, we were unable to include everything. We hope that this book will serve as an introduction to the topics discussed, and to some extent, as a guide to those areas not addressed. Annotated references are provided for those interested in the sources for our discussion, and for those who wish further detail.

As do other areas of medicine, pulmonary medicine rests on both science and empiricism. Some aspects of all of the topics discussed here are controversial or ambiguous. While specific references are too cumbersome for a brief text, we have tried to point out areas of uncertainty or disagreement. Our references include opinions from both sides of most controversies. In general, we have avoided blanket or definitive statements, presenting our view of the current consensus or of the state of available evidence.

Organization

This book is divided into relatively few chapters, given the breadth of pulmonary medicine. Topics are grouped by clinical affinity, which may occasionally separate related topics, such as various causes of pneumonia, but we hope this disadvantage is outweighed by an increase in clinical usefulness.

We have employed an outline format, but overall style is informal. As far as possible, topics of immediate clinical applicability are presented in tables or figures. We hoped to combine ready access with adequate explanation.

References

References include both reviews and primary articles. We have chosen these sources for currency, clarity, and in some cases, as examples of controversial opinion. Annotations are intended as guides to the most useful sources, rather than as summaries of the content of a reference.

Acknowledgments

We would like to acknowledge advice, encouragement, and comments from Drs. Steven Calderwood, Leo Ginns, Charles Hales, Robert Novelline, Ellen Williams, and our colleagues in the Pulmonary Unit, Massachusetts General Hospital. We thank John Gilchrist and Richard Laufer for editorial assistance.

Lawrence G. Miller, M.D.
Homayoun Kazemi, M.D.

1
Respiratory Physiology

The function of the lung in overall homeostasis is to arterialize venous blood; that is, to provide oxygen from the atmosphere and to remove carbon dioxide to the atmosphere. The two processes required to achieve this goal are **ventilation**, which provides the gas "substrate," and **gas exchange**, whereby concentrations of oxygen and carbon dioxide are altered. These processes will be considered individually, followed by discussions of the pulmonary vasculature, lung innervation and neural control, and acid-base equilibrium.

I. VENTILATION AND LUNG MECHANICS

Ventilation is the bulk movement of air to and from alveoli. Air is transported from the atmosphere to the alveoli; after gas exchange, altered air is returned to the atmosphere. Movement of air depends upon a pressure gradient: flow occurs from areas of higher to lower pressure. In inspiration, respiratory muscles generate a negative pressure relative to the atmosphere and thus a gradient **into** the lungs. In expiration, respiratory muscles and lung elastic recoil create a positive pressure relative to the atmosphere and an **outward** gradient. Three factors oppose gas flow in the respiratory system: **elastance**, due to elasticity of the pulmonary parenchyma; **resistance**, due to frictional resistance in the airways; and **inertance**, due to inertia of gas.

Inertia is usually negligible, so that the force required to move air through the lungs depends on elastance and resistance. Forces are usually analyzed in terms of pressure, force per unit area. The pressure necessary to bring air into the lungs is:

$$P_{lung} = P_{el} + P_{res}$$

Elastance, P_{el}, is a static property, changing with volume but not with flow. Conversely, resistance, P_{res}, is dynamic, related to flow and—to a lesser extent—volume. The factors that create and oppose flow will be considered sequentially: respiratory muscles, lung volumes, ventilation, static properties, dynamic properties, and distribution of ventilation.

A. **Respiratory muscles.** Respiratory muscles include the diaphragm, intercostals, and accessory muscles such as scalenes and sternocleidomastoids. In quiet inspiration, diaphragmatic movement accounts for about two-thirds of inspired volume. Contraction of the diaphragm leads to descent of its domes, increasing the vertical dimensions of the thoracic cavity. In addition, the lower ribs rise and move outward, due to the angle of insertion of diaphragmatic fibers. The intercostals also contract with inspiration, leading to expansion of the thoracic cavity. Lower ribs move outward, increasing transverse diameter, while upper ribs move laterally, increasing anteroposterior dimensions. Accessory muscles are primarily used at high levels of ventilation or with inflow obstruction. The scalenes elevate and fix the first and second ribs, while the sternocleidomastoids elevate the sternum.

Quiet expiration is passive, resulting from lung elastic recoil rather than muscular effort. During high levels of ventilation or outflow obstruction, internal intercostals act to depress the ribs. Abdominal muscles compress abdominal contents, pulling down the lower chest wall and depressing the lower ribs, thereby decreasing vertical and anteroposterior dimensions of the thoracic cavity.

B. **Volumes.** Static volumes of the lung are presented in figure 1-1, and a glossary of related terms is found in *table 1-1*. Total lung capacity is defined as the volume of the lungs when maximally expanded. With maximal expiration, some air remains in the lungs. Such an expiration is the vital capacity, and the remaining air is the residual volume. Tidal volume is the volume of each breath at rest, and functional residual capacity is the lung volume at the end (or beginning) of a resting breath. The remaining volumes are derived from the volumes described above.

C. **Ventilation.** Ventilation, the volume of air that enters or leaves the lungs, is often quantified in terms of minute

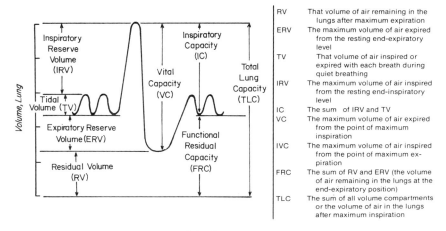

Figure 1-1. Static volumes of the lung.

ventilation, V_E, or the volume of air leaving the lung per minute:

$$V_E = V_T \times f$$

V_T is tidal volume (volume per breath) and f is respiratory rate per minute. Of this volume, a portion remains in the conducting airways and does not participate in gas exchange. Two compartments are therefore defined by gas exchange: dead space, V_D, which does not undergo gas exchange, and alveolar space, V_A, which does undergo gas exchange.

$$V_E = V_D + V_A$$

V_D, dead space, can be defined anatomically as the volume of conducting airways, and physiologically as the volume of the lung that functionally does not participate in gas exchange (including unperfused alveoli, as well as conducting airways). Anatomic dead space is defined pathologically. Physiologic dead space is defined by the Bohr equation:

$$V_D/V_T = (PA_{CO_2} - PE_{CO_2})/PA_{CO_2}$$

where Pa_{CO_2} is often substituted for PA_{CO_2}. This method depends on the fact that essentially all expired CO_2 comes from alveolar gas and none from dead space. The normal value for V_D/V_T is between 0.2 and 0.35.

V_A, alveolar ventilation, is defined above as minute ventilation minus dead space ventilation. Since gas exchange is the source of all expired CO_2, alveolar ventila-

Table 1-1
Glossary for Static Lung Volumes

Volume	Symbol	Definition
Residual volume	RV	That volume of air remaining in the lungs after maximum expiration
Expiratory reserve volume	ERV	The maximum volume of air expired from the resting end-expiratory level
Tidal volume	TV*	That volume of air inspired or expired with each breath during quiet breathing
Inspiratory reserve volume	IRV	The maximum volume of air inspired from the resting end-inspiratory level
Inspiratory capacity	IC	The sum of IRV and TV
Vital capacity	VC	The maximum volume of air expired from the point of maximum inspiration
Inspiratory vital capacity	IVC	The maximum volume of air inspired from the point of maximum expiration
Functional residual capacity	FRC	The sum of RV and ERV (the volume of air remaining in the lungs at the end-expiratory position)
Total lung capacity	TLC	The sum of all volume compartments or the volume of air in the lungs after maximum inspiration

*The symbol TV is traditionally used for tidal volume to indicate a subdivision of static lung volume. The symbol V_T is used in gas-exchange formulae.

tion may also be expressed in terms of a general clearance equation. For CO_2, this becomes:

$$V_A = FE_{CO_2} \times V_E / Pa_{CO_2}, \text{ or}$$
$$V_A = \dot{V}_{CO_2} / Pa_{CO_2} \times K$$

where K is a constant and $\dot{V}_{CO_2}$ is CO_2 production.

D. **Static properties.** The fundamental static property of the respiratory system is elastance, the tendency of a substance to return to its original shape after deformation by an external force. In the respiratory system, elastance can be subdivided into two parts: **lung recoil inward**, and **chest wall recoil** (outward at low volumes, inward at high volumes). In general, clinical discussion of these properties is in terms of compliance, the reciprocal of elastance:

Compliance = Change in volume/Change in pressure

In the lung, the structural basis for compliance is the elastin, and to a lesser extent, collagen, in the lung parenchyma, and the surfactant lining of the alveoli. Compliance is nonlinear. It is greater at mid-lung volumes and decreases at either extreme, as the pressure-volume curve in excised lungs illustrates (see figure 1-2). Compliance is the slope of any point on this curve. The position of the curve along the abscissa is determined by the elastic recoil of the lungs. Less compliant (less distensible) lungs, as in pulmonary fibrosis, might approximate curve B, while more compliant lungs, as in emphysema, better fit curve C.

The pressure-volume curve presented in figure 1-2 is that of one phase of the respiratory cycle. At a given volume, however, pressures vary between inspiration and expiration, as presented in figure 1-3. This phenomenon—the variation of pressures depending on volume history—is called hysteresis. It is classically demonstrated by comparing pressure-volume curves of excised lungs filled with saline and air. With saline, hysteresis is abolished and inspiration approximates expiration as seen in figure 1-3. With air, hysteresis is present due to surface forces at the alveolar-air interface, and also due to recruitment of alveoli closed at low lung volumes.

Thus, two types of forces determine compliance: tissue forces and surface forces. The relative contributions of these forces vary with volume. At low lung volumes, surface forces primarily determine compliance,

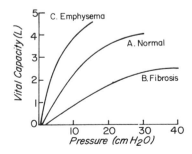

Figure 1-2. Pressure-volume characteristics of the lung.

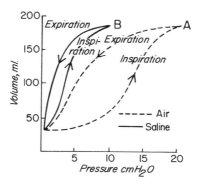

Figure 1-3. Hysteresis in the respiratory cycle.

but at high volumes tissue forces predominate. Particular characteristics of lung surface forces are determined by surfactant, a lecithin-based material lining the alveoli. Surfactant acts to decrease surface tension at low lung volumes, increasing lung compliance and facilitating inspiration from low volumes. Conversely, surfactant increases surface tension at high lung volumes, decreasing compliance and facilitating expiration.

In addition, surfactant promotes alveolar stability. In the absence of surfactant, surface tension is determined by the Laplace relationship: for spherical structures, $P = T/r$, where P = alveolar pressure, T = surface tension, r = alveolar radius. Smaller alveoli would therefore have higher pressures, emptying across a pressure gradient into larger alveoli. Partial lung collapse would result. Surfactant decreases surface tension in small alveoli, offsetting effects of the reduction in radius.

The chest wall also has elastance, although this is directed outward in the opposite direction of the elastic recoil of the lungs. The volume-pressure characteristics of the isolated chest wall are presented in figure 1-4. The chest wall is relaxed, that is, exerts no pressure, at about 60 percent of vital capacity. At volumes less than this value, the chest wall tends to recoil outward, exerting negative pressure on the lungs. At higher volumes, it recoils inward, exerting positive pressure. Summation of the pressures across the lung in figure 1-4 yields the pressure across the entire respiratory system. As figure 1-4 illustrates, pressure is 0 at FRC. The system is relaxed at the end of the normal respiratory cycle.

E. **Resistance.** Resistance is determined by rate of change

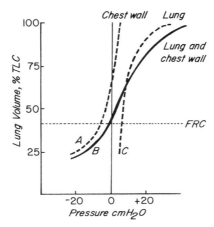

Figure 1-4. Pressure-volume characteristics of lung and chest wall.

of volume, is thus a dynamic property, and is defined as follows:

Resistance = Driving pressure/Flow rate

Two major types of resistance exist in the lung: airways resistance, which comprises about 80 percent of the total, and tissue resistance, which comprises the remaining 20 percent. Resistance equations for the lung, airways, and chest wall are presented in *table 1-2*. All resistance equations must be corrected for elastic recoil of the lung and chest wall.

Airways resistance can be partitioned among the structures of the respiratory tract. During quiet nasal breathing, the nose provides about 50 percent of resistance, increasing markedly at high flow rates. In quiet mouth breathing, the oropharynx and larynx account for about 30 to 40 percent of resistance, again increasing markedly at high flows. Within the tracheobronchial tree, large airways (greater than 2 mm in diameter) account for the bulk of resistance, while smaller airways provide only 10 to 20 percent of resistance.

Chest wall resistance during quiet mouth or nose breathing accounts for 40 and 20 percent of total lung resistance, respectively.

Airways resistance varies according to airway size and to the type of flow through the airways. In a straight cylindrical tube, resistance is proportional to radius to the fourth power. The presence of laminar or turbulent

Table 1-2
Pulmonary Resistance Equations

Lung	Airways	Chest Wall and Abdominal Structures
R_L = (Pao-Ppl)/Flow where Pao is pressure at the airway opening, and Ppl is pleural pressure	R_{AW} = (Pao-Palv)/Flow where Palv is alveolar pressure	R_W = (Ppl-Pbs)/Flow where Pbs is pressure at the body surface

flow also affects resistance. Laminar flow may be imagined as streamlined. Driving pressure (P) is proportional to flow rate ($\dot{V}$), $P = K_1 \dot{V}$. In turbulent flow, driving pressure is proportional to flow rate squared (i.e., $P = K_2 \dot{V}^2$). The Reynolds number, Re, indicates the presence of laminar or turbulent flow. Turbulence may occur at Re greater than 2000, usually in large tubes with high flow rates such as the trachea. True laminar flow probably occurs only in very small airways. Most flow in the tracheobronchial tree is transitional, a combination of laminar and turbulent ($P = K_1 \dot{V} + K_2 \dot{V}^2$).

Airways resistance is also affected by airway morphometry, lung volume, elastic recoil, and airway structure.

1. **Airway morphometry.** Airway branching leads to a marked increase in individual airway size, but a marked increase also in number of airways. Total cross-sectional area therefore increases from proximal to distal. There is a concomitant reduction in resistance.

2. **Lung volume.** As noted above, airways increase in diameter and length with lung inflation. Maximum diameter is achieved at beginning or early inspiration (near FRC), whereas length continues to increase up to TLC. This effect on resistance leads to rapid increases below FRC, but only gradual increases above this level.

3. **Elastic recoil.** In inspiration, flow is effort-dependent; that is, inspiratory flow increases with muscular effort at any volume. In expiration, flow is effort-independent; that is, further muscular effort at certain volumes does not increase expiratory flow. Flow-volume curves illustrate this distinction. Figure 1-5 presents a "family" of flow-volume curves during inspiration and expiration. In inspiration, flow increases with volume (as does respiratory muscle effort), but in expiration, flow is constant below a certain volume. This phenomenon is explained by dynamic compression of the airways. As lung volume decreases, intrathoracic airways narrow, resistance in-increases, and flow decreases.

Dynamic compression can be explained by reference to the equal pressure point (EPP) model. Figure 1-6 shows a schematic model of the lung during expiration. At rest, with no flow, pleural pressure is balanced by elastic recoil pressure, so alveolar

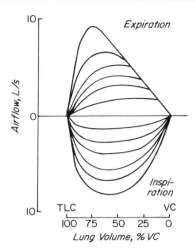

Figure 1-5. Flow-volume relations in the lung.

pressure is 0. During quiet expiration, pleural pressure becomes less negative, alveolar pressure rises, and flow occurs toward the airway opening, with alveolar pressure progressively dissipated by resistance. During forced expiration, pleural pressure becomes positive, concomitantly increasing alveolar pressure. But this pressure is dissipated in the airways, and at some point (the EPP), pleural pressure equals airway pressure, and dynamic compression occurs. Further increases in pleural pressure produce further compression, but do not increase flow.

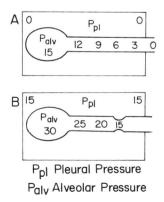

Figure 1-6. Equal pressure point model.

The upstream segment between the alveoli and the EPP determines flow, since driving pressure and resistance determine the position of the EPP. Driving pressure is P_{alv}-P_{pl}, the elastic recoil of the lung. Since the EPP usually lies in the lobar or segmental bronchi, resistance in the upstream segment is that of small airways. In this model, the downstream segment does not affect flow. Although oversimplified here, this model is generally accepted as the means of expiratory flow limitation.

4. Airways structure. Resistance also varies with bronchial wall smooth muscle tone and secretions in the airway lumen.

F. Distribution of ventilation. Regional variations occur in distribution of inspired volume, based on variations in compliance and resistance in the lung.

1. Pleural pressure. The weight of the lung and its mode of support in the thoracic cavity result in a gradient of pleural pressure down the lung of about 0.25 cm H_2O/cm. Thus, pleural pressure is less negative at the base than at the apex. At rest, basal alveoli are subject to less distending pressure and are smaller. During inspiration at lung volumes above FRC, basal areas receive more ventilation than apical areas. That is, for a similar change in pressure, basal areas operate on a steeper part of the volume-pressure curve, since the volume-pressure characteristics of the lung appear similar throughout. (see figure 1-7, part A).

At low lung volumes, between RV and FRC, basal pleural pressure remains less negative than apical pleural pressure. In this circumstance, basal lung units are compressed at rest, and ventilation does not occur until pleural pressure falls below atmospheric. Distribution of ventilation is reversed, with apical regions ventilating more than basal until FRC is reached (see figure 1-7, part B). Distribution of ventilation from apex to base is illustrated in figure 1-11 below.

2. Tracheobronchial asymmetry. Branching in the tracheobronchial tree is variable and asymmetric. Therefore, different quantities of dead space gas precede inspired air into lung units, leading to some variation among units.

3. Regional compliance and resistance. Distribution of inspired volume depends on resistance and compliance of lung units, expressed as their product, RC,

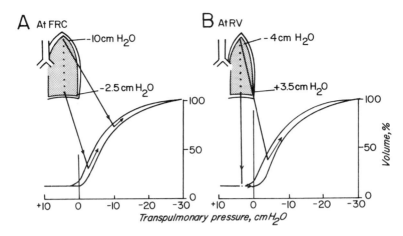

Figure 1-7. Vertical distribution of ventilation.

the time constant. A lung unit with a narrowed airway, for example, will have an abnormal time constant and will be less well ventilated than an adjacent unit with a normal airway (and time constant), whereas in normal persons unequal time constants occur, due to the pleural pressure gradient. Ventilation is minimally affected since a fourfold variation is required to detect asymmetry.

4. **Interdependence.** Contiguous areas of the lung are connected by the fibrous and elastic framework of the parenchyma. Thus, units do not move independently; rather, each influences adjacent units. This mechanism promotes more equal ventilation. A similar phenomenon occurs between lung and chest wall. Under dynamic conditions, pleural pressure may not change uniformly with time, resulting in "lag" between parts of the lung. Chest wall interdependence reduces this lag and promotes uniformity.

5. **Collateral ventilation.** Ventilation may occur between adjacent alveoli (via pores of Kohn) and lobules (via canals of Lambert). Collaterals are important in redistributing ventilation in airways obstruction, although their contribution in normal lungs is uncertain.

II. GAS EXCHANGE

Gas exchange, the primary function of the lung, involves uptake of oxygen from inspired air to blood, and transfer of carbon dioxide from blood to air. Both **ventilation**, providing air, and **perfusion**, providing blood, are necessary for gas exchange. Approximate volumes for ventilation and blood flow in a simple lung model are presented in figure 1-8.

A. **Normal gas exchange.** Normal gas pressures during inspiration are presented in *table 1-3*. Inspired air has an oxygen tension (P_{O_2})—at body temperature and humidity—of about 149 torr, whereas arterial blood P_{O_2} is about 95 torr. Four major steps account for this decrement in P_{O_2} between atmospheric gas and blood. The first three steps are illustrated in figure 1-9.

1. **Ventilation.** Upon inspiration into the lung, air undergoes gas exchange, with oxygen removed and carbon dioxide added. For normal levels of ventilation, blood flow, and tissue metabolism, an equilibrium is reached in the lung. This yields an alveolar P_{O_2} of about 105 torr. Decreased ventilation leads to decreased replacement of fresh gas and a greater decrement in P_{O_2} between atmosphere and alveoli.

Alveolar oxygenation can be assessed by means of the alveolar gas equation:

$$PA_{O_2} = Pi_{O_2} - (PA_{CO_2}/R) + F$$

where Pi_{O_2} is the partial pressure of inspired oxygen and F is a correction factor. R, the respiratory quotient or respiratory exchange ratio, represents the balance between oxygen consumption and carbon dioxide production:

$$R = \dot{V}_{CO_2}/\dot{V}_{O_2}$$

R normally varies between 0.7 and 1.0, depending on metabolic substrate and exertion.

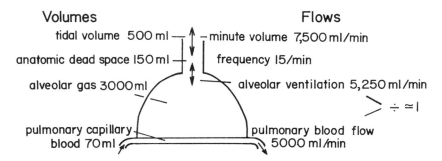

Figure 1-8. Volumes and blood flow in the lung.

Table 1-3
Gas Pressures in the Lung

(all pressures in torr)

Gas Pressure	Ambient Air	Conducting Airways	Terminal Units	Arterial Blood	Mixed Venous Blood
P_{O_2}	156	149	100	95	40
P_{CO_2}	0	0	40	40	46
P_{H_2O}	15	47	47	47	47
P_{N_2}	589	564	573	573	573
P total	760	760	760	755	706

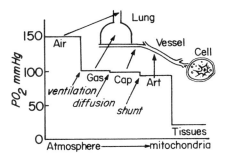

Figure 1-9. Decrements in respiratory oxygen transport.

2. **Diffusion.** Oxygen (and carbon dioxide) must traverse erythrocyte membrane, plasma, capillary endothelium, interstitium, and alveolar epithelium in diffusing between blood and gas. The last three structures are collectively termed the alveolar-capillary membrane. Diffusion is dependent on:
   a. "Patency" of alveolar-capillary membrane
   b. Pressure gradient from gas to blood
   c. Rate of combination of oxygen with hemoglobin
   d. Volume of blood in capillaries

   In normal individuals, these factors allow rapid diffusion between gas and blood, so that oxygen equilibrates in about 0.25 seconds. This represents one-third of the time blood remains in alveolar capillaries. The decrement in Pa_{O_2} caused by diffusion is therefore very small.

   In exercise or in limitation of capillary bed volume by disease, time spent by blood in the alveolar capillaries may decrease to the minimum required for equilibration. Diseases causing thickening of the alveolar-capillary membrane may increase the time required for diffusion. The two processes in conjunction may increase the decrement in Pa_{O_2} caused by diffusion.

3. **Shunt.** In normal individuals, a small proportion of arterial blood does not traverse the pulmonary capillaries and therefore does not undergo gas exchange in the lung. This includes blood from the bronchial circulation and the thebesian veins draining directly from the myocardium. Total shunt is about 2 percent of cardiac output. Admixture of this venous blood with arterialized blood from the lung results in a decrement in arterial P_{O_2} of about 5 torr.

In congenital heart disease, right-to-left shunting may lead to a further decrement. Intrapulmonary shunting may occur in cases of arteriovenous fistulas, or more commonly, in the presence of areas of the lung that are perfused but not ventilated. In this situation, shunting occurs despite passage of blood through the lung, since no gas exchange takes place.

Shunt, Qs/Qt, can be calculated using the Fick principle:

$$Qs/Qt = (Cc - Ca)/(Cc - Cv)$$

where Cc is the end capillary oxygen content, Ca is the arterial oxygen content, and Cv is the mixed venous oxygen content. In practice, end capillary oxygen content is calculated from alveolar P_{O_2}, assuming complete equilibration between gas and blood.

4. **Ventilation/perfusion (V/Q) inequality.** Gas exchange in a lung unit is determined by quantity of blood flow and ventilation. Different areas of the lung receive different proportions of blood flow and ventilation. If these are not exactly matched, some units may receive proportionately greater ventilation or perfusion, leading to inefficient gas exchange. Overall gas exchange represents the sum of all lung units. In normal persons, V/Q inequalities result in a decrement in arterial P_{O_2} of less than 5 torr.

V/Q inequalities in normal persons have their origin in gradients of perfusion and ventilation in the lung. The weight of the lung and its suspension in the thorax lead to gradients in perfusing pressure and blood flow from apex to base. Blood flow increases rapidly down the lung. West has divided the lung into three zones to illustrate the effects of this gradient (see figure 1-10). In the upper zone, alveolar pressure exceeds mean arterial pressure, hence the apex at rest is poorly perfused. Flow is independent of pulmonary venous pressure. The middle zone behaves as a Starling resistor, with dynamic compression of capillaries and venules by alveolar pressure. Flow therefore depends on the arterial-alveolar pressure difference and remains independent of venous pressure. In zone 2, arterial pressure, and therefore flow, increases. In zone 3, venous pressure exceeds alveolar pressure. Flow is then determined by arterial-venous pressure difference and is independent of alveolar pressure. At low lung volumes, large vessels

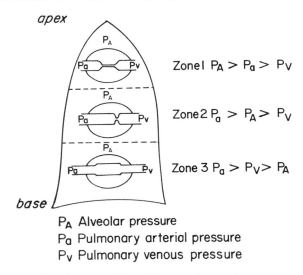

Figure 1-10. Distribution of blood flow in the lung.

in basal areas of zone 3 may be collapsed due to the weight of the lung, so that perfusion in this area may be limited below FRC.

Ventilation also decreases from base to apex, but at a much slower rate. Gravity is again responsible, as the weight of the lung results in a less negative pleural pressure at the base than at the apex. As previously noted, different areas of the lung therefore operate on different parts of the pressure-volume curve. This leads to a decrease in ventilation up the lung from FRC to TLC. At lower lung volumes, from RV to FRC, the gradient may be reversed. Distribution of ventilation and perfusion are presented in figure 1-11. V/Q ratios increase from base to apex. At the base, V/Q is about 0.6, increasing to 3.0 or greater at the apex. Overall V/Q is determined by blood flow and ventilation, which are 6 L/min and 5.1 L/min, respectively. Overall V/Q is thus about 0.85.

In disease, both ventilation and perfusion may be altered. If these are changed proportionately in the same region, V/Q will undergo little change. If changes in ventilation and perfusion are unequal for various lung units, a further decrement in P_{O_2} results. Physiologic mechanisms acting to limit the effects of V/Q inequalities include **hypoxic constriction**

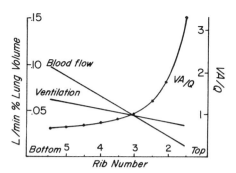

Figure 1-11. Ventilation and perfusion distribution.

of pulmonary vessels, a local response occurring when alveolar P_{O_2} is less than 50, and increases in airways resistance if perfusion is obstructed (a less vigorous response).

Measurement of V/Q inequalities is difficult. Arterial P_{O_2} may reflect other causes of hypoxemia, especially change in ventilation. A better index is the alveolar-arterial oxygen difference, $A\text{-}aD_{O_2}$. This is calculated using the alveolar gas equation and assuming similarity of alveolar and arterial P_{CO_2}. This index takes ventilation into account, but not shunt or diffusion limitation. The significance of $A\text{-}aD_{O_2}$ may vary depending upon the position on the oxygen-hemoglobin dissociation curve. An $A\text{-}aD_{O_2}$ of the same magnitude indicates greater compromise of lung function lower on the dissociation curve. Of other measurements, shunt calculation does not distinguish between shunt and V/Q contributions. Physiologic dead space indicates areas of very high V/Q, but includes conducting airways. Research techniques employ multiple inert gases to measure V/Q inequalities.

B. **Effects of increased oxygen concentration.** Breathing increased oxygen concentrations leads to partial resolution of several causes of hypoxemia. Hypoxemia due to hypoventilation is corrected by increasing alveolar oxygen concentration. Diffusion impairment, if present, is corrected by increasing the gradient across the alveolar-capillary membrane. Equilibration thus becomes more rapid. Shunt, however, is not affected by oxygen concentration, since shunted blood is not exposed to alveolar gas.

Effects of inspired oxygen concentration on V/Q inequalities are variable. Moderate concentrations may partially ameliorate V/Q inequalities by increasing oxygen exchange in alveolar units with low V/Q. Units with physiologic V/Q may increase oxygen exchange somewhat, but this is limited by oxygen-hemoglobin dissociation characteristics (see Chapter 7, figure 7-1). Hemoglobin is 95 percent saturated at 90 torr and 100 percent saturated at 150 torr, so that little additional oxygen can be added with increased alveolar P_{O_2}. If 100 percent oxygen (FI_{O_2} 1.0 atmospheres) is administered for a sufficient amount of time, oxygen will replace nitrogen in all ventilated units and V/Q inequalities will be virtually abolished.

Therefore, breathing 100 percent oxygen corrects all causes of hypoxemia except shunt, so $(A-aD_{O_2})$ 1.0 is often used as an index of shunting. Normal $(A-aD_{O_2})$ 1.0 is 30 to 50 torr, representing about 2 to 3 percent of cardiac output. Effects of various causes of hypoxemia on Pa_{O_2}, $A-aD_{O_2}$, and $(A-aD_{O_2})$ 1.0 are summarized in *table 1-4*.

Normal arterial P_{O_2} is about 100 torr, decreasing with age. It can be predicted from the formulas:

Seated Pa_{O_2} = 104.2 − 0.27 x age in years
Supine Pa_{O_2} = 103.5 − 0.42 x age in years

Normal $A-aD_{O_2}$ is about 5 to 8 torr, and can be predicted from the formula:

$A-aD_{O_2}$ = 2.5 + 0.21 x age in years

C. **Carbon dioxide exchange.** The model of gas exchange developed for oxygen also applies to carbon dioxide.

Table 1-4
Hypoxemia and the Alveolar-Arterial Oxygen Difference

Cause	PaO_2	$A-aDO_2$	$(A-aDO_2)$ 1.0
Hypoventilation	↓	No change	Resolved
Diffusion limitation	No change or ↓	No change or ↑	Resolved
Shunt	↓	↑	Persistent
V/Q inequalities	↓	↑	Resolved

Carbon dioxide is generated in tissues and removed by gas exchange in the lung. Mechanisms contributing to the difference between atmospheric and arterial oxygen may also lead to decrements in exchanging carbon dioxide, or hypercapnia.

1. **Hypoventilation.** The major cause of hypercapnia is insufficient ventilation. The inverse relation between ventilation and alveolar P_{CO_2} is illustrated in the alveolar ventilation equation:

$$Pa_{CO_2} = P_{CO_2}/V \times K$$

   where K is a constant. Since arterial P_{CO_2} is directly related to alveolar P_{CO_2}, hypercapnia results from hypoventilation. Hypoxemia can be ameliorated by increasing FI_{O_2} without a change in ventilation. In contrast, hypercapnia will not resolve without an increase in ventilation.

2. **Diffusion limitation.** Carbon dioxide probably is exchanged in about the same amount of time as oxygen. The effect of diffusion limitation on P_{CO_2} is uncertain, but apparently small.

3. **Shunt.** This rarely leads to hypercapnia, although in theory, blood not exposed to alveolar gas causes an elevation in arterial P_{CO_2}. Compensatory mechanisms usually increase ventilation in this situation, leading to normalization of arterial P_{CO_2}.

4. **V/Q inequalities.** This situation may lead to hypercapnia if ventilation cannot be appropriately increased. Lung units with low V/Q may have incomplete carbon dioxide exchange, leading to hypercapnia. Central chemoreceptor mechanisms act to increase ventilation, returning arterial P_{CO_2} to normal. Increased ventilation acts by two mechanisms. First, it may improve exchange in units with low V/Q. Second, units with physiologic V/Q are able to increase exchange, compensating for poorly ventilated units. The latter mechanism is not completely effective with oxygen, owing to oxygen-hemoglobin dissociation characteristics. However, carbon dioxide exchange is nearly linear in the physiologic range, so that increasing ventilation results in increased carbon dioxide removal. In certain patients with severe V/Q abnormalities, ventilation does not increase sufficiently and chronic hypercapnia develops.

Normal arterial P_{CO_2} is 37 to 43 torr, unaffected by age.

D. **Carbon dioxide transport.** Transport of oxygen is discussed in Chapter 7. Carbon dioxide is carried in the blood in several forms. About 5 percent is dissolved in blood, whereas most of the remainder enters erythrocytes and undergoes one of two reactions:

1. About 80 percent combines with water, catalyzed by carbonic anhydrase, to yield:

$$CO_2 + H_2O = H_2CO_3 = H^+ + HCO_3^-$$

2. About 10 percent combines with hemoglobin to form carbamino- compounds.

The relation between blood carbon dioxide content and carbon dioxide tension is different from that for oxygen. The carbon dioxide saturation curve is presented in figure 1-12. The two curves shown in figure 1-12 illustrate the Haldane effect. Oxygenated blood at any P_{CO_2} has less carbon dioxide content than reduced blood. This occurs since reduced hemoglobin is a weaker acid than oxyhemoglobin, so that more hydrogen ion can be bound and more bicarbonate ion formed. Also, deoxyhemoglobin binds more carbon dioxide in carbamino-compounds than does oxyhemoglobin. The Haldane effect promotes CO_2 loading in tissues, where hemoglobin is deoxygenated, and promotes CO_2 release in the lungs, where oxyhemoglobin predominates.

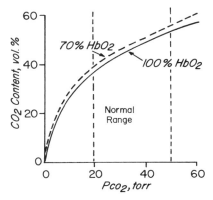

Figure 1-12. Carbon dioxide dissociation curve.

III. VASCULATURE

Gas exchange depends on a continuous blood supply to pulmonary capillaries. The pulmonary circulation provides this blood supply, and serves several nonrespiratory functions as well.

A. Nonrespiratory functions of the pulmonary circulation
 1. Supplying of substrate for alveolar lining cells
 2. Participation in cellular and humoral immune mechanisms
 3. Filtering of particulate matter in venous blood
 4. Release, removal, and biotransformation of substances in blood
 5. Water and protein exchange
 6. Fibrinolysis, and participation in anticoagulation

The pulmonary circulation receives virtually the entire cardiac output, with the exception of the small amount shunted through the bronchial vessels and thebesian veins. It is a low pressure system. Pressures at various sites are presented in *table 1-5.*

B. **Dynamic properties.** Resistance in the pulmonary vasculature appears more symmetrically distributed than in

Table 1-5
Hemodynamics of the Pulmonary Circulation

Measurement	Value
Blood flow, L/min	6.0
Blood flow, L/min/m^2	3.1
Blood pressures, torr (systolic/diastolic; mean)	
Right atrium	3/2; 2
Right ventricle	22/0
Pulmonary artery	22/9; 15
Pulmonary wedge	8
Left atrium	8/3; 5
Vascular resistance	
torr/ml/sec	0.1
(dyn sec)/cm^5	132.8

the systemic vessels, where resistance is primarily located in arterioles. Pressure drop appears similar before and after the capillary bed, and in the dog, 35 to 50 percent of total pulmonary resistance appears to lie in the capillary bed itself. Pulmonary vascular resistance is calculated as:

$$R = (Ppa - Pla)/Q$$

where Ppa is mean pulmonary artery pressure, Pla is mean left atrial pressure, and Q is blood flow through the lungs. However, resistance is not always proportional to pressure or inversely proportional to flow. A distinctive characteristic of the pulmonary vasculature is its response to changes in volume and pressure. In normal persons, the pulmonary vessels hold about 10 percent of circulating blood volume, or 290 ml/m^2. Increase in blood flow or pulmonary arterial pressure leads to a decrease in pulmonary vascular resistance. At low pressures, this appears to be due to recruitment. At rest, only about 25 percent of pulmonary capillaries are perfused, but as pressure rises, unperfused vessels begin to conduct blood. At high pressures, pulmonary capillaries appear to dilate, further decreasing vascular resistance.

Pulmonary vascular resistance is also affected by lung volumes and alveolar gas concentrations. Small vessels (less than 30 μ) are exposed to alveolar pressures and are compressed at low lung volumes. At high lung volumes, thin walls of these vessels are stretched, decreasing caliber and increasing resistance. Larger vessels (greater than 100 μ) are subject to pleural pressures, so that their resistance decreases as lung volumes increase. The net effect is to minimize resistance around FRC, with increasing resistance above and below this value. Alveolar gas concentrations exert local effects on resistance. Alveolar hypoxia increases local vascular resistance, and alveolar hypercapnia increases local resistance in animals. Acidemia produces a generalized, but less significant, increase in resistance.

Pulmonary muscular arteries are richly innervated, and therefore subject to central and peripheral nervous control. Neurologic, humoral, and hemodynamic effects on pulmonary vessels are summarized in *table 1-6*.

Flow in the pulmonary circulation is high, and is calculated by application of the Fick principle:

$$Q = V_{O_2}/(Ca_{O_2} - Cv_{O_2})$$

Table 1-6
Pulmonary Vascular Responses

Factor	Resistance
Hemodynamic	
Increased: Pulmonary artery pressure	Decreased
Left atrial pressure	Decreased
Pulmonary blood volume	Decreased
Whole blood viscosity	Increased
Pulmonary	
Lung volume (change from FRC)	Increased
Increased pulmonary interstitial pressure	Increased
Neural	
Sympathetic	Increased in animals
Parasympathetic	No change
Humoral	
Catecholamines, histamine, angiotensin, PGF	Increased
Acetylcholine, bradykinin, PGE	Decreased
Chemical	
Alveolar hypoxia	Increased
Alveolar hypercarbia	Increased
Acidemia	Increased

where V_{O_2} is oxygen consumption, Ca_{O_2} is arterial oxygen content, and Cv_{O_2} is mixed venous oxygen content. As previously discussed, flow increases from apex to base of the lung.

The bronchial circulation is arranged in parallel with the pulmonary vasculature, with many precapillary anastomoses between the two. Bronchial vessels are especially well innervated, and are notably sensitive to histamines and bradykinin. Beyond helping to supply substrate for airway metabolism, bronchial vessels may also help to humidify inspired air.

C. **Fluid and solute exchange.** As in any other vascular bed, liquid and solute movement is continuous in the lung. Liquids and small solutes leak through vascular endothelia. Since the alveolar epithelium is less permeable than capillary endothelium, fluid remains in the interstitial space, where it is drained by an extensive lymphatic network. Net fluid movement is determined by the balance of hydrostatic and oncotic pressures, as expressed in the Starling equation:

$$Qt = Kf\,([Pcap-Pis] - theta\,[PIpl-PIis])$$

where Pcap and Pis are capillary and interstitial hydrostatic pressures, respectively, and PIpl and PIis are plasma and interstitial oncotic pressures, respectively. Hydrostatic forces in pulmonary capillaries are about 10 torr, whereas oncotic pressure is about 25 torr. However, the interstitium also exerts oncotic pressure of about 19 torr, so that net fluid movement occurs from the pulmonary capillaries into interstitial spaces, and thence into lymphatics.

IV. INNERVATION AND NEURAL CONTROL

A. Lung and chest wall receptors. The major structures of the respiratory apparatus—the airways, lung parenchyma, chest wall, and vasculature—are innervated and interact with central and peripheral receptors. Innervation of the vasculature is discussed above. Three other types of receptors are associated with the lung: stretch, irritant, and "juxtacapillary." Stretch receptors are located in the smooth muscle of the trachea and larger airways. They are stimulated by deformation of the airway, with resulting changes in transmural airway pressure. Stimulation of stretch receptors increases expiratory duration, perhaps strengthens expiratory effort, and may lead to airway dilatation. Stretch receptors appear to be responsible for the apnea that occurs in animals with lung inflation—the Hering-Breuer reflex. These receptors adapt slowly, and afferent impulses are conducted through the vagus nerve.

Irritant receptors are found in airway epithelial lining, and are stimulated by rapid lung inflation or direct contact with a variety of substances, such as chemicals (ammonia, histamine), or irritant aerosols. Excitation in large airways leads to cough, and excitation in small airways produces tachypnea. Bronchoconstriction may occur throughout the airways. Adaptation of these receptors is rapid.

"Juxtacapillary" or "J" receptors are located in the pulmonary interstitium. They appear to cause tachypnea when stimulated by interstitial congestion. Characteristics of lung receptors are summarized in *table 1-7*.

The thoracic wall contains muscle spindles that respond to changes in muscle length. Their function is to

Table 1-7
Lung Neural Receptors

Receptor	Location	Stimuli	Responses
Pulmonary stretch	Smooth muscle of intrapulmonary airways	1. Lung inflation 2. Increased transpulmonary pressure	1. Bronchodilation 2. Hering-Breuer inflation (inhibition of breathing) 3. Increased heart rate 4. Decreased peripheral vascular resistance
Irritant	Epithelium of extrapulmonary airways (some intrapulmonary)	1. Irritants: NO_2, smoke 2. Mechanical 3. Anaphylaxis (histamine) 4. Pneumothorax 5. Hyperpnea 6. Pulmonary congestion	1. Bronchoconstriction 2. Hyperpnea 3. Laryngeal constriction 4. Cough
"J" receptor	Alveolar wall (juxtacapillary)	1. Interstitial congestion 2. Chemical injury 3. Microembolism	1. Rapid shallow breathing 2. Laryngeal constriction 3. Hypotension, bradycardia 4. Spinal reflex inhibition

Modified with permission of WB Saunders from *The Normal Lung* (p 68), by Murray JF, © 1976.

prevent overinflation and to coordinate muscle contraction.
B. **Respiratory control.** Respiration is regulated by both central and peripheral stimuli. The major regulatory center lies in the medulla, although its exact location is uncertain. Medullary center activity fluctuates with pH in the extracellular fluid, which at steady-state is similar to that of cerebrospinal fluid (CSF). In nonequilibrium conditions, extracellular fluid pH varies with arterial and CSF pH. Extracellular fluid pH is primarily influenced by the balance between P_{CO_2} and HCO_3^-. The blood-brain barrier is permeable to CO_2, but less so to ions such as H+ and HCO_3^-. Levels of both are related to cerebral blood flow, and some evidence suggests the existence of active transport of HCO_3^-.

Peripheral receptors influencing ventilation are located in the carotid bifurcation and the thoracic aorta. The carotid bodies respond to changes in arterial P_{O_2}, rather than P_{CO_2}, and to a lesser extent to variations in pH.

Increase in Pa_{CO_2} leads to a corresponding increase in ventilation, which is approximately linear. Above a certain level of Pa_{CO_2}, which varies in disease states, central nervous system depression occurs, and ventilation reaches a plateau. Hypocapnia in anesthetized humans produces apnea, but in conscious hyperventilating humans, ventilation continues. The effects of Pa_{CO_2} may be modulated by metabolic acidosis and alkalosis. In general, acidosis potentiates and alkalosis depresses ventilatory response to increased Pa_{CO_2}.

Decrease in Pa_{O_2} leads to increased ventilation, but the response is hyperbolic rather than linear. Ventilatory efforts are greater at low Pa_{O_2}. At very low Pa_{O_2} (less than 25 torr), central nervous system depression due to hypoxia may be counteracted by increased sensitivity to Pa_{CO_2}. Conversely, hypercapnia increases ventilatory response to hypoxia.

V. **ACID-BASE EQUILIBRIUM**

A. **Normal homeostasis.** Beyond its respiratory function, the lung plays a major role in maintaining acid-base equilibrium. Conversely, lung function is regulated by acid-base status, as noted above. Acid-base chemistry will be reviewed only briefly here. Acids are defined as hydrogen ion (H^+) donors, and bases, as H^+ acceptors. In conventional use, pH is substituted for H^+ concentration, and pH is related to acid-base dissociation by the Henderson-Hasselbalch equation:

$$pH = pK + \log(\text{base/acid})$$

where pK is the dissociation constant of the acid. For carbon dioxide, this equation becomes:

$$pH = 6.1 + \log(HCO_3^-)/(Pa_{CO_2} \times 0.03)$$

Carbon dioxide produced by cellular respiration combines with water to form carbonic acid, H_2CO_3, the primary volatile acid in the body. About 24×10^4 mEq/day of this acid are removed as CO_2 by the lungs. Fixed acids, such as lactate, sulfate, and phosphate are also produced by cells, and about 50 mEq/day of these acids and carbonic acid hydrogen ion are removed by the kidney.

B. **Alterations in equilbrium.** Derangements of acid-base metabolism are considered as processes—acidosis and alkalosis. These do not necessarily coincide with the pH status of the blood, referred to as acidemia and alkalemia. Metabolic alkalosis, for example, may coexist with respiratory acidosis, and the systemic pH may reflect overall acidemia. Normal blood pH is 7.38 to 7.44.

When acid-base equilibrium is altered, three regulatory mechanisms come into play:

1. **Buffers.** In order of importance, these are HCO_3^-, intracellular proteins, hemoglobin, plasma proteins, and bone constituents. These act immediately to limit changes in pH.
2. **Lungs.** CO_2 is excreted, driving carbonic acid reaction away from acid production. Effects on pH occur in minutes.
3. **Kidneys.** These organs excrete or reabsorb HCO_3^- or H^+. Effects on pH require hours to days.

Acid-base alterations are often divided into respiratory and nonrespiratory (metabolic), categories according to cause. A summary of these causes, and their effects on pH, Pa_{CO_2}, and HCO_3^-, is presented in *table 1-8*. The calculations presented are approximations, but may be useful in differentiating disorders and indicating chronicity or the presence of mixed disturbances. Graphic presentation of acid-base relations often simplifies analysis. Several types of diagrams relate the three common variables. An example of an HCO_3^--pH diagram is presented in figure 1-13.

Table 1-8
Alterations in Acid-Base Equilibrium

Process	Causes	pH	P_{CO_2}	HCO_3^-
Respiratory acidosis				
Acute	Hypoventilation	↓ $\Delta Pa_{CO_2} \times .007$	↑	↑ (slight) $\Delta Pa_{CO_2} \times 0.1$
Chronic	Decreased ventilatory drive Neuromuscular disease Asthma Emphysema	↓ $\Delta Pa_{CO_2} \times .003$	↑	↑ $\Delta Pa_{CO_2} \times 0.4$
Respiratory alkalosis				
Acute	Exercise Stimulants Hypoxemia Metabolic acidosis Restrictive disease	↑	↓	↓ (moderate) $\Delta Pa_{CO_2} \times 0.2$
Chronic	High altitudes	Little change	↓	↓ $\Delta Pa_{CO_2} \times 0.5$
Metabolic acidosis	Acid intake Bicarbonate loss (GI, renal) Endogenous production	↓	↓ $(1.5 \times HCO_3^- + 8)$	↓
Metabolic alkalosis	Acid loss (GI, renal) Bicarbonate intake	↑	Variable	Variable

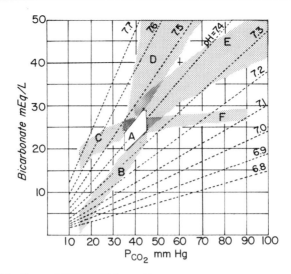

Figure 1-13. P_{CO_2}-HCO_3 acid-base diagram.

Concepts such as "standard bicarbonate" or "base excess" are sometimes used to estimate renal compensation in mixed disorders. These concepts, and the correction formulas cited above are, at best, approximations. Deficiencies are due to the fact that bicarbonate levels must be calculated using an assumed value for pK in the Henderson-Hasselbalch equation (since standard arterial blood gas measurements include P_{CO_2} and pH). Also, base deficit curves utilize an in vitro, and hence potentially inaccurate, dissociation curve. In replacing bicarbonate in clinical situations, these measures are further flawed. Calculations require knowledge of the "compartment" in which bicarbonate is distributed, an uncertain value. Also, evidence in animal studies suggests that the amount of bicarbonate needed to correct a metabolic acidosis depends on the rapidity of its infusion.

Approach to acid-base disorders should follow a pattern such as the one suggested below:
    a. Evaluate overall systemic pH.
    b. Identify primary acid-base disturbance using diagram or Henderson-Hasselbalch equation.
    c. Categorize primary disturbance as acute or chronic.
    d. Identify presence and type of compensation, using diagram or approximations suggested above.
    e. Identify secondary acid-base disturbance resulting in a mixed pattern.

f. Titrate changes in therapy using repeated measurements. Calculated values may be in error.

REFERENCES

I. General

Bates DV, Macklem PT, Christie RV: *Respiratory Function in Disease*, 2nd ed. Philadelphia, WB Saunders, 1971.

Comroe JH: *Physiology of Respiration*, 2nd ed. Chicago, Year Book Medical, 1974.

Cotes JE: *Lung Function*, 4th ed. New York, Oxford University Press, 1979.

Murray JF: *The Normal Lung: The Basis for Diagnosis and Treatment of Pulmonary Disease.* Philadelphia, WB Saunders, 1976.

Saunders KB: *Clinical Physiology of the Lung.* New York, Oxford University Press, 1977.

Tisi GM: *Pulmonary Physiology in Clinical Medicine.* Baltimore, Williams & Wilkins, 1980.

West JB: *Respiratory Physiology*, 2nd ed. Baltimore, Williams & Wilkins, 1979.

Bates and Comroe are older references than the others listed but remain excellent texts. Bates is more detailed than Comroe, with an emphasis on pulmonary function testing and disease states. Cotes is a detailed text with consideration of pulmonary function tests. The last four are introductory and much briefer. West is unparalleled as a brief, readable introduction. Murray is also easily accessible, with more detail. Tisi is more clinically oriented, but the sections on physiology are lucid and succinct. Saunders offers a more idiosyncratic but often useful approach, with an emphasis on systems analysis.

II. Mechanics

Altose MD: Pulmonary mechanics. In *Pulmonary Diseases and Disorders*. Edited by Fishman AP, New York, McGraw-Hill, 1980, pp 359-372.

Derenne JP, Macklem PT, Roussos C: The respiratory muscles: mechanics, control, and pathophysiology. *Am Rev Respir Dis* 118:119-123, 373-390, 1978.

Hoppin FG, Hildebrandt J: Mechanical properties of the lung. In *Bioengineering Aspects of the Lung*. Edited by West JB, New York, Dekker, 1977, pp 83-162.

Mead J, Turner JM, Macklem PT, et al: Significance of the relationship between lung recoil and maximum expiratory flow. *J Appl Physiol* 22:951-958, 1967.

Rodarte JR, Hyatt RE: Respiratory mechanics. *Basics of RD* 4:1-6, 1976.

Altose, Hoppin, and Rodarte are good introductions to current ideas in pulmonary mechanics. Mead presents an excellent exposition of the equal pressure point concept. Derenne et al. present an exhaustive summary of recent knowledge about respiratory musculature.

III. Gas exchange

Wagner PD, West JB: Changes in ventilation-perfusion relationships and gas exchange. In *The Lung in Transition Between Health and Disease.* Edited by Macklem PT, Permutt S, New York, Dekker, 1979, pp 183-226.

West JB, Wagner PD: Pulmonary gas exchange. In *Bioengineering Aspects of the Lung.* Edited by West JB, New York, Dekker, 1977, pp 361-458.

West JB: *Ventilation/Blood Flow and Gas Exchange,* 3rd ed. New York, Oxford University Press, 1977.

The West book is already a classic, notable for clarity and brevity. The other two chapters provide a brief review of the same material with some applications to disease.

IV. Vasculature

Conference on the pulmonary circulation: *Chest* 71:244-315, 1977.

Fishman AP: Regulation of the pulmonary circulation. In *Pulmonary Diseases and Disorders.* Edited by Fishman AP, New York, McGraw-Hill, 1980, pp 397-409.

Fishman AP, Renkin EM: *Pulmonary Edema.* Baltimore, Williams & Wilkins, 1979.

Fishman's chapter provides a good, brief summary. The book on pulmonary edema and the collection in *Chest* address more detailed aspects of the pulmonary circulation, with discussion of research methods.

V. Innervation and Neural Control

Cherniack NS, von Euler C: Central neural and reflex control of breathing. In *Pulmonary Diseases and Disorders.* Edited by Fishman AP, New York, McGraw-Hill, 1980, pp 275-281.

Mitchell RA, Berger AJ: Neural regulation of breathing. *Am Rev Respir Dis* 111:206-224, 1975.

Richardson JB: Nerve supply to the lungs. *Am Rev Respir Dis* 119:785-802, 1979.

Cherniack and Mitchell provide good brief discussions of the innervation of the lung and control of breathing. Richardson considers innervation in detail in animals and, to a lesser extent, in humans.

VI. Acid-Base Equilibrium

Davenport HW: *The ABC of Acid-Base Chemistry,* 6th ed. Chicago, University of Chicago Press, 1974.

Heinemann HO: The kidney and acid-base disorders in obstructive disease of the airways. In *Pulmonary Diseases and Disorders.* Edited by Fishman AP, New York, McGraw-Hill, 1980, pp 549-561.

Davenport is a brief classic, describing acid-base physiology as well as chemistry. Heinemann briefly considers general acid-base relations, and then presents a superb discussion of acid-base problems in chronic airways obstruction.

2
Pulmonary Function Tests

A variety of pulmonary function tests is available, many of which are performed as part of a battery of tests. As with any diagnostic procedure, a knowledge of technique, limitations, indications, and spectrum of results allows more discriminating and effective use of the data. Alterations in pulmonary function tests in specific diseases are discussed in subsequent chapters, and several types of tests are addressed in detail in other chapters, including tests of control of respiration and respiratory muscle function in Chapter 15, and tests that analyze individual lung function in Chapter 13.

I. VOLUMES

Subdivisions of lung volumes are presented in figure 1-1, and terms are defined in *table 1-1*. The technique commonly used for ascertaining volume is to measure FRC by helium dilution or plethysmography, and then to measure ERV, IC, and VC by spirometry. Other volumes are calculated. Helium dilution and plethysmographic volume determinations are presented in figure 2-1.

A. **Helium dilution.** In the helium dilution method, the patient breathes a known concentration of helium from a spirometer in a closed system. Carbon dioxide is held constant by absorption, and oxygen is maintained constant by adding an amount equal to the volume taken up by the subject. Content of all major gases in the system remains constant, since helium and nitrogen are not absorbed, oxygen is maintained, and carbon dioxide is eliminated. FRC may be calculated using initial and

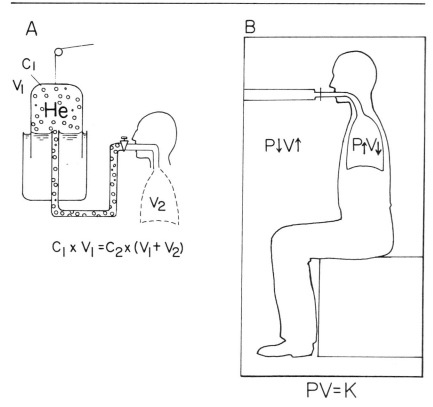

Figure 2-1. Helium dilution and plethysmographic volume determinations.

final helium concentrations, and total system volume (including spirometer and patient lung volume at FRC).

$$C_1 \times V_1 = C_2 \times (V_1 + V_2)$$

where C_1 and C_2 are initial and final helium concentrations, respectively, and V_1 is initial volume (spirometer volume) and V_2 is lung volume at FRC. Accuracy of this technique depends upon adequate equilibration. If helium is not distributed to poorly ventilated areas, underestimation of volume may result.

B. **Plethysmography.** Plethysmography is based on Boyle's law, which states that pressure times volume is constant in a system if the temperature remains constant. Both pressure-sensitive and volume-sensitive plethysmographs are available. To measure FRC by pressure plethysmography, the patient breathes quietly through a mouthpiece. At end expiration, a shutter is closed and the patient pants gently. Inspiratory and expiratory maneuvers cause oscillation in mouth and box pressures. By Boyle's law,

$$P_1 V = P_2 (V + \Delta V)$$

where P_1 and P_2 are mouth pressures before and after panting, V is volume at FRC, and ΔV is change in volume with panting. Since P_1, P_2, and ΔV are measured, V may be calculated. This method measures total volume of gas in the lung, including gas not communicating with airways. Unlike helium dilution, it is independent of distribution of ventilation.

Other volumes—IC, VC, and ERV—are measured by spirometry. The subject expires into a chamber, and chamber displacement is recorded. A pneumotachograph, which is a flow-sensing device, may be substituted for the volume chamber. Maneuvers are best performed slowly, to prevent airway collapse due to high pleural pressures.

II. FLOWS AND MECHANICS

A. Spirometry. Dynamic measurements, adding time as a variable, usually are achieved by spirometry or flow-volume curves. Spirometric flows are based on forced expiration from TLC. Forced vital capacity (FVC) is measured and divided into components such as FEV_1 (forced expiratory volume in 1 second). The forced mid-expiratory flow rate (FEF25-75%) is obtained from a line connecting points corresponding to 75 percent and 25 percent of the vital capacity. FVC is equal to slow vital capacity in normal individuals. In the presence of airways obstruction or air trapping, FVC may be reduced cause higher pleural pressures prevent complete emptying. Other spirometric measurements include peak expiratory flow rate (PEFR) and the ratio, FEV_1/FVC. To some extent, FEV_1/FVC allows correction for alterations in lung volumes. For example, decreased volumes lead to decreased flows, but in the absence of obstruction the ratio will be preserved.

B. Maximal expiratory flow-volume (MEFV) curves. The maximal expiratory flow-volume curve is obtained by plotting expiratory flow rates against expired lung volume during a forced vital capacity maneuver. By adding indicators of time, information similar to the results of spirometry is obtained. In addition, MEFV curves allow rapid visualization of reduction in expiratory flow at any volume. When this curve is superimposed on a curve obtained during quiet breathing, a visual impression of the total flow available to the subject is obtained. For example, subjects with marked flow limitation may have resting tidal volumes similar to maximal expiratory flows. MEFV curves also are useful in evaluating obstruction in small airways. Flow at low lung volumes depends upon small airways patency. Abnormalities in small airways function can be recognized by reduction in flow at 25 percent vital capacity ($V_{max}25\%$). Inspiratory components of MEFV curves may identify lesions of major airways, including trachea and larynx. Upper airway obstruction produces characteristic abnormalities in expiratory and inspiratory curves. Examples are presented in figure 2-2.

C. Patterns in disease. Whereas forced expiratory flow measurements are most often used to diagnose and follow obstructive disease, no single test measures airways obstruction alone, as airways and parenchyma are interdependent. All tests are sensitive to changes in overall elastic recoil, local airways characteristics, abnormalities in ventilation distribution, and overall airways resistance. Care must be taken in interpreting results of volume-time and flow-volume measurements, using clinical evaluation and volume measurements to arrive at a diagnosis.

Volume and flow measurements are combined to yield two general patterns of respiratory dysfunction:

1. Obstructive. Forced expiratory values are reduced. Lung volumes are normal or increased. RV often is increased more than TLC due to loss of elastic recoil and air trapping. The RV/TLC ratio is increased. Examples include emphysema, chronic bronchitis, asthma, and cystic fibrosis.

2. Restrictive. All volumes are decreased, VC and TLC more than RV. The RV/TLC ratio is thus normal or increased. Because flows are decreased proportionally to volumes, FEV_1/FVC may be normal. PEFR is often well preserved. Examples include kyphoscoliosis, pulmonary fibrosis, and congestive heart failure.

D. Bronchodilators. Response to bronchodilators is measured using MEFV or spirometric curves. Generally, spirometry is performed before and immediately after inhalation of small amounts of bronchodilator. An increase of 10 to 15 percent or more in FVC, FEV_1,

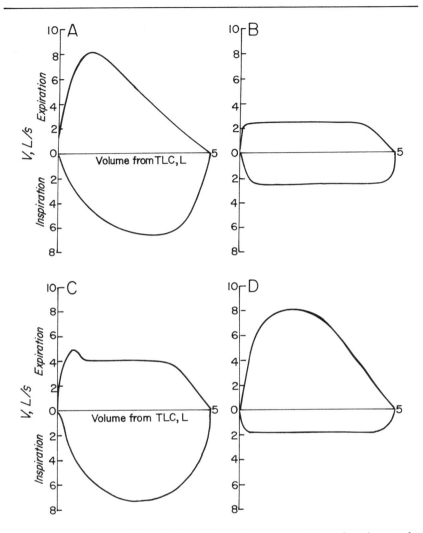

Figure 2-2. Maximal expiratory flow-volume curves in major airway obstruction. (A) Normal flow-volume curve. (B) Fixed lesion; e.g., tracheal stricture, either intrathoracic or extrathoracic. Expiration and inspiration are limited. (C) Variable intrathoracic lesion, e.g., lower tracheal malignancy. Dynamic compression occurs during expiration, but inspiration is relatively normal. (D) Variable extrathoracic obstruction; e.g., bilateral vocal cord paralysis. Forced expiration results in opening, but inspiration leads to closure.

$V_{max} 25\%$, or FEF25-75% is defined as significant. However, a negative result may be due to improper inhalation, inadequate dose, or daily variation. Use of oral bronchodilators with repeated measurements provides a more accurate assessment of response.

E. **Maximal voluntary ventilation.** Maximal voluntary ventilation, MVV, is the maximum volume of air a patient can move through the lungs in 12 or 15 seconds. It requires adequate patient cooperation and respiratory muscle function, and is also dependent upon airways resistance.

F. **Airways resistance.** Airways resistance occasionally is useful in documenting the cause of decreased expiratory flow. The panting maneuver in the plethysmograph allows measurement of alveolar pressure and flow. Resistance is the ratio of the two. It is usually expressed as its reciprocal, conductance, which is linearly related to lung volume.

G. **Small airways dysfunction.** Small airways dysfunction appears to be important in screening for respiratory disease. Inasmuch as small airways contribute only 10 to 20 percent of total airways resistance, dysfunction is difficult to detect. Tests designed to evaluate small airways include $V_{max}25\%$, dynamic compliance, closing volume, and volume of isoflow. $V_{max}25\%$ is obtained from MEFV curves, as noted above. The other tests are primarily research techniques.

III. GAS EXCHANGE

Arterial blood gas measurements are the basis for evaluation of gas exchange. Other tests include:

A. **Alveolar gas composition.** End tidal gas, presumed to reflect alveolar gas, may be measured, or FI_{O_2} and Pa_{CO_2} may be measured and used in the alveolar gas equation (see ch 1, section II A-1).

B. **Physiologic dead space.** P_{CO_2} in expired gas and arterial blood are entered into the modified Bohr equation (see ch 1, section I C).

C. **Alveolar-arterial oxygen difference.** A brief method, assuming similarity between PA_{CO_2} and Pa_{CO_2}, requires measurement only of Pa_{O_2} and Pa_{CO_2}, and knowledge of FI_{O_2}. Using a simplified alveolar gas equation:

$$PA_{O_2} = FI_{O_2} \times (760 - 47) - Pa_{CO_2}/0.8$$
$$A\text{-}aD_{O_2} = PA_{O_2} - Pa_{O_2}$$

D. Diffusing capacity (DLco, transfer factor). This test measures the ability of the lung to conduct gas from alveoli to blood. It is defined as the amount of gas removed per unit time, per unit pressure. Once ventilation occurs, three major processes determine oxygen diffusion:
1. Transfer across the alveolar-capillary membrane
2. Reaction with hemoglobin to form oxyhemoglobin
3. Removal of oxyhemoglobin from the vascular bed by blood flow

Therefore, tests of diffusion are sensitive to factors affecting transfer of gas, reaction rate, and blood flow, including
1. "Patency" of alveolar-capillary membrane
2. Time spent in pulmonary capillaries
3. Pulmonary capillary blood volume
4. Hemoglobin level
5. Cadiac output
6. Inadequate ventilation or V/Q inequalities

Carbon monoxide (CO) is used to measure diffusing capacity, since it diffuses in a similar fashion to oxygen, and its affinity for hemoglobin ensures that virtually all CO entering the blood reacts with hemoglobin. In the single breath method, the patient inspires a gas mixture of 0.3 percent CO and 10 percent helium. Expired gas is then collected, the initial portion discarded, and the final concentration of CO is used to determine diffusing capacity. In the steady-state method, gas containing 0.1 percent CO is breathed until uptake is constant, and measurements are made as before.

Neither method is clearly superior. The single-breath technique is less sensitive to V/Q inequalities due to small airways dysfunction and airway closure, since it utilizes maximal inspiration. The steady-state method relies on tidal breathing, so that V/Q inequalities may have a greater effect. Small airways dysfunction may decrease steady-state diffusing capacity.

Results of diffusing capacity in major respiratory disorders are presented in *table 2-1*.

IV. EXERCISE

Detailed consideration of exercise testing is beyond the scope of this discussion. A variety of exercise procedures is available, encompassing widely disparate technologies and vary-

Table 2-1
Diffusing Capacity in Disease

Factor	Process	Examples	Results Single-Breath	Results Steady-State
Alveolar-capillary membrane	Thickening	Interstitial pneumonitis Fibrosis	Nl or ↓	↓
	Alveolar filling	Pneumonia Granulomatous disease	↓	↓
	Destruction	Emphysema Fibrosis Lung resection	↓	↓
	Recruitment	Asthma	Nl or ↑	Nl or ↑
Time spent in alveolar capillary	Increased cardiac output	Exercise	↓	↓
	Destruction of capilary bed	As above	↓	↓
Pulmonary capillary blood volume	Obstruction of vascular bed	Pulmonary emboli Pulmonary hypertension Mitral stenosis	↓	↓
	Destruction of capillary bed	As above	↓	↓
	Left-to-right shunt	ASD, congenital heart disease	↑	↑
Hemoglobin level	Decreased	Anemia	↓	↓
	Increased	Polycythemia	↑	↑
Airway closure	Small airways dysfunction	Smoking	Nl or ↓	↓
Increased alveolar uptake	Hemoglobin in alveoli	Goodpasture's syndrome	↑	↑

ing needs for invasive monitoring. The choice of test should be based on the specific clinical question to be answered. Patients in whom exercise capacity or provocation of symptoms is at issue may undergo graded exercise, measuring heart rate and respiratory rate. More detailed information regarding level of respiratory and cardiac function may be obtained by measuring oxygen uptake and CO_2 output in expired gas. By adding arterial blood gas measurements, shunt may be calculated, and specific causes of hypoxemia suggested. In a few patients, cardiac and pulmonary contributions to symptoms may be difficult to differentiate. Use of a pulmonary artery catheter enables specific assessment of cardiac function.

REFERENCES

I. General

Bates DV, Macklem PT, Christie RV: *Respiratory Function in Disease*, 2nd ed. Philadelphia, WB Saunders, 1971.

Cherniack RM: *Pulmonary Function Testing*. Philadelphia, WB Saunders, 1977.

Metzger LF, Altose MD, Fishman AP: Evaluation of pulmonary performance. In *Pulmonary Diseases and Disorders*. Edited by Fishman AP, New York, McGraw-Hill, 1980, pp 1751-1777, 1796-1804.

Tisi GM: *Pulmonary Physiology in Clinical Medicine*. Baltimore, Williams & Wilkins, 1980.

    Bates is a comprehensive text, integrating discussion of measurement and physiology. Cherniack is detailed, primarily discussing measurement. Metzger and Tisi are briefer, more basic discussions. Both are lucid and clearly illustrated.

II. Volumes and mechanics

Cosio M, Ghezzo H, Hogg JC, et al: The relations between structural changes in small airways and pulmonary-function tests. *N Engl J Med* 298:1277-1281, 1978.

Hyatt RE, Black L: The flow-volume curve. *Am Rev Respir Dis* 107:191-198, 1973.

Mead J: Problems in interpreting common tests of pulmonary mechanical function. In *The Lung in Transition Between Health and Disease*. Edited by Macklem PT, Permutt S, New York, Dekker, 1979, pp 43-52.

Pride NB: Analysis of forced expiration—return to the recording spirometer? *Thorax*, 34:144-149, 1979.

    Cosio presents pathologic correlations between tests of small airways function and biopsy specimens. Hyatt summarizes theoretical and early experimental bases for flow-volume curves. Mead's brief article is an excellent critique of the non-specificity of pulmonary function tests. Pride's brief editorial traces the history of tests of forced expiration, presenting useful criticisms of various tests.

III. Gas exchange

Cotes JE: *Lung Function*, 4th ed. Oxford, Oxford University Press, 1979, pp 23-50.

West JB: *Ventilation/Blood Flow and Gas Exchange*, 3rd ed. Oxford, Blackwell, 1977.

Cotes's text is generally clear, and is especially useful in discussing gas exchange and measurement of diffusing capacity. West primarily considers physiology, but measurement of V/Q abnormalities is presented in a final chapter.

IV. Exercise testing

Jones NL: Exercise tests. In *Pulmonary Diseases and Disorders*. Edited by Fishman AP, New York, McGraw-Hill, 1980, pp 1796-1804.

Wasserman K, Whipp BJ: Exercise physiology in health and disease. *Am Rev Respir Dis* 112:219-249, 1975.

Wasserman presents a general discussion of changes in cardiopulmonary function during exercise. Jones is a brief introduction to exercise testing using the four-quadrant diagram.

3
Asthma

I. DEFINITION

The term **asthma** describes a broad clinical syndrome rather than a specific disease. The American Thoracic Society definition of asthma indicates the breadth of the term: "... increased responsiveness of the tracheobronchial tree to a variety of stimuli ... manifested by widespread narrowing of the airways that changes in severity either spontaneously or as a result of therapy." This definition implies three criteria for the diagnosis of asthma:

A. Functional abnormality of bronchial smooth muscle

B. Partial or complete reversibility of physiologic abnormalities

C. Chronicity of disease

Recent evidence also indicates that peripheral eosinophilia is characteristic of asthma, and may help to distinguish asthma from other chronic diseases associated with reversible bronchospasm, such as chronic obstructive pulmonary disease (COPD).

II. PATHOPHYSIOLOGY

The pathogenesis of airway narrowing in asthma is poorly understood. Both airway constriction and mechanical obstruction by secretions are clearly involved. Pathophysiology may differ in various subgroups of patients categorized by etiology (e.g., allergen-mediated) or functional abnormality (e.g., location and degree of bronchoconstriction). Cellular and molecular events have been most clearly described in **extrinsic asthma**, asthma mediated by allergens through a Type I immediate hypersensitivity reaction. Briefly, inhaled allergens (antigens) interact with specific IgE antibodies fixed to mast cells and basophils in the tracheobronchial tree. These cells in turn release preformed and synthesized mediators leading to bronchoconstriction and other manifestations of asthma, as presented in figure 1. Unanswered questions in this scheme include the site of antigen-mast cell interaction, the precise structure and contribution of various mediators, the specific function of the eosinophil in the reaction, and the role of prostaglandin receptors.

Other evidence suggests that autonomic dysfunction contributes to asthma in some patients. Theories of an imbalance between alpha- and beta-adrenergic responsiveness in asthma are supported by data showing decreased beta receptors on lymphocytes from asthmatic patients, and excessive alpha, but diminished beta, response to catecholamines in such patients. Further data point to excess cholinergic responsiveness in asthma, such as altered sweat response and the reversal of antigen-induced bronchospasm by atropine in animals and some patients. Other neural contributions to asthma, perhaps mediated by "irritant" receptors in the lung, are indicated by the onset of hyperventilation in asthmatic

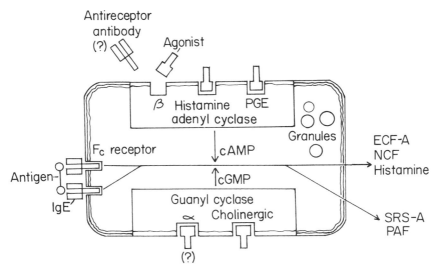

Figure 3-1. Mediators of bronchospasm in asthma.

patients soon after antigen exposure, but before apparent bronchospasm. Pathophysiology of exercise-induced asthma has been clarified on a more macroscopic level. Careful studies demonstrate that stimuli that lead to airway cooling precipitate bronchospasm in susceptible patients. The fundamental problem therefore appears to be heat transfer: inspired air must be warmed and hydrated, both of which processes entail heat loss. Thus, not only exercise but also hyperventilation or breathing cold or dry air may exacerbate asthma.

III. ETIOLOGY

Asthma is often divided into two broad etiological categories, intrinsic and extrinsic. Characteristics of these two groups are presented in *table 3-1*. Therapy is generally similar for both types, although demonstration of extrinsic asthma due to a specific antigen allows avoidance of that agent. An alternative classification is based on the following, more specific, causes:

A. Allergen-mediated
  1. Common agents (e.g., animal dander, dust, pollen)
  2. Occupational agents
  3. Pollution (Tokyo-Yokohama)
B. Exercise-induced
C. Infection: allergic bronchopulmonary aspergillosis
D. Medication
  1. Idiosyncrasy or side effect
  2. Aspirin sensitivity/nasal polyposis

Table 3-1
Extrinsic Versus Intrinsic Asthma

Characteristic	Extrinsic	Intrinsic
Allergens as precipitants	Yes	No
Immediate skin tests	Positive	Negative
Elevated IgE	Common	Uncommon
Childhood onset	Common	Uncommon
Other allergies	Common	Uncommon
Family history of multiple allergies	Common	Uncommon

E. Systemic disease
1. Polyarteritis nodosa (rare manifestation)
2. Churg-Strauss syndrome (bronchospasm, vasculitis)

These etiologies are by no means exclusive; many patients develop symptoms in response to a variety of stimuli.

IV. DIAGNOSIS

The diagnosis of asthma in an adult is usually not difficult. Patients often give a history of childhood disease or of prior episodes of dyspnea and wheezing. These symptoms are the hallmarks of asthma, although intermittent cough may appear prior to episodes of wheezing. In some patients, cough may supplant wheezing as the primary symptom, and asthma should be suspected in patients in whom there is no clear etiology for chronic cough. The differential diagnosis of asthma is presented in *table 3-2*.

Although forced expiratory maneuvers showing an obstructive ventilatory defect are definitive in evaluating the severity of asthma, similar results may be obtained in other causes of bronchospasm. If the diagnosis is in doubt, laboratory evidence useful in establishing the diagnosis of asthma includes **sputum and peripheral eosinophilia** and **positive re-**

Table 3-2
Differential Diagnosis of Acute Asthma

Diagnosis	Differential Characteristics
Upper airway obstruction (e.g., laryngeal spasm)	Stridor
Obstruction of proximal bronchus (e.g., foreign body, tumor)	Localized wheezing, contralateral mediastinal shift on chest x-ray
COPD (chronic bronchitis, emphysema)	History of same, abnormal chest x-ray, lack of eosinophilia
Tracheobronchitis/bronchiolitis	No asthma history, evidence of infection, toxin inhalation
Pulmonary edema	Abnormal chest x-ray and ECG
Pulmonary embolism	No asthma history, evidence for DVT, ECG changes
Aspiration	Altered mental status, abnormal chest x-ray
Other: sarcoid, tuberculosis, extrinsic alveolitis	History of same, usually abnormal chest x-ray

sponse to inhalation challenge. Inhalation challenge, performed using metacholine or histamine and monitoring forced expiratory parameters, demonstrates the presence of reactive airways. Such tests are especially valuable when symptoms are atypical, or other causes of bronchospasm coexist. In acute asthma, diagnosis must be followed by assessment of the severity of the episode. *Table 3-3* presents a summary of clinical parameters used to monitor severity of asthma. Forced expiratory maneuvers, either FEV_1 and FVC or MEFR, define the severity of asthma and should be measured to assess efficacy of therapy in the acute illness and in chronically treated patients. Arterial blood gas measurements are especially useful in the acute illness; Pa_{O_2} correlates closely with severity of bronchospasm, and elevated Pa_{CO_2} may suggest the need for further observation or aggressive therapy.

V. ALTERATIONS IN LUNG FUNCTION

Regardless of precipitant, similar abnormalities in lung function occur in asthma. A unifying hypothesis posits airway

Table 3-3
Assessment of Severity in Asthma

Data	Assessment
1. Subjective	
Patient's perception of severity	Often underestimated; many patients feel no symptoms at FEV_1 less than 50% predicted
2. Objective	
Cyanosis	Rare; may be masked by alkalosis if present
Signs of CO_2 retention (headache, agitation, wide pulse pressure	Masked by anxiety accompanying episode
Wheezing/inspiratory: expiratory ratio	Dependent on tidal volume; may be masked with very low tidal volumes
Pulsus paradoxus	May correlate with severity of obstruction; evidence conflicting
Use of accessory muscles of respiration (e.g., sternocleidomastoids, trapeziuses)	Correlates with severe disease

narrowing or closure as the primary abnormality in asthma. Subsequent events include elevated lung volumes, increased airways resistance and higher airways pressures, and exacerbation of V/Q inequalities and hypoxemia.

A. **Volumes.** TLC and RV are increased during an episode of asthma. Air trapping is not sufficient to explain increased TLC, since this abnormality occurs rapidly after inhalation challenge. Increase in RV is due to decreased elastic recoil and early airway narrowing or closure. This leads to reduced flow, and perhaps, decreased muscle power.

Forced expiratory volumes and flow rates are also decreased. Mechanisms for these complex alterations include airway narrowing due to bronchoconstriction, loss of lung units due to airway closure, changes in bronchial compliance, and decreased elastic recoil. FEV_1 returns to normal relatively early in the course of therapy, but TLC and especially RV remain elevated for several additional days.

B. **Mechanics.** Airways resistance is increased in asthma (and specific conductance is therefore decreased), leading to higher airway pressures. This is due in part to bronchoconstriction. The roles of other factors, such as inspissated secretions and mucosal edema, are suggested by pathologic studies and by the presence of persistent abnormalities during the resolution of asthma. Specific conductance improves early in the course of therapy, whereas dynamic compliance remains abnormal for several additional days.

C. **Gas exchange.** Acute asthma is usually accompanied by hypoxemia, hypocarbia, and alkalemia. Hypoxemia parallels airflow obstruction, whereas hypocarbia is less directly related to obstruction. Pa_{CO_2} rises only when FEV_1 falls below 20 percent of the predicted level. Hypoxemia is due to V/Q inequalities, with little or no shunting. Washout studies demonstrate two distinct populations of alveoli, with normal and low V/Q ratios, respectively. In a presumably diffuse disease, collateral ventilation may be important in maintaining lung units with normal V/Q properties.

Gas exchange is also affected by ventilatory pattern: an increase in ventilation, perhaps neurologically mediated, accompanies acute asthma. Once hypoxemia occurs, some evidence indicates that asthmatic patients have a decreased ventilatory response to this stimulus.

During therapy, hypoxemia persists after improvements occur in lung mechanics. Pa_{O_2} returns slowly to normal, presumably due to persistent, small airways obstruction and resulting V/Q inequalities.

D. **Vasculature.** Inhomogeneous ventilation in asthma leads to hypoxic vasoconstriction and redistribution of pulmonary blood flow. Vasoconstriction may be partially reversed by the adrenergic effects of some bronchodilators. Increased V/Q inequalities and exacerbation of hypoxemia may result from these agents, although clinical significance of this finding is uncertain.

VI. **TREATMENT**

The mainstays of therapy in asthma, regardless of severity or etiology, are bronchodilators and corticosteroids. Although the medications themselves are similar, regimens and routes of administration vary with the severity and time course of the disease.

A. **Acute asthma.** Patients with mild, acute onset of asthma may be treated with subcutaneous epinephrine or terbutaline sulfate alone. If this fails, or if disease is judged to be more severe, more aggressive therapy is warranted.

1. **Theophylline.** A frequently cited dosage regimen for parenteral aminophylline is a loading dose of 5.6 mg/kg over 20 to 30 minutes and a maintenance infusion of 0.9 mg/kg. These doses are based on data from relatively young, healthy patients. Recent evidence indicates that these maintenance doses may be excessive, especially in older, debilitated patients. Revised dosage schedules are presented in *table 3-4*. The maximum rate of loading dose infusion is 25 mg/min. Adjustments in maintenance dose should be based on clinical response and serum levels. Therapeutic levels are approximately 10-20 μg/ml. Side effects include anxiety, headache, nausea, vomiting, tachycardia, and arrhythmias; at high serum levels, usually greater than 40 μg/ml, seizures may occur.

2. **Sympathomimetics.** Parenteral agents available in the United States are epinephrine and terbutaline sulfate. Parenteral terbutaline sulfate has not been demonstrated to be more $beta_2$-selective than epinephrine. Bronchodilator effects and side effects are similar in both agents; they include anxiety, tremor, nausea, headache, tachycardia, hypertension, and arrhythmias. Dosage regimens vary, but some phy-

Table 3-4
Parenteral Aminophylline Dosage

Group	Loading Dose (mg/kg)	Maintenance for Next 12 Hours (mg/kg/hr)	Maintenance Beyond 12 Hours (mg/kg/hr)
Children 6 mos-9 yrs	6	1.2	1.0
Children 9 yrs-16 yrs and young adult nonsmokers	6	1.0	0.8
Otherwise healthy, nonsmoking adults	6	0.7	0.5
Older patients and patients with cor pulmonale	6	0.6	0.3
Patients with congestive heart failure or liver disease	6	0.5	0.1-0.2

Note: Weight based on estimated lean or ideal body weight, since theophylline is not distributed into adipose tissue.

sicians administer epinephrine as frequently as every 20 to 30 minutes, monitoring cardiac side effects. Terbutaline sulfate should be given less frequently, probably no more than every 4 hours after one repetition.

Inhaled agents include epinephrine, isoproterenol, metaproterenol sulfate, and isoetharine. Epinephrine should be avoided due to its alpha-adrenergic effects, but the other three agents are similar in the acute illness. Dosage schedules vary, with isoproterenol given as often as every 20 to 30 minutes. There is no apparent benefit in administering inhaled agents by means of intermittent positive pressure breathing (IPPB) rather than nebulization; indeed, IPPB may increase mortality. *Table 3-5* summarizes use of sympathomimetics.

3. **Other agents.** Corticosteroids have not been demonstrated to affect the course of acute asthma in the first 6 hours. They should not be withheld on this basis, but rather administered with the expectation of longer-term effects. Inhaled corticosteroids and cromolyn sodium are not effective in the acute illness.

Asthma 51

Table 3-5
Sympathomimetics in the Treatment of Asthma

Generic Name	Trade Name	How Supplied	Dose	Onset	Peak	Duration
Parenteral						
Epinephrine		1:1000	.2-.5 ml sc q20-30 min	10-15 min	1 hr	up to 4 hr
Terbutaline sulfate		1 mg/ml	.25 mg sc repeat 30 min x1, then q4-6h	5-15 min	0.5-1 hr	1.5-4 + hr
Aerosols						
Epinephrine	Medihaler Primatene Bronkaid	0.3 mg/puff 0.2 mg/puff	1-2 puff q4-6h	1-5 min	double; 5 and 90-120 min.	2-3 hr
Isoproterenol	Mistometer Medihaler	0.125 mg/puff 0.75 mg/puff 1:100 or 1:200	up to 20 qid (1:100)	2-5 min	5-30 min	1-3 hr
Metaproterenol sulfate	Alupent Metaprel	0.65 mg/puff	up to 16 qid	2-10 min	30-90 min	1-5 hr
Isoetharine	Bronkosol Bronkometer		up to 16 qid	5 min	15-60 min	1.5-3 hr
Albuterol	Ventolin Proventil	90 μg/puff	2 qid	5 min	60 min	3-5 hr
Oral						
Terbutaline sulfate			2.5-5 tid-qid	30 min	2-4 hr	4-6 hr
Metaproterenol sulfate			10-20 tid-qid	30 min	2-2.5 hr	1-5 hr
Ephedrine			15-50 q4h	60 min	2-3.5 hr	3-5 hr

4. **Hydration.** Aggressive hydration is required to compensate for increased respiratory water loss and to prevent drying of secretions.
5. **Oxygen.** Humidified oxygen should be administered at appropriate concentrations depending on the degree of hypoxemia and on associated conditions, such as hypercapnia. Hypoxemia may be worsened by bronchodilator therapy; increasing inspired oxygen counteracts this problem.
6. **Summary of emergency therapy of acute asthma.** Measure FEV_1 or FVC or MEFR; if greater than 50 percent of predicted, administer epinephrine 0.3 ml (1:1000) sc, recheck FEV_1 or FVC in 30 minutes. If little improvement or if initial FEV_1 or FVC or MEFR was less than 50 percent of predicted:
   a. Administer heated humidifed oxygen.
   b. Begin hydration at 200-400 ml/hr, depending on clinical status.
   c. Begin aminophylline loading dose and maintenance infusion as discussed above.
   d. Begin isoproterenol aerosol by compressed air nebulizer 0.5 ml in 2 ml normal saline; repeat q 30 minutes, monitoring pulse, blood pressure, and symptoms for 3 to 5 doses.
   e. Repeat epinephrine 0.3 ml sc q 30 minutes, monitoring pulse, blood pressure, and symptoms for 3 to 5 doses.
   f. Measure FEV_1 or FVC or MEFR q 30 minutes to 1 hour.
   g. If patient appears severely ill, measure ABG; consider initiating corticosteroid treatment.
7. **Hospitalization.** The decision to hospitalize a patient with acute asthma is often difficult. In a few situations, such as the presence of other severe illness (e.g., cardiac disease or pneumonia), hypercapnia, or patient fatigue, admission should be routine. In other cases, no threshold exists, and the decision is based on clinical evaluation. Response to therapy is probably the most accurate guide, although little evidence is available concerning the type and duration of therapy preceding hospitalization. One report suggests that lack of response to one dose of subcutaneous epinephrine indicates that the patient should be hospitalized. Another study suggests the need for longer emergency therapy (3 hours or more) and reports a correlation of change in FEV_1 during

this period with eventual response to therapy. General criteria for hospitalization in acute asthma follow:
- a. FEV_1 less than 0.5 L with little response to therapy
- b. FVC less than 1.0 L with little response to therapy
- c. Cyanosis
- d. Pa_{O_2} less than 60 or Pa_{CO_2} greater than 40
- e. ECG abnormalities suggesting ischemia or serious arrhythmia

B. **Therapy of hospitalized patients.** Treatment is similar to emergency therapy. Adequate hydration and oxygenation remain crucial objectives. Aminophylline is the mainstay of therapy, with sympathomimetics as adjuncts. Longer acting agents, such as terbutaline sulfate and metaproterenol sulfate, isoetharine, or albuterol may be more convenient than epinephrine in hospitalized patients. Aminophylline should be given as described previously, with monitoring of serum levels to minimize toxicity.

Despite the well-known side effects of long-term corticosteroid therapy, a brief course of these agents is often useful in hospitalized patients. There is little information to govern choice, dose, or duration of therapy. Given variable biologic half-lives, no single agent has precedence based on duration of action. Frequency of administration is equally uncertain; many physicians use divided doses in severe disease, returning to single morning doses as improvement occurs. One series demonstrated the need for 4 mg/kg of hydrocortisone, given frequently to maintain therapeutic serum levels, but failed to correlate these levels with functional improvement. Although not universally accepted, serial total eosinophil counts probably enable monitoring of adequacy of steroid therapy. Magnitude of eosinophil count correlates with severity of disease, and steroid doses should be chosen to suppress eosinophilia totally, if the clinical situation warrants.

Other agents occasionally used in acute asthma include atropine, 0.5 to 1 mg inhaled every 4 to 6 hours. Anticholinergic side effects, especially tachycardia, may limit its use. Isoproterenol can be administered parenterally at a dose of 0.5 to 2 μg/min, but experience with adults is limited and tachycardia occurs frequently.

Anxiety and agitation, sometimes extreme, may accompany acute asthma. Sedation should be avoided if at all possible, since depression of respiration and reduced clearance of secretions may occur; these may, in turn, predispose to respiratory failure.

C. **Respiratory failure.** Most hospitalized asthmatic patients pose no management problems. Rarely, patients develop acute respiratory failure. In recent series, about 1 to 3 percent of hospitalized patients required mechanical ventilation.

1. **Patients at risk.** Prospective identification of high-risk patients is difficult. Retrospective data suggest that several characteristics are likely to be associated with respiratory failure or sudden death:
   a. History of severe asthma with prior assisted ventilation
   b. Fluctuating hospital course with marked diurnal variation in symptoms and Pa_{CO_2}
   c. Long delay in seeking therapy
   d. Withholding, or late initiation, of corticosteroids
   e. Overuse of sedation

   Respiratory failure is not clearly associated with patient age or with etiology of asthma.

2. **Need for intubation.** No firm laboratory criteria supplant clinical evaluation. Indications are generally similar to those in other causes of respiratory failure: hypoxemia, deteriorating mental status, and inability to clear secretions. Unlike chronic lung disease, hypercapnia in acute asthma is an ominous sign. The consensus is that patients with Pa_{CO_2} greater than 60 torr, or rising faster than 5 torr/hr, should be intubated. In some patients, lesser degrees of hypercapnia may also require ventilatory support.

3. **Therapy for respiratory failure:**
   a. Intubate with endotracheal tube 8 mm or greater, internal diameter.
   b. Use volume-cycled ventilator.
   c. To ensure adequate alveolar ventilation without hypercapnia or hypocapnia
      (1) Decrease tidal volume as tolerated to allow lower cycling pressures.
      (2) Decrease respiratory rate as tolerated to allow adequate duration of expiration.
   d. Supply heated, humidified oxygen to maintain Pa_{O_2} at 60 to 90 torr.
   e. Sedate—only if absolutely necessary—with benzodiazepines and pancuronium bromide, rather than opiates or succinylcholine chloride.

f. Monitor progress with FVC if patient is cooperative, and with ventilator peak pressures or compliance if patient is unable to cooperate.
g. Administer aminophylline to maintain serum level 10 to 20 mg/L; administer terbutaline sulfate sc and inhaled isoproterenol, isoetharine or albuterol q 4h as tolerated.
h. Administer corticosteroids in divided doses to suppress total eosinophil count completely.
i. Administer frequent chest physiotherapy and encourage patient to cough; suction as necessary.

More detailed information concerning assisted ventilation can be found in Chapter 5.

4. **Complications.** High airway pressures and mucus plugging may be responsible for complications of assisted ventilation in asthma. In one series, pneumothorax, alveolar hypoventilation, pneumonia, and endotracheal tube malfunction occurred more often in asthma than in cases of respiratory failure with other causes. All were associated with increased mortality. Additional complications are similar to those occurring in cases of respiratory failure with other causes.

5. **Course.** As duration of intubation is usually less than 10 days, tracheostomy is seldom required. Mortality in recent series ranges from 10 to 40 percent of those requiring assisted ventilation.

D. **Therapy for chronic asthma.** Outpatient management of asthma has three goals: return of normal lung function; prevention of severe episodes; prevention of hospitalization. Each patient requires diagnostic evaluation and a specific therapeutic program.

1. **Diagnostic evaluation.** This should include a careful history, seeking precipitating factors such as animals, occupational agents, or drugs. Skin testing for specific allergens is indicated if the history is suggestive, and perhaps in the presence of severe asthma that is refractory to conventional therapy. If skin tests indicate a specific allergen, avoidance of that allergen should be suggested, as desensitization is of questionable value. Multiple drugs and inhaled agents have been implicated in asthma. The more common agents are presented in *table 3-6*.

Laboratory evaluation should include total eosinophil count and forced expiratory maneuvers. Other tests should be dictated by symptoms and associated

Table 3-6
Common Precipitants of Asthma

1. Medications

    Pharmacologic action
    Beta-adrenergic blockers (e.g., propranolol, metoprolol, nadolol)
    Cholinergic agents (e.g., pilocarpine, neostigmine)

    Allergy or idiosyncrasy
    Antibiotics (e.g., penicillin, cephalosporins, erythromycin, tetracyclines, streptomycin, sulfonamides, ethionamide
    Organic iodides
    Intravenous anesthetics
    Monoamine oxidase inhibitors
    Antiserums/vaccines
    Steroids (uncommon)
    Anti-inflammatory agents (e.g., aspirin, indomethacin, ibuprofen)
    Local irritation (acetylcysteine, cromolyn sodium)

2. Occupational Agents

Animal dander	Plastics fumes
Castor beans	Proteolytic enzymes
Exhaust fumes	Red cedar
Formaldehyde	Textiles
Grains	Tobacco
Isocyanates	
Metals (nickel, platinum, tungsten, vanadium)	

conditions. Patients with a history of intermittent fever, eosinophilia, and pulmonary infiltrates should be evaluated for allergic bronchopulmonary aspergillosis (ABPA). Diagnosis is supported by positive skin tests, positive sputum cultures, and specific precipitin titers.

2. **Therapy.** Except in patients with mild intermittent disease, lung function should be maintained as close to normal as possible. A stepwise approach is usually effective, beginning with theophylline and a sympathomimetic aerosol; adding an oral sympathomimetic; following with a corticosteroid aerosol; and finally, using oral steroids, if necessary. Although

combination drug preparations should be avoided, regimens often require the use of several drugs at submaximal doses, to limit side effects.

Long-acting theophylline preparations achieve sustained serum levels when given several times per day, although cost is greater than generic aminophylline. Table 3-7 compares various oral theophyllines. Rectal theophylline preparations are erratically absorbed and should be avoided except in rare cases of intolerance to oral theophylline.

Of the sympathomimetics, oral ephedrine should be replaced by more selective beta agents, such as terbutaline sulfate or metaproterenol sulfate. Isoproterenol aerosol has been epidemiologically associated with increased asthma mortality; it probably should be replaced by metaproterenol sulfate, isoetharine or albuterol.

The side effects of corticosteroids, including weight gain, hypertension, osteoporosis, and cataracts, are well known. There is no apparent increase in the incidence of tuberculosis in asthmatic patients taking steroids. Corticosteroids should be used when patients remain moderately symptomatic on bronchodilators alone. In addition, exacerbations of disease in patients with confirmed ABPA should be treated with steroids.

Constant effort should be made to reduce and then discontinue corticosteroid treatment. Whenever possible, every-other-day regimens should be used to minimize hypophyseal-adrenal suppression. Recently, steroid aerosols have proved effective in the therapy of chronic asthma, although not in the acute illness. Whether steroid aerosols cause less hypophyseal-adrenal suppression than every-other-day regimens using oral steroids is controversial. Nonetheless, in some patients aerosols may allow tapering and even discontinuation of oral steroids; therefore, all such patients should have a trial of beclomethasone dipropionate. To increase effectiveness and limit absorption, patients should be instructed to take inhaled steroids immediately after an inhaled sympathomimetic, and to gargle after use to prevent swallowing of pharyngeal deposits. Side effects, beyond those of systemic absorption, include mild hoarseness and oral candidiasis, which usually responds to local antifungal therapy.

Cromolyn sodium is not a bronchodilator per se, but appears to prevent mediator release from mast cells in vitro. It is effective as prophylaxis against asthma but

Table 3-7
Oral Theophylline Preparations

Generic Name	Trade Name	Available Theophylline	Peak Effect	Dose Interval
Theophylline	Aerolate	100%	3-8h	bid
	Elixophyllin		1-2h	tid
	Slo-Phyllin		1h	qid
	Slo-Phyllin gyrocaps		3-5h	bid-tid
	Theo-Dur		6-10h	bid
	Theolair		1-2h	qid
Aminophylline	(enteric)	86%	1-3h	tid-qid
	Aminodur		5-6h	bid-tid
			5h	
Oxtriphylline	Choledyl	64%	3h	qid
Dyphylline	Lufyllin	70%	1-3h	tid-qid

not in treating the acute illness. Cromolyn sodium is most effective in childhood asthma, whether allergic or exercise-induced. Side effects are uncommon, but include exacerbation of bronchospasm. The cost of cromolyn is a limiting factor for some patients. Therapeutic effect should be monitored, especially in patients on complicated regimens, by serial forced expiratory maneuvers. Total eosinophil counts should be obtained to monitor steroid effect. Viral—but not bacterial—respiratory infections appear to exacerbate asthma, and affected patients should be monitored closely. Telephone contact may be useful in adjusting regimens and averting the need for hospitalization. Therapy of chronic asthma is summarized as follows:

  a. **Mild intermittent asthma:** give metaproterenol sulfate, isoetharine, or albuterol inhaler prn, 2-4 puff qid.
  b. **Mild chronic asthma:** ADD aminophylline or long-acting theophylline 800-1,200 mg per day in divided doses; adjust for cardiac or hepatic disease.
  c. **If uncontrolled,** ADD terbutaline sulfate 10-20 mg per day in divided doses or, if side effects develop, use metaproterenol sulfate 40-80 mg per day in divided doses.
  d. **If still uncontrolled,** ADD beclomethasone dipropionate 2 puff PO qid after sympathomimetic inhaler.
  e. **If still uncontrolled,** ADD oral corticosteroids (prednisone, methylprednisolone). Use qd if possible; monitor therapy with expiratory maneuvers, total eosinophil count.
  f. **Consider trial of cromolyn sodium** in severe asthma or in exercise- or allergen-induced asthma.

VII. NATURAL HISTORY AND PROGNOSIS

Outcome of childhood asthma has been studied prospectively. About one-half of patients have no recurrence of disease as adults, 20 percent have chronic symptoms, and about 30 percent have intermittent symptoms. Whether childhood asthma leads to emphysema or chronic bronchitis is uncertain. The natural history of adult-onset asthma is less clear. One prospective study comparing asthmatic patients to controls with pharyngitis disclosed a greater long-term mortality among asthmatic persons from coronary artery disease and malignancies, but not from lung disease. Whether asthmatic adults sustain chronic loss of lung function is also uncertain.

REFERENCES

I. General

Lichtenstein LM, Austen KF (eds): *Asthma: Physiology, Immunopharmacology, and treatment.* New York, Academic Press, 1977.

Stein M (ed): *New Directions in Asthma.* Park Ridge, Illinois, American College of Physicians, 1975.

Weiss EB, Segal MS (eds): *Bronchial Asthma.* Boston, Little, Brown, 1976.

    Lichtenstein and Stein are similar, containing brief sections on a variety of topics related to asthma, often directed toward research. Weiss is more clinically oriented. All are somewhat dated with regard to therapy.

II. Pathophysiology

Boushey HA, Holtzman MJ, Shellar JR, et al: Bronchial hyperreactivity. *Am Rev Respir Dis* 121:389-413, 1980.

Henderson WR, Shelhamer JH, Reingold DB, et al: Alpha-adrenergic hyperresponsiveness in asthma. *N Engl J Med* 300:642-647, 1979.

McFadden ER, Ingram RH: Exercise-induced asthma. *N Engl J Med* 301:763-769, 1979.

    Boushey discusses bronchial wall structure and response to various stimuli (Mediators of hypersensitivity are more completely addressed in Lichtenstein above.) Henderson adds support to the adrenergic imbalance theory of asthma. McFadden is an excellent summary of the heat flux hypothesis in the pathogenesis of exercise-induced asthma.

III. Acute and hospital therapy

Josephson GW, MacKenzie EJ, Lietman PS, et al: Emergency treatment of asthma. *JAMA* 242:639-643, 1979.

McFadden ER, Kaser R, DeGroot WJ: Acute bronchial asthma: relations between clinical and physiological manifestations. *N Engl J Med* 228:221-225, 1973.

McFadden ER, Ingram RH: A controlled study of the effects of single doses of hydrocortisone on the resolution of acute attacks of asthma. *Am J Med* 60:52-59, 1976.

Paterson JW, Woolcock AJ, Shenfield GM: Bronchodilator drugs. *Am Rev Respir Dis* 121:1149-1188, 1979.

Powell JR, Vozeh S, Hopewell P, et al: Theophylline disposition in acutely ill hospitalized patients. *Am Rev Respir Dis* 118:229-238, 1978.

Rossing TH, Fanta CH, Goldstein DH, et al: Emergency therapy of asthma. *Am Rev Respir Dis* 122:365-371, 1980.

Scoggin CH, Sahn SA, Petty TL: Status asthmaticus *JAMA* 233:1158-1162, 1977.

    Josephson and Rossing indicate that sympathomimetic agents may be superior to theophylline in acute asthma. McFadden correlates use of accessory muscles of respiration with severity of asthma, and also finds steroids of no benefit in the early therapy of acute asthma. Paterson describes pharmacokinetics of bronchodilators, whereas Powell documents decreased metabolism in seriously ill patients. Scoggin et al. review their experience with severely ill patients requiring mechanical ventilation; hypoventilation, tube malfunction, pneumothorax, and pneumonia contributed to mortality.

IV. Chronic Therapy

Bernstein IL, Johnson CL, Tse CS: Therapy with cromolyn sodium. *Ann Intern Med* 89:228-233, 1978.

Horn BR, Robin EO, Theodore J, et al: Total eosinophil counts in the management of bronchial asthma. *N Engl J Med* 292:1152-1155, 1975.

Litchtenstein LM: An evaluation of the role of immunotherapy in asthma. *Am Rev Respir Dis* 117:191-197, 1978.

Wolfe JD, Tashkin DP, Calvarese B, et al: Bronchodilator effects of terbutaline and aminophylline alone and in combination in asthmatic patients. *N Engl J Med* 298:363-367, 1978.

Wyatt R, Waschek J, Weinberger M, et al: Effects of inhaled beclomethasone dipropionate and alternate day prednisone on pituitary-adrenal function in children with chronic asthma. *N Engl J Med* 299:1387-1392, 1978.

Bernstein reviews mechanisms of, and results with, cromolyn, suggesting that the agent is effective in younger patients with allergic or exercise-induced asthma. Horn indicates that response to steroids may be gauged by suppression of eosinophil counts in some patients. Lichtenstein finds no rigorous evidence supporting immunotherapy in asthma. White describes additive effects of bronchodilators: combinations led to decreased toxicity. Wyatt showed similar pituitary-adrenal suppression with inhaled and alternate-day steroids; both appeared equally effective.

V. Natural history

Blair H: Natural history of childhood asthma. *Arch Dis Child* 52:613-619, 1977.

Karetzky MS: Asthma mortality: an analysis of one year's experience. *Medicine* 54:471-484, 1975.

Robinelle CD, Froumeni JF: Asthma and subsequent mortality in World War II veterans. *J Chron Dis* 31:619-624, 1978.

Westerman DE, Benetar SR, Potgieter PD, et al: Identification of the high-risk asthmatic patient. Experience with 39 patients undergoing ventilation for status asthmaticus. *Am J Med* 66:565-572, 1979.

In the group followed by Blair, about one-half were free of disease as adults, and about one-fifth worsened. Karetzky suggests that intermittent positive pressure breathing is associated with increased mortality. Robinelle found greater mortality among asthmatic patients than in controls, but this was due to coronary artery disease and cancer rather than lung disease. Westerman identified high-risk patients retrospectively; their disease was labile, and most required mechanical ventilation within 24 hours of hospitalization.

4
Chronic Airways Obstruction

I. DEFINITIONS

Chronic bronchitis and emphysema are the two major disease entities in the category often referred to as chronic obstructive pulmonary disease (COPD). These diseases share the common physiologic manifestation of obstruction to expiratory flow. They are further characterized by chronicity, in contrast to asthma, a disease of episodic exacerbations and remissions. Despite this physiologic resemblance in diagnosis and treatment, and the frequent coexistence of the two in individual patients, chronic bronchitis and emphysema are fundamentally different in pathology, pathogenesis, and natural history. Differences in pathogenesis, while incompletely understood, may eventually lead to the establishment of more specific therapies. The approach taken here will be to consider the diseases concurrently, emphasizing the distinctive aspects of each.

The American Thoracic Society's formal definitions of chronic bronchitis and emphysema are asymmetric; chronic bronchitis is defined clinically, and emphysema, pathologically, as follows:

Chronic bronchitis: " . . . excessive mucus secretion in the bronchial tree . . . manifested by chronic or recurrent productive cough." **Emphysema:** " . . . anatomic alteration of the lung characterized by an abnormal enlargement of the airspaces distal to the terminal nonrespiratory bronchiole."

Antemortem diagnosis of emphysema is often assumed, based on: a history of exposure to a precipitant, such as cigarette smoke; obstructive physiology; and lack of symptoms of bronchitis. This practice underlines a point made by Fishman: the two diseases constitute parts of a spectrum of obstructive lung diseases, with differences, but without clear distinctions.

II. ETIOLOGY AND PATHOGENESIS

A. Etiology. Current theories of the etiologies of both chronic bronchitis and emphysema involve an interaction between noxious inhalants and genetic predisposition.
1. Smoking. Cigarette smoking is clearly associated with the development of chronic bronchitis and emphysema. Epidemiologic evidence indicates that risk is increased approximately 10 times among cigarette smokers and 1.5 to 3 times among pipe and cigar smokers. Occurrence and severity of both diseases are related to duration and quantity of smoking. A "threshold" of about 20 "pack-years" appears to exist before chronic bronchitis and emphysema become apparent. Nonetheless, young, asymptomatic smokers develop alterations in pulmonary function that appear to precede the clinical development of chronic bronchitis and emphysema. Particular smoking habits, such as lighting and relighting and leaving cigarettes in the mouth, also increase the risk of disease.
2. Pollutants. Large-scale population studies indicate an increased risk of chronic bronchitis and emphysema in areas of high pollution, and have found alterations in lung function consistent with early stages of disease in these areas. Specific pollutants implicated epidemiologically and in animal models include sulfur dioxide, cadmium, nitrogen dioxide, and black particulate matter.
3. Other inhaled agents. Dust exposure, particularly cereal grain dust, is associated with chronic bronchitis in the absence of smoking.
4. Age. Incidence of emphysema increases with age. In postmortem studies, mild emphysema is common among elderly nonsmokers, although severe disease is rare.
5. Genetic predisposition. Familial factors in the development of chronic bronchitis and emphysema are indicated by the clustering of chronic bronchitis cases within families. Genetic influence is suggested by higher correlations of FEV_1 between relatives than between spouses, and greater prevalence in

monozygotic than dizygotic twins. Specific manifestations of disease, such as hypoventilation, also appear to have familial components.

6. **Alpha$_1$-antitrypsin deficiency.** Alpha$_1$-antitrypsin is a glycoprotein protease inhibitor found in normal human serum. While specific genetic loci are unknown, there appear to be two codominant alleles, known as Pi (protease inhibitor). Three phenotypic variations have been identified electrophoretically: M (normal), Z (deficient), and S (intermediate). Between 1 in 5000 and 1 in 2000 people are homozygous for the Z phenotype (PiZZ). These patients almost uniformly have very low protease inhibitor levels, and a markedly increased risk of developing emphysema as young adults. PiSZ patients occasionally have low inhibitor levels, and probably are susceptible to emphysema as well. Despite extensive investigation, the evidence relating PiMZ and PiSS alleles to clinical lung disease is conflicting. It appears that heterozygotes have an increased risk of alterations in pulmonary function, but not of clinical disease.

B. **Pathogenesis.** Three major structural abnormalities contribute to the expiratory flow obstruction characteristic of chronic bronchitis and emphysema: **decreased size of the bronchial lumen** (both diseases); **increased collapsibility of bronchial walls** (both diseases); and **decreased elastic recoil** of the lung parenchyma (primarily in emphysema).

1. **Decreased bronchial lumen diameter**, which is prominent in chronic bronchitis, may develop as a consequence of irritant inhalants that lead to bronchial, and later bronchiolar, injury. In susceptible patients, submucosal gland hypertrophy occurs, leading to mucus hypersecretion and reversible obstruction in bronchioles and small bronchi. Partial obstruction and stasis due to depression of mucociliary clearance predispose to infection, which may exacerbate obstruction. Recurrent inhalational injury, perhaps abetted by infection, produces chronic pathologic changes, such as the following:

    a. Increased mucus in airways
    b. Increased wall thickness due to submucosal gland hypertrophy
    c. Secretory cell (goblet cell) proliferation
    d. Mucosal edema
    e. Bronchial smooth muscle hypertrophy

All contribute to obstruction to expiratory flow, and to the clinical course characterized by sputum production and recurrent infection. As described here, the disease is primarily confined to airways. Only in susceptible patients do parenchymal destruction and concomitant emphysema occur.

2. Emphysema is characterized by **increased collapsibility of bronchial walls** and **decreased parenchymal elastic recoil**. The discovery of the association between emphysema and $alpha_1$-antitrypsin deficiency stimulated research relating the disease to an imbalance between proteolytic enzymes and protease inhibitors, in which destruction of elastin results. Beyond the discovery of $alpha_1$-antitrypsin deficiency, several lines of evidence support this hypothesis:
    a. Decreased elastin in animal models of emphysema, but not in humans
    b. Increased elastase levels in neutrophils and alveolar macrophages of smokers
    c. Animal models of emphysema produced by intratracheal injection of elastolytic enzymes

    Further evidence linking smoking and elastase imbalance includes production of neutrophil chemotactic factor by sensitized alveolar macrophages and decreased elastase inhibition and functionally reduced $alpha_1$-antitrypsin activity in smokers. A pathogenetic scheme begins with cigarette smoke and other inhalants attracting alveolar macrophages to the lung. Inhalants also stimulate elastase release from macrophages and neutrophils and inactivate elastase inhibitors. Elastin disruption, although not frank destruction, occurs in the lung parenchyma.

    Two pathologically distinct types of emphysema are recognized: centrilobular and panlobular. Centrilobular has in the past been associated with smoking. However, present evidence indicates that most clinically significant disease, regardless of etiology, is panlobular. Bronchitis may be superimposed on either type.

3. **Airflow obstruction** in emphysema is due to:
    a. Increased compliance and decreased elastic recoil, due to elastin alteration
    b. Increased airway collapsibility due to diminished tethering action of the parenchyma on airways, especially noncartilaginous peripheral bronchioles.

Pure emphysema is therefore a parenchymal lesion, causing expiratory obstruction in the absence of airway lesions. Most patients exhibit a combination of chronic bronchitis and emphysema, with flow obstruction due to both airway and parenchymal disease. In some patients, the processes remain distinct, pursuing individual natural histories. Chronic bronchitis remains a disease of mucus hypersecretion without emphysematous changes, while emphysema is manifested by obstruction but little cough or sputum. In both, the primary site of obstruction to flow, whether directly or by decreased tethering, is the small (2-3 mm) airways, as determined by postmortem retrograde catheterization.

Theories of the pathogenesis of chronic bronchitis and emphysema are illustrated in figure 4-1.

III. CLINICAL MANIFESTATIONS AND DIAGNOSIS
  A. Symptoms and signs

  Given their common pathophysiologic basis, and coexistence in many patients, it is not surprising that clinical manifestations of chronic bronchitis and emphysema are generally similar. Nonetheless, the distinction suggested some years ago by Dornhorst, between "blue bloaters" (chronic bronchitics) and "pink puffers" (emphysematous patients) has some validity. The patient with predominant chronic bronchitis is husky, with marked cyanosis, and primary symptoms of cough, sputum production, and frequent upper respiratory infections. In contrast, the emphysematous patient is thin, even emaciated, usually noncyanotic, but with marked dyspnea and little cough or sputum. Infections are less common with emphysema, but when present are more likely to be life-threatening.

  Other than cyanosis, signs are similar in chronic bronchitis and emphysema. In both diseases there may be an expanded thoracic cage, with increase in anteroposterior diameter, that is more prominent in emphysema. Breath sounds are diminished in both disorders. Wheezing on unforced expiration appears to correlate with the severity of disease, although forced expiratory wheezing does not. Hoover's sign, retraction of the lower ribs with inspiration, is presumably due to flattening and change in angle of insertion of the diaphragm..It is more common in emphysema. Signs of right heart failure, such as jugular venous distention, hepatomegaly, and pedal edema, are more common in chronic bronchitis.

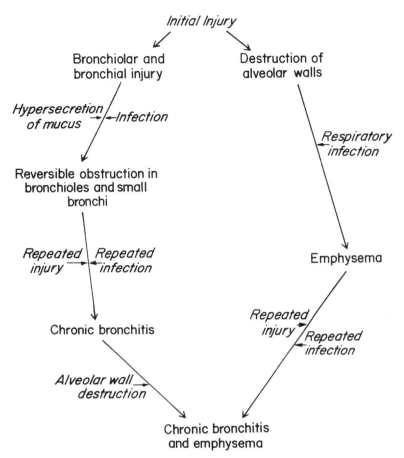

Figure 4-1. Pathogenesis of chronic bronchitis and emphysema.

B. Laboratory findings

Laboratory abnormalities are more often related to severity of disease and complications than to underlying disease process. If hypoxemia is severe and prolonged, erythrocytosis may develop. Electrolyte abnormalities usually are due to diuretic intake or to salt and fluid restriction. Arterial blood gases in early stages of either disease reveal mild-to-moderate hypoxemia, normocapnia, and normal pH. With progression of disease, some patients, usually those with chronic bronchitis or combined disease, develop hypercapnia and corresponding respiratory acidosis.

Electrocardiographic changes are also nonspecific. Atrial arrhythmias are common, especially in exacerbations of disease. Once right ventricular dysfunction occurs, most commonly in chronic bronchitis, increased P-wave voltage, right P-wave axis and right QRS-axis deviation, and right ventricular hypertrophy may ensue. Neither emphysema nor chronic bronchitis is diagnosed radiographically. Chest x-rays are usually nonspecific, and may sometimes appear normal. Diffusely increased markings and tubular shadows are common, but by no means universal, in chronic bronchitis. Increased markings and vascular deficiency are common in emphysema, but nondiagnostic. Severity of disease, but not type, can be roughly gauged from flattening of the diaphragm (below the 7th rib anteriorly), enlargement of the retrosternal space (greater than 4.4 cm), and decreased transverse heart size (less than 11.5 cm).

Other techniques, such as bronchography in chronic bronchitis, are rarely necessary. Clinical and laboratory features of chronic bronchitis and emphysema are summarized in *table 4-1*.

C. Diagnosis

Diagnosis of chronic bronchitis and emphysema depends on the presence of symptoms, and on abnormal pulmonary function tests. Bedside measurements, such as the match test or duration of forced expiration, have been supplanted by more accurate and widely available spirometry. Routine spirometric and plethysmographic measurements pose no serious risks to patients with these diseases.

As emphasized above, obstruction to expiratory flow is the hallmark of both chronic bronchitis and emphysema. In early, subclinical disease, this appears to be manifested in small airways, as measured by increased closing volume, decreased maximal midexpiratory flow, and decreased flow at 25 percent vital capacity. However, these tests are also sensitive to elastic recoil, so early emphysema without significant airways disease might mimic the findings of small airways dysfunction. Once chronic bronchitis and emphysema are clinically apparent, FEV_1 and FVC are decreased, as is the ratio FEV_1/FVC. Lung volumes are increased in both chronic bronchitis and emphysema, but diagnosis is dependent upon spirometry.

In summary, chronic bronchitis is diagnosed in patients with chronic cough and sputum production, and reduced FEV_1 and FVC. Emphysema is diagnosed by the presence of dyspnea, mild-to-moderate cough with

Table 4-1
Clinical and Laboratory Findings in
Emphysema and Chronic Bronchitis

Characteristic	Chronic Bronchitis	Emphysema
Age	40-55	50-75
Primary symptom	Cough	Dyspnea
Sputum	Moderate to copious	Small amount
Signs		
Breath sounds	Moderately diminished	Markedly diminished
Cyanosis	Marked	Slight
Laboratory		
Chest x-ray	Nl diaphragm position Nl or increased markings	Low, flat diaphragms Radiolucent areas
ECG	Right heart strain	Strain in advanced disease
Hemoglobin	Commonly increased	Increased in advanced disease

scant sputum, and reduced spirometric values. The presence of both cough with sputum and marked obstruction suggests a combination of the two processes.

IV. ALTERATIONS IN LUNG FUNCTION

A. **Volumes.** TLC, RV, and FRC are usually increased in both chronic bronchitis and emphysema. In emphysema, increases are due to decreased elastic recoil. In chronic bronchitis, TLC and RV are increased to a lesser extent, and the increases are due to trapping of air in obstructed airways. FRC may be normal if measured statically in chronic bronchitis, but prolongation of expiration may result in the beginning of inspiratory flow before FRC is reached. A "dynamic" increase in FRC therefore occurs.

B. **Mechanics.** Elastic recoil is diminished in emphysema, but preserved in chronic bronchitis. Compliance is therefore increased in emphysema. Airways resistance is increased in both diseases, due to airway collapse and increased secretions.

Flows are diminished in chronic bronchitis by the mechanisms of increased airways resistance cited above. In emphysema, flows are reduced due to decreased elastic recoil and increased airway collapsibility. Increased resistance in large airways may mask abnormalities in small airways function. Tests such as volume of isoflow may be normal in emphysema and chronic bronchitis.

C. Gas exchange. Both chronic bronchitis and emphysema lead to hypoxemia, which is often more severe in bronchitis. In both disorders, ventilation is nonhomogeneous due to alterations in resistance and compliance. These in turn lead to V/Q inequalities as the primary cause of hypoxemia. V/Q patterns differ in the two diseases. In emphysema, many units have high V/Q, while in chronic bronchitis, units with low V/Q predominate. Shunt appears uncommon in emphysema, but may occur in severe chronic bronchitis or combined disease. No direct evidence exists for diffusion limitation in airways obstruction. V/Q data suggest that the reduced diffusing capacity common in emphysema can be accounted for by V/Q inequalities. Diffusion limitation may result from destruction of the capillary bed in emphysema. This would account for the reduction in Pa_{O_2} with exercise in this disorder. Hypoventilation also contributes to hypoxemia in some patients.

Exaggerated changes in Pa_{O_2} and Pa_{CO_2} occur during sleep in both chronic bronchitis and emphysema. In rapid eye movement (REM) sleep, Pa_{O_2} decreases by 10 to 15 torr, or at least 10 percent saturation, and Pa_{CO_2} increases by about 10 torr. These changes are presumably caused by hypoventilation and respiratory asynchrony.

D. Vasculature and cardiac function. Increased pulmonary vascular resistance, with concomitant pulmonary hypertension, is common in chronic bronchitis, and occurs to a lesser extent in emphysema. Hypoxia appears to be the primary cause, although acidosis and hypercapnia may contribute. Right ventricular hypertrophy and dilatation, with eventual failure, may occur if resistance remains elevated. Controversy over left ventricular function in the presence of chronic bronchitis and emphysema persists, but there is little evidence for left ventricular dysfunction unless other myocardial disease is present.

E. Respiratory control. A wide variety of hypoxic and hypercapnic responses occurs in chronic bronchitis and emphysema. The most striking is the chronic hypercapnia developed by some patients, despite the fact that others are normocapnic. Hypercapnic patients have increased respiratory frequency and decreased tidal volume as compared to normocapnic patients. Dead space is approximately equal in both groups, leading to decreased alveolar ventilation in those with hypercapnia.

In general, patients with chronic bronchitis and emphysema have diminished ventilatory responses to hypoxia and hypercapnia. The mechanism of these abnormalities is uncertain. Blunted response to external resistive loads in both diseases suggests the participation of mechanoreceptors. Disordered breathing patterns are common in sleep, contributing to hypoxemia and pulmonary hypertension.

In emphysema, ventilation increases markedly with exercise, primarily via increased respiratory rate. Vd/Vt therefore increases. In chronic bronchitis, ventilatory response to exercise is especially limited in patients with chronic hypercapnia.

Alterations in lung function in chronic bronchitis and emphysema are summarized in *table 4-2*.

V. TREATMENT

Therapy in chronic bronchitis and emphysema is directed toward arresting progress of the disease, treating reversible abnormalities, treating exacerbations, attempting rehabilitation, and preventing complications.

A. **Disease progression.** Although both bronchitis and emphysema are chronic processes, removal of precipitating factors may lead to stabilization of pulmonary function and even mild improvement. Epidemiologic studies indicate two subgroups of smokers with chronic bronchitis and emphysema:
   1. Patients with symptoms and a moderately increased rate of deterioration in pulmonary function
   2. Patients with symptoms and an accelerated deterioration in pulmonary function

   Both groups improve when smoking is stopped—in fact, pulmonary function returns to that found in nonsmokers. The group with accelerated deterioration in function is of particular concern. Much morbidity and mortality could be prevented by identifying these people and convincing them to stop smoking. Whether similar improvement will occur in those with other types of chronic bronchitis and emphysema must await a better understanding of other causes.

Table 4-2
Functional Abnormalities in Chronic Bronchitis and Emphysema

Measurement	Predominant in Chronic Bronchitis	Predominant in Emphysema
Volumes		
RV	Moderate ↑	Marked ↑
TLC	Slight ↑	Moderate ↑
FRC	Nl or slight ↑	Marked ↑
Flows		
FEV_1	Decreased	Decreased
FVC	Decreased	Decreased
Pressures		
Compliance	Nl or slight ↓	Nl or ↑
Elastic recoil	Nl or ↑	Decreased
Gas exchange		
Pa_{O_2}	Moderate to Marked ↓	Slight to moderate ↓
Pa_{CO_2}	Commonly ↑	Nl or slight ↑
DL_{CO}	Nl or decreased	Decreased
Vasculature		
PA pressure	Increased	Nl or slight ↑
Ventilatory drive		
Rest	Decreased to P_{O_2}, P_{CO_2}	Decreased to P_{O_2}, P_{CO_2}
Exercise	Mild increase	Moderate increase
Sleep	Disordered pattern	Disordered pattern

B. **Reversible abnormalities.** The primary physiologic defect in chronic bronchitis and emphysema is obstruction to flow. In both diseases, obstruction secondary to bronchoconstriction may be partially reversible, although this supposition remains unproved. Abnormal results on pulmonary function tests with inhaled bronchodilators, peripheral eosinophilia, or sputum eosinophilia, all may indicate presence of reversible bronchoconstriction. Even if these findings are absent, patients with moderate or severe disease should have a finite trial of bronchodilators, with monitoring of clinical response and pulmonary function. Although various tests of pulmonary function are adequate to monitor effects of therapy, FEV_1 is simple and as sensitive as other measurements. Apparent clinical response to bronchodilators may occur even in the absence of objective change in pulmonary function. Recent data suggest that response may be due to improved cardiac or respiratory muscle function.

1. **Bronchodilators.** Theophylline preparations and sympathomimetics are the mainstays of therapy, although not all patients respond. Theophylline should be used cautiously, with monitoring of clinical response and serum levels. Dosage schedules for parenteral aminophylline are presented in Chapter 3. Oral dose should approximate the same amount per day, in divided doses. Therapeutic serum levels are between 10 and 20 µg/ml. In addition to bronchodilation, theophylline may improve right and left ventricular performance and perhaps also improve diaphragmatic function.

    Sympathomimetic agents are described in Chapter 3. They may be useful in chronic bronchitis and emphysema, although side effects of tachycardia and tremor frequently are limiting factors in elderly patients.

2. **Corticosteroids.** The role of corticosteroids in chronic bronchitis and emphysema is less clear than in asthma. A number of uncontrolled studies exists, but of three uncontrolled, double-blind trials, two indicated no response and one found improvement with steroids. The latter, more recent study, found an improvement in FEV_1 in one-third of patients with chronic bronchitis treated with prednisone 30 mg/day. Response to steroids could be predicted more accurately by sputum, than by blood, eosinophilia. Patients with moderate or severe disease and eosinophilia probably should have a finite trial of steroids. Patients with severe disease, or life-threatening exacerbations of either bronchitis or emphysema, may also be given a brief course of steroids.

3. **Physiotherapy.** Along with bronchoconstriction, mucus hypersecretion may contribute to airways obstruction in chronic bronchitis and, to a lesser extent, in emphysema. Studies employing a variety of techniques have attempted to determine the value of chest physical therapy in chronic bronchitis. Several studies in which patients were encouraged to cough and to use postural drainage demonstrated an increase in sputum clearance and improvement in flow

measurements or specific conductance. In one study, however, cough alone produced similar results, and in another, physical therapy led to a decrement in FEV_1. Induced cough and physical therapy are probably useful in patients with chronically increased sputum volume, greater than 30 ml/day, or in patients with exacerbations of disease and increased sputum production. Patients with predominant emphysema and mild cough probably benefit little, other than from increased attention. Intermittent positive pressure breathing (IPPB) has shown no advantage over physical therapy or aerosol bronchodilatation, and may increase hyperinflation. It should not be used routinely.

4. **Supplemental oxygen.** Supplemental oxygen must be used with caution in both acute and chronic settings of bronchitis and emphysema. In the acute exacerbation of either disease, usually caused by infection, oxygen is often necessary to maintain adequate Pa_{O_2}. Patients with chronic hypercapnia, and some patients with normocapnia, may be especially sensitive to increased alveolar oxygen. Their borderline or diminished ventilatory drive is further suppressed by increasing Pa_{O_2}, and coma or apnea may result. Oxygen should be given in a stepwise, controlled fashion, monitoring clinical status, Pa_{O_2}, and if necessary, Pv_{O_2}, as discussed in Chapter 7.

Oxygen therapy for severe hypoxemia in chronic bronchitis and emphysema has been advocated to limit systemic consequences. Common abnormalities in hypoxemic patients are summarized in *table 4-3*.

Early, uncontrolled studies generally treated pa-

Table 4-3
Abnormalities in Hypoxemic Patients

Physical	Psychosocial
Pulmonary hypertension	Mood alterations
Erythrocytosis	↓ Cognitive function
↓ Exercise tolerance	↑ Hospitalization
	↓ Quality of life

tients who had Pa_{O_2} less than 50 to 55 torr with low flow oxygen at 1-3 L/min. At least 12 hours/day of therapy were necessary to achieve beneficial effects, which included improved neuropsychologic function, increased exercise tolerance, decreased hospitalization, and a subjectively improved quality of life. Several studies also demonstrated decreased erythrocytosis and pulmonary hypertension in some patients. Unanswered questions included the effect on mortality and the duration of daily therapy required to produce results. Complications were mild—primarily a subclinical increase in Pa_{CO_2}. No clinical or pathologic evidence of oxygen toxicity was found.

Recently, two controlled studies addressed the issues of mortality and daily therapy. A preliminary finding from a British study is decreased mortality with 15 hours/day of therapy, in patients with chronic bronchitis. An American study compared 12- versus 24-hour low-flow oxygen therapy in patients with both chronic bronchitis and emphysema. Subjects had Pa_{O_2} less than 55 torr, or 59 torr with erythrocytosis or right heart failure. Pa_{O_2} was maintained above 60 torr, and follow-up after more than 12 months showed decreased mortality in the group treated with continuous oxygen. Both groups showed improved neuropsychologic function, decreased hematocrit, decreased pulmonary vascular resistance, and an increase in the quality of life, confirming prior studies. All effects were greater in continuous, than in 12-hour, therapy.

At present, patients with hypoxemia conforming to the criteria noted above probably should be offered low-flow oxygen for at least 15 hours/day. This may be administered by compressed gas, room-air enrichment devices, or portable liquid oxygen systems. Several studies suggest that oxygen therapy for chronic disease is most effective as part of a comprehensive treatment program.

C. **Exacerbations of disease.** Exacerbations of chronic airways obstruction are common, and may be life-threatening, given the patient's compromised status. Vigorous treatment should begin as early as possible to prevent respiratory failure. Therapeutic measures are supportive and intended to maintain adequate respiratory function while the precipitating factor of the episode is being dealt with. Precipitants of and treatment for exacerbations of chronic airways obstruction follow:

1. Precipitants
   a. Infection (e.g., tracheobronchitis, pneumonia)
   b. Respiratory center depression (e.g., drugs, oxygen)
   c. Superimposed pulmonary disease
      (1) Pulmonary edema
      (2) Pulmonary embolism
      (3) Chest trauma
      (4) Pneumothorax
   d. Abdominal insults
      (1) Surgery
      (2) Trauma
      (3) Inflammatory process (e.g., cholecystitis, pancreatitis)
      (4) Pain due to other process (e.g., peptic ulcer disease)
   e. Systemic compromise (e.g., sepsis)
   f. Altitude
   g. Metabolic imbalance (e.g., severe acidemia or alkalemia)
2. Treatment
   a. Correct hypoxemia
   b. Manage secretions
      (1) Physiotherapy and suctioning
      (2) Hydration
      (3) Humidify inspired gas
   c. Decrease airways resistance with bronchodilators
   d. Correct acid-base imbalance
   e. Maintain adequate nutrition
   f. Treat underlying cause (e.g., infection)

D. **Rehabilitation.** Physical training programs for patients with chronic bronchitis and emphysema are based on the premise that improved ventilatory and cardiac muscle function might compensate for nonreversible lung disease. Evidence for beneficial effects of such programs is limited, because: most studies have been short term and uncontrolled; training is often combined with other techniques, such as physical therapy; and different types of physical training have been used. Overall training, usually by treadmill or bicycle, appears to lead to decreased oxygen consumption with exercise, and increased work capacity. Effects on Pa_{O_2} and pulmonary function are uncertain. More specific ventilatory muscle training has similar effects, without evident change in pulmonary function. At present, exercise and ventilatory muscle training are research techniques rather than clinical methods of rehabilitation.

VI. COMPLICATIONS

A. **Infection.** Patients with chronic bronchitis sustain an increased frequency and severity of upper respiratory infections. This appears true to a lesser extent in patients with emphysema. Impaired mucociliary clearance, decreased cough effectiveness due to airway collapse, and systemic debility, all have been suggested as predisposing factors to infection. Isolation of pathogenetic organisms in chronic bronchitis and emphysema is often difficult. Viral cultures are laborious and insensitive, viral titers may be confounded by multiple serotypes, and bacterial colonization may occur in the absence of infection. At least one-third of exacerbations of chronic bronchitis are due to viruses or mycoplasmas. The range of such viruses is similar to that in normal individuals, and include rhinovirus, coronavirus, respiratory syncytial virus, adenovirus, parainfluenza virus, and influenza virus. However, in these patients, viral infections are associated with more symptoms than in normal persons, and influenza virus is associated with increased mortality. Furthermore, influenza and parainfluenza infections lead to prolonged decrements in pulmonary function, whereas other viral infections produce only transient declines. Severity of chronic bronchitis does not correlate with frequency of infection.

The role of bacterial infection in chronic bronchitis and emphysema is difficult to assess. Inasmuch as the upper respiratory tract is often colonized by gram-negative pathogens in such patients, sputum must be analyzed with care. In exacerbations of disease, the lower respiratory tract appears also to harbor pathogens, but in the absence of consolidation their role is uncertain. Bacteria probably are responsible for increases in sputum volume and purulence, but their effects on airway mucosa are unknown. Antibiotics are often administered to patients who have exacerbations of disease without consolidation. The efficacy of this treatment remains to be proved.

Bacteria commonly involved in exacerbations of chronic bronchitis are *S. pneumoniae* and *H. influenzae*. Other gram-negative organisms are found in institutionalized or recently treated patients. Choosing antibiotics empirically is probably as effective as examining sputum for organisms. A defined course of ampicillin, tetracycline, or sulfamethoxazole-trimethoprim may be used. If symptoms and sputum purulence persist, cultures should be performed and antibiotics changed. Resistance by *H. influenzae* remains uncommon. In some areas, 5 percent of these organisms are resistant to ampicillin and 6 percent to tetracycline; all remain sensitive to chloramphenicol. Almost all pneumococci are sensitive to ampicillin, although tetracycline does not always eradicate this organism.

Beyond attempted treatment of bacterial agents, no effective strategy exists for **preventing** infection. Prophylactic antibiotics appear to shorten duration of symptoms from infections, but do not affect frequency of infection, overall decline in pulmonary function, or other bacterial effects on pulmonary function. Prophylactic measures remain of uncertain value at present. If respiratory therapy or oxygen equipment is used, careful cleaning may prevent colonization by pathogens.

B. **Acid-base and electrolyte disturbances.** Hypercapnic patients with chronic bronchitis and emphysema often have metabolic alkalosis compensating for chronic respiratory acidosis. Chloride depletion occurs in these patients from salt restriction and diuretics prescribed for right heart failure. Potassium depletion results from use of diuretics. Both chloride and potassium depletion contribute to increased metabolic alkalosis and alkalemia. Chloride depletion limits renal excretion of bicarbonate, since an anion must accompany sodium reabsorption. Potassium depletion promotes distal hydrogen ion secretion and proximal ammonia formation. Diuretic-induced volume depletion also favors bicarbonate retention with sodium reabsorption. Mechanical ventilation in such patients may rapidly induce similar changes. Pa_{CO_2} is normalized quickly, but renal elimination of chronically retained bicarbonate requires hours to days.

In either setting, the resulting alkalemia may promote arrhythmias and bronchospasm, depress ventilatory drive, and interfere with regional pulmonary vasoconstriction. Improvement in hypoxemia and hypercapnia occurred in a small series of patients in whom alkalosis was reversed. Patients with hypercapnia and metabolic alkalosis should have diuretic therapy only if absolutely necessary. Chloride and potassium should be replaced with KCl. Acetazolamide and ammonium chloride are of uncertain benefit. Despite anecdotal evidence supporting the use of both agents, reliable information concerning risks and benefits is lacking. Use of HCl should be restricted to critically ill, mechanically ventilated patients in whom KCl cannot be used owing to elevated serum potassium levels. HCl should be given with great care, with frequent pH monitoring to prevent acidosis.

C. **Respiratory failure.** Acute respiratory failure in chronic bronchitis and emphysema is discussed in Chapter 5. Treatment is similar to that of other causes of respiratory failure, except that oxygen must be used with care, and positive end-expiratory pressure (PEEP) and continuous positive airway pressure (CPAP) present greater risks.

D. **Cor pulmonale.** Cor pulmonale designates heart disease caused by pulmonary disorders. Specifically, it refers to right ventricular enlargement (hypertrophy or dilatation) secondary to pulmonary disease. Chronic bronchitis and emphysema are the most common causes of chronic cor pulmonale, although chest wall, interstitial, and vascular diseases may lead to similar pathology. Right ventricular hypertrophy or dilatation, the hallmark of cor pulmonale, is caused by pulmonary hypertension. In chronic airways obstruction, this is due to hypoxia. Hypoxia is an extremely potent vasoconstrictor, and chronic hypoxia leads to arteriolar muscle hypertrophy and probably hyper-reactivity. Chronic hypercapnia has little direct effect on pulmonary vascular resistance (PVR), although consequent acidemia exerts both direct and indirect pressor effects on pulmonary vessels.

Since hypoxemia is usually more severe in chronic bronchitis than in other disorders leading to cor pulmonale, PVR is greater and cor pulmonale more common in patients with chronic bronchitis. Destruction of the pulmonary vascular bed in emphysema may also increase PVR by limiting recruitment. However, reversibility of pulmonary hypertension with oxygen in emphysema, argues against loss of vasculature as a major contributor.

Pulmonary vascular resistance represents right ventricular afterload. Increase in afterload leads to hypertrophy, especially of the free wall. If increase in afterload is sufficiently severe and prolonged, right ventricular dilatation and failure result, with intravascular volume expansion and systemic venous congestion. Unlike left ventricular failure, cardiac index is often preserved at rest, but increases little with exertion, despite elevated right ventricular filling pressures. The left ventricle is probably unaffected in cor pulmonale, in the absence of other myocardial disease. Pathogenesis of cor pulmonale is illustrated in figure 4-2.

Incidence of cor pulmonale is related to the underlying disease process. In emphysematous patients, right ventricular dilatation and failure are uncommon except

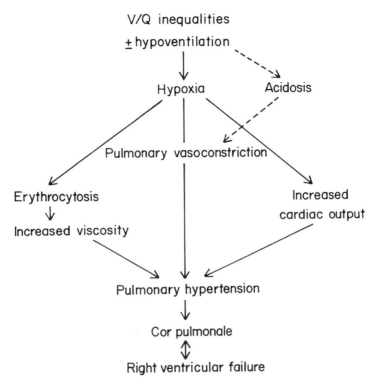

Figure 4-2. Pathogenesis of cor pulmonale. (Note: processes are intermittent in exacerbations of emphysema and chronic in chronic bronchitis.)

when precipitated by acute hypoxemia. In patients who have chronic bronchitis with right ventricular hypertrophy alone, symptoms and signs reflect the overall disease process rather than hypertrophy per se. Right ventricular dilatation in either disease leads to the characteristic findings of cor pulmonale: cyanosis, jugular venous distention, hepatomegaly, and pedal edema.

Treatment of cor pulmonale is based on the underlying disorder. Use of digitalis and diuretics is controversial. Digitalis might exert an inotropic effect on the failing right ventricle, but evidence supporting this hypothesis is scant. Risks of arrhythmias are significant in these hypoxemic patients. Diuretics, although useful in treating symptomatic edema, are of uncertain hemodynamic benefit. Hypokalemia and alkalosis resulting from their use may exacerbate respiratory problems, as noted above.

E. **Bullous Disease.** Emphysema is often accompanied by bullae, cavities formed by coalescence of air spaces after parenchymal destruction. Bullae are defined by reference to other types of noninfectious lung cavities, as follows:

1. **Bleb.** Space abutting the visceral pleura, usually 1 to 2 cm in diameter
2. **Cyst.** Space lined by epithelium, usually developmental or inflammatory
3. **Bulla.** Emphysematous space exceeding 1 cm in diameter

Three types of bullae are defined pathologically, as presented in figure 4-3.

Bullae alter lung mechanics via a "mass" effect. Large bullae cause a reduction in airway diameter due to decreased radial traction on airways. In addition, bullae may become clinically evident through several complications: **pneumothorax**, especially after positive pressure breathing; **infection**; and **hemorrhage**. Diagnosis is based on chest x-ray, and occasionally, lung scan. Pulmonary function tests are altered by large bullae. FRC by helium dilution may be decreased due to lack of communication between bullae and airways. Airways resistance may increase due to decreased traction, as noted above.

Significant bullae usually occur in relatively severe emphysema. Increases in mortality in patients with bullous disease may reflect severity of underlying disease

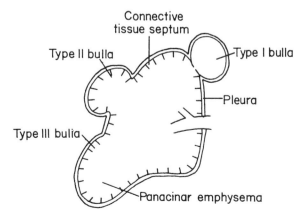

Figure 4-3. Types of bullous disease. (Used with permission of Reid L from *The Pathology of Emphysema* (p 212), JB Lippincott Co., 1967.

process. Occasionally, resection is attempted if hemorrhage, recurrent infection, or "mass" effect is thought clinically significant. Improvement after resection appears unpredictable. Other therapy includes antibiotics for infection and avoidance of positive pressure breathing.

F. Summary of therapy for chronic airways obstruction and its complications
1. Halt disease progression
   a. Discontinue smoking
   b. Remove from other potentially toxic agents
2. Treat reversible abnormalities
   a. Bronchoconstriction
      (1) Theophylline preparations for defined course
      (2) Sympathomimetics for defined course
      (3) Corticosteroids, if severe disease or no response from above
   b. Hypoxemia: continuous low-flow oxygen if criteria are satisfied
   c. Mucus hypersecretion: physical therapy in selected patients or for exacerbations of disease
3. Prevent complications
   a. Infection: possibly prophylactic antibiotics
   b. Acid-base and electrolyte disturbances
      (1) Maintain normal pH by use of chloride supplements
      (2) Avoid diuretics and salt restriction, if possible
   c. Cor pulmonale: treat hypoxemia

VII. NATURAL HISTORY AND PROGNOSIS

Chronic bronchitis and emphysema appear to progress in stages paralleling the pathogenesis of these diseases. The initial insult, usually cigarette smoke, causes mucosal thickening in small airways with concomitant pulmonary function abnormalities, but few symptoms. With continued exposure beyond a threshold, probably about 20 "pack-years," susceptible patients develop large airways disease leading to chronic bronchitis, emphysema, or both. One subgroup of patients develops mucus hypersecretion, manifested as chronic bronchitis. Cough and sputum production are prominent, but relatively little obstruction occurs. A second subgroup primarily develops emphysema, with little cough but significant obstruction. A third subgroup develops evidence of both processes. All three groups have some symptoms referable to these diseases. Cessation of exposure, before severe systemic manifestations occur, leads to stabilization of symptoms and pulmonary function. Flows return to levels of the population at large. Continued exposure augments the decline in pulmonary function, and in a minority of patients, leads to rapid deterioration in flows. A model of the natural history of emphysema and chronic bronchitis is presented in *table 4-4*.

Rate of decline of FEV_1, in several series of mixed emphysema and chronic bronchitis patients, was 50 to 60 ml/yr, although this probably underestimates the actual value. Corresponding rates in normal persons are 20 to 30 ml/yr. Other parameters also show progressive decline, but deterioration is less predictable and evidence is limited. Hypoxemia increases with time, although much less in emphysema than chronic bronchitis. Nonetheless, when FEV_1 reaches 1.0 L, almost all patients develop resting hypoxemia and hypercapnia. Pulmonary hemodynamics also vary with type of disease. Cardiac output remains low in the absence of hypoxemia, but increases if oxygenation is compromised.

Mortality in chronic bronchitis and emphysema is variable; pooled data indicate overall mortality only slightly

Table 4-4
Natural History of Chronic Bronchitis and Emphysema

Age	Smoking (pk-yrs)	Symptoms	Pulmonary Function
15-25	0-10	None	Normal
25-35	10-20	Decreased exercise tolerance	Small airways disease (Vmax 25, frequency-compliance, etc)
35-45	20-40	Bronchitis: productive cough Emphysema: mild DOE	Decreased FEV_1, FEF 25-75
45-55	30-60	Bronchitis: cough, infections Emphysema: increasing DOE	Decreasing FEV_1
55+	50+	Moderate-to-severe limitation in activity	Decreasing FEV_1; increasing PA pressures

greater than that of the general population. More specific projections can be made based on FEV_1 at initial measurement:

FEV_1 1.4 L: median survival 10 years
FEV_1 1.0 L: median survival 4 years
FEV_1 0.5 L: median survival 2 years

Survival expectation is decreased by evidence of cor pulmonale, and especially, by high levels of PVR. Effects of therapy on the course of disease are uncertain. As noted above, continuous oxygen therapy in hypoxemic patients appears to ameliorate symptoms and may improve chances for survival. Whether other types of therapy affect survival is unknown at present.

REFERENCES

I. General

Fishman AP: The spectrum of chronic obstructive disease of the airways. In *Pulmonary Diseases and Disorders*. Edited by Fishman AP, New York, McGraw-Hill, 1980, pp 458-469.

Hugh-Jones P, Whimster W: The etiology and management of disabling emphysema. *Am Rev Respir Dis* 117:343-378, 1978.

Petty TL (ed): *Chronic Obstructive Pulmonary Disease*. New York, Dekker, 1980.

Reid L: Chronic obstructive lung diseases. In *Pulmonary Diseases and Disorders*. Edited by Fishman AP, New York, McGraw-Hill, 1980, pp 503-525.

Fishman locates chronic bronchitis and asthma on a continuum of obstructive diseases. Hugh-Jones offers an extensive discussion of emphysema with few references to chronic bronchitis. Petty's book is a recent compilation of reviews, emphasizing rehabilitation and outpatient therapy. Reid presents a concise review, especially useful for pathology and pathogenesis.

II. Etiology and Pathogenesis

Defels R, Rokaw SN, Coulson AH, et al: The UCLA population studies of chronic obstructive respiratory disease: methodology and comparison of lung function in areas of high and low pollution. *Am J Epidemiol* 109:33-58, 1979.

Kimbel P, Kueppers F: The biochemical basis of emphysema: the oxidant effect of cigarette smoke? *Ann Intern Med* 92:564-566, 1980.

Morse JO: $Alpha_1$ antitrypsin deficiency. *N Engl J Med* 299:1045-1048, 1978.

Mountain R, Zwillich C, Weil J: Hypoventilation in obstructive lung disease. *N Engl J Med* 298:521-525, 1978.

Defels presents evidence from a large study implicating pollution in some aspects of obstructive disease. Kimbel presents a brief review of one theory of pathogenesis of emphysema, whereas Morse reviews evidence concerning alpha$_1$-antitrypsin. Mountain documents familial abnormalities in ventilation in patients with obstructive lung disease.

III. Diagnosis

Burki NK, Krumpelman JL: Correlation of pulmonary function with the chest roentgenogram in chronic airway obstruction. *Am Rev Respir Dis* 121:217-223, 1980.

Ingram RH, Jr, McFadden ER, Jr: Pulmonary performance in chronic bronchitis and emphysema. In *Pulmonary Diseases and Disorders*. Edited by Fishman AP, New York, McGraw-Hill, 1980, pp 542-548.

Fraser RGF, Pare RG: *Diagnosis of Diseases of the Chest*. Philadelphia, WB Saunders, 1979, pp 1352-1406.

Burki points out the general lack of sensitivity and specificity of the chest x-ray; Fraser discusses diagnosis, with emphasis on radiologic techniques. Ingram concentrates on the role of pulmonary function abnormalities in the diagnosis of these diseases.

IV. Alterations in Lung Function

Parot S, Saunier C, Gautier H, et al: Breathing pattern and hypercapnia in patients with obstructive pulmonary disease. *Am Rev Respir Dis* 121:985-991, 1980.

Wagner PD, et al: Ventilation/perfusion inequality in chronic obstructive pulmonary disease. *J Clin Invest* 59:203-216, 1979.

Wynne JW, Block AJ, Hemenway J, et al: Disordered breathing and oxygen desaturation during sleep in patients with chronic obstructive lung disease (COLD). *Am J Med* 66:573-579, 1979.

Pulmonary mechanics are discussed in the general reviews in the first section above. Parot points out the lack of correlation between mechanics and ventilatory pattern, and Wynne demonstrates transient desaturation during sleep in a small group. Wagner finds several V/Q patterns, with no evidence for a role for diffusion limitation.

V. Treatment

Alexander MR, Dull WL, Kasik JE: Treatment of chronic obstructive pulmonary disease with orally administered theophylline. *JAMA* 244:2286-2290, 1980.

Aubier M, De Troyer A, Sampson M, et al: Aminophylline improves diaphragmatic contractility. *N Engl J Med* 305:249-252, 1981.

Belman MJ, Mittman C: Ventilatory muscle training improves exercise capacity in chronic obstructive pulmonary disease patients. *Am Rev Respir Dis* 121:273-280, 1980.

Gracey DR, Divertie MB, Didier EP: Preoperative pulmonary preparation of patients with chronic obstructive pulmonary disease. *Chest* 76:123-129, 1979.

Lertzman MM, Cherniack RM: Rehabilitation of patients with chronic obstructive pulmonary disease. *Am Rev Respir Dis* 114:1645-1665, 1976.

Murray JF: The ketchup-bottle method. *N Engl J Med* 300:1155-1156, 1979.

Nocturnal Oxygen Therapy Trial Group: Continuous or nocturnal oxygen therapy in hypoxemic chronic obstructive lung disease: a clinical trial. *Ann Intern Med* 93:391-398, 1980.

Sahn SA: Corticosteroids in chronic bronchitis and pulmonary emphysema. *Chest* 73:389-396, 1978.

Alexander suggests that, contrary to common belief, theophylline is of little benefit to most patients. Aubier shows improved diaphragmatic function in normal persons treated with aminophylline. Gracey and Murray discuss possible benefits from physical therapy. Lertzman briefly reviews this subject as well as supplemental oxygen and exercise training. The nocturnal oxygen therapy trial group and Belman document the utility of these last two modes of therapy. Sahn reviews prior studies concerning steroids. At present, evidence is inconclusive.

VI. Complications

Fishman AP: Chronic cor pulmonale. *Am Rev Respir Dis* 114:775-794, 1976.

Heinemann HO: The kidney and acid-base disorders in obstructive disease of the airways. In *Pulmonary Diseases and Disorders*. Edited by Fishman AP, New York, McGraw-Hill, 1980, pp 549-561.

Smith CB, Golden CA, Kanner R, et al: Association of viral and mycoplasma pneumonia infections with acute respiratory illness in patients with chronic obstructive pulmonary disease. *Am Rev Respir Dis* 21:225-232, 1980.

Tager I, Speizer FE: Role of infection in chronic bronchitis. *N Engl J Med* 292:563-571, 1975.

Fishman presents a comprehensive review, not recently surpassed. Heinemann offers an excellent summary of renal compensation for respiratory acid-base imbalance. Smith and Tager present data on causative organisms in infections, and inconclusive data concerning prophylactic antibiotics.

VII. Natural History

Bates DV: The fate of the chronic bronchitic. *Am Rev Respir Dis* 108:1043-1077, 1973.

Fletcher C, et al: *The Natural History of Chronic Bronchitis and Emphysema*. New York, Oxford University Press, 1976.

Traver GA, Cline MG, Burrows B: Predictors of mortality in chronic obstructive pulmonary disease. *Am Rev Respir Dis* 119:895-902, 1979.

All three references, together with the chapter by Burrows in the Petty collection above, establish the natural history of these diseases. Bates notes the presence of a group with accelerated deterioration, and Fletcher distinguishes between patients with outflow obstruction and those with mucus hypersecretion. Traver establishes rates of decline in FEV_1, and notes a wide variation in survival.

5
Respiratory Failure

I. **DEFINITION**

   Respiratory failure is a condition of insufficient gas exchange to meet metabolic demands. This definition presupposes no threshold level of oxygenation. Rather, it depends on the role of the lung in overall homeostasis: respiratory failure always involves other organ dysfunction. Respiratory failure may be defined operationally with reference to arterial blood gases (ABG):

   Pa_{O_2} less than 50 torr
   Pa_{CO_2} greater than 50 torr

   Acute respiratory failure entails new symptoms related to these abnormalities. Patients with chronic respiratory failure may have little change in symptoms with these ABG values.

II. **PATHOPHYSIOLOGY**

   Respiratory failure invariably involves hypoxemia, but can be further subdivided by level of Pa_{CO_2} and ventilation:

   A. Hypoxemia with hypercapnia

      1. **Decreased ventilation.** Decreased alveolar ventilation leads to both hypoxemia and hypercapnia. It occurs in patients with depression of central respiratory output due to drugs or central nervous system lesions, or respiratory muscle dysfunction, as in paralysis or trauma. The gas exchange apparatus is often well preserved in such patients.

      2. **Normal or increased ventilation.** Hypercapnia due to V/Q inequalities leads to compensation by in-

creased ventilation. When, owing to severe V/Q inequalities and increased work of breathing, ventilation can no longer increase, hypercapnia and hypoxemia result. Causes are primarily the obstructive diseases, such as emphysema, chronic bronchitis, and asthma. Such patients almost invariably have intrinsic lung disease.

B. **Hypoxemia with normocapnia or hypocapnia.** Hypoxemia is usually due to shunt or V/Q inequalities, but ventilation remains sufficient to exchange carbon dioxide. This occurs in the adult respiratory distress syndrome (ARDS), which involves alveolar filling and collapse, or in specific disorders leading to alveolar filling, such as pneumonia. In addition, chronic restrictive disease, such as fibrosis, may lead to hypoxemia and hypocapnia.

Physiologic and anatomic abnormalities in these categories of respiratory failure are summarized in *table 5-1*.

III. **DIAGNOSIS**

A. **History and symptoms.** Evidence for the presence and etiology of respiratory failure includes a history of chronic lung, cardiac, or neuromuscular disease. Symptoms are nonspecific, including dyspnea, cough, and chest pain. Presence and severity of symptoms do not help distinguish between respiratory compromise and failure.

B. **Signs.** Signs of respiratory failure are nonspecific. Respiratory, cardiovascular, and central nervous systems are most often affected.

1. **Central nervous system.** Effects range from alterations of mood to profound coma, with common symptoms including headache, confusion, agitation, and drowsiness. Level of consciousness is especially important in patients with chronic airways obstruction (CAO). One large series found no coma or semicoma unless Pa_{CO_2} was greater than 75 torr, or Pa_{O_2} less than 35 torr. Other neurologic dysfunction can, of course, occur within this range.

2. **Respiratory.** Signs of respiratory distress, such as tachypnea and labored breathing, are common but not always present.

3. **Cardiovascular.** Tachycardia and mild systemic hypertension are common. Signs of pulmonary hyper-

Table 5-1
Pathophysiologic Patterns in Respiratory Failure

Gas Exchange	Causes	Abnormalities	
		Physiologic	Anatomic
Hypoxemia, hypercapnia			
Normal or increased ventilation	COPD	V/Q inequalities	Airways and parenchyma
	Asthma	V/Q inequalities	Airways
Decreased ventilation	Respiratory center depression	Hypoventilation	Central nervous system
	Neuromuscular disease	Hypoventilation	Chest wall
	Kyphoscoliosis	Hypoventilation	Chest wall
	Trauma	Hypoventilation	Chest wall
	Obesity	Hypoventilation	Chest wall
Hypoxemia, normocapnia	ARDS	V/Q inequalities and shunt	Vasculature
	Pulmonary edema	V/Q inequalities and shunt	Vasculature
	Pneumonia	V/Q inequalities and shunt	Parenchyma

tension and right ventricular failure occur in long-standing disease.
4. **Other.** Cyanosis is common, but not always present.

C. **Arterial blood gases (ABG).** The diagnosis of respiratory failure requires knowledge of ABG patterns, which are presented in *table 5-2*.

D. **Other laboratory findings.** Chest x-rays may indicate a specific etiology such as pneumonia or lymphangitic carcinoma, or may be nonspecific, as in ARDS. Other laboratory findings relate to underlying disease, rather than to the presence of respiratory failure per se.

IV. **ALTERATIONS IN LUNG FUNCTION**

A. **Volumes.** Changes in lung volumes vary with etiology of respiratory failure. In ARDS, alveolar collapse leads to decreased FRC. In asthma and CAO, airway obstruction and closure may lead to increased FRC. Patients with neurologic or chest wall dysfunction often have normal lung volumes.

B. **Mechanics.** Independent of premorbid state, total pulmonary resistance is usually increased in respiratory failure. This is due to increased airway resistance secondary to secretions, and increased parenchymal resistance secondary to increased lung water. Increased lung water also results in decreased lung compliance. These abnormalities lead to higher airway and transpulmonary pressures.

C. **Gas Exchange.** Hypercapnia is due to hypoventilation, exacerbated by V/Q inequalities. Hypoxemia may be

Table 5-2
Arterial Blood Gas Patterns in Respiratory Failure

Gas Exchange	Pa_{O_2} (torr)	Pa_{CO_2} (torr)	pH	HCO_3 (mEq/L)
Hypoxemia, hypercapnia				
Normal or increased ventilation	<50	>50	~7.38	>30
Decreased ventilation	<50	>50	<7.30	~24
Hypoxemia, normocapnia	<50	<40	~7.44	~24

due to hypoventilation, shunt, or V/Q inequalities. The contribution of diffusion limitation probably is small. Physiologic dead space, V_D/V_T, represents volume of conducting airways and unperfused alveoli, and indicates adequacy of gas exchange. It is usually increased in respiratory failure in patients with intrinsic lung disease.

D. **Vasculature.** Increased pulmonary vascular resistance with concomitant pulmonary artery hypertension is a hallmark of severe respiratory failure, even after correction of hypoxemia. Possible causes include active vasoconstriction, decreased lung volume, increased interstitial pressure, microembolism, and fibrosis. Elevated pressure may in turn lead to right ventricular dysfunction.

V. **TREATMENT OF RESPIRATORY FAILURE**

A. **Primary therapy.** This consists of reversing the most life-threatening consequences of respiratory failure: **hypoxemia** and **respiratory acidosis.** Hypoxemia is reversed by providing supplemental oxygen, and respiratory acidosis by increasing alveolar ventilation, and if necessary, by providing bicarbonate. Initial therapy is directed toward establishing and maintaining an airway, providing oxygen, and initiating mechanical ventilation. In addition, efforts to diagnose and treat the underlying disease should begin as soon as possible.

B. **Mechanical ventilation.** The decision to proceed with endotracheal intubation and mechanical ventilation is based on clinical and ABG evaluation, and varies with etiology and gas exchange pattern.
  1. **Hypoxemia, hypercapnia.** Patients with obviously inadequate ventilatory effort may require mechanical assistance before ABG results are available. Patients with apparently adequate ventilation, especially in the setting of chronic disease, should be carefully evaluated for level of consciousness and ABG. Alterations of consciousness, or hypoxemia unrelieved by careful oxygen supplementation, are causes for intubation. Systemic pH may suggest a change from a chronic compensated state: ventilatory support is generally required for pH less than 7.20.
  2. **Hypoxemia, hypocapnia.** Evidence of extreme hypoxemia or extreme tachypnea occasionally may lead to intubation before ABG results are known. Hypoxemia unrelieved by supplemental oxygen, as determined by ABG, is the usual criterion for support.

Other parameters, such as V_D/V_T, alveolar-arterial oxygen difference $(A\text{-}aD_{O_2})$, or inspiratory force, are difficult to obtain unless the patient is intubated, and are therefore more useful in weaning from mechanical ventilation. Abnormalities usually associated with the need for ventilatory support are presented in *table 5-3*.

C. Initiating mechanical ventilation

Mechanical ventilation utilizes several types of apparatus with the potential for dysfunction. Ventilatory support should be initiated and monitored in a systematic fashion. A suggested procedure for beginning mechanical ventilation is presented below.

1. Endotracheal tube
   a. Type
      (1) Nasotracheal or orotracheal
      (2) Greater than 7.5 mm internal diameter, if possible
      (3) Low pressure cuff (less than 30 torr)
   b. Position: check with chest x-ray
2. Mechanical ventilator
   a. Volume-cycled
      (1) Tidal volume: 10-15 ml/kg
      (2) Respiratory rate: 10-20/min to maintain gas exchange

Table 5-3
Indications for Mechanical Ventilation in Respiratory Failure

Measure	Normal Value	Ventilation Indicated
Mechanics		
Respiratory rate (/min)	12-20	>35
Vital capacity (ml/kg)	65-75	<15
FEV_1 (ml/kg)	50-60	<10
Inspiratory force (cm H_2O)	75-100	<25
Gas exchange		
Pa_{O_2}	75-100 (air)	<60
$A\text{-}aP_{O_2}$	25-65	>450
Pa_{CO_2}	37-43	>55 (except chronic)
V_D/V_T	0.25-0.40	>0.6

(3) Inspiratory duration: 1-3 sec (less than 1/3 cycle)
(4) Inspiratory pressure: less than 50-60 torr
(5) Alarm on continuously
b. Pressure-cycled
(1) Tidal volume: in normal lungs, approximately 80 ml gas/10 cm H_2O
(2) Rate: 10-20/min
3. Monitoring
a. Frequent vital signs
b. Cardiac monitor
c. ABG: Pa_{O_2} 60-90 torr; pH 7.35-7.50
d. Hemoglobin
e. Essential organ system function, especially CNS and renal

D. **Ventilator management.** Positive pressure ventilation, maintaining mean positive alveolar pressure, is used to ventilate almost all patients. Two types of positive pressure ventilators are available: pressure-cycled and volume-cycled. The former delivers a variable volume of gas up to a preset pressure; the latter delivers a preset volume of gas up to a designated safety or "pop-off" pressure. Volume ventilators are preferable, since minute ventilation can be controlled more carefully, and precise oxygen concentrations can be delivered. In addition, pressure-cycled ventilators may be unable to deliver adequate tidal volumes in patients with noncompliant lungs or those with high airways resistance. With both types of ventilator, expiration is passive, dependent on lung elastic recoil and chest wall recoil.

One of two types of ventilation pattern is generally used: controlled and assisted. In controlled ventilation, a preset number of breaths is delivered by the ventilator without contribution from the patient. This is necessary in apneic patients, and may be achieved through sedation and paralysis if the patient's own respiratory efforts interfere with effective ventilation. Assisted ventilation allows the patient to initiate respiratory efforts, which may then be supplemented by the ventilator, with a preset volume of gas. Patterns of alveolar pressure with these types of ventilation are compared with spontaneous breathing in figure 5-1.

Theoretical advantages of assisted ventilation include less risk of hypocapnia and alkalosis from excessive ventilation, lower mean intrathoracic pressures and thus less hemodynamic compromise, lack of need for sedation, and maintenance of the patient's respiratory

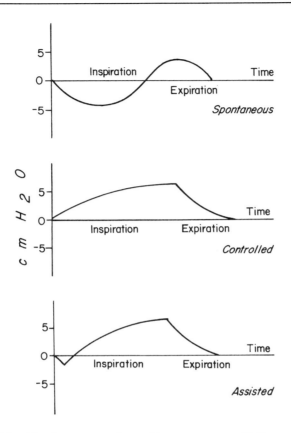

Figure 5-1. Alveolar pressure in positive pressure ventilation.

muscle tone. A third type of ventilation, intermittent mandatory ventilation (IMV), is discussed below.

Numerous studies have established an optimal pattern of ventilation for patients in respiratory failure. This pattern includes large tidal volumes and physiologic respiratory rates as presented above. The use of intermittent hyperinflations, or sighs, is controversial, but probably unnecessary when large tidal volumes are used. All patients receiving mechanical ventilation should have inspired gas humidified to saturation at body temperature (44 ml H_2O/L gas). This prevents drying of secretions and subsequent airway obstruction.

E. **Oxygenation.** Supplemental oxygen should be administered to maintain adequate arterial oxygen content. Other factors, such as cardiac output and hemoglobin concentration, affect oxygen transport to tissues, as discussed in Chapter 7. Hazards of supplemental oxygen are also discussed in Chapter 7. Pulmonary oxygen toxicity clearly occurs with high inspired oxygen concentrations, probably greater than 0.6 atmospheres. Every effort should be made to decrease inspired oxygen below this level by treating the underlying disease process and adding positive end-expiratory pressure (PEEP) in appropriate situations. High concentrations of oxygen may also replace nitrogen in lung units, leading to "absorption atelectasis," with a resulting increase in V/Q inequalities.

In patients with chronic hypercapnia, supplemental oxygen may depress oxygen-dependent respiratory drive, decreasing spontaneous ventilation. Such patients are often chronically hypoxemic, and oxygen must be administered carefully. Pa_{O_2} should be raised to chronically maintained levels rather than to an arbitrary normal value.

F. **Sedation.** Sedatives should be used with caution in respiratory failure, due to side effects of decreased respiratory effort, decreased cough, and occasional systemic hypotension. In some situations, the patient's own respiratory efforts interfere with those of the ventilator, resulting in inadequate tidal volume delivery, excessive inspiratory pressure, and inadequate oxygenation. Reassurance alone may suffice in alert patients, but if asynchrony persists, sedation may be required.

In the extreme case, muscle paralysis will also be necessary to achieve effective ventilation. A nondepolarizing agent such as pancuronium bromide or D-tubocurarine should be used, and an opiate or benzodiazepine sedative should always be used concurrently. The use of sedation and paralysis requires added attention to physiotherapy and pulmonary toilet, because they depress clearance of secretions. Theoretical exacerbation of V/Q inequalities by paralysis is of uncertain clinical significance. Situations in which sedation and paralysis are most often necessary include ARDS and severe asthma.

G. **Weaning from mechanical ventilation.** Efforts to decrease and ultimately discontinue mechanical ventilation should be initiated as soon as possible after intubation, owing to the inherent risks of ventilatory support.

Criteria for "weaning" are generally similar to those for initiating mechanical ventilation. More sophisticated measurements are possible because they are easier to perform on intubated patients. Clinical status, such as level of consciousness, ability to clear secretions, and dysfunction of other organ systems, also must be considered before weaning. Criteria for weaning follow:

1. Primary criteria
   a. P (A-aD$_{O_2}$ 1.0) less than 300 torr
   b. Alveolar ventilation able to maintain pH greater than 7.25
   c. Inspiratory force greater than 20 cm H$_2$O
   d. Vital capacity 8-10 ml/kg
2. Secondary criteria
   a. Pa$_{O_2}$ greater than 60 torr with FI$_{O_2}$ = 0.4 or less
   b. V$_D$/V$_T$ less than 0.6
   c. Resting minute ventilation less than 10 L/min; doubles with maximal effort.

Fulfillment of these criteria has been shown to predict successful extubation; the first four criteria are especially well studied.

Weaning may be accomplished by one of two methods: progressive removal from ventilatory support, and intermittent mandatory ventilation (IMV). In the former technique, once weaning criteria are met, the patient is disconnected from the ventilator and allowed to breathe spontaneously. If the clinical status and Pa$_{CO_2}$ remain stable for approximately one-half hour, the patient may be extubated. If not, the patient may be returned to the ventilator and the procedure repeated until extubation is considered appropriate. Extubation is contraindicated in the presence of symptoms and signs of respiratory failure, such as confusion and agitation.

IMV provides a gradual approach to weaning. Ventilators with this capacity deliver a preset volume at a variable rate. If the patient does not make the requisite number of efforts, then a preset number of breaths are delivered, as in controlled ventilation. In synchronized IMV (SIMV), if the patient breathes faster than the ventilator rate, then a preset number of breaths are assisted, as in assisted ventilation. With this technique, the respiratory rate can be decreased gradually, allowing the patient to assume more of the work of breathing. Extubation can proceed once a patient demonstrates stability on low respiratory rates or off the ventilator. Theoretical advantages of IMV include decreased mean intrathoracic pressures and improved respiratory muscle tone. No rigorous evidence supports the superiority of IMV over standard weaning techniques in adults. PEEP is probably useful in weaning. A decrease in VC and FRC almost always occurs in the first hours after extubation. In some patients this may lead to distress, and occasionally, the necessity for resumption of mechanical ventilation. Some evidence indicates that patients weaned from low levels of PEEP or continuous positive airway pressure (CPAP) maintain better postextubation VC, FRC, and oxygenation.

Complications of successful weaning include some degree of **hypoxemia**, which can usually be managed by increasing supplemental oxygen; mild **hypercapnia**, with a mean increase in Pa_{CO_2} of 8 torr, usually returning to normal within 24 hours; and occasional **hypervolemia** and **congestive heart failure**, the result of increased venous return upon discontinuation of mechanical ventilation.

Findings in patients who fail to wean are presented below:

H. Failure to wean from assisted ventilation
  1. Clinical findings
     a. Rise in previously normal pulse to greater than 120/min
     b. Increase in mean arterial blood pressure greater than 15 torr
     c. Bradycardia or hypotension
     d. Marked anxiety or agitation
  2. Arterial blood gas
     a. Increased P $(A\text{-}aD_{O_2}\ 1.0)$ to greater than 350 torr
     b. Pa_{O_2} less than 70 torr (except in chronic hypoxemia)
     c. Increased Pa_{CO_2} greater than 2 torr/min
     d. Arterial pH less than 7.25

I. Effects of mechanical ventilation
  1. Mechanics. Changes in volumes vary with the etiology of respiratory failure. In most instances, volumes are increased, including VC and FRC. Anatomic dead space is also increased, since increased lung volume leads to radial traction on airways. Changes in

pressures are also variable. In most cases, airway pressures are increased by mechanical ventilation.
2. **Gas exchange.** If previously elevated, Pa_{CO_2} is decreased, due to increased alveolar ventilation. Pa_{O_2} is increased, due to increased ventilation and supplemental oxygen. While changes in overall V/Q inequalities may vary, physiologic dead space is often increased. Raised airway pressures divert blood flow from ventilated regions, creating areas of high V/Q. The increase in physiologic dead space is of variable clinical significance. It can be countered, if necessary, by increasing minute ventilation.

J. Complications of mechanical ventilation
1. **Barotrauma.** This complication is due to the use of high pressures necessary to ventilate diseased lungs, especially in ARDS, and includes pneumothorax, pneumomediastinum, and subcutaneous emphysema. Markedly different rates of such complications have been reported in several series. A recent apparent decrease in incidence of barotrauma may be ascribed to greater familiarity and experience with positive pressure techniques. One recent series found only one pressure-induced complication in 200 cases. Pneumothorax in patients on mechanical ventilation may rapidly assume tension characteristics and become life-threatening.
2. **Ventilator malfunction.** Common problems include leaks, insensitive triggering mechanisms, and faulty oxygen mixing. To help avoid such complications, direct measurements of minute ventilation, tidal volume, delivered pressure, and oxygen concentration should be made. All ventilators should have an alarm indicating inadequate ventilation. Inappropriate ventilator settings, despite proper ventilator function, may result in alveolar hypoventilation or hyperventilation. Alveolar hypoventilation is of particular concern, because of its association with increased mortality.
3. **Endotracheal tube malfunction.** Common problems include intubation of the right main stem bronchus, cuff leak, and self-extubation. As the former two complications were associated with increased mortality in a large series, tube position should be checked after intubation. Expired tidal volume should be compared frequently with delivered volume to exclude cuff leak.

4. **Injury to the larynx and trachea.** Laryngeal ulcerations have been reported as early as 6 hours after intubation. Tracheal injury leading to tracheomalacia or stenosis may occur after several days of intubation. These complications may be minimized by careful attention to endotracheal tube position, use of low pressure/high volume cuffs, and tracheostomy, if long-term ventilation is required. The maximum duration of endotracheal intubation before tracheostomy is necessary is uncertain. Estimates range from 6 or 7 days, to 14 days. There are indications that low-pressure cuffs and careful nursing care allow intubation for 10 to 14 days with a low risk of late tracheal damage.

5. **Water retention.** Patients receiving mechanical ventilation retain salt and water. This is due in part to redistribution of intrarenal blood flow toward medullary junction glomeruli, and to release of aldosterone and antidiuretic hormone (ADH). Volume status must be monitored carefully to prevent left ventricular failure and cardiogenic pulmonary edema superimposed on respiratory compromise.

6. **Electrolyte imbalance.** As discussed in Chapter 4, patients with chronic hypercapnia often develop metabolic alkalosis during mechanical ventilation. Chloride replacement usually is necessary to correct alkalosis and should be provided as NaCl if volume status allows, or as KCl if serum potassium allows. In rare cases, HCl is necessary to correct alkalosis; it should be given carefully, with frequent monitoring of pH. No more than half the calculated H^+ deficit should be given in 24 hours (H^+ deficit − $[HCO_3^- - 25]$ x total body water). Acetazolamide in high doses is less easily regulated, and in low doses its effect may be limited by establishment of a new but persistently alkalotic equilibrium. If hepatic function is normal, ammonium chloride may be given either enterally or parenterally.

7. **Nosocomial infection.** Loss of upper airway defenses, compromise of lower tract defenses by disease, and in some cases, systemic immunocompromise, all render patients with respiratory failure susceptible to infection. Incidence of infection increases with duration of ventilation. Organisms are often multiply-resistant, and may colonize imperfectly cleaned respiratory equipment. Prevention must include meticulous cleaning of equipment, and sterile technique

in suctioning and tube manipulation. Patients who extubate themselves and are then reintubated may be at higher risk of infection.

8. **Gastrointestinal bleeding.** Prospective studies indicate an increased risk of upper gastrointestinal bleeding in respiratory failure, presumably due to stress ulceration. Controlled trials have shown the efficacy of antacids in preventing this complication, if gastric pH is titrated to 5.0. All patients should therefore receive prophylactic antacids. Histamine-receptor blocking agents have not been shown to be equally effective.

9. **Miscellaneous.** Gastric distention, presumably due to small air leaks, is not uncommon and is treated with nasogastric suction. Acute onset of distention should suggest cuff leak. Cuff testing should be performed, and the endotracheal tube replaced if necessary. Nasal necrosis arises occasionally with the use of nasotracheal tubes and may necessitate orotracheal intubation.

K. Adjunctive therapy
1. **Fluid management.** Positive fluid balance associated with ventilation occurs as described above. The use of colloid versus crystalloid solutions in maintaining fluid balance is controversial. In theory, colloids are preferable in hypoalbuminemic patients. Informed fluid management often necessitates the placement of a pulmonary artery catheter to allow measurement of pulmonary capillary wedge pressure (PCWP) as an index of intravascular volume.

2. **Chest physical therapy.** Percussion and vibration, change in body position, and postural drainage all are used to help mobilize secretions in patients with respiratory failure. These techniques are of added importance in patients who are unable to aid in clearing secretions. When necessary, deep endotracheal suction should be performed, with sterile technique. Preliminary treatment with supplemental oxygen reduces the frequency of arrhythmias resulting from this procedure. Suctioning should be performed for only 5 to 10 seconds per effort.

3. **Nutrition.** Patients with respiratory failure sustain severe catabolic stress and often receive little nutrition except small amounts of parenteral dextrose.

Despite a lack of controlled evidence, conservative management dictates maintenance of proper nutrition to prevent further complications, such as infection. Adequate calories and protein should be given as early as possible in the hospitalization period, preferably by the enteral route, but parenterally if necessary.

4. Electrolytes. Hypophosphatemia may interfere with effective muscle contraction. Phosphate should, therefore, be maintained in the normal range.

5. Extracorporeal membrane oxygenation (ECMO): This technique involves diverting a portion of the venous blood through an external membrane oxygenator and returning it to the circulation. By this method, gas exchange can be continued in the presence of severely diseased lungs. Controlled studies have thus far demonstrated the capability of this system in maintaining gas exchange, but not in decreasing mortality.

VI. RESPIRATORY FAILURE IN SPECIAL SITUATIONS

A. Carbon monoxide poisoning. Carbon monoxide (CO) binds to hemoglobin with an affinity approximately 210 times that of oxygen. Thus, high inhaled CO concentrations may displace oxygen and severely depress blood oxygen content. Because dissolved oxygen level is unchanged, Pa_{O_2} may remain normal. Oxygen content rather than Pa_{O_2}, therefore, should be measured. CO poisoning should be suspected from a history of exposure to automobile or other exhaust fumes. Patients are seldom "cherry red" as occasionally described, but rather exhibit pallor or even mild cyanosis. Treatment consists of administration of as high concentrations of oxygen as can be delivered, at least 100 percent, and preferably two or three atmospheres, if hyperbaric therapy is available. Such concentrations help displace CO from hemoglobin and increase dissolved oxygen concentrations. Carbon dioxide administration is not helpful.

B. Asthma. The decision to begin mechanical ventilation and the choice of ventilator settings for asthma are considered in Chapter 3. Once ventilation is begun, high cycling pressures due to diffuse bronchospasm may limit minute ventilation. If necessary, sedation and paralysis can be used to decrease chest wall resistance and prevent unsynchronized respiratory effort. Reduction of inspiratory flow rate decreases peak pressures, but also prolongs inspiration. This measure is usually unnecessary.

C. **Chronic airways obstruction.** Respiratory failure in chronic airways obstruction is discussed in Chapter 4. Efforts should be made to minimize inspired oxygen concentration and thus maintain hypoxic ventilatory drive. PEEP has little role in such situations, since adequate oxygenation is usually attainable. Moreover, PEEP incurs an increased risk of barotrauma. Metabolic alkalosis should be treated vigorously. Pharmacologic stimulants or analeptics currently available in the United States are of little benefit for these patients.

D. **Altered chest wall configuration.** Management of respiratory failure in these patients is generally the same as that of patients with normal anatomy. Since patients may be especially prone to atelectasis, periodic hyperinflation by incentive spirometry or positive pressure breathing is useful. Hypercapnia often complicates late stages of these disorders, therefore careful attention must be paid to oxygenation, acid-base equilibrium, and cardiac function.

E. **Obesity.** Obese patients may develop respiratory failure without associated lung disease, although this is uncommon. Most of these patients are best managed conservatively. A small percentage are truly "Pickwickian," exhibiting a decreased respiratory response to increasing Pa_{CO_2}. These patients often retain CO_2 in response to oxygen therapy, and therefore should be maintained on low oxygen concentrations. Central respiratory stimulants, such as progesterone, may be helpful in some cases.

F. **Postoperative.** Surgery of the chest and abdomen leads to a decrease in VC and FRC, with subsequent respiratory failure in susceptible patients. Upper abdominal surgery causes the greatest decrement—up to 50 percent VC—whereas lower abdominal surgery may lead to a 30 percent decrease in VC. In the early postoperative period, ventilation may also be depressed by perioperative sedation. Later problems include atelectasis and infection. Management is conservative, with early efforts directed toward weaning and spontaneous ventilation.

G. **Pneumothorax.** Mechanical ventilation not only poses

risks of pneumothorax, but patients who develop a bronchopleural fistula for any reason become more difficult to ventilate. Primary therapy of the pneumothorax, by aspiration or chest tube, is unchanged. If positive pressure ventilation is required, inflation pressures should be minimized. A second chest tube may be inserted if resolution does not occur, and thoracotomy may be necessary if the fistula persists.

VII. RESPIRATORY DISTRESS IN PATIENTS RECEIVING MECHANICAL VENTILATION

Acute respiratory distress in patients receiving mechanical ventilation is often life-threatening because of the compromised status of these patients. Two major problems occur: complications of the underlying disorder, and malfunction of the ventilator system. Diagnosis of distress in ventilated patients is especially difficult and requires meticulous evaluation, keeping the following factors in mind:

A. **Symptoms are often masked** by artificial airway or sedation. An alert patient may communicate dyspnea by writing or making signs. If patient is not alert, increase in agitation may signify distress.

B. **Signs include cyanosis and diaphoresis.** Change in respiratory rate or pattern ("fighting" the ventilator) may also indicate distress.

C. **Monitoring** of tidal volume, airway pressure, ABG, PCWP, ECG, and cardiac output may all help to locate causes of distress. *Table 5-4* and figure 5-2 present the differential diagnosis and schematic evaluation of ventilated patients with respiratory distress.

VIII. NATURAL HISTORY AND PROGNOSIS

Different outcomes of respiratory failure are reported in various series. Data relating survival to etiology are scant. Overall survival of hospitalization is about 40 to 70 percent. Accelerated mortality continues after discharge, and five-year survival ranges from 5 to 30 percent. As expected, younger patients seem to have better long-term prognoses. Patients surviving respiratory failure are usually at increased risk of further episodes, hence aggressive rehabilitation measures are important. Pulmonary function after respiratory failure is related to etiology. Follow-up data are too limited to predict recovery or deterioration in pulmonary function.

Table 5-4
Respiratory Distress in Patients Receiving Assisted Ventilation

Problem	Causes	Diagnosis	Therapy
Artificial airway	Main stem bronchus intubation	Decreased breath sounds on exam; chest x-ray	Reposition ET tube, check chest x-ray
	Cuff leak	Check cuff pressure, expired and delivered V_T, ventilator V_T	Reinflate or replace tube
	Herniation of cuff	Increased peak airway pressure; difficult suctioning	Deflate cuff, replace tube
Airway secretions	Obstruction of central bronchus	Atelectasis on exam, chest x-ray; no change with manual ventilation	Chest physiotherapy, bronchoscopy
Pneumothorax	Abscess, ARDS	Increased peak pressure, decreased dynamic compliance	Emergent: percutaneous needle Definitive: chest tube
Pulmonary edema	Fluid overload vs. ARDS	Difficult; chest x-ray often not helpful; check PCWP	Diuresis vs treatment of ARDS
Pulmonary embolism		Signs of DVT; hypoxemia; right ventricular strain on ECG Definitive: angiography	Anticoagulation or thrombolytic agents
Decreased systemic oxygen transport	Decreased cardiac output (e.g., MI); anemia	Check ECG, CO if possible; stool guaiac test, check Hb	Pressors, oxygen, transfusion as necessary
Ventilator malfunction	Leak; faulty oxygen concentration; abnormal triggering	Measure exhaled, delivered, ventilator V_T; measure triggering pressure	Repair or change ventilator

A. PATIENT APPEARS SEVERELY ILL

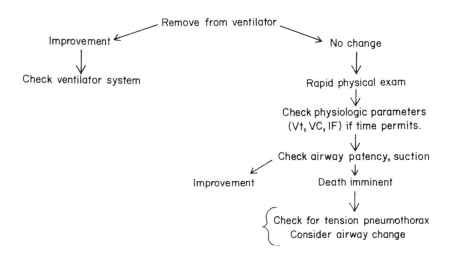

B. PATIENT APPEARS MODERATELY ILL

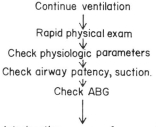

For continued deterioration, remove from ventilator as above.

Figure 5-2. Evaluation of respiratory distress in ventilated patients.

REFERENCES

I. General

Pontoppidan H, Geffin B, Lowenstein E: *Acute Respiratory Failure in the Adult.* Boston, Little, Brown, 1973.

Pontoppidan H, Wilson RS, Rie MA, et al: Respiratory intensive care. *Anesthesiol* 47:96-116, 1977.

Rogers RM, Juers JA: Physiologic considerations in the treatment of acute respiratory failure. *Basics of RD.* 3:1-6, 1975.

Pontoppidan (1973) is a classic monograph describing pathophysiology and therapy; surprisingly little has changed since this time. Pontoppidan (1977) incorporates more recent approaches. Rogers is a brief introduction to the physiology of respiratory failure.

II. Mechanical Ventilation—General

Kirby RR: Mechanical ventilation: facts, fiction and fallacies. *Curr Probl Anesthesiol Crit Care Med* 41:5, 1977.

Tisi G: Physiologic basis of ventilator therapy. In *Pulmonary Physiology in Clinical Medicine.* Edited by Tisi G, Baltimore, Williams & Wilkins, 1980, pp 225-245.

These are both succinct discussions of various types of ventilators and their effects on lung physiology. Kirby also discusses IMV and PEEP.

III. Mechanical Ventilation—Complications

Cullen DJ, Caldera DL: The incidence of ventilator-induced pulmonary barotrauma in critically ill patients. *Anesthesiol* 50:185-190, 1979.

Zwillich CW, Pierson DJ, Creagh CE, et al: Complications of assisted ventilation. A prospective study of 354 consecutive episodes. *Am J Med* 57: 161-170, 1974.

Cullen is a retrospective series, describing a low incidence of barotrauma. Zwillich is a prospective study of 18 common complications, three of which are associated with increased mortality.

IV. Mechanical Ventilation—Weaning

Feeley TW, Hedley-Whyte J: Weaning from controlled ventilation and supplemental oxygen. *N Engl J Med* 292:904-906, 1975.

Kirby RR, Graybar GB (eds): Intermittent mandatory ventilation. *Int Anesthesiol Clin* 18:1-196, 1980.

Sahn SA, Lakshminarayan S, Petty TL: Weaning from mechanical ventilation. *JAMA* 235:2208, 1976.

Feeley discusses "standard" weaning technique, including evidence for the use of positive pressure. Kirby is a collection of articles, primarily describing IMV, and includes a critique. Sahn discusses both methods, including a critique of IMV.

V. Other Therapy

Priebe HJ, Skillman JJ, Bushnell LS, et al: Antacid versus cimetidine in preventing acute gastrointestinal bleeding. *N Engl J Med* 302:426-430, 1980.

Zapol WM, Snider MT, Hill JD, et al: Extracorporeal membrane oxygenation in severe acute respiratory failure. *JAMA* 242:219-226, 1979.

Priebe documents the occurrence of upper gastrointestinal bleeding and its prophylaxis with antacids. Zapol summarizes the ECMO trial, demonstrating efficacy of the technique but no change in mortality.

VI. Specific Etiologies

Bergofsky EH: Respiratory failure in disorders of the thoracic cage. *Am Rev Respir Dis* 119:643-669, 1979.

Bone RC, Pierce AK, Johnston RL: Controlled oxygen administration in acute respiratory failure in chronic obstructive pulmonary disease. *Am J Med* 65:896-902, 1978.

Skillman JJ: Postoperative respiratory failure. In *Pulmonary Diseases and Disorders*. Edited by Fishman AP, New York, McGraw-Hill, 1980, pp 1682-1694.

Bergofsky recommends conservative therapy in patients with kyphoscoliosis. Bone presents an algorithm for selecting oxygen concentrations in COPD. Skillman discusses the effects of surgery on respiration, and general aspects of respiratory failure.

VII. Natural History

Asmundsson T, Kilburn KH: Survival after acute respiratory failure. *Ann Intern Med* 80:54-57, 1974.

This article reviews previous studies, and describes a retrospective series of 146 patients.

6
Adult Respiratory Distress Syndrome

I. DEFINITION

Adult respiratory distress syndrome (ARDS) is the term often given to respiratory failure involving peripheral gas exchange units (alveoli, capillaries, interstitium). ARDS is further characterized by clinical evidence of **respiratory distress, hypoxemia** requiring high inspired oxygen concentrations, and **diffuse infiltrates** on chest x-ray.

ARDS can result from a variety of heterogeneous causes. It is related only in name and pathologic appearance to respiratory distress syndrome of the neonate. The relative uniformity of clinical findings and of therapy justifies the notion of a syndrome rather than multiple diseases categorized by etiology.

II. PATHOGENESIS

　A. Etiology

　　A wide variety of insults may lead to ARDS, as summarized below:
　　1. Shock of any etiology
　　2. Infection
　　　a. Sepsis
　　　b. Viral or bacterial pneumonia
　　　c. Fungal or protozoal pneumonia
　　3. Trauma
　　　a. Fat embolism
　　　b. Pulmonary contusion
　　　c. Nonthoracic trauma with hypotension

4. Aspiration
   a. Gastric contents
   b. Fresh and salt water (drowning)
   c. Hydrocarbons
5. Drug overdose
   a. Opiates (heroin, methadone, propoxyphene)
   b. Barbiturates
   c. Colchicine
6. Inhaled toxins
   a. Oxygen
   b. Smoke
   c. Corrosive chemicals (NO_2, Cl_2, NH_3, phosgene)
7. Hematologic disease
   a. Disseminated intravascular coagulation (DIC)
   b. Massive blood transfusion
   c. Postcardiopulmonary bypass
8. Metabolic
   a. Pancreatitis
   b. Uremia
9. Miscellaneous
   a. Lymphangitis carcinomatosa
   b. Elevated intracranial pressure
   c. Eclampsia
   d. Postcardioversion
   e. Radiation pneumonitis

B. Pathophysiology

The common lesion appears to be diffuse lung injury resulting in alveolar-capillary membrane damage and concomitant pulmonary edema. Loss of pulmonary vascular bed and increased pulmonary vascular resistance soon follow. Alveolar and interstitial edema, and therefore increased lung water, are hallmarks of ARDS.

Factors contributing to edema include **increased capillary permeability, decreased plasma oncotic pressure,** and **decreased lymphatic drainage in the lung.** Increased capillary permeability and decreased surfactant appear especially important in the physiologic derangements induced in ARDS.

1. **Increased capillary permeability.** This may be due to vasoactive peptides released as a result of the initial injury. Alternatively, deposition of microemboli may lead to capillary damage and subsequent release of vasoactive substances. Increased permeability has been demonstrated by the finding of high alveolar albumin concentrations in pulmonary edema induced

by heroin and endotoxin. Increased permeability, in turn, causes leaking of plasma and erythrocytes into interstitial and alveolar spaces.

The roles of platelets and microemboli are uncertain. Angiographic studies suggest the presence of small distal clots. However, results of labeling techniques are equivocal in demonstrating the presence of platelets in the lung in ARDS.

2. **Decreased surfactant.** The increase in surface forces in ARDS suggests a lack of surfactant, but decreased surfactant levels have not been demonstrated clearly. Various abnormalities in ARDS might account for reduced surfactant effect: loss of formed surfactant into pulmonary edema fluid; combination of surfactant with plasma proteins leaked from capillaries; or decreased production of surfactant due to high tidal volume ventilation, high oxygen concentrations, or ischemia with damage to Type I cells. The result is increased surface forces and atelectasis.

These theories of the pathogenesis of ARDS are summarized in figure 6-1.

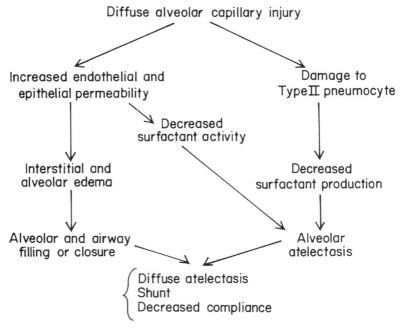

Figure 6-1. Proposed pathogenesis of ARDS.

C. **Pathology.** Pathologic changes are usually nonspecific, revealing the presence of the syndrome rather than its specific etiology. One series defined three stages of ARDS by biopsy:
1. **Early.** Interstitial and alveolar edema, with proteinaceous and cellular debris and hemorrhage into alveoli.
2. **Middle.** Hyperplasia and organization of debris, with increased Type II pneumocytes, increased interstitial cellularity, and hyaline membrane formation.
3. **Late.** Cuboidal transformation of alveolar epithelium with fibrosis, loss of capillary bed volume, and muscular hypertrophy of pulmonary arterioles.

III. DIAGNOSIS

A. **Symptoms.** The onset of dyspnea and tachypnea is characteristically insidious. Dyspnea increases, followed by exhaustion and central nervous system symptoms. Mild, usually dry, cough may also be present.

B. **Signs.** Tachypnea increases with time, and is often, in later stages, accompanied by cyanosis. Physical examination is otherwise unrevealing.

C. **Laboratory findings.** Early in the course, chest x-ray may be normal. Within 24 to 48 hours, diffuse hazy infiltrates appear and progress to involve most of the lung fields. Early ABG results may show mild- to-moderate hypoxemia and hypocapnia, with resulting alkalosis. As the syndrome progresses, hypoxemia worsens. Onset of the full-blown syndrome usually occurs hours to several days after the initial insult. Diagnosis is based on evaluation of the clinical course and chest x-ray, and on the presence of hypoxemia and reduced lung compliance.

A common dilemma in the diagnosis of ARDS is how to distinguish it from pulmonary edema secondary to increased left atrial pressure ("cardiogenic"). This is especially problematic in patients who have received large volume infusions for hypotension, or who have underlying cardiac disease. Resolution of the problem often requires a pulmonary artery catheter. A low pulmonary capillary wedge pressure (PCWP) suggests the presence of ARDS rather than cardiac dysfunction.

IV. ALTERATIONS IN LUNG FUNCTION

A. **Volumes.** A consistent finding in ARDS is a **reduction**

in functional residual capacity (FRC). This may be caused by the following factors:
1. Interstitial fluid reducing transmural airway pressure, leading to collapse and distal atelectasis
2. Alveolar edema and increased surface forces leading to further atelectasis
3. Decreased compliance leading to decreased expansion at a given pressure

B. Mechanics. Decreased lung compliance is characteristic of ARDS. Causes include:
1. Decreased tissue elasticity with increased lung water
2. Increased alveolar surface forces due to reduced surfactant activity
3. Decreased lung volume (an indirect cause)

Late in the course of the syndrome, fibrosis results in a further reduction in compliance.

C. Gas exchange. Severe hypoxemia is invariable in ARDS. The common pathologic findings, regardless of specific etiology, are pulmonary edema and atelectasis. These, in turn, cause hypoxemia through two mechanisms, shunt and V/Q inequalities.
1. Shunt. Pulmonary edema, with subsequent flooding and closure of small airways and alveoli, results in areas of the lung that are perfused but not ventilated. This, in turn, leads to intrapulmonary shunting of blood, a hallmark of ARDS.
2. V/Q inequalities. Several factors contribute to V/Q inequalities in ARDS:
   a. Atelectasis in some lung areas may affect adjacent zones through mechanical deformation.
   b. Interstitial fluid accumulation, even without accompanying alveolar edema, reduces both airway and vascular transmural pressure, and thus decreases the diameter of both structures. Airways in dependent zones may narrow or collapse, reducing ventilation and exacerbating V/Q inequalities.

   The pattern of V/Q inequalities appears to change with time. Late in the course of the syndrome, as fibrosis and capillary obliteration occur, units with high V/Q ratios increase and those with low V/Q ratios correspondingly de-

crease. This shift results in decreased CO_2 excretion and hypercapnia, unless counterbalanced by an increase in minute ventilation.

The contribution of diffusion limitation to the hypoxemia of ARDS is uncertain. Structure-function correlations can be made based on biopsy results and response to increased oxygen concentrations, as presented in *table 6-1*.

D. Vasculature. Patients with ARDS have increased pulmonary vascular resistance. Possible etiologies include hypoxia with reactive vasoconstriction, infarction, microvascular thrombosis, and destruction of alveolar capillary bed. Elevated pulmonary vascular resistance in turn raises pulmonary artery pressure, and may lead to right ventricular strain, dilatation, or failure.

In summary, characteristic functional abnormalities in ARDS are hypoxemia, reduced compliance, reduced FRC, and increased vascular resistance.

V. TREATMENT

Therapeutic measures in ARDS have two major goals: defining and treating the causes of the syndrome, and reversing hypoxemia by expanding distal gas exchange units and preventing further airway and alveolar collapse.

A. Treating etiological factors. Hypotension should be treated with volume, taking care to avoid excessive volume administration. Measurements of PCWP may be useful in titrating volume replacement. Sepsis should be treated aggressively with antibiotics. Most other causes

Table 6-1
Pathophysiologic Subgroups in ARDS

Gas Exchange	Response to Therapy	Pathology
Severe hypoxemia (large fixed shunt)	Little response to increased F_{IO_2} or PEEP	Severe interstitial alveolar edema; slight fibrosis
Less severe hypoxemia (moderate shunt)	Slow response to increased F_{IO_2} or PEEP	Extensive fibrosis
Least severe hypoxemia (moderate shunt)	Rapid response to PEEP	Moderate edema, no fibrosis

of ARDS are managed conservatively, by removing the precipitant, if possible, and providing respiratory support.

B. Oxygenation
1. **Indications for intubation and ventilation.** The full-blown syndrome of ARDS invariably requires ventilatory support. Patient exhaustion and inadequate oxygenation, despite maximum mask-oxygen concentrations, are clear indications for intubation. In general, strong clinical evidence of the presence of ARDS should lead to early intubation.
2. **Mechanical ventilation.** Optimal ventilation is similar to that in other causes of respiratory failure: high tidal volumes, 10-15 ml/kg; physiologic respiratory rates, 10-20/minute; and FI_{O_2} less than 0.6 atmospheres, if possible.
3. **Oxygen delivery.** The presence of shunt as the primary gas exchange abnormality in many patients with ARDS renders oxygenation difficult. Despite high, often toxic, levels of inspired oxygen, shunt persists, and arterial oxygenation may remain inadequate. Continuous positive pressure ventilation is used to enhance oxygenation, and is generally employed when Pa_{O_2} is less than 60 torr with FI_{O_2} greater than 0.6.

C. **Continuous positive pressure ventilation** represents the major therapeutic advance of the last decade in the management of ARDS. Two modalities, positive end-expiratory pressure (PEEP) and continuous positive airway pressure (CPAP) are used.

PEEP is artificial maintenance of positive pressure of selected magnitude at end expiration. CPAP is maintenance of pressure above ambient levels throughout the respiratory cycle.

In general, PEEP is used in the ventilated patient. PEEP in spontaneously breathing patients requires the generation of substantial negative pressure with inspiration, and thus increases the work of breathing. CPAP minimizes work of breathing, but increases mean intrathoracic pressure. It is generally used in spontaneously breathing patients. Effects of PEEP and CPAP on airway pressure are shown in figure 6-2.
1. Pulmonary effects of PEEP
   a. **Volumes.** The primary effect of PEEP is to in-

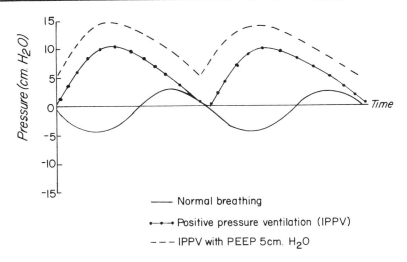

Figure 6-2. Effect of positive pressure ventilation on airways pressure.

       crease FRC. Positive pressure presumably increases transmural pressure across airways and alveoli, preventing and reversing collapse. This, in turn, increases FRC.

  b. **Pressures.** PEEP increases airway and pleural pressures as noted above. In addition, PEEP results in improved compliance within appropriate limits. Prevention and reversal of atelectasis leads to improved lung distensibility, and thus, compliance.

  c. **Gas exchange.** PEEP results in decreased shunt and increased Pa_{O_2}. Studies of V/Q profiles in patients with ARDS indicate that this is due to recruitment (opening) of closed alveoli. Ventilation of closed lung units results in decreased shunt.

       PEEP does not alter pathophysiologic abnormalities in ARDS. Total lung water remains increased despite PEEP, and cellular inflammatory response is not affected.

2. **Circulatory effects of PEEP.** Decreased cardiac output is a recognized complication of PEEP. Increased airway pressure caused by PEEP decreases venous return (preload) in proportion to the resulting rise in pleural pressure. Although not universally accepted, patients with stiff, noncompliant lungs probably

transmit less pressure to the pleural space, and therefore are less affected by PEEP. In general, the greater the increase in FRC with PEEP, the greater will be the depression of preload and cardiac output. The underlying intravascular state determines circulatory response to changes in pleural pressure, and therefore to changes in PEEP. Studies in animals and patients demonstrate that hypervolemia may attenuate or even abolish adverse circulatory effects of PEEP, preserving cardiac index at pre-PEEP levels.

Elevation of mean airway pressure with PEEP increases pulmonary vascular resistance in the presence of normal vasculature. This is presumably also true in ARDS. The resulting increase in right ventricular afterload may therefore contribute to decreased cardiac output. Increased transmural pressures across right and left ventricular walls caused by PEEP might also depress cardiac output.

In summary, PEEP acts to decrease cardiac output by decreasing venous return, and perhaps by increasing right ventricular afterload. Preload effects of PEEP are moderated by decreased lung compliance and increased circulatory volume.

3. **Use and monitoring of PEEP.** The complexity of pulmonary and circulatory interactions involved makes it impossible to predict the presence and magnitude of hemodynamic response to PEEP in an individual patient. Salutary and adverse effects must therefore be balanced. One study, for example, documented increased FRC, decreased shunt, and increased Pa_{O_2} in all patients, but cardiac output was reduced in half the patients, and oxygen delivery reduced in one-third of patients. As enhanced oxygen delivery to tissues is the fundamental goal of therapy, measurements of Pa_{O_2} alone may be misleading. Clinically, circulatory compromise from PEEP may be suspected from peripheral vasoconstriction, hypotension, tachycardia, or oliguria. More accurate assessment of the effects of PEEP can be made by measurements of:

   a. **Cardiac output.** Direct determination of cardiac output by dye dilution or thermodilution can be combined with data on gas exchange. This is done by multiplying cardiac output and arterial oxygen content to yield an index of systemic oxygen transport ($S_{O_2}T$). The goal of PEEP is to maximize transport.

b. **Compliance.** Maximal oxygen transport appears to correlate with optimal static compliance. This can be determined using the ventilator plateau phase. PEEP for any given tidal volume is then set below the level at which compliance begins to decline.
c. **Mixed venous oxygen.** This may also correlate with maximal oxygen transport. $P\bar{v}_{O_2}$ can be measured with a pulmonary artery catheter. PEEP is then adjusted to maximize this value. Pa_{O_2}, or ideally, the arteriovenous oxygen difference, should also be followed to ensure that arterial oxygen content and tissue oxygen uptake are normal. In general, $P\bar{v}_{O_2}$ (normal = 40 torr) less than 35 torr suggests inadequate tissue oxygenation.
d. **Shunt (Qs/Qt).** One series suggests that decrease in shunt may be used to predict optimal PEEP, especially in the setting of high PEEP and intermittent mandatory ventilation (IMV). Experience with this measurement is controversial.

Optimal levels of PEEP vary among patients and also vary during the course of an individual patient's illness. Levels generally used range from 5 to 15 cm H_2O. Higher levels—up to 45 cm H_2O—have been reported useful in patients receiving intermittent mandatory ventilation (IMV), which allows lower mean airway pressure by letting the patient generate subambient pressure with inspiration. Deleterious effects on cardiac output were not found, but the advantages of this method over continuous positive pressure ventilation, with lower levels of PEEP, are uncertain.

Practically, PEEP may be initiated at a level of 5 cm H_2O and increased in increments of 2-3 cm H_2O until Pa_{O_2} and circulatory function are adequate on FI_{O_2} less than 0.6. Should the level of PEEP required result in significant circulatory compromise, volume or pressors may be used to maintain cardiac output while PEEP is increased to allow nontoxic concentrations of oxygen.

4. **Volume status and PEEP.** The use of a pulmonary artery catheter is strongly recommended in ARDS to help adjust circulatory volume and allow measurement of cardiac output and mixed venous oxygenation. Without direct atrial cannulation, PCWP is the most accurate reflection of left atrial pressure (LAP).

However, this measurement may be unreliable in the presence of PEEP. At less than 10 cm H_2O, PEEP does not significantly alter PCWP. However, at higher levels of PEEP (10 cm H_2O or more), PCWP may not reflect LAP. This discrepancy may be due to catheter position or a relative isolation of the pulmonary vasculature from alveolar pressure in severe ARDS. PCWP measurements must therefore be made in the absence of PEEP, or carefully correlated with measurements of circulatory function, such as cardiac output.
5. **PEEP and chest x-ray.** PEEP results in increased lung volumes on chest film, in turn leading to apparent "clearing" of lung fields. Cessation of PEEP results in return to prior radiographic appearance.
6. Complications of PEEP
   a. **Overdistention, decreased compliance, and circulatory compromise** may result from overly enthusiastic use of PEEP without attention to pulmonary and volume status, as noted above.
   b. **Barotrauma** appears to be more common in patients receiving PEEP, owing to increased airway pressures induced by PEEP. The actual contribution of PEEP to pneumothorax and pneumomediastinum is unknown.
   c. **Impaired oxygenation** may, in rare cases, result from PEEP. This has been reported in cases of marked regional lung disease, and is probably due to shift in blood flow from normal to diseased lung.
7. **Weaning from PEEP.** Weaning probably should not begin at levels of PEEP above 10 cm H_2O. Below this level, weaning may proceed as in other instances of assisted ventilation. Positive pressure at 5 to 8 cm H_2O is often used to prevent atelectasis postextubation. *Table 6-2* summarizes the effects of PEEP in ARDS.

D. Adjunctive therapy in ARDS
   1. **Fluid.** Careful attention to fluid management is crucial in ARDS. Excessive intravascular fluid administration may result in cardiogenic pulmonary edema superimposed on the edema of ARDS. Patients with capillary damage from ARDS may be especially susceptible to leakage into alveolar spaces. Major problems in fluid administration include:

Table 6-2
Effects of PEEP in ARDS

Pulmonary
 Increased mean airway pressure
 Increased functional residual capacity
 Increased compliance
 Decreased shunt
Circulatory
 Decreased venous return (preload, moderated by volume and compliance)
 Possibly, increased pulmonary vascular resistance (right ventricular afterload)
Radiographic
 Increased lung volumes, "clearing" of lung fields
Complications
 Unreliable pulmonary capillary wedge pressure (PCWP) above 10 cm H_2O
 Possible increased incidence of pneumothorax and pneumomediastinum

    a. **Monitoring.** Clinical parameters such as pulse, urine output, and peripheral vasoconstriction are subject to a myriad of influences. Central venous pressure (CVP) determination is not a reliable index of LAP. A pulmonary artery catheter and serial determinations of PCWP offer an important practical guide.
    b. **Quantity of fluid.** In most situations, maintenance of PCWP at 10-15 torr provides adequate, but not excessive, intravascular volume. Relative hypervolemia may be required to sustain high levels of PEEP, but care must be taken to prevent "unmasked" hypervolemia when PEEP is discontinued.
    c. **Type of fluid.** Briefly, colloid should be used in hypoalbuminemic patients, and crystalloid in other situations.
2. **Diuretics.** Combinations of loop diuretics and 25% albumin have been proposed to decrease lung water and promote systemic diuresis. No rigorous evidence exists to support this practice.
3. **Transfusion.** Hematocrit should be maintained above 30% and hemoglobin above 10 g, but optimal levels have not been established.

4. **Corticosteroids.** The use of corticosteroids is controversial. Possible benefits in ARDS, such as decreased edema, stabilization of lysosomal membranes, and reduction in subsequent fibrosis, remain speculative. Of the specific causes of ARDS, steroids may be justified in fat embolism, but no rigorous data are available.
5. **Heparin.** Use of anticoagulants is based on the hypothesis that microvascular emboli contribute to alveolar-capillary damage in ARDS. Little evidence exists concerning benefits of heparin, and its well-known risks argue against its use.
6. **Infection.** Infection may lead to, or complicate, ARDS. Sputum should be examined daily, and invasive methods such as transtracheal aspiration and bronchoscopy or lung biopsy may be required if infection is not controlled.

VI. **NATURAL HISTORY AND PROGNOSIS**

A. **Hospital mortality.** Because ARDS is variably defined, survival rates in different series are difficult to compare. Most studies have shown survival rates of 30 to 50 percent from the early 1970s to the present. Several studies address specific aspects of mortality:
1. **Etiology.** In ARDS secondary to sepsis, one series found a 90 percent mortality rate, as compared to 50 percent mortality in sepsis uncomplicated by ARDS.
2. **Pathology.** Open lung biopsy results have been correlated with pulmonary function. Patients with severe edema or fibrosis (fixed shunt and little response to PEEP) had the worst prognosis: 8 and 23 percent survival, respectively. Patients with moderate edema (moderate shunt and rapid response to PEEP) had the best prognosis, with 48 percent survival.
3. **Effect of PEEP.** Anecdotal evidence suggests the value of PEEP in many patients with ARDS. One retrospective series compared patients treated with and without PEEP, finding little difference in patient population. PEEP recipients had a prolonged hospital survival rate, but no change in overall in-hospital mortality.

B. **Long-term survival.** Few long-term studies of ARDS survivors exist. One small series found four of nine patients with normal pulmonary function test results and two with improvement of restrictive changes after ARDS. This and another series noted bronchial hyper-reactivity in many ARDS survivors, perhaps as a consequence of the syndrome.

REFERENCES

I. General

Fishman AP: Adult respiratory distress syndrome. In *Pulmonary Diseases and Disorders.* Edited by Fishman AP, New York, McGraw-Hill, 1980, pp 1667-1681.

Hopewell PC, Murray JF: The adult respiratory distress syndrome. *Ann Rev Med* 25:343-351, 1976.

Both references provide excellent brief summaries of pathophysiology, pathogenesis, and therapy.

II. Pathophysiology

Anderson RR, Holliday RL, Driedger AA, et al: Documentation of pulmonary capillary permeability in the adult respiratory distress syndrome accompanying human sepsis. *Am Rev Respir Dis* 121:869-877, 1979.

Bachofen M, Weibel ER: Alterations of gas exchange apparatus in adult respiratory insufficiency associated with septicemia. *Am Rev Respir Dis* 116:589-565, 1977.

Dantzker DR, Brook CJ, Dehart P, et al: Ventilation perfusion distributions in the adult respiratory distress syndrome. *Am Rev Respir Dis* 120:1039-1052, 1979.

Lamy M, Fallat RJ, Koeniger E, et al: Pathologic features and mechanisms of hypoxemia in ARDS. *Am Rev Respir Dis* 114:267-284, 1976.

Anderson found more radiolabeled albumin appearing in lung secretions in sepsis than in cardiogenic pulmonary edema, suggesting increased capillary permeability in ARDS. Bachofen, in a pathologic study, found no anatomic correlate in capillary endothelium to explain increased permeability. Dantzker confirms the origin of hypoxemia in ARDS as shunt and units with very low V/Q. Lamy correlated biopsy data, shunt, response to PEEP, and prognosis in 45 patients; three groups emerged from biopsy results and response to PEEP.

III. Effects of PEEP

Lozman J, Powers SR Jr, Older T, et al: Correlation of pulmonary wedge and left atrial pressures. A study in the patient receiving positive end-expiratory pressure ventilation. *Arch Surg* 109:270-277, 1974.

McCloud TC, Barash PG, Ravin CE: PEEP: radiographic features and associated complications. *Am J Roentgen* 129:209-213, 1977.

Powers SR, et al: Physiologic consequences of PEEP ventilation. *Ann Surg* 178:265-272, 1973.

Qvist J, et al: Hemodynamic responses to mechanical ventilation with PEEP: the effect of hypervolemia. *Anesthesiology* 42:45-55, 1975.

Robotham JL, Lixfeld W, Holland L, et al: The effects of PEEP on right and left ventricular performance. *Am Rev Respir Dis* 121:677-683, 1980.

Suter PM, Fairley HB, Isenberg MD: Optimum end-expiratory airway pressure in patients with acute pulmonary failure. *N Engl J Med* 292:284-289, 1975.

Zapol WM, Snider MT: Pulmonary hypertension in severe acute respiratory failure. *N Engl J Med* 298:476-480, 1977.

Lozman found a good correlation between LAP and PCWP at PEEP of 5 cm, but little correlation above this level. McCloud describes the apparent increase in lung volumes on chest films. Powers's article is among the early reports that PEEP may result in decreased peripheral oxygen delivery due to depression of cardiac output. Qvist found that PEEP decreases cardiac index in dogs, but hypervolemia attenuates this effect. Robotham, also working with dogs, found that PEEP exerts a non-neuronal adverse effect on right and left ventricular performance. Suter, in a widely cited study, defines optimum PEEP as maximum oxygen transport. Zapol describes the marked pulmonary hypertension and possible right ventricular dysfunction accompanying ARDS; etiology is uncertain.

IV. Natural history

Lakshminarayan S, Hudson LD: Pulmonary function following the adult respiratory distress syndrome (editorial). *Chest* 74:489-490, 1978.

Simpson DL, Goodman M, Spector SL, et al: Long-term follow-up and bronchial reactivity testing in survivors of the adult respiratory distress syndrome. *Am Rev Respir Dis* 117:449-454, 1978.

Lakshminarayan summarizes previous data, indicating a 40 percent mortality rate and frequent abnormal pulmonary function in survivors. Simpson describes follow-up in nine patients, three of whom had bronchial hyperreactivity.

7
Oxygen Therapy

Aerobic metabolism requires the presence of oxygen in mitochondria for use in energy generation. Aerobic species must, therefore, transport oxygen to tissues and limit its toxicity. Oxygen transport and oxygen toxicity will be considered individually. Recent evidence indicates that cellular oxygen metabolism is also important in regulation of oxygen use and adaptation to disease. This topic has been reviewed by Robin (1980).

I. OXYGEN TRANSPORT

    A. **Physiologic.** At the level of the organism, oxygen transport involves four major processes: pulmonary gas exchange, binding of oxygen to hemoglobin, cardiac output, and distribution of output to organs and cells.

        1. **Pulmonary gas exchange** is discussed in detail in Chapter 1.

        2. **Binding of oxygen to hemoglobin.** At atmospheric conditions, a very small amount of oxygen is dissolved in plasma (.003 ml/100 ml per torr of O_2). The bulk of oxygen is transported bound to its carrier molecule, hemoglobin (Hb). This is an ideal carrier owing to its associative properties allowing maximum transport between lungs and tissues. Normal human hemoglobin, when 10 percent saturated, contains 1.36 ml O_2/g hemoglobin. Oxygen binding to hemoglobin is depicted in the O_2-Hb dissociation curve in figure 7-1.

           The position of the curve along the abscissa reflects the affinity of oxygen for hemoglobin; this is often expressed as the P_{50}, or partial pressure at

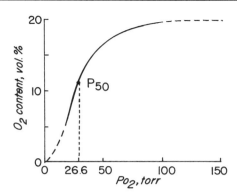

Figure 7-1. Oxygen-hemoglobin dissociation curve.

which hemoglobin is 50 percent saturated. Increases in P_{50} tend to increase tissue oxygen delivery if arterial oxygen content is adequate. Decreases in P_{50} permit greater oxygen uptake, but may limit oxygen release in the periphery. Factors that alter P_{50} include 2,3-DPG, pH, carbon dioxide, and temperature.

a. **2,3-DPG.** This molecule stabilizes the deoxyform of hemoglobin and lowers intracellular pH; P_{50} therefore increases. 2,3-DPG is ordinarily present in erythrocytes in the same molar quantity as hemoglobin. Levels may be altered by pH, serum phosphate, erythrocyte enzymes, and hormones.

b. **pH.** Increased plasma and therefore erythrocyte—hydrogen ion (decreased pH), leads to increased P_{50}.

c. **CO_2.** Increased blood CO_2 content primarily lowers pH through carbonic acid production; however, CO_2 also has a direct effect (the Bohr effect) through binding and stabilizing deoxyhemoglobin, thereby increasing P_{50}.

d. **Temperature.** Increased temperature leads to increases in P_{50}.

In normal circumstances, changes during circulation promote oxygen binding in the lungs and oxygen release in the periphery. Blood flowing through tissues receives carbon dioxide and metabolic acids; pH falls, leading to decreased hemoglobin affinity for oxygen and increased oxygen release to tissues. Blood returning to the pulmonary capillaries releases carbon dioxide, leading to increased pH, increased hemoglobin affinity for oxygen, and increased oxygen uptake in the lung. Furthermore, metabolically active tissues function at higher temperatures, promoting decreased hemoglobin-oxygen affinity and improving oxygen release. Alveolar air has a lower temperature, allowing improved oxygen uptake in the lung. Factors affecting hemoglobin affinity for oxygen are summarized in *table 7-1*.

3. **Cardiac output** depends upon myocardial function, blood volume, blood viscosity, and peripheral resistance. Oxygen delivery varies directly with cardiac output.
4. **Distribution of cardiac output.** Blood flow is apportioned to various organs by complex neurohumoral mechanisms. When oxygen transport is marginal, redistribution toward heart and brain may lead

Table 7-1
Factors Affecting P_{50} of Hemoglobin

Factor	P_{50}	O_2 Affinity
2,3-DPG: increased	↑	↓
decreased	↓	↑
pH: increased	↓	↑
decreased	↑	↓
P_{CO_2}: increased	↑	↓
decreased	↓	↑
Temperature: increased	↑	↓
decreased	↓	↑
Abnormal hemoglobin:		
Acquired: carboxyhemoglobin	↓	↑
methemoglobin	↓	↑
Congenital: HbS	↑	↓
Hb Seattle	↑	↓
Hb Kansas	↑	↓
Fetal	↓	↑
Hb Bart's	↓	↑
Hb Chesapeake	↓	↑
Erthyrocyte enzyme abnormalities:		
Pyruvate kinase deficiency	↑	↓
Hexokinase deficiency	↓	↑

to hypoxia elsewhere, especially the gastrointestinal tract or kidney.

B. Response to stress. In normal subjects, oxygen transport can increase markedly in response to stress. This is accomplished through increased gas exchange and increased cardiac output. Gas exchange increases, from the usual resting rate of 4 ml/kg O_2/min, up to three times this value, and cardiac output increases, from the resting index of 3 L/min/m^2, up to four times this value.

On a more chronic basis, oxygen transport may be limited by dysfunction in any of the four processes described above. Dysfunction, in turn, evokes several compensatory mechanisms acting to restore oxygen transport to adequate levels:

1. Cardiac failure causes increased 2,3-DPG, change in blood flow distribution, and increased pulmonary oxygen loading.
2. Decreased gas exchange leads to increased 2,3-DPG, increased cardiac output, and increased erythropoiesis.
3. Anemia causes increased cardiac output and increased pulmonary oxygen loading.
4. Increased tissue oxygen demands result in increased cardiac output and increased pulmonary oxygen loading.

C. Hypoxia. If dysfunction in oxygen transport is severe, or compensation inadequate, hypoxia results. The body stores a small amount of oxygen, approximately 20 ml/kg, in the lungs and blood. The basal metabolic requirement is 4 ml/kg/min. Stores provide enough oxygen for 2 to 4 minutes of anoxia before irreversible damage occurs. Effects of acute hypoxia occur in the cardiovascular, renal, and nervous systems.

1. Central nervous system effects include headache, clouding of sensorium, somnolence, and seizure.
2. Cardiovascular manifestations include tachycardia and hypertension if hypoxia is mild; hypotension and bradycardia, if severe.
3. Renal dysfunction leads to sodium retention. Central nervous system function is especially sensitive to hypoxia. Dysfunction begins at 4 to 6 seconds of anoxia, and loss of consciousness, at 10 to 20 seconds.

II. SUPPLEMENTAL OXYGEN

A. **Apparatus.** Oxygen may be delivered by various devices; oxygenation in the intubated patient is discussed in Chapter 5. In the nonintubated patient, oxygen is delivered by nasal cannulas, face tents, and several types of face masks. Oxygen delivery is dependent on four factors: minute ventilation, duration of inspiration, inspiratory flow rate, and oxygen flow rate.

Adequate minute ventilation and inspiratory duration must be maintained regardless of the means of oxygen delivery. The balance between inspiratory flow rate and oxygen flow rate determines the efficiency of delivery devices. These devices can be grouped into two broad categories: those of variable, and those of fixed, performance.

1. **Variable performance devices** deliver gas at a flow rate less than the patient's peak inspiratory flow rate. This category includes nasal cannulas, face tents, and simple masks with oxygen flow less than 4 to 6 L/min. In early and late inspiration, when patient flow rates are low, high concentrations of oxygen are inspired. In the remainder of inspiration, the patient's inspiratory flow rate is greater than that of the device, so that oxygen will be mixed with room air. The degree of mixing is variable between inspirations in any patient and among individual patients.

2. **Fixed performance devices**, such as the Venturi mask, deliver gas at a flow rate greater than the patient's peak inspiratory flow rate. These devices entrain room air with oxygen, resulting in high flow rates; further mixing is precluded, so that specific oxygen concentrations can be provided. Above 40% oxygen concentrations, however, mask flow rates decrease below the inspiratory rates of many patients, so that room air mixing occurs, and the devices become variable in performance.

The actual concentration of oxygen delivered by various devices depends upon measurement technique. Accurate measurements must be made below the larynx or from standardized arterial oxygen concentrations in individual patients. Measurements obtained by these techniques in small numbers of normal subjects at rest are presented in *table 7-2*. Venturi masks deliver relatively constant oxygen concentrations, whereas other methods are more variable.

Patients in whom concentrations of oxygen must be

monitored carefully, such as those with chronic hypercapnia, should be treated with Venturi masks if at all possible. Nasal cannulas are often better tolerated, but they deliver low flows, are altered by oral versus nasal breathing, and often lead to uncomfortable drying of the nasal mucosa. Face tents are probably the least accurate method of providing oxygen, as the widely disparate figures from two groups illustrate, (see *table 7-2*).

Oxygen concentrations above 40 percent can be delivered by these devices or by combinations, such as cannulas and masks. However, all such devices perform variably, and are especially susceptible to hyperventilation and other manifestations of disease.

B. **Monitoring.** Oxygen therapy should be monitored to ensure efficacy and prevent toxicity. In general, arterial blood gas measurements provide an accurate guide in assessing oxygenation.

The amount of oxygen required for an individual patient depends on clinical status and the hemoglobin-oxygen dissociation curve (see figure 7-1). As the curve illustrates, hemoglobin is 90 percent saturated at Pa_{O_2} 60 torr, and 100 percent saturated at Pa_{O_2} 150 torr. Be-

Table 7-2
Oxygen Delivery from Common Apparatus

	Expected $F_{I_{O_2}}$	Tracheal	Corrected Arterial
Venturi mask	0.24 (atm)	0.22 (atm)	0.25 (atm)
	0.28	0.23	0.28
	0.35	0.30	0.35
	0.40	0.33	0.38
Nasal cannulae	2 L/min	0.22	
	3	0.24	
	4		0.30
	5	0.25	
Face tent	15 L/min	0.88	
	1.0 (atm)	0.46	
Aerosol mask	0.40 (8 L/min)		0.40
	0.70 (14 L/min)		0.51
	1.00 (14 L/min)		0.69
	0.44 (10 L/min)	0.33	
	0.60 (10 L/min)	0.50	
	1.00 (10 L/min)	0.52	

Note: Values in atmospheres except as otherwise indicated.

yond 100 percent saturation, increasing Pa_{O_2} adds only to dissolved oxygen and therefore increases oxygen content only slightly at atmospheric conditions. However, in rare circumstances, such as carbon monoxide poisoning, this increase may be desirable. A Pa_{O_2} of 90 torr represents 95 percent saturation, so that further increases in Pa_{O_2} add little to oxygen content; this represents a convenient upper limit for oxygen therapy. Below Pa_{O_2} 60 torr (90 percent saturation), oxygen content decreases rapidly, so that this value is a practical lower limit for effective oxygenation, except in patients with chronic hypercapnia.

Patients with chronic hypercapnia may rely on hypoxic respiratory drive to maintain adequate alveolar ventilation. Excessive oxygen administration can suppress this drive, in turn leading to increased hypercapnia, hypoxemia, and respiratory failure. In acute exacerbations, oxygen should be given very cautiously, with careful attention to mental status. It is often difficult to achieve Pa_{O_2} 60 torr without respiratory depression; the patient's chronic Pa_{O_2} may serve as a goal for oxygen therapy.

Another approach is to use mixed venous oxygenation as an index of adequacy of therapy. Since this measurement is rarely available, one series suggests that Pa_{O_2} greater than 50 in patients with chronic hypercapnia results in $P\bar{v}_{O_2}$ greater than 33, in turn ensuring an adequate level of oxygenation. Chronic low flow oxygen therapy often benefits such patients. Use of this therapy is described in Chapter 4.

Goals for oxygen therapy are summarized in *table 7-3*.

III. TOXICITY

A. Natural history. The toxicity of high concentrations of oxygen has been clearly demonstrated, although the exact concentration and duration of therapy leading to toxicity remain uncertain. In normal subjects breathing high FI_{O_2} (greater than 0.9), adverse effects of oxygen are evident in as early as 3 hours, when bronchoscopy demonstrates decreased tracheal mucus velocity. At 6 hours, tracheitis is evident, although its clinical significance is uncertain. Most studies show no physiologic abnormalities in the first 24 hours of exposure. Beyond this point, virtually all humans appear to show some signs of toxicity.

Table 7-3

Goals for Oxygen Therapy

a. Normocapnia

Pa_{O_2} maintained between 60 torr and 90 torr
or
$P\bar{v}_{O_2}$ greater than 35 torr

b. Chronic Hypercapnia

Pa_{O_2} at chronic level if greater than 50 torr
or
Pa_{O_2} greater than 50 torr (implies $P\bar{v}_{O_2}$ greater than 35 torr)

Onset of oxygen toxicity is insidious. Early symptoms such as cough or chest pain may be present, followed by anorexia, nausea, or headache. Physical signs are similarly nonspecific. Chest x-ray is rarely helpful; it often remains normal for 24 to 36 hours except for decreased lung volumes.

Pathophysiologically, oxygen toxicity may be divided into two phases, the acute exudative and the chronic proliferative. Characteristics of these phases are presented in *table 7-4*.

The long-term effects of high oxygen concentrations are unknown, since all exposed patients have other pulmonary disease. In animals, changes resolve slowly and scarring may be present months after exposure.

The extent of oxygen toxicity at FI_{O_2} less than 0.9 is uncertain. Lower concentrations, FI_{O_2} 0.4 or less, have been tolerated for several weeks with no ill effects. Studies using high oxygen concentrations are confounded by possible alterations in sensitivity of the diseased lung, marked individual variation, and the potential for development of tolerance. Present consensus appears to be that FI_{O_2} less than 0.5 is safe, FI_{O_2} between 0.5 and 0.6 is uncertain, and FI_{O_2} greater than 0.6 for more than 24 to 48 hours is toxic.

B. **Mechanism.** The mechanism of oxygen toxicity has been partially elucidated. Most oxygen is reduced by mitochondrial cytochrome *c* oxidase to water. Other reactions produce hydrogen peroxide, superoxide (which

Table 7-4
Effects of Oxygen Toxicity

Type	Physiologic Effects	Pathologic Effects
Acute	6 hours: Decreased VC 24 hours: Decreased protein synthesis 30 hours: Decreased compliance; interstitial edema 36-48 hours: Alveolar edema; decreased D_{LCO}	Endothelial cell and Type I pneumocyte necrosis
Chronic	Decreased lung volumes	Thickening of alveolar septa; Type II pneumocyte proliferation

can, in turn, produce hydroxyl radical), and singlet oxygen. Hydrogen peroxide is probably well tolerated. Superoxide has been shown to alter DNA configuration, depolymerize polysaccharides, and interfere with lipid peroxidation. Singlet oxygen and hydroxyl radical are highly reactive, perhaps causing direct cytotoxicity. Defenses against oxygen toxicity include enzymes such as superoxide dismutase, catalase, and glutathione peroxidase, which neutralize superoxide. Antioxidants, such as reduced glutathione, alpha-tocopherol (vitamin E), and ascorbate (vitamin C), may serve to absorb free radicals. Pharmacologic manipulation of these defenses is of uncertain value at present.

Interaction of drugs, chemicals, and metabolic products with oxygen is under extensive investigation in animals. Chemicals such as paraquat accelerate superoxide formation, potentiating oxygen toxicity. Conversely, hypothermia and hypothyroidism may limit oxygen radical formation and exert a protective effect. Endotoxin appears to enhance tolerance to oxygen, perhaps by inducing protective enzymes. Disulfiram exacerbates oxygen toxicity by an unknown mechanism. The clinical application of these interactions is uncertain.

REFERENCES

I. General

Comroe JH: *Physiology of Respiration*, 2nd ed. Chicago, Year Book Medical, 1974, pp 183-200.

Finch CA, Lenfant C: Oxygen transport in man. *N Engl J Med* 296:407-415, 1972.

Robin ED: Of men and mitochondria: coping with hypoxic dysoxia. *Am Rev Respir Dis* 122:517-531, 1980.

Comroe and Finch offer concise summaries of normal and altered oxygen transport. Robin presents a provocative discussion of adaptations to hypoxia, concentrating on cellular metabolism.

II. Inspired oxygen

Gibson RL, Comer PB, Beckham RW, et al: Actual tracheal oxygen concentrations with commonly used oxygen equipment. *Anesthesiology* 44:71-73, 1976.

Redding TS, McAfee DD, Parham AM: Oxygen concentrations received from commonly used delivery systems. *South Med J* 71:169-172, 1978.

These articles discuss oxygen delivery apparatus, including fixed versus variable performance devices.

III. Monitoring of oxygen therapy

Mithoefer JC: Oxygen therapy. In *Pulmonary Diseases and Disorders*. Edited by Fishman AP, New York, McGraw-Hill, 1980, pp 1581-1586.

Mithoefer JC, Ramirez C, Cook W: The effect of mixed venous oxygenation on arterial blood in chronic obstructive lung disease. *Am Rev Respir Dis* 117:259-264, 1978.

In both references, Mithoefer discusses the use of arterial blood gases and mixed venous oxygen measurements, particularly in patients with chronic hypercapnia.

IV. Oxygen toxicity

Deneke SM, Fanburg BL: Normobaric oxygen toxicity of the lung. *N Engl J Med* 303:76-86, 1980.

Frank L, Massaro D: Oxygen toxicity. *Am J Med* 69:117-126, 1980.

Mustafa MG, Tierney DF: Biochemical and metabolic changes in the lung with oxygen, ozone, and nitrogen dioxide toxicity. *Am Rev Respir Dis* 118:1061-1090, 1978.

Sackner MA: Pulmonary effects of oxygen breathing. *Ann Intern Med* 82:40-43, 1975.

These papers review oxygen toxicity; Deneke, Frank, and Mustafa present biochemically-based data, and Sackner offers bronchoscopic observations.

8
Pneumonia

I. DEFINITION

Acute pneumonia, or pneumonitis, is an inflammatory process of the lung parenchyma. Pneumonia may be caused by a variety of infectious and noninfectious agents, including inhaled toxins, aspirated material, bacteria, viruses, rickettsiae, chlamydiae, mycoplasmas, and fungi. By far the most common causes of pneumonia are infections due to bacteria or viruses, which will form the subject matter of this chapter. Pneumonias caused by mycobacteria, and those occurring in immunocompromised hosts, pose unique problems and will be addressed in Chapters 10 and 9, respectively. Finally, noninfectious pneumonitides are discussed in Chapter 11.

II. PATHOGENESIS

Since the lung parenchyma in normal humans is sterile, the occurrence of pneumonia represents an imbalance between host defenses and infectious agents. Pathogenesis of pneumonia therefore depends upon **status of host defenses, acquisition of infectious agents, mode of spread of infection,** and **characteristics of infecting organism.**

A. **Host defenses.** The upper respiratory tract in humans, including the mouth, nasopharynx, oropharynx, and supralaryngeal airway, is colonized by aerobic and anaerobic bacteria. In addition to serving as a source of infection, these flora also aid host defenses by inhibiting colonization by more virulent agents. Below the larynx, mechanical branching, mucociliary clearance, and cough help to limit the extent of colonization and maintain sterility distal to the respiratory bronchioles. Infectious agents routinely gain access to the lower tract, primarily by inhalation of droplet nuclei or by aspiration of oropharyngeal contents. The latter process occurs more commonly in persons with depressed gag reflex or glottic dysfunction. However, it is probable that most normal persons aspirate small amounts during sleep. Lower respiratory tract defenses include:

1. Cellular and humoral immunity regulated by lymphocytes.
2. Phagocytosis and cell killing by macrophages and neutrophils.
3. Complement-mediated cell lysis.

B. **Acquisition of infectious agents.** The type of organism causing pneumonia varies with circumstances of acquisition. This is most obvious in epidemics, such as influenza leading to postinfluenzal staphylococcal pneumonia, or in closed populations, such as streptococcal pneumonia affecting military recruits. Etiology also varies with place of acquisition, in particular, community versus hospital flora. Community-acquired pneumonias most often are caused by viruses, mycoplasmas, and bacteria. Relative incidence of each type of agent is difficult to assess, especially for viruses. Several series of patients hospitalized for community-acquired pneumonia indicate about 60 percent bacterial etiology, usually pneumococcal, and 35 percent viral or mycoplasmal etiology. The latter two agents probably account for a larger percentage of pneumonias in patients not requiring hospitalization. Gram-negative bacteria are relatively uncommon causes of community-acquired pneumonia, although they are more likely to occur in patients with compromised defenses, such as those with chronic respiratory disease, ethanol abuse, or diabetes, as well as patients receiving antibiotics and those who are bed-ridden. As noted above, bacterial pneumonia appears to follow aspiration of oropharyngeal flora. Viruses and mycoplasmas are transmitted by inhalation of droplet nuclei.

Hospital-acquired, or nosocomial, pneumonia occurs in 0.5 to 5 percent of hospitalized patients. Predominant organisms responsible for nosocomial pneumonia have changed markedly in the last decades with the advent of antimicrobial therapy. In the 1950s, nosocomial pneumonia was predominantly due to *S. pneumoniae, H. influenzae*, and *S. pyogenes.* In the 1960s, it was primarily caused by *S. aureus.* In the 1970s, gram-negative organisms, especially *Pseudomonas* and *Enterobacteriaceae*, were largely responsible. Viruses and fungal agents most often affect the compromised host.

Pathogenesis of nosocomial pneumonia appears to involve endogenous aspiration with the following sequence of events:

1. Normal pharyngeal flora are altered by disease or antibiotics.
2. Oropharynx is colonized with hospital organisms.
3. Microaspiration into the tracheobronchial tree initiates lower tract colonization.
4. Impaired clearance of aspirated organisms leads to infection.

In some circumstances, "exogenous" aspiration occurs due to bacterial colonization of nebulization equipment or ventilators. Transmission may also occur via hospital personnel or by bacterial seeding from another source of infection. Patients in other types of institutions, such as nursing homes, also develop gram-negative pneumonias due to altered pharyngeal flora; *Klebsiella* and *Staphylococcus* species are more common in these patients. Among institutionalized patients, colonization and subsequent pneumonia are more common in the presence of severe underlying disease. In one study, 45 percent of patients in an intensive care unit became colonized with gram-negative bacteria, and 12 percent developed pneumonia.

C. **Mode of spread of infection.** Virtually all organisms may cause pneumonia on occasion, and characteristic patterns occur with different types of agents.
  1. **Airspace or alveolar.** This is most common with gram-positive bacteria. Organisms gain access to alveoli, leading to accumulation of fluid and debris. Neutrophils migrate to the area, followed by macrophages.
  2. **Conducting airways.** Gram-negative agents and staphylococci initiate an inflammatory response in airways and contiguous parenchyma, leading to diffuse patchy involvement.
  3. **Interstitium.** Viruses and mycoplasmas often affect interstitial tissues preferentially, leading to a diffuse process with less exudation and little consolidation.

D. **Characteristics of organism.** Specific clinical patterns caused by various agents are presented below. Organisms affect lung parenchyma according to general category. Viruses and mycoplasmas usually do not destroy alveolar septa, although necrosis and fibrosis occasionally occur. In general, overall lung architecture is preserved in these infections and the lung returns to its previous state after resolution of pneumonia. *Streptococcus pneumoniae* usually has similar characteristics. In contrast, pneumonia due to gram-negative bacilli or staphylococci is frequently necrotizing, leading to septal and parenchymal destruction and abscess formation. The latter is especially characteristic of anaerobic organisms. Invasive measures are often necessary to eradicate these organisms, and residual scarring is the rule.

III. **DIAGNOSIS**

The *sine qua non* for the diagnosis of pneumonia is the chest x-ray. The presence of an infiltrate establishes the diagnosis, although an infectious etiology and a specific etiologic agent must be demonstrated by other means.

A. **History.** Most pneumonias are due to alterations in host defenses, often associated with systemic disease. In one large series, only 18 percent of 292 patients hospitalized with pneumonia had no underlying disease. Several diseases are associated with particular etiologic agents, as presented in *table 8-1*.

B. **Symptoms and signs.** Symptoms may suggest the presence of respiratory infection, although not specifically lower tract infection. Symptoms of upper respiratory

Table 8-1
Illnesses Predisposing to Specific Pneumonias

Disease	Etiologic Agent
Influenza	*Staphylococcus aureus*
Emphysema or chronic bronchitis	*Streptococcus pneumoniae; Hemophilus influenzae*
Alcoholism	*Klebsiella pneumoniae*; other gram-negative bacilli
Cystic fibrosis	*Pseudomonas aeruginosa*; staphylococci
Pulmonary alveolar proteinosis	*Nocardia asteroides*

infection precede pneumonia in 35 to 50 percent of patients. Causal relation is uncertain except in staphylococcal superinfection following influenza. Once pneumonia is present, common symptoms include fever, rigors, cough, pleuritic pain, and dyspnea. Their occurrence in various types of pneumonia is discussed below. Signs are equally nonspecific and less often present. One series found a correlation between chest x-ray and physical findings in only 42 percent of patients. When present, signs include localized dullness, rales, and pleural rub. Fever and tachypnea are common, but not invariable.

C. **Sputum.** Since the lower respiratory tract is not directly accessible to investigation, primary concerns in the evaluation of pneumonia must be **obtaining sputum and assessing the degree to which it reflects lower respiratory tract processes.** Sputum is best obtained in cooperative patients by encouraging deep cough and expectoration. Physiotherapy and nebulization may be helpful in some patients. Patients unable to cough may be suctioned nasotracheally, using sterile technique.

Macroscopic examination of sputum is occasionally helpful. Sputum is characteristically, but not invariably, thin or watery in nonbacterial infection, and mucoid in bacterial infection. Color is often rusty in alveolar infection, especially pneumococcal, and dark red and thick in *Klebsiella* infection.

Microscopic examination and culture form the basis of sputum evaluation.

1. **Gram stain.** Sensitivity and specificity vary with technique and etiologic agent. In routinely obtained samples, gram stain is 50 to 70 percent sensitive for pneumococcal infection, but only 11 to 71 percent specific in several series. Adequacy of specimens can be assessed by presence of neutrophils, epithelial cells, and organisms. Presence of many neutrophils, few epithelial cells, and abundant organisms increased diagnostic yield to 70 percent sensitivity and 85 percent specificity for pneumococcal pneumonia in one series.

2. **Culture.** Sputum culture is especially prone to contamination by colonizing flora. To limit this effect, sputum should be cultured rapidly; gram stain should be examined simultaneously to ensure adequacy of specimens. The presence of fewer than 10 epithelial cells—and of more than 25 neutrophils—per high power field correlates with accuracy of culture results. Even with careful technique, cultures appear

only 50 percent sensitive for pneumococcal disease, and 35 to 50 percent sensitive for pneumonia caused by *Hemophilus influenzae*. Specificity is less certain, but about 30 percent of samples in these patients appear to be contaminated with gram-negative bacilli. Washing samples to remove colonizing flora is of uncertain value. Although countercurrent electrophoresis to detect pneumococcal antigen was shown to be useful in one study, the technique is not widely available and is of uncertain value.

In order to avoid oropharyngeal contamination and to increase yield of lower tract flora, several invasive techniques have been developed for obtaining lower respiratory secretions.

3. **Transtracheal aspiration.** In this procedure, the cricothyroid membrane is punctured and a polyethylene catheter introduced into the trachea. Injection and aspiration of sterile saline is then performed. Sensitivity and specificity are increased over expectorated sputum. Sensitivity is 80 to 90 percent, with false negatives usually occurring in patients previously treated with antibiotics. Specificity is 70 to 80 percent, with false positives probably due to tracheobronchial colonization.

Risks include hemoptysis (1 percent in one series), pneumomediastinum (3 percent), subcutaneous emphysema (19 percent), and saline aspiration or soft tissue infection in occasional patients. Despite increased accuracy, the procedure should be reserved for seriously ill or compromised patients in whom adequate sputum is not available.

4. **Fiberoptic bronchoscopy.** Although this technique offers direct access to the lower respiratory tract, contamination with oropharyngeal flora limits its utility. Several studies suggest that careful sampling with a double lumen brush may decrease contamination.

5. **Needle aspiration.** Direct percutaneous aspiration establishes a diagnosis in 35 to 70 percent of patients. The major risk is pneumothorax (5 to 17 percent); the technique should be performed by experienced clinicians in critically ill patients for whom other procedures are nonproductive.

6. **Open lung biopsy.** Direct sampling yields a diagnosis in about 60 to 70 percent of critically ill patients on

whom it is performed. Risks are those associated with general anesthesia and thoracotomy. In summary, sputum gram stain results should be used to determine initial therapy. Sputum culture may be less reliable unless the sample is known to be adequate. If adequate sputum is not available and the patient appears seriously ill, transtracheal aspiration should be performed. Fiberoptic bronchoscopy, needle aspiration, and open biopsy should be reserved for critically ill or immunocompromised patients.
Pleural fluid, if present, should be aspirated and examined. Careful radiologic studies disclose effusions in 40 to 60 percent of patients with pneumococcal pneumonia, and in a variable number of patients with other types of pneumonia. In pneumococcal disease, pleural fluid is usually sterile, although the finding of organisms on gram stain will establish the diagnosis. Infected effusions usually require drainage via chest tube. Recent evidence suggests that pleural fluid pH less than 7.20 signifies the need for drainage even if no organisms are seen.

D. **Chest x-ray.** As previously noted, an abnormal chest x-ray is required for the diagnosis of pneumonia. While the chest film cannot establish an etiologic diagnosis, patterns of involvement suggest types of organisms and occasionally, specific agents. Most pneumonias involve the lower lobes, presumably owing to mechanical factors that promote deposition of aspirated particles in dependent areas. Three general radiographic patterns correspond roughly with theories of pathogenesis described above: **lobar** corresponds to gram-positive organisms, with primary airspace focus; **bronchopneumonia** corresponds to gram-negative organisms, with multiple bronchiolar foci; and **interstitial** corresponds to viruses or mycoplasmas, with primary interstitial focus. Appearance of each of these patterns, especially lobar consolidation, may be altered by:
   1. **Age.** Diminished lung volumes and prior disease with residual scarring may render consolidation difficult to detect or to distinguish from pre-existing disease.
   2. **Emphysema.** Destruction of alveolar architecture may alter lobar or segmental consolidation.
   3. **Hydration.** Anecdotally, dehydration has been im-

plicated in diminishing the radiographic appearance of pneumonia. "Hidden" pneumonias are said to appear after rehydration. However, one careful study in dogs contradicts this observation, so that the importance of hydration is uncertain.

Chest x-ray evaluation is most useful when supplemented by clinical findings. About two-thirds of pneumonias can be correctly identified as viral or bacterial from chest films alone. Radiographic characteristics of specific types of pneumonia are presented in *table 8-2*.

E. **Clinical syndromes.** Clinical syndromes characteristic of various etiologic agents often help in confirming the diagnosis and predicting the natural history of pneumonia. A useful clinical categorization of pneumonia is based first on the availability of sputum for examination, and second on the type of organism seen in sputum.
1. Pneumonias without sputum production
   a. Mycoplasmal pneumonia
      (1) **Incidence.** About 20 percent of all pneumonias, 4 to 9 percent of those leading to hospitalization, are mycoplasmal.
      (2) **Clinical findings.** Subacute onset, with prominent sore throat, dry cough, and headache, is typical.

Table 8-2
Radiographic Patterns of Specific Pneumonias

Characteristic	Type of Pneumonia
Location	
Multilobar	Viral, legionellosis
Upper lobes	*Klebsiella*, mycoplasmal
Supra basilar segment of lower lobe	Aspiration
Posterior segment of upper lobe	Aspiration
Consolidation	Bacterial
Cavitation	Bacterial, especially *Pseudomonas;* aspiration
Nodular	Staphylococcic
Interstitial	Viral, mycoplasmal
Effusion	Bacterial (especially if large)

(3) **Laboratory findings.** WBC is usually normal. Chest x-ray shows patchy lower lobe infiltrates, with transient effusion in 20 percent. Sputum is scant; polymorphonuclear leukocytes (PMN) are present—smear is nonspecific. Cold agglutinins show a fourfold elevation in 50 to 60 percent of mycoplasmal pneumonias. At the bedside, agglutinin studies may be performed by placing 0.5 ml blood in heparinized tube on ice; clumping correlates with titer of 1:64 or greater. Using this method, positive agglutinins occur in about 20 percent of nonmycoplasmal infections.
(4) **Complications.** Widespread systemic manifestations have been reported, as presented in *table 8-3*.
(5) **Treatment.** Erythromycin, if given early in the course, shortens duration of symptoms and radiographic abnormalities, but does not eradicate the organism.

Table 8-3
Extrapulmonary Manifestations of *Mycoplasma pneumoniae* Infections

Organ or System	Disorders
Dermatologic	Erythema multiforme, Stevens-Johnson syndrome, bullous meningitis (uncommon in acquired cases), possibly erythema nodosum
Hematologic	Autoimmune hemolytic anemia, thrombocytopenia, disseminated intravascular coagulation
Cardiac	Pericarditis, myocarditis, pericardial effusion, conduction defects
Neurologic	Meningitis, meningoencephalitis, transverse myelitis, peripheral and cranial neuropathy, cerebellar ataxia
Gastrointestinal	Gastroenteritis, anicteric hepatitis, pancreatitis
Musculoskeletal	Arthralgias, myalgias, polyarthritis
Renal	Interstitial nephritis, glomerulonephritis
Miscellaneous	Lymphadenopathy, splenomegaly

Modified with permission of WB Saunders Company from Murray HW, Tuazon C: Atypical pneumonias. *Med Clin North Am* 64:512, 1980.

(6) **Course.** Symptoms persist 1 to 3 weeks; chest x-ray usually becomes normal within this period.
  b. **Viral pneumonia: influenza**
    (1) **Incidence.** Primarily occurs as winter epidemics.
    (2) **Clinical findings.** Three clinical syndromes follow acute influenzal infection: **acute, rapidly progressing pneumonia; upper respiratory infection with secondary bacterial infection,** usually by staphylococci or hemophiluses; and **concurrent viral and bacterial pneumonia.** Symptoms are those of upper respiratory infection (URI), with dry cough.
    (3) **Laboratory findings.** WBC is usually normal. Chest x-ray shows diffuse infiltrates in purely viral disease, and alveolar infiltrates in bacterial involvement. Sputum is nonspecific. Serologic results showing fourfold rise in antibody titers is diagnostic.
    (4) **Prophylaxis.** Active immunization for high-risk patients; amantadine hydrochloride for closed populations, concurrent with immunization if influenza A is implicated.
  c. **Other viral pneumonias.** Adenovirus and rhinovirus infections occur in closed populations and varicella and parainfluenza viruses cause pneumonia in occasional patients. Other agents are more likely to affect compromised hosts.
  d. **Bacterial:** *Legionella pneumophilia* and similar organisms
    (1) **Incidence.** Nonpneumonic form (Pontiac fever) occurs in epidemics; pneumonia can be epidemic or sporadic.
    (2) **Clinical findings.** Prodrome with 1 to 2 days malaise, myalgias, headache; mild fever occurs first, followed by high fever, recurring rigors, and dry cough; pleuritic pain occurs in 20 to 40 percent of affected patients. Diarrhea or altered mental status is uncommon but suggestive when present.
    (3) **Laboratory findings.** WBC is increased with shift to left in 75 percent of patients. Chest x-ray is abnormal in 90 percent of patients, bilateral in 35 percent. Multiple infiltrates occur with occasional consolidation or small

effusion. Sputum shows few PMN; occasionally, organisms are seen by immunofluorescence. Serum phosphorus is often decreased.
- (4) **Diagnosis.** Accomplished through serology, by fluorescent antibody or microagglutination methods. A positive result is a fourfold rise in titer, or a titer at 1:128, 20 to 60 days after onset of symptoms. Sputum occasionally reveals organisms via fluorescent antibody technique. Lung biopsy, stained with Dierterle silver, appears sensitive, but not completely specific.
- (5) **Complications.** Hypotension and renal failure may occur.
- (6) **Course.** There is a 15 to 20 percent mortality rate. Chest x-ray evidence of resolution usually requires more than 2 weeks.
- (7) **Treatment.** Erythromycin 2 to 4 g daily promotes defervescence and radiographic improvement. Limited evidence indicates that therapy results in decreased morbidity and mortality.

Differential diagnosis of these so-called "atypical" pneumonias is presented in *table 8-4.*

2. Pneumonias with sputum production
   a. Gram-positive bacteria
   (1) *Streptococcus pneumoniae*
   - (a) **Incidence.** Usually sporadic, 1-2/1000/yr, especially in patients with chronic disease, hypogammaglobulinemia, splenectomy, or sickle cell anemia.
   - (b) **Clinical findings.** A URI prodrome for several days is common. Eighty percent have single rigor, then fever, cough, and pleuritic pain. Abdominal symptoms are common in lower lobe disease.
   - (c) **Laboratory findings.** WBC is commonly increased. Chest x-ray shows lobar or segmental infiltrate, with pleural effusion in up to 50 percent. Sputum shows PMN, diplococci. Blood cultures are positive in 25 to 30 percent of cases.
   - (d) **Treatment.** Penicillin is curative in

Table 8-4
Differential Diagnosis of Atypical Pneumonias

Epidemiology
  Epidemics: influenza, legionellosis
  Closed populations: adenovirus
  Exposure: *Chlamydia psittaci* — avian species
    Coxiella burnetii — livestock

Symptoms
  Prominent headache: mycoplasma, *C. psittaci, C. burnetii*
  Confusion: legionellosis
  Diarrhea: legionellosis
  High fever: legionellosis, influenza

Laboratory results
  WBC elevated: legionellosis
  WBC normal: influenza, mycoplasmas, *C. psittaci, C. burnetii*
  Hematuria: legionellosis
  Abnormal liver function: legionellosis, *C. psittaci, C. burnetii*
  Cold agglutinins: mycoplasmas, occasionally viral

Systemic manifestations
  Bullous meningitis: mycoplasma
  Rash:
    Erythema multiforme mycoplasma, viruses
    Chickenpox — varicella
    Herpes — zoster
    Measles

minimum doses of about 80,000 U/day. The usual dose is up to 2 million U per day to limit superinfection from higher doses; increased doses are required in empyema, abscess, splenectomy. For patients allergic to penicillin, if allergy is manifested in rash or fever, use a cephalosporin or erythromycin; if allergy is anaphylactic, use erythromycin or clindamycin. Aminoglycosides are not useful.

(e) Complications. Abscess occurs rarely.
(f) Course. Symptoms improve after 12 to 36 hours of therapy, but 50 percent

of patients require 4 days for defervescence. Chest x-ray evidence of parenchymal infiltrates usually disappears in 6 to 8 weeks, but pleural disease may persist.
- (2) *Streptococcus pyogenes* (Group A)
  - (a) **Incidence.** Usually is epidemic.
  - (b) **Clinical findings.** Fever, cough, and pleuritic pain occur, with associated pharyngitis in 30 to 65 percent of cases. Acute glomerulonephritis may occur, but not rheumatic fever. Pericarditis is uncommon. Empyema occurs frequently (in 60 to 80 percent of patients).
  - (c) **Laboratory findings.** WBC usually increases, but to less than $12,000/mm^3$. Chest x-ray shows either interstitial lower lobe pattern or, less commonly, lobar pneumonia. Pharyngeal cultures are positive as above, and blood cultures are positive in 2 to 12 percent of cases. Antistreptolysin O and anti-DNase are often positive.
  - (d) **Treatment.** Penicillin; if patient is allergic to penicillin, cephalosporins or erythromycin should be given, as noted above.
  - (e) **Course.** Insignificant mortality rate; fever persists greater than 7 days in 60 percent of cases.
- (3) *Staphylococcus aureus*
  - (a) **Incidence.** This organism causes 3 to 10 percent of pneumonia requiring hospitalization. Incidence is increased in patients with diabetes mellitus and chronic renal failure, and those who are immunocompromised or involved in drug abuse.
  - (b) **Clinical findings.** Two major types of primary lung infection occur: superinfection, usually postviral, and primary airspace disease. Hematogenous seeding also occurs. Symptoms and onset are variable, usually with preceding URI symptoms if postviral. Disease may be rapidly progressive.
  - (c) **Laboratory findings.** WBC is usually

elevated to greater than 15,000/mm³. Chest x-ray in primary pneumonia shows a variable pattern, with infiltrates, cavitation, pneumatocoele, and empyema occurring. Bacteremic pneumonia usually appears as small peripheral densities; bacteremia occurs in less than 20 percent of cases.
- (d) **Treatment.** Prolonged course of semisynthetic penicillin (e.g., nafcillin); cephalosporin for mild allergy; and vancomycin for anaphylaxis or methicillin-resistant species.
- (e) **Course.** Defervescence in 48 to 72 hours; mortality rate, depending on patient's prior status, ranges from 9 to 67 percent.

b. **Gram-negative aerobic bacteria.** Overall, these organisms account for 2 percent of community-acquired, and 40 to 60 percent of hospital-acquired pneumonias.

(1) *Hemophilus influenzae*
- (a) **Incidence.** This is uncertain, but apparently it has been increasing. Predisposing factors are age, chronic lung disease, and alcoholism.
- (b) **Clinical findings.** A preceding URI is common, followed by fever and productive cough.
- (c) **Laboratory findings.** WBC is usually elevated. Chest x-ray reveals bronchopneumonia, or occasionally, a lobar or segmental pattern; pleural effusion is common. Bacteremia occurs in 40 to 60 percent of cases, especially with encapsulated strains.
- (d) **Treatment.** Ampicillin is used; if patient is allergic to the drug or strain is resistant, cefamandole or chloramphenicol should be substituted.

(2) *Klebsiella pneumoniae*
- (a) **Incidence.** Disease has a higher than normal incidence in patients who suffer from alcoholism or diabetes mellitus, or who are institutionalized.
- (b) **Clinical findings.** Acute onset with fever, productive cough, is usual.
- (c) **Laboratory findings.** WBC is usually

elevated. Chest x-ray shows lobar consolidation, usually in the right upper lobe; however, in 50 percent of patients, more than one lobe is involved. Sputum occasionally is tenacious and red ("currant jelly").
- (d) **Complications.** Abscess occurs in 10 to 50 percent of cases.
- (e) **Treatment.** Cephalosporin is used, sometimes with additional aminoglycoside; chloramphenicol is also used.

(3) *Escherichia coli*
- (a) **Incidence.** Patients with diabetes mellitus and those with pyelonephritis are especially susceptible.
- (b) **Clinical.** Hematogenous spread from gastrointestinal or genitourinary tracts is common.
- (c) **Laboratory.** A lower lobe bronchopneumonia is present on chest x-ray
- (d) **Complications.** Abscess and empyema are common.
- (e) **Treatment.** Ampicillin, or a cephalosporin with an aminoglycoside, is used.

Characteristics of other gram-negative pneumonias, including *Pseudomonas* and *Acinetobacter*, are discussed in Chapter 9.

c. **Anaerobes.** Anaerobes are the predominant flora in oropharyngeal secretions, which contain approximately 10^7 aerobes and 10^8 anaerobes/ml. The most common route of infection with these agents is aspiration, as noted above.
- (1) **Incidence.** Infections occur in patients with altered consciousness, periodontal disease, and gingivitis.
- (2) **Clinical findings.** Major syndromes are necrotizing pneumonia and abscess.
- (3) **Laboratory findings.** Chest x-ray findings vary from localized infiltrate to diffuse consolidation and cavity formation. Sputum gram stain is unreliable. Transtracheal aspirate is more sensitive although nonspecific; about 25 percent are false positives. Carefully performed cultures show *Bacteroides fusiformis*, peptostreptococci, and microaerophilic streptococci. Blood cultures are rarely positive.

(4) Treatment. For community-acquired disease, use penicillin, despite the presence of in vitro resistant *Bacteroides fragilis*. If no response, use clindamycin or chloramphenicol. For hospital-acquired disease, use a semisynthetic penicillin plus an aminoglycoside to treat staphylococci and aerobic gram-negative agents. For abscess and empyema, see below.

(5) Course. Gradual resolution occurs, often with residual scarring. If aspiration is severe, adult respiratory distress syndrome (ARDS) may evolve.

IV. ALTERATIONS IN LUNG FUNCTION

A. **Volumes.** In severe pneumonia, filling and collapse of alveoli lead to decreased volumes. This is much less evident with uncomplicated pneumonia.

B. **Pressures.** In severe pneumonia, increased lung water and secretions lead to decreased compliance and increased alveolar and airways pressures. This effect is attenuated in less severe disease.

C. **Gas exchange.** Fluid and debris within alveoli prevent effective gas exchange, leading to V/Q inequalities and increased shunt. In general, V/Q inequalities are the major cause of hypoxemia, with less contribution from shunt and little (if any) from diffusion limitation.

V. TREATMENT

A. **Antibiotics.** Antibiotics are the mainstay of therapy for acute pneumonia. Specific agents should be chosen on the basis of etiology, as noted in the previous sections. If no sputum is available and pneumonia appears uncomplicated, erythromycin, followed by tetracycline, are effective against mycoplasmas as well as common bacteria that cause pneumonia. Empiric treatment of the hospitalized or compromised patient depends on the extent of pneumonia and on the patient's overall status. In the immunocompromised patient, broad-spectrum antibiotics are often begun empirically if no etiologic agent is found (see Chapter 9).

Treatment of bacterial pneumonias is summarized in *table 8-5* (pp. 153-154).

B. **Physiotherapy.** The role of chest physiotherapy in has-

Table 8-5
Antibiotic Therapy of Bacterial Pneumonias

Etiologic Agent	First Choice	Second Choice
Gram-positive		
Streptococcus pneumoniae	Penicillin	Cephalosporin or erythromycin
Streptococcus pyogenes	Penicillin	Cephalosporin or erythromycin
Staphylococcus aureus	Semisynthetic penicillin	Cephalosporin or vancomycin
Gram-negative		
Hemophilus influenzae	Ampicillin	Chloramphenicol or cefamandole
Klebsiella pneumoniae	Cephalothin or cefamandole plus aminoglycoside	
Enterobacteriaceae	Aminoglycoside plus cefamandole	Carbenicillin or ticarcillin
Escherichia coli	Aminoglycoside plus ampicillin	Cephalosporin
Proteus mirabilis	Ampicillin	Carbenicillin or ticarcillin
Proteus vulgaris	Aminoglycoside plus carbenicillin or ticarcillin	Cefamandole

(Table 8-5 continued next page)

(Table 8-5 continued)

Etiologic Agent	First Choice	Second Choice
Pseudomonas aeruginosa	Aminoglycoside plus carbenicillin or ticarcillin	
Serratia marcescens	Aminoglycoside plus carbenicillin or ticarcillin	Cefoxitin
Acinetobacter calcoaceticus	Aminoglycoside plus carbenicillin or ticarcillin	
Legionella pneumophila	Erythromycin	Possibly rifampin

tening resolution of pneumonia is uncertain. Anecdotal evidence supports its use, but one carefully documented series found no change in fever, chest x-ray resolution, mortality, or duration of hospitalization. As in chronic bronchitis, physiotherapy might be reserved for patients with large volumes of secretions or diminished spontaneous cough.

C. **Prevention.** Pneumococcal vaccine, introduced in 1978, includes polysaccharide antigens from 14 pneumococcal types implicated in over 70 percent of human pneumonias. The vaccine induces antibody response in more than 75 percent of healthy adults. The antibodies formed are not bactericidal, but rather enhance phagocytosis. The adequacy of antibody response in compromised patients is uncertain. Patients treated for Hodgkin's disease show little response to vaccination. Recent analyses indicate that the vaccine is more than 60 percent effective in preventing pneumococcal disease in adults.

Current recommendations are to vaccinate the following: patients older than 50 years of age; patients with chronic cardiopulmonary, hepatic, or renal disease; patients with splenic dysfunction or splenectomy; those with diabetes mellitus; and those who are chronically institutionalized. The major contraindication is pregnancy. Duration of antibody response is uncertain, but appears to be at least 2 years. Influenza vaccination may also help prevent infection and subsequent pneumonia in patients at risk.

Patients in intensive care units have a high incidence of serious nosocomial infections. While endotracheally administered antibiotics have failed to cure established pneumonia, conflicting evidence surrounds their use in prophylaxis.

VI. **NATURAL HISTORY AND PROGNOSIS**

Resolution of pneumonia is usually defined radiographically as clearing of pneumonic infiltrates. Rate of resolution is uncertain. One series found virtually complete clearing of 87 percent of pneumonias in hospitalized patients within 4 weeks. An additional 12 percent cleared within 8 weeks. No difference was noted between pneumococcal pneumonia and those of other etiologies. Bacteremic pneumococcal pneumonia appears to clear more slowly than the nonbacteremic form. Infiltrates in the latter often resolve in 2 weeks, whereas persistence of up to 6 weeks is common in bacteremic pneumonia. Stranding and pleural disease often persist even at 6 weeks. Streptococcal pneumonia and mycoplasmal pneumonia in young patients usually resolve in 4 weeks.

Resolution may be delayed by underlying systemic disease or other pulmonary lesions, such as malignancy or bronchiectasis. An approach to nonresolving pneumonia is presented in figure 8-1.

Recovery from pneumonia depends upon the infecting organism and the overall status of the patient. Patients with viral, mycoplasmal, or pneumococcal pneumonia usually sustain no long-term effects. In contrast, necrotizing pneumonias due to staphylococci, gram-negative bacilli, or anaerobes frequently lead to scarring and permanent dysfunction. This is especially true in systemically ill patients, who sustain more severe disease, and thus more severe destruction.

Mortality is similarly dependent upon the patient's underlying disease. Of infectious agents, overall mortality from gram-negative pneumonia is much greater than that for gram-positive pneumonia.

VII. PNEUMONIA IN SPECIAL SITUATIONS

A. **Recurrent pneumonia.** Recurrent pneumonia—multiple episodes of pneumonia in an individual patient—suggests

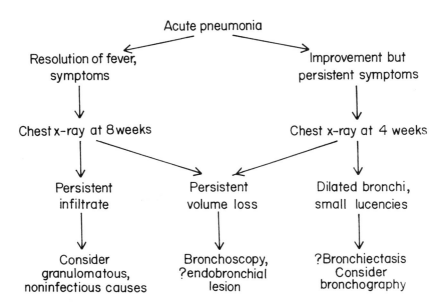

Figure 8-1. Flow chart for the evaluation of nonresolving pneumonia.

the need for further evaluation. One series found underlying disease in 93 percent of patients with recurrent pneumonia. Of these patients, 23 percent had intrathoracic disease (chronic bronchitis or emphysema, congestive heart failure, bronchiectasis), 33 percent had systemic disease (alcoholism, diabetes mellitus, or cancer), and 36 percent had both. Immunodeficiency was uncommon, and focal pulmonary lesions were present only if recurrence was limited to one lobe or segment. This suggests a low diagnostic yield in patients with recurrent pneumonia unless the location is also recurrent. In these patients, bronchoscopy or bronchography should be performed as dictated by history and chest x-ray.

B. Right middle lobe syndrome. The right middle lobe syndrome describes a heterogeneous group of disorders leading to a small, atelectatic right middle lobe (RML). Three general processes lead to RML volume loss:

1. Endobronchial lesions, causing complete or partial RML obstruction, with subsequent atelectasis and infection.
2. Chronic infections, causing hilar adenopathy with external compression of the RML bronchus.
3. Chronic RML infection, leading to destruction of alveolar architecture and scarring.

Although the role of endobronchial lesions seems clear, the relative importance of hilar node compression and chronic scarring is less certain. Studies in normal persons demonstrate markedly decreased collateral ventilation in the RML relative to other lobes, which apparently renders it susceptible to collapse, infection, and scarring.

Diagnosis is based on chest x-ray findings of volume loss in the RML. With total collapse, the RML moves medially with loss of the minor fissure on PA film and a linear density on lateral film. Complete re-expansion may occur after resolution of an infectious process, and the cycle of collapse and re-expansion may be repeated. Alternatively, partial or complete collapse may become chronic, with no interval re-expansion.

Causes of chronic RML volume loss in two series included neoplasm in 15 to 38 percent, bronchiectasis in 10 to 27 percent, tuberculosis in 10 to 12 percent, and recurrent pneumonia in 5 to 13 percent. Symptoms were usually those of recurrent pneumonia, although about 40 percent of patients had hemoptysis. Evaluation should include bronchoscopy to exclude neoplasm, and careful cultures for tuberculosis. Therapy is directed at the underlying disease, and the superimposed pneumonia, if present. Occasionally, lobectomy may be required for malignancy, recurrent hemoptysis, or recurrent pneumonias that compromise overall function.

C. **Aspiration pneumonia.** Aspiration of gastric contents occurs frequently in severely ill, hospitalized patients. Predisposing factors include altered mental status of any etiology, depressed gag reflex, general anesthesia, tracheostomy, and nasogastric tubes. Nasotracheal or orotracheal tubes do not appear to promote aspiration. Consequences of aspiration depend on the nature of gastric contents:

1. **Volume.** Regardless of type, increased volume of aspirate leads to more severe functional derangements.
2. **Acid.** A threshold pH of 2.5 appears to separate acid from nonacid injury in experimental aspiration. Above pH of 2.5, little necrosis occurs. Alveolar fluid leads to reflex airway closure and decreased surfactant, but these changes are easily reversed. Below pH 2.5, atelectasis occurs, followed by pulmonary edema, hemorrhage, and type II cell necrosis. The alveolar-capillary "membrane" may be damaged, leading to exudation, and in severe cases, ARDS. Hypoxia ensues due to airway closure, decreased surfactant, and exudation. Initially, pulmonary artery pressure rise, but they soon fall to normal.
3. **Food.** Food particles initiate a granulomatous reaction, with eventual clearing.
4. **Bacteria.** Oropharyngeal secretions almost always are included in the aspirate. Whether these initiate primary infection, or secondary infection supervenes in the damaged lung, is uncertain. Infection appears to play little part in the initial complications of aspiration; nevertheless, over 50 percent of patients with documented aspiration become infected.

Aspiration should be suspected in a predisposed patient who develops fever and pulmonary infiltrates. Prominent bronchospasm and hypoxemia may also suggest the diagnosis. Whereas a chemical pneumonitis usually becomes manifest several hours after aspiration, bacterial infection often is not apparent for several days. Areas of the lung most commonly involved depend on patient's position at time of aspiration: posterior segments of upper lobes, if supine, lower lobes if erect. Consolidation may appear rapidly, or the infiltrate may remain inhomogenous. Sputum is nonspecific, often purulent, but with few or mixed organisms. Transtracheal aspirate also reveals PMN with multiple organisms, often including anaerobes. Sputum cultures in one series of community-acquired aspiration pneumonia showed 63 percent aerobic flora, 7 percent anaerobic, and 30 percent mixed. In hospital-acquired infections, about 50 percent are mixed aerobes and anaerobes. Careful culture techniques may increase the yield of anaerobes.

Treatment of aspiration pneumonia is primarily supportive, replacing lost fluid and supplementing oxygenation and ventilation as necessary. In observed aspiration, immediate endotracheal suctioning may limit volume of aspirate. Corticosteroids have been advocated immediately after aspiration, but no conclusive animal or clinical data support their use. Prophylactic antibiotics, before the onset of fever or purulent sputum, have also been suggested, but no rigorous evidence supports this practice. Once infection is diagnosed, penicillin should be used in community-acquired pneumonia, with clindamycin or chloramphenicol as alternatives. For hospital-acquired infections, a semisynthetic penicillin and an aminoglycoside often are used to treat staphylococci and gram-negative aerobic organisms.

D. Lung abscess. A primary lung abscess is an area of parenchymal necrosis, usually a complication of anaerobic infection generally resulting from aspiration. Abscesses are most common in patients with altered mental status or depressed gag reflex. Symptoms include recurrent fever or copious sputum production, although the course may occasionally be indolent. Radiographic diagnosis is based on evidence of cavitation, which implies communication with the airways. Differential diagnosis is that of empyema, pneumatocele, or bullae:

1. **Abscess:** A spherical cavity within an alveolar infiltrate, appearing similar on PA and lateral films and sparing the pleura
2. **Empyema:** Usually not spherical, often appearing different on PA and lateral views
3. **Pneumatocele:** A rapidly growing, thin-walled air mass, due to intermittent airway obstruction rather than necrosis, with rapid resolution
4. **Bullae:** Vesicles, usually seen prior to infection that exhibit a smooth inner wall with little change during the course of infection

If radiographic definition is equivocal, ultrasonography may distinguish abscess from empyema. Occasionally, neoplasms may undergo central necrosis, simulating abscess. Lack of response to antimicrobial therapy usually signals the need for tissue diagnosis. Etiologic diagnosis may be established from sputum or transtracheal aspirate. Two series found that most infections were mixed, with anaerobes occurring in the great majority of cases. Therapy consists of antibiotics, and perhaps, postural drainage. Antibiotic choice depends upon organism and sensitivity, but usually includes an agent effective against such anaerobes as penicillin, clindamycin, chloramphenicol, or cefoxitin. Duration and route of therapy are uncertain, although most sources agree that 4 to 6 weeks is the minimum required. Oral antibiotics may follow initial parenteral therapy. Cavity resolution may be monitored by chest x-ray, and is complete in 70 percent of patients by 3 months. Surgical therapy is rarely necessary. It should be reserved for patients with delayed resolution, or perhaps with very large abscesses or bronchiectasis and inadequate clearance of abscess material. Bronchoscopic drainage probably should be reserved for similar circumstances.

E. **Empyema.** Empyema is defined as the presence of infected fluid (pus) within the pleural space. The most common cause of empyema is direct extension from adjacent structures, as in pneumonia, subphrenic infection, or esophageal rupture. Empyema may also result from metastatic seeding in systemic infection, or penetration by trauma, surgery, or diagnostic procedures. Pleural effusions are common in pneumonia, but empyemas are uncommon—they occur most often in debilitated patients. Differentiation of effusion and empyema rests on:

1. **Physical exam.** Local pain suggests empyema rather than effusion.
2. **Purulence.** Empyema is usually distinguished from an infected effusion by purulence, although both harbor organisms.
3. **Gram stain and culture.** Presence of organisms by either technique establishes infection.
4. **Culture.** Bacterial growth confirms empyema.
5. **Pleural fluid pH.** In parapneumonic effusions, pH less than 7.20 suggests loculation or empyema.

Thoracentesis should be performed if empyema is suspected, or in compromised patients in whom signs of empyema, such as fever or leukocytosis, might be absent.

Gram-negative bacilli are the major etiologic agents in recent years, reflecting a trend similar to that in pneumonias. One series found infecting organisms, in order of incidence, to be: gram-negative bacilli, mixed aerobes, *Streptococcus pneumoniae*, and *Staphylococcus aureus*. Another study, using careful isolation techniques, found a much higher incidence of anaerobes and mixed aerobic/anaerobic infections.

Therapy is that of closed-space infection: drainage and antibiotics. Small empyemas may be managed by thoracentesis, but large collections or empyemas causing fever that persists for more than 24 hours should be drained via chest tube. Choice of antibiotics is based on gram stain and culture results.

REFERENCES

I. General

Donowitz GR, Mandell GL: Acute pneumonia. In *Principles and Practice of Infectious Diseases.* Edited by Mandell GL, New York, John Wiley & Sons, 1980, pp 489-502.

Fraser RG, Pare JAP: *Diagnosis of Diseases of the Chest.* Philadelphia, WB Saunders, 1978, pp 683-731.

Stamm WE: Nosocomial pneumonia. In *Pulmonary Diseases and Disorders.* Edited by Fishman AP, New York, McGraw-Hill, 1980, pp 1041-1051.

Donowitz presents an excellent review, concentrating on diagnostic techniques. Stamm discusses incidence and pathogenesis; Fraser reviews specific organisms, with emphasis on radiologic patterns.

II. Pathogenesis

Fekety FR, Caldwell J. Gump D, et al: Bacteria viruses, and mycoplasmas in acute pneumonia in adults. *Am Rev Respir Dis* 104:499-507, 1971.

Johanson WG, Pierce AK, Sanford JP, et al: Nosocomial respiratory infections with gram-negative bacilli. *Ann Intern Med* 77:701-706, 1972.

Fekety documents the predominance of pneumococcal disease in cases of community-acquired pneumonia. Johanson reports the frequency of colonization and subsequent pneumonia in ill, hospitalized patients.

III. Diagnosis

Bartlett JA: Diagnostic accuracy of transtracheal aspiration: bacteriologic studies. *Am Rev Respir Dis* 115:777-782, 1977.

Davidson M, Tempest B, Palomar DL: Bacteriologic diagnosis of acute pneumonia: comparison of sputum, transtracheal aspirate, and lung aspirates. *JAMA* 235:158-163, 1976.

Goodman LR, Goren RA, Teplick SK: The radiographic evaluation of pulmonary infection. *Med Clin North Am* 64:553-574, 1980.

Murray PR, Washington JA: Microscopic and bacteriologic analysis of expectorated sputum. *Mayo Clin Proc* 50:339-344, 1975.

Wimberley N, Faling LJ, Bartlett JG: A fiberoptic bronchoscopy technique to obtain uncontaminated lower airway secretions for bacterial culture. *Am Rev Respir Dis* 119:337-343, 1979.

Bartlett and Davidson demonstrate the superiority of transtracheal aspirate over expectorated sputum for diagnostic purposes. Direct aspiration is rarely necessary. Murray correlates sputum gram stain with culture results, and Wimberley provides a preliminary report of bronchoscopy yielding uncontaminated secretions. Goodman discusses classic and atypical radiographic presentations.

IV. Clinical

Cordes LG, Fraser DW: Legionellosis. *Med Clin North Am* 64:395-416, 1980.

Finland M: Pneumonia and pneumococcal infections, with special reference to pneumococcal infection. *Am Rev Respir Dis* 120:481-502, 1979.

Knight V: Respiratory viral infections. In *Pulmonary Diseases and Disorders*. Edited by Fishman AP, New York, McGraw-Hill, 1980, pp 119-127.

Murray HW, Tuazon C: Atypical pneumonias. *Med Clin North Am* 64:507-528, 1980.

Reyes MP: The aerobic gram-negative bacillary pneumonias. *Med Clin North Am* 64:363-383, 1980.

Tuazon C: Gram-positive pneumonias. *Med Clin North Am* 64:343-361, 1980.

Wallace RJ, Musher DM: *Hemophilus influenzae* pneumonia in adults. *Am J Med* 64:87-93, 1978.

All are reviews of the clinical presentation of pneumonias by etiologic agent. The Finland article is primarily historical, discussing changes in incidence and treatment over the last decades.

V. Treatment

Austrian R: Pneumococcal vaccine: development and prospectus. *Am J Med* 67:547-549, 1979.

Graham WGB, Bradley DA: Effect of chest physiotherapy and IPPB in the resolution of pneumonia. *N Engl J Med* 299:624-627, 1978.

Murray BE, Moellering RC: Antimicrobial agents in pulmonary infections. *Med Clin North Am* 64:319-342, 1980.

Austrian briefly reviews indications and evidence for the use of pneumococcal vaccine. Graham finds no clear benefit from IPPB and physiotherapy. Murray reviews pharmacology and spectrum of antimicrobials.

VI. Natural history

Boyd DHA: Failure of resolution of pneumonia. *Br J Dis Chest* 69:259-266, 1975.

Jay SJ, Johanson WG, Pierce AK: The radiographic resolution of *Streptococcus pneumoniae* pneumonia. *N Engl J Med* 293:798-801, 1975.

Lerner AM: Systemic effects of pulmonary infections. In *Pulmonary Diseases and Disorders.* Edited by Fishman AP, New York, McGraw-Hill, 1980, pp 1065-1070.

Boyd and Jay document clearing of most pneumonias in 8 weeks. Lerner provides morbidity and mortality estimates by etiologic agent.

VII. Special situations

Albo RH, Grimes OF: The middle lobe syndrome: a clinical study. *Dis Chest* 50:509-518, 1966.

Bartlett JG, Gorbach SL, Finegold SM: The bacteriology of aspiration pneumonia. *Am J Med* 56:202-207, 1974.

Bartlett JG, Gorbach SL, Tally FP, et al: Bacteriology and treatment of primary lung abscess. *Am Rev Respir Dis* 109:510-518, 1974.

Inners CR, Terry PB, Traystman RJ, et al: Collateral ventilation and the right middle lobe syndrome. *Am Rev Respir Dis* 118:305-310, 1978.

Potts DE, Levin DC, Sahn SA: Pleural fluid pH in parapneumonic effusions. *Chest* 70:328-330, 1976.

Sherman MM, Subramian V, Berger RL: Management of thoracic empyema. *Am J Surg* 113:474-479, 1977.

Winterbauer RH, Bedon GA, Ball WC, Jr; Recurrent pneumonia—predisposing illness and clinical patterns in 158 patients. *Ann Intern Med* 70:689-700, 1969.

Wynne J, Modell J: Respiratory aspiration of stomach contents. *Ann Intern Med* 87:466-474, 1977.

Albo presents a series of cases of the RML syndrome, while Inners provides evidence that decreased collateral ventilation may be one cause of the syndrome. Wynne reviews experimental and clinical evidence on the pathogenesis of aspiration pneumonia. Bartlett and Gorbach find a preponderance of anaerobes in these patients. Bartlett et al discuss medical management of lung abscess. Potts suggests pleural fluid pH less than 7.20 as indication for drainage. Sherman advocates drainage and antibiotics for empyema. Winterbauer finds a lack of focal pulmonary pathology in recurrent pneumonias, except those recurring in the same area.

9
Pulmonary Disease in the Immunocompromised Patient

I. DEFINITION

Pulmonary disease in the immunocompromised patient poses unique diagnostic and therapeutic dilemmas: First, these patients often have infiltrates with several potential etiologies; second, diagnosis is difficult owing to the lack—or nonspecificity—of sputum and serum; and third, therapy must be chosen promptly, because of the rapid dissemination of disease, and carefully in order to avoid adverse drug effects. As noted in Chapter 8, most patients who develop pneumonia have underlying systemic disease, and thus might be said to be "compromised." Immunocompromised patients differ in the degree of dysfunction in host defenses. This, in turn, alters the natural history of pulmonary disease.

II. PATHOGENESIS

Pulmonary disease in the immunocompromised patient may be classified broadly as either infectious or noninfectious.

A. Infectious. Five major mechanisms aid in host defense against infection. Diseases affecting one or more of these defenses predispose to infection.

1. Granulocyte function. Neutrophils serve primarily to phagocytize infecting organisms, especially bacteria. The most common defect is a decrease in the number of circulating granulocytes, usually because of hematologic malignancy or drugs. The number of neutrophils required to prevent infection is unknown, but risk is clearly increased if the count is below $1000/mm^3$, and markedly increased below

500/mm^3. Functional defects in neutrophils, including impaired chemotaxis, adhesion, phagocytosis, and bactericidal activity, occur congenitally, or secondary to a variety of diseases or drugs. Both quantitative and qualititative defects predispose to bacterial infection.

2. **Humoral immunity and complement.** Roles of antibody in host defense include opsonization of organisms and bactericidal activity. Depressed levels of functional antibody are found most commonly in defects of B-cell lineage, such as multiple myeloma or chronic lymphocytic leukemia. In addition, selective IgA deficiency may impair mucocutaneous defenses (see below). Hypogammaglobulinemia predisposes affected persons to bacterial infection, especially pneumonia, sinusitis, and bacteremia; parasitic infestations, such as giardiasis, also occur more frequently. Defense against viral and fungal infections is minimally affected, except possibly for poliomyelitis and viral hepatitis. Complement deficiency, usually congenital, results in decreased bactericidal activity and similar immune defects.

3. **Cell-mediated immunity.** T lymphocytes are primarily involved in defense against intracellular infection, and to a lesser extent, as adjuncts to humoral immunity. T-cell defects are most often seen in the presence of lymphomas and immunosuppressive drugs. Incidence of fungal (especially *Candida*) and viral (especially herpesvirus) infections is increased. In addition, bacteria that establish chronic intracellular infection, such as *Mycobacteria*, *Nocardia*, *Listeria*, and *Salmonella*, occur more frequently in association with T-cell defects, as do some parasites such as *Pneumocystis carinii*, *Toxoplasma gondii*, and *Strongyloides stercoralis*.

4. **Mucocutaneous barriers.** The common portals of entry for infection in immunocompromised patients are breaks in the gastrointestinal mucosa, indwelling cannulas, and the upper respiratory tract. In the gastrointestinal tract, normal host flora serve as a common source for pathogens. These bacteria also prevent colonization and potential infection by other, more virulent, organisms. Secretory antibody, IgA, helps prevent entry of normal or colonizing flora. Indwelling cannulas allow entry of skin and external flora. Impairments of upper respiratory defenses al-

lowing bacterial access to the lower respiratory tract include:

    a. Intubation bypassing the upper respiratory tract
    b. Massive inhaled inocula from contaminated respiratory therapy equipment
    c. Impaired ciliary clearance, as in cystic fibrosis

5. **Reticuloendothelial function.** The least understood of defense mechanisms is the monocyte-macrophage system and the network of phagocytic cells in reticuloendothelial tissue. These cells apparently are important in preventing metastatic infection, clearing organisms with polysaccharide capsules (e.g., *S. pneumoniae*, *H. influenzae*, type B), and perhaps, removing some parasites. Splenectomy reduces reticuloendothelial system function; chronic hemolysis with subsequent pigment overload, as in sickle cell anemia or beta-thalassemia, results in similar dysfunction.

Nutrition is not a specific defense mechanism but rather impinges on all defenses described above. Protein-calorie malnutrition, a frequent result of neoplastic disease or immunosuppressive therapy, leads to depression of phagocytic function, cell-mediated immunity, and mucocutaneous integrity.

Table 9-1 presents a compilation of diseases causing defects in host defenses, and lists the pulmonary infections commonly seen with each defect.

B. **Noninfectious.** A variety of noninfectious processes may lead to pulmonary infiltrates in the immunocompromised patient, including neoplasia, radiation, drugs, pulmonary edema, pulmonary emboli, leukoagglutinin reactions, and hemorrhage. Pathogenesis is similar to that in normal hosts, and will be discussed briefly below.

III. CLINICAL PRESENTATION

Symptoms, such as dyspnea or cough, and signs, such as fever, may suggest the onset of pulmonary disease. Infiltrates on chest x-ray localize disease to the lung and indicate the need for further evaluation. Etiology of pulmonary infiltrates in immunocompromised patients varies with underlying disease, extent of therapy, and individual hospital. *Table 9-2* summarizes etiologies of pulmonary infiltrates found in four recent series. Differences in methodology, patient population, and time period may account for differences in incidence, but the lists of diagnoses are similar. Major causes

Table 9-1
Immune Defects and Infection in the Compromised Patient

Defect	Cause	Pathogen

Decreased granulocyte function	Myelocytic leukemia
	Chronic granulomatous disease
	Drug-induced granulocytopenia
	Corticosteroids
	Acidosis
	Malnutrition
	Uremia
	Possibly diabetes mellitus
		Bacteria
		  Pseudomonas
		  Serratia
		  Staphylococcus
		  Nocardia
		Fungi
		  Aspergillus
		  Candida

Decreased humoral immunity	Multiple myeloma
	Lymphocytic leukemia
	Congenital or acquired hypogammaglobulinemia
	Cytotoxic or antineoplastic drugs
	Radiation
	Complement deficiency
		Bacteria
		  S. pneumoniae
		  H. influenzae type B
		  Pseudomonas
		Protozoa
		  Possibly *Pneumocystis*

Decreased cellular immunity	Hodgkin's disease
	Lymphoma
	Corticosteroids
	Uremia
	Sarcoidosis
	Radiation
	Cytotoxic or antineoplastic drugs
		Bacteria
		  Listeria
		  Mycobacteria
		Viruses
		  Herpes
		  Measles
		Fungi, esp.
		  Candida
		Protozoa
		  Pneumocystis
		  Toxoplasma
		  Strongyloides

Mucocutaneous barriers	Mucositis, decubitus, ulceration
	Intravenous catheter
	Urethral catheter
	Intubation
	IgA deficiency
	Alterations of normal flora
	Respiratory therapy contamination
		Bacteria
		  Oral flora
		  E. coli
		  Klebsiella
		  Pseudomonas
		Fungi
		  Candida

Reticuloendothelial dysfunction	Splenectomy
	Chronic hemolysis
	Possibly, malaria
		Bacteria
		  S. pneumoniae
		  H. influenzae type B
		  Salmonella

Table 9-2
Etiology of Pulmonary Infiltrates in Immunocompromised Patients in Four Studies

Etiology	Tenholder, Hooper	Ramsey, et al	Rubin	Singer, et al
		(in percentages)		
Infection	49	66	73	41
Bacterial	23	22	26	1
Fungal	13	26	16	4
Viral	1	16	11	1
Protozoan	2	2	6	26
Mixed	?	?	14	9
Mycobacterial	0	0	1	0
Radiation	0	0	7	?
Drug	0	0	5	?
Pulmonary edema	10	11	1	0
Neoplasm	10	0	8	9
Leukoagglutinin	0	0	2	0
Pulmonary embolus	0	17	3	0
Hemorrhage	15	0	1	5
Fibrosis	1	0	0	12
Other	0	0	0	2
No diagnosis	16	6	0	18

Note: Tenholder and Hooper: all leukemia, 94% fever;
Ramsey, et al: all renal transplant, all fever;
Rubin: all malignancy, all fever, diagnosis in all;
Singer, et al: all malignancy, 86% fever, all diffuse infiltrates.

of infiltrates will be discussed briefly according to etiologic category.

A. Infection

1. Bacterial. Bacteria remain the most common cause of infectious infiltrates in the immunocompromised patient. Of bacterial pneumonias, about 90 percent occurring in hospitalized patients are caused by gram-negative organisms, primarily *Klebsiella*, *Pseudomonas*, *E. coli*, and *Serratia*. Fever is common, although other symptoms and signs are variable. Unlike normal hosts, cough may be dry, especially in neutropenic patients. Similarly, chest x-ray may be negative early in the course of disease, especially in the presence of neutropenia. Radiographic findings do not correlate with etiology. Several gram-negative pathogens, important in immunocompromised as

well as normal hosts, such as *Klebsiella*, *E. coli*, and *Legionella*, are discussed in Chapter 8.
  a. *Pseudomonas aeruginosa* (aerobic gram-negative bacillus)
    (1) **Predisposition.** Granulocyte defect, cystic fibrosis
    (2) **Portal of entry.** Endogenous aspiration from colonization in upper respiratory tract; occasionally from contaminated respiratory therapy equipment
    (3) **Clinical findings.** Symptoms include fever, chills, dyspnea, cough with yellow or green sputum; ecthyma gangrenosum is associated with bacteremia.
    (4) **Laboratory findings.** WBC is usually elevated, and bacteremia is common. Chest x-ray shows diffuse, often bilateral bronchopneumonia, or occasionally, nodular infiltrates. Sputum is usually purulent.
    (5) **Diagnosis.** Sputum gram stain, culture
    (6) **Therapy.** Carbenicillin or ticarcillin, and an aminoglycoside
  b. *Acinetobacter* species (pleomorphic, encapsulated, gram-negative coccobacillary forms)
    (1) **Predisposition.** Tracheostomy, endotracheal tube
    (2) **Portal of entry.** Oropharyngeal colonization
    (3) **Clinical findings.** Nonspecific symptoms and signs
    (4) **Laboratory findings.** Chest x-ray shows multilobar bronchopneumonia. Sputum shows organisms of variable morphology, often suggesting *Neisseria* or enteric forms.
    (5) **Diagnosis.** Sputum gram stain, culture
    (6) **Therapy.** Carbenicillin or ticarcillin, and an aminoglycoside
  c. *Serratia marcescens* (aerobic gram-negative bacillus)
    (1) **Predisposition.** Granulocyte defect
    (2) **Portal of entry.** Contaminated respiratory therapy equipment; oropharyngeal colonization
    (3) **Clinical findings.** Fever, chills, cough
    (4) **Laboratory findings.** Chest x-ray usually shows bronchopneumonia.
    (5) **Diagnosis.** Sputum gram stain, culture

(6) Therapy. Organisms are of variable sensitivity; use aminoglycoside plus cefoxitin or trimethoprim-sulfamethoxazole
   d. *Listeria monocytogenes* (aerobic gram-positive rod)
      (1) Predisposition. Altered cell-mediated immunity
      (2) Portal of entry. Inhalation, or through gastrointestinal tract
      (3) Clinical findings. Often subacute onset with nonspecific symptoms
      (4) Laboratory findings. Variable chest x-ray pattern
      (5) Diagnosis. Sputum gram stain, culture; associated meningitis
      (6) Therapy. Ampicillin or penicillin
   e. *Nocardia* species (usually *N. asteroides*)
      (1) Predisposition. Altered cell-mediated immunity
      (2) Portal of entry. Inhalation
      (3) Clinical findings. Often subacute or chronic presentation, with nonspecific symptoms. Central nervous system disease occurs in one-third to one-half of cases, and skin disease occurs occasionally.
      (4) Laboratory findings. Chest x-ray shows bronchopneumonia or nodules, often with cavitation; empyemas occur in up to 25 percent of patients.
      (5) Diagnosis. Sputum gram stain, modified acid-fast stain
      (6) Therapy. Sulfonamides

2. Mycobacterial. These organisms are discussed at length in Chapter 10. In the immunocompromised patient, tuberculosis is usually due to reactivation rather than primary infection. Differences from normal hosts include decreased skin reactivity (PPD-negative in 4 of 12 in one series) and greater mortality (17 percent in one series). Atypical mycobacteria are usually Runyon classes I and III, *M. kansasii* and *M. fortuitum*.

   Diseases associated with tuberculosis include squamous cell carcinoma of the head and neck, lung carcinoma, lymphoma, and Hodgkin's disease. Presentation is similar to that in normal hosts. Disease may be especially severe in patients receiving corticosteroids. Therapy usually includes three drugs. Isoniazid prophylaxis has been advocated for compromised patients with positive tuberculin reactivity, but evidence for its efficacy is limited.

3. **Fungal.** Fungi account for 15 to 20 percent of pneumonias in immunocompromised patients, and about 30 percent of total mortality from pneumonia. Opportunistic fungi rarely cause pneumonia in normal hosts. On the other hand, common causes of fungal pneumonia in normal persons, such as histoplasmosis, coccidioidomycosis, and blastomycosis, are infrequent pathogens in compromised patients.
   a. *Aspergillus* species (usually *A. fumigatus* or *A. flavus*)
   (1) **Predisposition.** Altered cell-mediated immunity; granulocyte defect, especially in leukemia or transplants
   (2) **Portal of entry.** Inhalation
   (3) **Clinical findings.** Invasive form produces a necrotizing bronchopneumonia with small vessel invasion and hemorrhagic infarction. Symptoms include dyspnea and cough with little sputum
   (4) **Laboratory findings.** Chest x-ray is variable, with interstitial or nodular infiltrates, often with cavitation and rapid progression. Dissemination occurs in 20 to 50 percent of patients.
   (5) **Diagnosis.** Sputum cultures are positive in 10 to 30 percent of patients; serologic results are nonspecific. Biopsy and culture usually are required.
   (6) **Therapy.** Amphotericin B
   b. *Cryptococcus neoformans* (yeast-like fungus)
   (1) **Predisposition.** Altered cell-mediated immunity, especially Hodgkin's disease, sarcoidosis
   (2) **Portal of entry.** Inhalation
   (3) **Clinical findings.** Subacute or chronic presentation, one-third of patients with no symptoms, about one-half with cough. Dissemination to meninges is common.
   (4) **Laboratory findings.** Chest x-ray shows variable patterns, especially mass lesion or segmental consolidation, usually involving one lobe. Effusion is uncommon.
   (5) **Diagnosis.** Sputum culture is often falsely

positive. Serum antigen appears specific in interstitial pneumonitis if rheumatoid factor is negative. Biopsy may be required, or evidence of meningeal disease, such as organism or antigen in cerebrospinal fluid.
- (6) Therapy. Amphotericin B with flucytosine
- c. *Phycomycetes.* *(Rhizopus, Mucor, Absidia* species)
  - (1) Predisposition. Altered cell-mediated immunity, altered granulocyte function, especially leukemia, lymphoma
  - (2) Portal of entry. Inhalation
  - (3) Clinical findings. Invasive form leads to vascular invasion with infarction. Symptoms are variable, and dissemination is common.
  - (4) Laboratory findings. Chest x-ray shows variable patterns, including fungus balls (mycetoma).
  - (5) Diagnosis. Biopsy is required.
  - (6) Therapy. Amphotericin B
- d. *Candida* species (dimorphic fungi, especially *C. albicans* and *C. tropicalis*)
  - (1) Predisposition. Altered cell-mediated immunity; mucocutaneous barriers
  - (2) Portal of entry. Normal commensals; entry by endogenous aspiration, breaks in mucocutaneous barriers, or hematogenous seeding
  - (3) Clinical findings. An uncommon cause of pneumonia; symptoms are variable
  - (4) Laboratory findings. Chest x-ray findings are variable.
  - (5) Diagnosis. Serology not useful, biopsy is required.
  - (6) Therapy. Amphotericin B
4. Viral. As in normal persons, influenza viruses are common pathogens in immunocompromised patients. Major opportunistic organisms are herpes viruses.
   - a. Herpes simplex (types 1 and 2)
     - (1) Predisposition. Altered cell-mediated immunity.
     - (2) Portal of entry. Inhalation
     - (3) Clinical findings. Spectrum ranges from tracheobronchitis to pneumonia; symptoms are not specific.

(4) Laboratory findings. Chest x-ray usually shows diffuse interstitial disease.
(5) Diagnosis. Fourfold rise in titer is sensitive but nonspecific; biopsy is required for confirmation.
(6) Therapy. Role of adenosine arabinoside (Ara-A) is uncertain.
b. Herpes varicella-zoster
(1) Predisposition. Altered cell-mediated immunity, especially due to lymphoma or transplant
(2) Portal of entry. Inhalation
(3) Clinical findings. Variable symptoms, often characteristic rash; 16 to 30 percent of adults have pulmonary involvement, with dissemination to other viscera in 6 to 26 percent.
(4) Laboratory findings. Chest x-ray shows diffuse nodular infiltrate.
(5) Diagnosis. Presence of rash, biopsy
(6) Therapy. Zoster immune globulin prophylaxis in children, within 72 hours of exposure; adenosine arabinoside in adults with visceral dissemination. The role of interferon is uncertain.
c. Cytomegalovirus
(1) Predisposition. Altered cell-mediated immunity, especially due to renal or bone marrow transplant.
(2) Portal of entry. Uncertain.
(3) Clinical findings. Dry cough, dyspnea.
(4) Laboratory findings. Chest x-ray pattern is variable, usually with interstitial or small nodular infiltrate.
(5) Diagnosis. Serologic studies are sensitive but nonspecific; biopsy is required for confirmation.
(6) Therapy. Role of interferon prophylaxis is uncertain.

5. Parasitic. Although *Pneumocystis carinii* has received wide attention as a pathogen in the immunocompromised patient, its incidence is geographically variable. Other parasites, such as *Toxoplasma* and *Strongyloides*, are rare causes of opportunistic infections.
   a. *Pneumocystis carinii*
      (1) Predisposition. Altered cell-mediated im-

munity, especially due to corticosteroids or cyclophosphamide
(2) **Portal of entry.** Uncertain
(3) **Clinical findings.** Subacute onset of fever, cough, and dyspnea
(4) **Laboratory findings.** Chest x-ray shows interstitial or reticulonodular infiltrate, usually perihilar. Eosinophilia is uncommon.
(5) **Diagnosis.** Sputum is only 5 percent sensitive, while transtracheal aspirate has only 15 percent yield; biopsy is usually required.
(6) **Therapy.** Trimethoprim-sulfamethoxazole, or alternatively, pentamidine isethionate

b. *Toxoplasma gondii*
(1) **Predisposition.** Altered cell-mediated immunity, especially Hodgkin's disease
(2) **Clinical findings.** Uncommon infection; subacute or chronic onset
(3) **Laboratory findings.** Chest x-ray shows diffuse interstitial infiltrate.
(4) **Diagnosis.** Serologic results are often false positive, although suggestive if levels are markedly elevated; biopsy is required.
(5) **Therapy.** Pyrimethamine, sulfonamides

B. **Progression of underlying disease.** Underlying diseases, usually neoplastic, may involve lung parenchyma, giving rise to infiltrates in the immunocompromised patient. Radiographic characteristics may suggest a neoplastic origin for infiltrates. Discrete or nodular infiltrates are more common in metastases from solid tumors, whereas diffuse infiltrates are more likely to result from hematologic malignancy, lymphangitic extension, or occasionally, primary lung neoplasm.

1. **Hodgkin's disease.** Approximately 30 percent of cases have pulmonary involvement, usually by extension from the mediastinum. Effusions occur in about 30 percent of patients at some time during the course of disease.

2. **Non-Hodgkin's lymphomas.** Pulmonary disease often takes the form of multiple nodular lesions, especially in the lower lobes.

3. **Leukemia.** At autopsy, 50 percent of patients have mediastinal involvement, and 25 percent have pulmonary parenchymal disease. As many as half of these cases are not recognized before death. Infil-

trates are usually diffuse, bilateral, reticular patterns resembling lymphangitic carcinoma.
4. **Multiple myeloma.** Pulmonary involvement is rare, occasionally occurring by direct extension from a rib or as a solitary plasmacytoma.
5. **Solid tumors.** As many as 30 percent of neoplasms metastasize to the lung, although lesions less than 1 centimeter in diameter usually are not visible on chest x-ray. Symptoms from metastases are uncommon. Effects are usually those of the neoplasm on overall host defenses.

C. **Radiation pneumonitis.** Pulmonary parenchyma is often included in the radiation portal for hematologic, mediastinal, breast, and primary lung neoplasms. Approximately 40 percent of patients irradiated for breast carcinoma develop radiographic evidence of radiation disease, although only 8 percent are symptomatic. Patients irradiated for lung neoplasms and lymphomas have a variable incidence of disease, although only 5 to 15 percent have clinical manifestations. Some patients appear to be "hyper-reactive" to radiation, developing pneumonitis at relatively low doses. Clinical aspects of radiation pneumonitis are presented in Chapter 11.

D. **Drug-induced pneumonitis.** Drug effects on the lung are discussed in Chapter 11. The most common causes of pulmonary infiltrates are oxygen, antineoplastics, and antibiotics. Common drug effects in immunocompromised patients are summarized in *table 9-3*.

E. **Pulmonary emboli.** Conditions predisposing to pulmonary emboli are common in immunocompromised patients, including bed rest, thrombocythemia, and hypercoagulability. Radiographic manifestations are variable, as described in Chapter 13, including oligemia, atelectasis, and consolidation. Clinical presentation is similar to that in normal hosts.

F. **Leukoagglutinin reaction.** An uncommon complication of transfusions, in both normal and immunocompromised patients, is pulmonary edema, presumably due to leukoagglutinins. This syndrome, occurring in mid-transfusion or immediately post-transfusion, includes fever, chills, tachycardia, cough, and dyspnea. Chest x-ray shows nodular, perihilar, and lower lung field infiltrates without cardiomegaly. Eosinophilia is common, and fever

Table 9-3
Drug Effects on the Lung in Immunocompromised Patients

Reaction	Drug	Frequency*
Alveolar and Interstitial infiltrates	Bleomycin	C
	Busulfan	C
	Nitrofurantoin	C
	Cyclophosphamide	C
	Methotrexate	C
	Chlorambucil	R
	Azathioprine	R
	Melphalan	R
	Sulfasalazine	R
	Procarbazine	R
Alveolar infiltrates	Penicillin	U
	Sulfonamides	R

*C = common, U = uncommon, R = rare

and infiltrates persist up to 48 hours. Resolution is spontaneous.

G. **Pulmonary edema due to congestive heart failure.** Interstitial or alveolar edema due to left atrial hypertension must be considered in the immunocompromised patient. The leading causes of pulmonary edema are common disorders, such as left ventricular dysfunction and mitral or aortic valve disease. In addition, immunocompromised patients are predisposed to congestive heart failure because of
   1. Fluid overload, due to chemotherapeutic agents or treatment of hypercalcemia
   2. Cardiomyopathy, secondary to drugs such as doxorubicin
   3. Uremia

H. **Pulmonary hemorrhage.** Coagulation abnormalities in some immunocompromised patients, especially those with acute leukemia, render them susceptible to hemorrhage. This may occur in the lung in the absence of other disease, or when precipitated by emboli or infection. Dense consolidation with fever is the usual presentation.

IV. DIAGNOSIS

A. **Approach.** Because of multiple etiologies for pulmonary infiltrates and the potential for rapid deterioration, thorough evaluation in immunocompromised patients is imperative. Systematic evaluation includes consideration of:
  1. Epidemiologic factors
     a. **Remote exposure.** Careful history should be sought for exposure to tuberculosis, histoplasmosis, coccidioidomycosis, or blastomycosis.
     b. **Recent exposure.** History of contacts or recent travel should be sought.
     c. **Site of acquisition.** As in infectious pneumonia in normal hosts, etiologic organisms vary with site of acquisition. Community-acquired pneumonia is more likely to be pneumococcal or influenzal in origin; hospital-acquired disease is more often due to a gram-negative or opportunistic pathogen.
     d. **Epidemic vs endemic organism.** Community epidemics of diseases such as influenza should suggest this diagnosis. Outbreaks of nosocomial pneumonia may also occur in hospitalized patients. In addition, organisms appear prevalent in some hospitals but not in others, as is the case with *P. carinii*.
  2. **Past history.** Information about prior illness or evidence for extension of a current illness should be sought, as well as information on exposure to drugs or radiation. One recent series found varying significance of radiographic findings, depending upon stage of treatment, in leukemias. Those with infiltrates prior to, or soon after, the start of chemotherapy appeared to respond to diuretics or empirical antibiotics. Those with diffuse infiltrates during treatment were more likely to harbor opportunistic pathogens.
  3. **Physical examination.** The presence or absence of fever does not differentiate infectious from noninfectious disease. Other aspects of the exam are generally unrevealing, except in the presence of lesions associated with specific infections, such as ecthyma gangrenosum (*Pseudomonas*) or erythema nodosum (tuberculosis, fungal infection, sarcoidosis).

Presence of deep venous thrombosis should suggest pulmonary embolism.
4. Laboratory findings
   a. Hematologic. Marked leukocytosis with left shift suggests bacterial infection, while marked thrombocythemia predisposes to embolic disease. Coagulation disorders increase risk of hemorrhage.
   b. Sputum is often unavailable, owing to debility and neutropenia. If sputum is present, gram stain and culture may establish the diagnosis of bacterial or mycobacterial infection. Sputum is rarely helpful in the diagnosis of viral, protozoan, fungal, or noninfectious pulmonary infiltrates. Transtracheal aspiration may increase diagnostic yield in bacterial or protozoan infection.
   c. Serologic study for various organisms is often sensitive but nonspecific. Further diagnostic evaluation is almost always necessary despite positive serologic findings. Especially helpful serologic findings include elevated cytomegalovirus and *Legionella* titers.
5. Pulmonary function. Most causes of diffuse infiltrates decrease lung compliance and, in later stages, lung volumes as well. Interference with oxygenation and subsequent hypoxemia is common in most causes of diffuse infiltrates. Exceptions are neoplasia, fungi, and tuberculosis. These diseases seldom cause overwhelming pneumonia, hence oxygenation is preserved until late in the course.
6. Chest x-ray. Radiographic presentations do not correlate with specific etiologies, although characteristic x-ray findings may occur, as presented in *table 9-4*.
7. Progression. Rate of progression of infiltrates, and overall clinical status, may suggest specific etiologies, especially when coupled with radiographic findings. Correlation of disease progression, radiographic appearance, and etiology is presented in *table 9-5*.

B. Biopsy. Even intensive evaluation using the methods described above yields a diagnosis in only a minority of immunocompromised patients with pulmonary infiltrates. If disease is sufficiently severe, direct access to lung tissue by biopsy should be considered. Published

Table 9-4
Radiographic Findings in Immunocompromised Patients

Pattern	Etiology
Multiple masses	Fungi, staphylococci, *Pseudomonas*, septic emboli, anaerobes
Diffuse infiltrate	Viruses, protozoa, leukoagglutinin reactions, drug reactions, radiation
Cavitation	Fungi, *Nocardia*, tuberculosis, anaerobes
Sharp margins	Radiation pneumonitis

reports of diagnostic yields of various techniques in immunocompromised patients vary widely. Yields for bronchoscopy appear to be about 60 to 70 percent if biopsy is performed. Yield may be increased somewhat by concurrent brushings. Yield in needle aspiration is similar or slightly lower. Open lung biopsy, despite offering direct access to tissue, increases yield only moderately. About 20 to 30 percent of biopsies are nonspecific, regardless of technique.

In summary, the diagnostic approach to pulmonary infiltrates in the immunocompromised patient should include a careful search for etiologies, considering predisposing factors, time course, and results of noninvasive studies. If the patient appears well, empiric therapy for a clearly defined course may obviate the need for further diagnostic measures. If the patient is severely ill, if empiric therapy has little effect, or if disease progresses rapidly, early biopsy should be considered.

V. THERAPY

Therapy of pulmonary disease in the immunocompromised patient is based on etiologic diagnosis. Agents recommended for specific processes are presented above. If no etiologic diagnosis can be made and the patient appears stable, a brief course (2 to 5 days) of empiric therapy may be started. If volume overload is suspected, diuretics should be used. If infection is suspected, antibiotics should be started. Although studies have not specifically addressed pulmonary disease, trials of antibiotics in febrile, immunocompromised patients confirm the efficacy of synergistic antibiotics, usually a cephalosporin or semisynthetic penicillin and an aminoglycoside. Use of adjunctive measures, such as granulocyte transfusions in neutropenic patients or interferon, is uncertain.

Table 9-5
Differential Diagnosis Based on Radiographic Pattern and Course

Chest X-ray Finding	Acute Conditions	Subacute or Chronic Conditions
Consolidation	Bacteria Thromboemboli Hemorrhage (Pulmonary edema)*	Fungi *Nocardia* Neoplasms Tuberculosis (Radiation reactions) (Drug reactions) *(Pneumocystis)* (Viruses)
Interstitial	Leukoagglutinin reactions Pulmonary edema (Bacteria)	Viruses *Pneumocystis* Radiation reactions Drug reactions (Neoplasms) (Fungi) *(Nocardia)* (Tuberculosis)
Nodular	(Bacteria) (Pulmonary edema)	Neoplasms Fungi *Nocardia* Tuberculosis

*Diagnoses in parentheses represent unusual presentations
Modified with permission of McGraw-Hill Book Company from *Current Clinical Topics in Infectious Disease*, vol 1. (p 298) by Remington JS, Swartz MN, © 1980 McGraw-Hill Inc.

Prevention of infection remains a primary goal, in light of associated high morbidity and mortality. Preventive measures include the following:

A. **Prevent colonization** of pathogenic organisms by
  1. Isolating patients with virulent pathogens
  2. Avoiding use of antibiotics unless necessary
  3. Altering diet
B. **Prevent invasion** across mucocutaneous barriers by avoiding placement of intravenous and urethral catheters, if possible.
C. **Maintain host defenses** by ensuring adequate nutrition.
D. **Prophylactic antibiotics**, including oral nonabsorbable agents and trimethoprim-sulfamethoxazole, appear ef-

fective in reducing overall incidence of infection in neutropenic patients. Present evidence warrants treatment of neutropenic patients with trimethoprim-sulfamethoxazole 5-20 mg/kg/day.

E. The contribution of **protected environments** to prevention is uncertain.

VI. NATURAL HISTORY AND PROGNOSIS

Natural history of pulmonary disease in immunocompromised patients depends on both the pulmonary process and the underlying illness. Fulminant acute infections, such as *Pseudomonas* or *Pneumocystis* pneumonias, progress rapidly, with high mortality. In subacute infections or radiation pneumonitis, an underlying malignancy may lead to mortality before the pulmonary process does. Overall mortality of immunocompromised patients with pulmonary infiltrates is high, ranging from 45 to 76 percent. The effect of therapy or prophylactic measures on mortality in these patients is uncertain.

REFERENCES

I. General

Bode FR, Pare JAP, Fraser RG: Pulmonary disease in the compromised host. *Medicine* 53:255-293, 1974.

Ramsey PG, Rubin RH, Tolkoff-Rubin NE, et al: The renal transplant patient with fever and pulmonary infiltrates: etiology, clinical manifestations, and management. *Medicine* 59:206-222, 1980.

Rubin RH: The cancer patient with fever and pulmonary infiltrates: etiology and diagnostic approach. In *Current Clinical Topics in Infectious Disease.* Edited by Remington JS, Swartz MN, New York, McGraw-Hill, 1980, pp 288-303.

Williams DM, Krick JA, Remington JS: Pulmonary infection in the compromised host. *Am Rev Respir Dis* 114:359-394, 593-627, 1976.

All discuss slightly different patient populations, as noted in the titles. Bode, Ramsey, and Rubin consider infection as well as other etiologies; Williams deals primarily with infection.

II. Etiology and Pathogenesis

Bodey GP, Rodriguez V, Chang HY, et al: Fever and infection in leukemic patients: a study of 494 consecutive patients. *Cancer* 41:161-222, 1978.

Dauber JH, Fogarty CM: Immune-deficiency states and recurrent respiratory tract infections. In *Pulmonary Diseases and Disorders.* Edited by Fishman AP, New York, McGraw-Hill, 1980, pp 997-1009.

Matthay RA, Greene WH: Pulmonary infections in the immunocompromised patient. *Med Clin North Am* 64:529-551, 1980.

Tenholder MF, Hooper RG: Pulmonary infiltrates in leukemia. *Chest* 78: 468-473, 1980.

Dauber presents a brief review of immune defense mechanisms. Matthay correlates these with specific diseases, and Bodey and Tenholder provide representative series of patients with hematologic malignancies.

III. Clinical

Abdullah P, Mark J, Merigan T: Diagnosis of cytomegalovirus pneumonia in compromised hosts. *Am J Med* 61:326-332, 1976.

Gross NJ: Pulmonary effects of radiation therapy. *Ann Intern Med* 86:81-92, 1977.

Hughes WT: Pneumocystis carinii pneumonia. *N Engl J Med* 297:1381-1383, 1977.

Kaplan MH, Armstrong D, Rosen P: Tuberculosis complicating neoplastic disease. *Cancer* 33:850-858, 1974.

Kilburn KH: Pulmonary disease induced by drugs. In *Pulmonary Diseases and Disorders*. Edited by Fishman AP, New York, McGraw-Hill, 1980, pp 707-724.

Masur H, Rosen PP, Armstrong D: Pulmonary disease caused by *Candida* species. *Am J Med* 63:914-925, 1977.

Meyer RD, Rosen P, Armstrong D: Phycomycosis complicating leukemia and lymphoma. *Ann Intern Med* 77:871-879, 1972.

Pennington JE: Aspergillosis pneumonia in hematologic malignancy. *Arch Intern Med* 137:769-771, 1977.

Phillips JC, Wyatt JP: Radiation fibrosis. In *Pulmonary Diseases and Disorders*. Edited by Fishman AP, New York, McGraw-Hill, 1980, pp 658-674.

Rosenow EC: The spectrum of drug-induced pulmonary disease. *Ann Intern Med* 77:977-991, 1972.

Valdivieso M, Gil-extremera B, Zarnoza J, et al: Gram-negative bacillary pneumonia in the compromised host. *Medicine* 65:241-254, 1977.

Ward HN: Pulmonary infiltrates associated with leukoagglutinin transfusion reactions. *Ann Intern Med* 73:689-694, 1970.

Young LS, Armstrong D, Blevins A, et al: *Nocardia asteroides* infections complicating neoplastic disease. *Am J Med* 50:356-357, 1971.

All describe specific etiologic agents for, and presentation of, pulmonary disease in the immunocompromised patient.

IV. Diagnosis

Cunningham JH, Zavala DC, Corry RJ, et al: Trephine air drill, bronchial brush, and fiberoptic transbronchial lung biopsies in immunosuppressed patients. *Am Rev Respir Dis* 115:213-220, 1977.

Lauver GL, Hasan FM, Morgan RB, et al: The usefulness of fiberoptic bronchoscopy in evaluating new pulmonary lesions in the compromised host. *Am J Med* 66:580-585, 1979.

Leight GS, Michaelis LL: Open lung biopsy for the diagnosis of acute, diffuse pulmonary infiltrates in the immunosuppressed patient. *Chest* 73:477-482, 1978.

Matthay RA, Farmer WC, Odero D: Diagnostic fiberoptic bronchoscopy in the immunocompromised host with pulmonary infiltrates. *Thorax* 32:539-545, 1977.

Nishio JN, Lynch JP: Fiberoptic bronchoscopy in the immunocompromised host: the significance of a "nonspecific" transbronchial biopsy. *Am Rev Respir Dis* 121:307-312, 1980.

Pennington JE, Feldman NT: Pulmonary infiltrates and fever in patients with hematologic malignancy. *Am J Med* 62:581-587, 1977.

Singer C, Armstrong D, Rosen PP, et al: Diffuse pulmonary infiltrates in immunosuppressed patients. Prospective study of 80 cases. *Am J Med* 66:110-120, 1978.

All present series documenting utility of various biopsy techniques in slightly differing groups of patients. Nishio also considers outcome of nonspecific biopsies (e.g., inflammation, fibrosis). In about half of these, diagnosis was eventually made by other means.

V. Therapy

EORTC International Antimicrobial Therapy Project Group: Three antibiotic regimens in the treatment of infection in febrile granulocytopenic patients with cancer. *J Infect Dis* 137:14-29, 1978.

Gurwith MJ, Brunton JL, Lank BA, et al: A prospective controlled investigation of prophylactic trimethoprim-sulfamethoxazole in hospitalized granulocytopenic patients. *Am J Med* 66:248-256, 1979.

Hughes WT, Kuhn S, Chaudhary S, et al: Successful chemoprophylaxis for *Pneumocystis carinii* pneumonitis. *N Engl J Med* 297:1419-1426, 1977.

Rodriguez V, Bodey GP, Freireich EJ, et al: Randomized trial of protected environment—prophylactic antibiotics in 145 adults with acute leukemia. *Medicine* 57:253-266, 1978.

The first article demonstrates the superiority of synergistic antibiotics, while the latter three document efficacy of prophylactic antibiotics in neutropenic patients.

10
Mycobacterial and Fungal Diseases

PART 1
MYCOBACTERIAL DISEASES

I. DEFINITION AND INCIDENCE

Over 99 percent of mycobacterial infections involving the lung are due to *M. tuberculosis*. Occasionally, other organisms, such as *M. avivum* and *M. intracellulare*, are the cause. In 1977, there were 30,415 cases of active tuberculosis in the United States, with 2,968 fatalities. Of these cases, approximately 85 percent occurred primarily in the lung, and the balance were primarily extrapulmonary. Positive skin tests, suggesting infection but not clinical disease, occur in about 7 percent of the United States population. About 40,000 new infections are reported each year.

II. ETIOLOGY AND PATHOGENESIS

A. **Organism.** Mycobacteria are nonmotile, nonsporulating, gram-positive rods classified in the order Actinomycetales. The tubercle bacillus, *M. tuberculosis* (other tubercle bacilli are *M. bovis* and *M. africanum*), causes the vast majority of pulmonary infections. It is an obligate parasite, distinctive among bacteria in that it establishes a lifelong symbiosis with the human host. After the initial infection is controlled by host defenses, mycobacteria may remain dormant for years, "reactivating" in response to immunosuppression or other stimuli. Although tubercle bacilli may infect any organ, they are obligate aerobes, with a predilection for areas of high oxygen tension, such as alveolar air at the lung apices, or high blood flow, such as in the kidney, brain, and epiphyses.

B. Natural history of infection. The mycobacterium's capacity for symbiosis involves two distinct phases of involvement: **subclinical infection,** the presence of mycobacteria in the body with minimal or no symptoms or signs; and frank **tuberculosis,** the result of multiplication and dissemination of organisms sufficient to cause clinical manifestations.

Infection occurs primarily via airborne human-to-human contact. Infection via gastrointestinal tract or skin is rare, and fomites play an insignificant role in transmission. Tuberculous infection thus begins with exposure to a person harboring and transmitting the organism. Factors that affect transmission fall into two categories:

1. Index case: **Number of organisms expelled,** in turn dependent upon extent of involvement, cough frequency, and site of involvement (increased with cavitary or laryngeal tuberculosis).

2. Host: **Duration and nature of exposure,** usually close, prolonged contact. Also, HLA Bw15 status and AB blood type appear to predispose to infection.

Communicability is variable, and usually very low. The average newly diagnosed case of tuberculosis has seven close contacts, 21 percent of whom are infected, but less than 1 percent of whom have active disease.

Infection begins with inhalation of organisms contained in droplet nuclei, particles 1 to 10 microns in diameter that, owing to their size, remain airborne. They contain several tubercle bacilli. When inhaled, they may bypass upper respiratory defenses, usually depositing in the lower lobes or anterior segments of the upper lobes, due to upright ventilatory pattern. As little as 1 organism may initiate infection. Organisms multiply slowly, forming a localized pneumonia even after ingestion by phagocytes. Drainage of the area may cause unilateral hilar adenopathy. The original site of infection, when calcified and viewed radiographically, is termed a Ghon lesion. When unilateral hilar adenopathy is also noted, a Ranke complex is said to be present.

Before immune mechanisms can contain infection, lymphohematogenous dissemination takes place. Seeding occurs in multiple sites, including liver, kidney, and lung upper lobes. Lung foci are often located in apical or posterior segments, areas of high oxygen tension. These are termed Simon's foci when seen on chest x-ray. Pathologically, areas of infection are characterized by mononuclear cell infiltration, with giant cell formation and tissue necrosis. Cell death and tissue damage appear to be due to the effects of delayed hypersensitivity, rather than the organism per se. In about 5 percent of infected individuals, immune defenses are unsuccessful and organisms multiply in the lung parenchyma, leading to active tuberculosis. In others, infection is contained, with subsequent healing and granuloma formation. Granulomas in the lung usually contain dormant but viable organisms. This process constitutes infection, usually with few symptoms or clinical findings.

Dormant organisms may be reactivated and may resume multiplication at any time during the life of the host, most commonly in the first year after infection. Four-to-five percent of infected persons develop tuberculosis in this period, with much lower incidence in ensuing years. Factors predisposing to reactivation include immunosuppression, silicosis, diabetes mellitus, gastrectomy, and jejunoileal bypass.

The majority of cases of tuberculosis in adults—probably about 90 percent—represent reactivation rather than primary infection. Prior infection confers relative immunity to exogenous reinfection; however, multiple infections occasionally occur, as documented by the isolation of several strains of *M. tuberculosis* in the same patient.

The natural history of tuberculous infection is summarized in *table 10-1*.

III. DIAGNOSIS AND CLINICAL PRESENTATION

A. Subclinical infection. As noted above, tuberculous infection produces nonspecific or minimal symptoms. Patients may report mild fatigue, lethargy, or malaise, but this rarely suggests the diagnosis unless an infected contact is discovered. Tuberculous infection is diagnosed by skin testing, the injection of a tuberculous antigen (tuberculin) intradermally. This procedure relies on the presence of a delayed hypersensitivity (type IV) response in infected hosts, rather than the detection of organisms. The diagnosis is therefore presumptive. If cell-mediated immunity functions adequately, characteristic induration occurs. This response appears 2 to 10 weeks after infec-

Table 10-1
Natural History of Tuberculous Infection

Stage	Process	Symptoms and Signs
Inhalation	Airborne droplet nuclei via human-to-human contact	None
Bronchopneumonia	Organisms lodge in alveoli of lower lobes or anterior segments of upper lobes	
	Regional multiplication; occasionally hilar adenopathy	Few or mild constitutional symptoms
Dissemination	Lymphohematogenous dissemination, including extrapulmonary sites	
Host response	Failure of host response with diffuse disease	Tuberculin conversion 4-8 wks
Miliary tuberculosis		Fever, anorexia, dyspnea
Parenchymal tuberculosis	Parenchymal multiplication continued	Fever, cough with sputum
Healing with granuloma	Infection persists; no disease 4-5% incidence of disease in 1 year Possibility of remote reactivation	None

tion, and persists for the duration of infection, usually the life of the host.
1. Types of tuberculin
   a. **Old tuberculin (OT).** This antigen is manufactured from heat-stabilized cultures of *M. tuberculosis*, and contains multiple tuberculous antigens and extraneous material. False positive reactions may occur, and it is seldom used except in tine testing.
   b. **Purified protein derivative (PPD).** This is an extracted antigen from *M. tuberculosis*, which appears more specific than OT for tuberculous infection. It is stabilized in a detergent—polysorbate—to prevent adsorption.
2. Techniques of administration
   a. **Multiple puncture (tine).** This technique is used for population screening, and results in multiple small punctures containing either OT or PPD. Tine testing appears to be both less sensitive and less specific than Mantoux administration.
   b. **Mantoux.** This technique employs a syringe with a number 26 or smaller needle to inject 0.1 cc of PPD intradermally, usually in the volar forearm. A wheal should appear, indicating intradermal injection. Otherwise, the antigen probably is in the subcutaneous tissues. PPD is supplied in three strengths: 1, 5, and 250 tuberculin units (TU). Five TU is the diagnostic standard. "Second strength" (250 TU) increases sensitivity at the expense of specificity. If negative, 250 TU may be useful in excluding tuberculosis if the patient is not anergic or harboring disseminated disease. One TU is poorly standardized and should not be used. A local reaction occasionally occurs to 5 TU, which may be treated with topical corticosteroids.
3. **Interpretation.** Both tests are read at 48 and 72 hours, and induration rather than erythema is evaluated. Induration is best assessed by touch, either by hand or by a pen run to the edge of the indurated area from opposite sides. Accepted diagnostic criteria are:

    Greater than 10 mm—positive
    5 to 9 mm—doubtful
    Less than 5 mm—negative

Since the range of Mantoux reactions in those with infection comprises a normal distribution, some infected patients may fall below this limit. The average reaction in immunocompetent infected patients is 16 mm, with a range from 8 to 24 mm. The most common cause of a doubtful result is cross-reaction with nontuberculous mycobacteria. In regions where these organisms are common, such as the southeastern United States, a larger reaction may be required to maintain specificity. Conversely, in other areas, smaller reactions may indicate infection.

4. Errors in tuberculin testing
   a. False positive reactions
      (1) **Bacille Calmette-Guérin (BCG) vaccination.** This usually causes induration less than 12 mm in diameter.
      (2) **Nontuberculous mycobacterial infection.** This is the most common cause of a false positive result, due to cross-reacting antigen. PPD prepared for specific organisms may be helpful in children, but use in adults is uncertain.
      (3) **Interpretation.** Measurement of erythema rather than induration may incorrectly suggest a large reaction.
      (4) **"Booster effect."** The booster effect is defined as an increase in the size of the tuberculin reaction with repeated testing. Apparently, it is due to stimulation of an anamnestic immune response in subjects with a waning or cross-reacting PPD. Thus, repeated testing may increase the size of a small reaction, producing a positive result. The booster effect occurs more commonly with advancing age. It occurs rarely if the interval between tests is less than 1 week, and peak effect occurs at 1 to 5 weeks. Duration of the booster effect is variable; in a few cases it has gone beyond one year, but most subjects revert to their original PPD status within 6 months. If periodic skin testing is to be performed, the booster effect may be managed as follows:
         (a) If the initial PPD is negative, repeat PPD at 1 week.
         (b) If the repeat PPD is positive, assume this is accurate.

(c) If the repeat PPD is negative, compare later tests to this result.
  b. False negative reactions
    (1) **Age.** Reactions to PPD wane with age, even in the presence of normal immune function, although they rarely vanish.
    (2) **Anergy.** Dysfunction of immune system components required for delayed hypersensitivity may render a reaction temporarily negative. Tuberculin reaction returns if immunocompetence is restored.
    (3) **Infection.** Rubeola infections may temporarily blunt tuberculin response, for unknown reasons. Whether other viral illnesses or vaccines have a similar effect is uncertain.
    (4) **Recent mycobacterial infection.** As noted above, several weeks are required for the development of specific delayed hypersensitivity and a positive tuberculin result.
    (5) **Promptly treated infection.** Occasionally, treatment of infection soon after tuberculin conversion will return response to negative, perhaps indicating the eradication of organisms.
    (6) **Inadequate PPD.** Improper preparation, standardization, or storage may result in false negative reactions.
    (7) **Administration.** Diagnostic standards for PPD are based on intradermal injection of 0.1 cc. Despite anecdotal evidence supporting the use of this technique in quantifying reactions, one recent study found no less induration with 0.05 cc or with subcutaneous injection. Nonetheless, careful technique should be attempted.
    (8) **Interpretation.** Reading at other than 48 and 72 hours may cause a missed positive reaction.
B. **Tuberculosis**
  1. **Clinical presentation.** Unlike subclinical tuberculous infection, tuberculosis usually is suspected due to clinical presentation, and diagnosed by isolation of the organism. As previously noted, two types of tuberculosis are recognized:
    a. **Primary** (childhood): the occurrence of disease soon following infection.

b. **Secondary** (postprimary, reactivation): The development of disease after an interval of dormancy.

The bulk of adult disease is secondary, resulting from multiplication of organisms in a previously established focus. Predisposing conditions include diabetes mellitus, ethanol abuse, silicosis, and renal failure. Immunosuppressive drugs also may lead to disease reactivation, and may perhaps enable primary infection to take place. Presence of malignancy predisposes to tuberculosis, presumably by depressing host immune defenses. The relation to sarcoidosis is uncertain.

Distinction between primary and secondary tuberculosis cannot be made clinically, but some manifestations occur differentially. Primary tuberculosis is uncommon in adults, accounting for 14 percent of cases, most often in patients under 30 years of age. Symptoms usually are mild and nonspecific; disease is often diagnosed by radiographic abnormalities in a recent PPD converter. When present, symptoms include fever, cough malaise, and occasionally, sputum production. Signs are uncommon; in a large Norwegian series, erythema nodosum occurred in 15 percent of patients. However, this sign appears less commonly in the United States.

In secondary tuberculosis, symptoms are equally nonspecific. Cough with sputum is more likely to occur, occasionally accompanied by minor hemoptysis and pleuritic chest pain. Signs are uncommon in pulmonary disease, with occasional rales on chest exam. Dyspnea and tachypnea are unusual except in severe, disseminated disease.

2. **Chest x-ray.** Presentation is variable. Usually a small lesion is present in the upper lung fields, in the apical or posterior segments of the right upper lobe, or in the apical-posterior segment of the left upper lobe. Less commonly, a lesion is present in the superior segment of the lower lobes. Hilar adenopathy, which is common in primary tuberculosis and almost always is unilateral, usually resolves within months. Effusion is more characteristic of primary than secondary tuberculosis, resolving spontaneously except for rare progression to empyema. Other presentations include apical cavitary lesions, localized pneumonias, and single or multiple tuberculomas. The range of presentations makes the chest x-ray an ad-

junct, rather than a definitive procedure, in the diagnosis of tuberculosis.
3. Laboratory findings are similarly nonspecific. Mild hypoproliferative anemia is common, and the WBC is often normal. Hypercalcemia is common in patients with active disease (20 to 30%), as is hyponatremia (10% in one series). Both conditions are presumably due to humoral mediators, resolving with treatment of the disease. Liver function tests are usually normal, and ESR is variable.
4. Diagnosis of tuberculosis requires isolation and culture of the organism, most often from sputum in pulmonary tuberculosis.
   a. Sputum. Sputum may be coughed spontaneously or induced by aerosol inhalation. A smear should be made and examined microscopically if tuberculosis is suspected, although sensitivity of smears depends upon the extent of disease. Approximately 10,000 bacteria/ml are required for a positive smear, a concentration most likely to occur in cavitary disease. Staining techniques include Ziehl-Neelsen's and auramine-rhodamine fluorochrome stain, the latter increasing sensitivity. Specificity is limited by the presence of other acid-fast organisms: nontuberculous mycobacteria, rhodocrous, *Nocardia*, and the Pittsburgh pneumonia agent. Although controversy exists about overall specificity, sputum smears remain useful if other clinical evidence is present. Smears allow treatment to begin pending culture results, since chemotherapy does not affect culture results for 7 to 10 days. Smears also are useful in establishing contagiousness, and probably in determing duration of therapy.
   Sputum culture is more sensitive than smear, requiring fewer bacilli for a positive result. Moreover, cultures are more specific in allowing a distinction to be made between tubercle bacilli and other acid-fast organisms. About 70 percent of tuberculosis cases will be diagnosed by three sputum culture specimens and 80 percent by five specimens. Diagnostic yield on the basis of subsequent samples is low.
   b. Other. If sputum is unobtainable or negative, other techniques can be used, including gastric aspiration, transtracheal aspiration, and bron-

choscopy. Gastric aspiration to recover swallowed organisms in a morning specimen is primarily useful in children. Smears are nonspecific, and cultures in adults are rarely positive if sputum is negative. Transtracheal aspiration and bronchoscopy are not necessary routinely, but both may allow diagnosis if sputa are negative and tuberculosis is suspected.
   c. **Pleural fluid.** Pleural effusion in tuberculosis is usually exudative, with 300-3000 leukocytes/ mm^3, and pH less than 7.25. It is uncommon for cultures of pleural fluid to grow tubercle bacilli. However, pleural biopsy increases yield dramatically, with positive cultures in 50 to 60 percent of cases and positive histologic results in an additional 20 percent. Pleural biopsy therefore should be performed if a tuberculous effusion is suspected.
   d. **Skin testing.** Although the *sine qua non* for diagnosing infection, the PPD is less reliable in tuberculosis. Five to 10 percent of patients with pulmonary tuberculosis have PPD less than 10 mm with 5 TU, and about 1 percent have nondiagnostic reactions to 250 TU. Negative results may be due to generalized anergy, or specific anergy to tuberculosis. Specific anergy may result from serum inhibitors, suppressor cells, or compartmentalization of the immune response.
5. **Differential diagnosis** of tuberculosis is that of chronic pneumonia, or occasionally, acute pneumonia. Infectious diseases to be considered are fungal, especially histoplasmosis, coccidioidomycosis, and blastomycosis, and those of higher bacteria, such as *Nocardia*. These organisms may occasionally coexist with tuberculosis. Neoplasia also may present with similar radiographic findings, with anergy confounding PPD results. If cultures are negative, and no other process is evident in a patient suspected of having tuberculosis, a trial of chemotherapy may confirm the diagnosis and eliminate the infection.

C. **Miliary tuberculosis.** Named because of the "millet-sized" lesions sometimes visible on chest x-ray, miliary tuberculosis is clinically defined as acute, diffuse dissemination of tubercle bacilli via the blood. Usually it is an early complication of primary tuberculosis, occurring in the first 3 to 6 months after infection. Miliary tuberculosis may also occur in the same time period after reactivation of dormant disease. In either case, bacilli undergo embolization to capillary beds and are not contained by host defenses. Predisposing factors include ethanol abuse, neoplasia, diabetes mellitus, and pregnancy.

Clinical presentation is nonspecific. Symptoms include weakness, anorexia, fever, and weight loss over weeks or months. Headache and abdominal pain should suggest meningitis and peritonitis, respectively. Common signs include fever, tachycardia, and tachypnea. Signs of pericarditis may be present, and choroidal tubercles are found on eye exam in 7 percent of adults. PPD (5 TU) is positive in 80 percent of cases, and chest x-ray shows a miliary pattern in over 90 percent. Radiographic lesions are usually small, less than 2 mm in diameter, and diffuse. "Cryptic" presentation, with negative chest x-ray, may occur in the first weeks after dissemination.

Laboratory findings include mild anemia, normal white blood cell count with left shift, mildly abnormal liver function tests, and occasional hyponatremia. Unlike localized pulmonary tuberculosis, oxygenation may be seriously impaired and spirometry may show a restrictive pattern. Diagnosis of miliary tuberculosis is established by smear and culture of sputum, transtracheal aspirate, or bronchial brushing. Occasionally, lung biopsy may be necessary if cultures are negative. Granulomas on liver biopsy are nonspecific, and yields in both marrow and urine culture are low (about 20 percent.) Treatment consists of mulitple drugs, but mortality remains about 15 percent, perhaps due to late diagnosis. Death usually is caused by respiratory failure.

IV. TREATMENT

Treatment of tuberculous disease varies with the stages in its natural history.

A. Prophylaxis. The goal of prevention is to define populations at high risk and to prevent tuberculous infection in these groups. In the United States, high risk occurs in household contacts of those with active tuberculosis, and in certain institutionalized populations where tuberculosis is common. In the first group, treatment with isoniazid (INH) probably prevents infection by eliminating organisms very early during multiplication. In the second group, INH may be used in the same fashion. In addition, BCG, a live attenuated strain of *M. tuberculosis*, may be used as a vaccine. Careful trials of BCG have been hampered by variability in populations and in strains of the vaccine. BCG is probably effective in endemic areas, but use in the United States should be restricted to groups in whom other methods have failed.

B. **Infection.** Treatment of tuberculous infection does not eradicate the organism, except in rare cases. Rather, treatment prevents progression to disease by killing most organisms. The marker of infection, PPD, is not reversed by treatment. Also, treatment prevents recrudescence of tuberculosis in patients with radiographic evidence of old disease and no prior therapy. INH is used to treat infection, usually with daily doses of 300 mg for 1 year.

Because infection per se poses no problem to the host, the long-term risk of developing tuberculosis must be weighed against the immediate risk of INH-induced hepatitis (see below). Current guidelines[1] for INH use follow, in the order of priority listed:

1. Household contacts of active cases
2. Tuberculin reactors with radiographic findings of inactive parenchymal tuberculosis
3. Newly infected cases (recent PPD convertors)
4. Tuberculin reactors with the following drug histories and diseases:
    a. Prolonged corticosteroid use
    b. Use of immunosuppressive drugs
    c. Leukemia, lymphoma, Hodgkin's disease
    d. Diabetes mellitus
    e. Silicosis
    f. Subtotal or partial gastrectomy
    g. Age under 35 years

These guidelines are based on inconclusive evidence; controversy exists concerning treatment of patients with positive PPD and old fibrotic lesions, as well as the age at which those patients with PPD of indeterminate duration should be treated.

C. **Tuberculosis.** The goals of treatment of tuberculosis are to halt disease progression and limit contagion. Treat-

---

[1] From *Am Rev Resp Dis* 110:371-374, 1974.

ment differs from that of tuberculous infection in that much larger numbers of bacilli must be killed. In tuberculosis patients, two populations of bacilli exist:
1. A large, actively multiplying, usually extracellular population
2. A smaller, slowly replicating, often intracellular population

Drugs must be chosen to eliminate both groups, and to prevent development of drug resistance, which is more common with large numbers of organisms. For example, about 1 in 10^5 bacilli is primarily resistant to INH. Since there are about 10^5 organisms in a cavity and 10^3 in a nodule, multiple drugs are necessary to prevent emergence of a resistant population. The 10 drugs used to treat tuberculosis in the United States are presented in *table 10-2*.

Primary drugs are most effective and form the basis of most regimens. Secondary drugs are less effective and generally more toxic, while tertiary drugs are used only when other agents fail or are contraindicated.

Duration and frequency of dosage vary with different regimens. In the last decade, intermittent and short-course regimens have been demonstrated to be effective in several studies. Intermittent regimens rely on standard drugs and duration, and are designed to allow supervised administration, decreased toxicity, and lower cost. Most regimens employ an initial daily phase to kill the majority of bacilli, followed by intermittent administration to eliminate slow-growing organisms. Dosage interval in intermittent therapy is uncertain. In those metabolizing INH rapidly (rapid acetylators), INH must be given twice per week with streptomycin, and three times per week with ethambutol. If rifampin is used, or if patient is a slow acetylator, INH may be given twice per week, or perhaps even once per week, depending upon initial daily dose.

Short-course regimens require bactericidal drugs—those able to kill nondividing organisms, such as rifampin or pyrazinamide, and to a lesser extent, INH and streptomycin. These drugs are given daily for 6 to 9 months in an effort to eliminate rapidly both dividing and quiescent organisms. Duration of short-course therapy is uncertain. For smear-positive tuberculosis, 9 months of two drugs and 6 months of four drugs appear adequate. For smear-negative disease, between 3 and 6 months of three or four drugs appears adequate. One recent study combined intermittent and short-course therapy, using INH and

Table 10-2
Drugs Used in the U.S. for Tuberculosis Treatment

Drug	Daily Dose	Side Effects	Monitor	Treatment
I. Primary Drugs				
Isoniazid	300 mg	Peripheral neuritis		Pyridoxine 50-100 mg; prophylaxis 10 mg
		Hepatitis	Symptoms; SGOT if high-risk	D/C drug
		CNS: convulsions, optic neuritis, dizziness, ataxia		
		Interactions: decreased clearance of phenytoin	Phenytoin levels	
Rifampin	600 mg	Orange urine, tears, saliva		
		Flu-like syndrome		
		Hepatitis	SGOT for symptoms	D/C drug
		Thrombocytopenia		
		Hemolysis		
		Renal failure		
		Interactions: increased catabolism of warfarin, oral contraceptives, methadone, and corticosteroids		

II. Secondary Drugs

Ethambutol	15-25 mg/kg	Optic neuritis (at 25 mg/kg)	Visual acuity; red-green discrimination
Para-aminosalicylic acid (PAS)	12-15 g	Rash Anorexia, nausea, hypersensitivity, hepatotoxicity Sodium load	SGOT for symptoms
Pyrazinamide	20-35 mg/kg to 3 gm	Hyperuricemia (gout rare)	Uric acid
Streptomycin	0.75-1 g	8th cranial nerve symptoms Nephrotoxicity	Hearing, with audiogram; vestibular function BUN/creatinine

III. Tertiary Drugs

Capreomycin	1 g	Similar to streptomycin Hypokalemia	Potassium
Cycloserine	750 mg	CNS: somnolence, headache, tremor, dysarthria, vertigo (increased with dose, ethanol)	
Ethionamide	0.75-1 g	Anorexia, nausea, vomiting; postural hypotension, rash, hepatotoxicity	SGOT
Kanamycin	0.5-1 g	Similar to streptomycin	

rifampin for 9 months. Results are preliminary but encouraging.

Several representative chemotherapeutic regimens are presented in *table 10-3*.

D. **Toxicity and monitoring.** Toxicity and side effects of antituberculous drugs are summarized in *table 10-2*. Of special importance is the toxicity of INH, the mainstay of treatment. The most serious side effect of INH is hepatitis, which presents in a fashion similar to viral hepatitis. Pathogenesis appears to be related to toxic metabolites, perhaps acetylhydrazine. Metabolite production is, in turn, related to rapidity of degradation of the drug. Two general phenotypes for INH metabolism exist: rapid and slow acetylators. Although rapid acetylators may be more likely to contract hepatitis, evidence does not yet warrant identification of this population.

In persons developing hepatitis, mortality is significant—as high as 10 percent in one series. Therefore, all patients on INH should be followed carefully, with monitoring of symptoms such as abdominal discomfort, bloating, and anorexia. INH should be discontinued in patients with these findings or other evidence of hepatitis. At present, consensus appears to favor monitoring of serum glutamic-oxaloacetic transaminase (SGOT) in patients at high risk: those with liver disease, and those who are over 35, ethanol abusers, or users of other hepatotoxic drugs. While 20 to 30 percent will have one or more abnormal values, persistent elevations 3 to 5 times normal will occur in about 5 percent of patients and should lead to discontinuation of the drug.

Rifampin may also cause hepatitis, although its toxicity is additive to that of INH, rather than synergistic. Symptoms should be monitored in patients taking the drug, although the value of routine SGOT monitoring is uncertain. In one series, SGOT increased in 44 percent of patients taking INH and rifampin.

E. **Failure of therapy.** Depending upon series and locale, 10 to 40 percent of patients treated for tuberculosis either fail to clear the organism from sputum, or suffer relapse after therapy. Reasons for failure are presented in *table 10-4*.

Careful diagnosis and follow-up are the most important factors in limiting treatment failures. Measures to prevent bacteriologic failures include:
1. Surveillance for primary resistance in patients who have lived abroad

Table 10-3
Chemotherapeutic Regimens for Tuberculosis

Type of Therapy	Medication
Prophylaxis	Isoniazid 300 mg daily for 1 year
Conventional	Isoniazid 300 mg and ethambutol 15 mg/kg daily for 18 months
	Isoniazid 300 mg and rifampin 600 mg daily for 9 months
Intermittent	Isoniazid 14 mg/kg and streptomycin 27 mg/kg or ethambutol 50 mg/kg twice weekly for 18 months, after daily therapy, until culture is negative
	Isoniazid 300 mg and rifampin 900 mg twice weekly for 8 months, after daily therapy for 1 month
Short course (experimental)	Isoniazid 300 mg and rifampin 600 mg and streptomycin 1 g and pyrazinamide 1.5 g daily for 2 months, followed by same regimen minus streptomycin for 4 months

2. Choice of drug regimen adequate to treat initial bacillary load
3. Adequate retreatment regimens for those partially treated. In one study, 41 percent of patients previously treated were resistant to one or more drug. Resistance was greatest among those treated initially with one drug, and those with increased duration of

Table 10-4
Treatment Failure in Tuberculosis

	Percentage of patients treated
Bacteriologic	5
Initial resistance of organisms	1-3
Inadequate regimen (resistance develops during therapy)	1-2
Bacillary load or host incompetence (disease progresses in severely ill or debilitated patients)	0-1
Toxicity (Side effects force discontinuation)	2-5
Noncompliance (Patients discontinue)	10

prior therapy. Approaches to therapy in these patients include the use of prior drugs if multiple drugs were used for less than 4 weeks and organisms are susceptible in vitro. Also recommended is the use of regimens of four drugs, including two new drugs (pending sensitivities), if one drug was used, or multiple drugs used for greater than 4 weeks.

    4. Selective use of drug susceptibility tests in
       a. Patients who received prior treatment
       b. Patients whose sputum smear does not clear after 2 to 3 months, or whose sputum cultures are positive at 4 to 6 months
       c. Patients at risk for primary resistance (i.e., those having lived abroad or contacts of patients with resistant organisms)

Toxicity and side effects can be minimized by reassurance, attention to dose, and use of alternative regimens. Noncompliance, the major reason for failure, may be reduced by supervised administration and the use of intermittent or short-course therapy.

F. **Location of therapy.** Careful study of household contacts demonstrates that the vast majority of infections occur in persons exposed to tuberculosis before it is diagnosed in the index case. Infectivity appears minimal after treatment begins. Therefore, tuberculosis may be treated at home if the patient is compliant, despite smear-positive or culture-positive sputum. If the diagnosis is made in the hospital, treatment may begin in either location. Frequently, patients remain hospitalized until symptomatic improvement occurs, usually in 10 to 20 days. No change in chest x-ray should be expected in this interval.

Hospitalized patients in whom tuberculosis is suspected, but treatment is not yet begun, should be isolated, and masks should be worn by all contacts. These precautions may be discontinued after treatment begins.

G. **Follow-up.** If sputum clears rapidly and patients complete the full course of chemotherapy, long-term follow-up is unnecessary. While relapse occurs occasionally, several studies indicate that relapses are not detected by routine surveillance procedures. Patients with complicated courses, resistant organisms, or disseminated disease probably should have continued follow-up. Sputum cultures and chest x-rays are often used, but the value of these tests is uncertain.

H. **Special situations**
1. **Pregnancy.** INH and ethambutol appear to be safe. Data concerning rifampin are limited.
2. **Renal failure.** Doses of INH and rifampin are unchanged. Ethambutol and aminoglycosides should be avoided if possible.
3. **Liver disease.** Doses of INH and rifampin are reduced. Serum levels may be helpful.
4. **Critically ill patients.** Multiple drugs are clearly indicated. Some evidence favors use of corticosteroids to limit destruction due to the inflammatory response.

V. **NONTUBERCULOUS MYCOBACTERIA**

These organisms also may cause pulmonary disease, frequently indistinguishable from that due to *M. tuberculosis*. While virtually all species have been reported to infect the lung, pulmonary disease is most often caused by *M. kansasii* and *M. avium-intracellulare* (Runyon groups I and III).

Nontuberculous mycobacterial disease most often occurs in: patients with underlying lung disease, especially silicosis; patients with malignancy; and possibly, patients with chronic aspiration. Pathogenesis is uncertain. Whether primary and secondary forms occur is controversial.

A. **Clinical presentation** usually is similar to that of tuberculosis, although the course is often more indolent. Chest x-ray findings, although not specific for nontuberculous mycobacteria, may nonetheless aid in identifying these infections. Radiographic findings include:
1. Relative increase in cavitation for extent of disease
2. Thin-walled cavities with surrounding, less dense, infiltrate
3. Contiguous, rather than bronchogenic, spread
4. Apical and anterior segment of upper lobe involvement
5. Marked pleural thickening in involved areas
6. Clustered opacities around irregular translucent areas

Differential skin testing with antigens prepared from

various mycobacteria may be of value in children, but its use in adults is uncertain. Examination of both smears and histology generally is nonspecific; cultures are necessary to establish the diagnosis firmly.

B. **Therapy** varies with the organism isolated. *M. kansasii* is sensitive to rifampin and only slightly resistant to other antituberculous agents. *M. avium-intracellulare* is resistant to most agents in vitro. Drugs used include ethambutol, ethionamide, and cycloserine. Surgery may be useful in localized disease if medical therapy has failed. Given the frequently indolent course of nontuberculous mycobacterial disease, therapy may be modulated according to the rapidity of disease progression, in order to limit drug-related toxicity.

PART 2
FUNGAL DISEASES

Three major pulmonary mycoses occur in immunocompetent hosts: histoplasmosis, coccidioidomycosis, and blastomycosis. Several additional mycoses, such as aspergillosis, candidiasis, and cryptococcosis, are more common in the immunocompromised and are discussed in Chapter 9. These infections are the result of dimorphic fungi present in the environment. Epidemiology and clinical findings differ among the mycoses.

I. COCCIDIOIDOMYCOSIS

A. **Epidemiology.** This is a disease caused by the fungus *Coccidioides immitis*, a soil-based organism endemic to the southwestern United States, and especially, the San Joaquin valley of California. It is acquired by inhalation of arthrospores.

B. Clinical findings
1. **Primary infection.** Exposure to *C. immitis* usually produces an immunologic response, with positive skin tests but no symptoms in 60 percent of cases. Of those with symptoms, cough, chest pain, or headache are common. Signs include toxic erythema (a diffuse macular exanthem) in up to 50 percent of cases, and erythema nodosum in 15 to 20 percent of cases, especially women. Peripheral eosinophilia is common. Chest x-ray is variable, most often showing a soft, hazy infiltrate and occasionally, unilateral hilar adenopathy. Primary disease generally is self-limited, with symptoms resolving in 2 to 3 weeks.
2. **Pneumonia.** An occasional complication of primary infection, acute pneumonia presents with prolonged symptoms, including cough and sputum production. Radiographic infiltrates are more extensive than in the absence of pneumonia, and adenopathy is common. An exudative effusion occurs in 2 to 6 percent of cases. Occasionally, infiltrates and symptoms continue for more than 6 weeks, leading to "persistent" pneumonia. Rarely, slow progression of infiltrates occurs over years, producing chronic pneumonia. Cavities associated with acute pneumonia may grow rapidly, in some cases causing bronchopleural fistulas. Late cavities due to scarring are usually asymptomatic unless superinfected by other organisms.

3. **Other.** Infection disseminates in about 4 percent of cases. Residual mid-lung nodules, 1 to 4 cm in diameter, often calcify, and later may raise suspicion of carcinoma.

C. **Diagnosis.** The organism must be recovered from sputum or tissue in order to establish diagnosis, although presumptive diagnosis may be made based on immunoreactivity. Skin testing is valuable in suggesting exposure: 0.1 ml of 1:100 coccidioidin is injected intradermally, and the result read at 36 hours. Greater than 5 mm of induration is positive. False negatives are not uncommon, but specificity appears good. Skin testing does not alter results of serologic tests, which include precipitin and immunodiffusion for IgM, and complement fixation and immunodiffusion for IgG. Positive IgM response indicates recent infection, although sensitivity is uncertain. Positive IgG response suggests well-established or disseminated infection. Latex agglutination, reacting with both IgG and IgM, is sensitive, but nonspecific. False positives occur in up to 15 percent of tests.

D. **Treatment.** Primary infection usually is self-limited, requiring no therapy. Chronic disease, severe acute pneumonia, dissemination, and perhaps, cavities, require treatment with amphotericin B. This drug is fungistatic, and onset of action is slow. Total dose required depends upon response to therapy.

Surgery probably should be limited to patients with bronchopleural fistulas, hemorrhage, symptomatic mycetoma, or rapidly expanding cavities.

II. **HISTOPLASMOSIS**

A. **Epidemiology.** The etiologic agent is the fungus *Histoplasma capsulatum*, a soil-based organism endemic to the Mississippi and Ohio River valleys. Infection occurs by spore inhalation.

B. **Pathogenesis.** Primary infection usually is subclinical, and similar to tuberculous infection in that localized pneumonia is followed by lymphohematogenous dissemination and subsequent containment within granulomas.

C. Clinical findings

1. **Acute histoplasmosis.** Acute disease is primary in about 90 percent of cases, occurring 10 to 23 days

after heavy exposure to spores. Symptoms include malaise, fever, and cough. Scattered infiltrates are present on chest x-ray, and the course of the disease usually is self-limited. Occasionally, heavy exposure may cause reinfection, with a shorter incubation period, and disseminated granulomas on chest x-ray similar to those seen in miliary tuberculosis.

2. Chronic pulmonary histoplasmosis. This entity usually complicates prior structural lung disease, especially emphysema. It may present as pneumonia or cavitary disease. Pneumonia usually resolves spontaneously, with frequent recurrences. Cavities resemble those in chronic pulmonary tuberculosis.

3. Other. Disseminated histoplasmosis especially affects the elderly or immunocompromised patient, with variable pulmonary involvement. Histoplasmomas—usually solitary peripheral nodules—may later calcify. Remote problems may occur due to mediastinal fibrosis or granulomas.

D. Diagnosis. Definitive diagnosis requires isolation of the organism from sputum or tissue. Sputum positivity is most common in chronic cavitary disease, less common in chronic pneumonia, and unusual in acute histoplasmosis. Presumptive diagnosis is based on immunologic response. Skin tests become positive 2 to 3 weeks after exposure, but are not specific for active disease. Greater than 5 mm induration at 48 hours after injection of 0.1 ml histoplasmin is a positive result. Skin tests should be performed after serum is collected, since marked increases in titers may occur. Complement fixation titers are elevated in 85 percent of primary infections, but in fewer reinfections. Serial titers 4 weeks apart may be useful if the diagnosis is uncertain. Complement fixation in chronic histoplasmosis is less helpful. Only 35 percent are positive, and 40 percent more are suggestive.

E. Treatment. Necessity for therapy is uncertain, except in disseminated disease. Amphotericin B has been advocated for cavitary disease as well, but evidence and dose are uncertain.

III. BLASTOMYCOSIS

This disease is caused by the fungus *Blastomyces dermatitidis*. It occurs in the south central and Great Lakes regions of the United States, presumably due to spore inhalation. Natural history is poorly understood, but the sequence probably resembles that of histoplasmosis.

Primary infection is usually without symptoms, although fever, chills, malaise, and cough may occur. Chest x-ray findings are nondiagnostic, revealing patchy infiltrates. Most infections are self-limited, but on occasion progressive or disseminated disease occurs. Diagnosis is made by sputum culture, which is often positive in acute or chronic pneumonias. Skin tests and complement fixation titers are insensitive.

Amphotericin B should be used in patients with persistent symptoms; it appears effective in doses of 2 g or more.

Major characteristics of pulmonary mycoses are summarized in *table 10-5*.

REFERENCES

I. General

Addington WW (ed): Tuberculosis. *Arch Intern Med* 139:1375-1340, 1979.

Glassroth J, Robins AG, Snider DE: Tuberculosis in the 1980s. *N Engl J Med* 32:1441-1450, 1980.

Reichman LB (ed): International conference on tuberculosis. *Chest* 76(suppl): 737-787, 1979.

Glassroth provides an excellent brief summary of current issues in tuberculosis. Reichman's conference summary is a superb review concentrating on diagnosis and therapy; Addington's collection is more comprehensive.

II. Etiology and Pathogenesis

Dannenberg AM: Pathogenesis of tuberculosis. In *Pulmonary Diseases and Disorders*. Edited by Fishman AP, New York, McGraw-Hill, 1980, pp 1264-1281.

Geppert EF, Leff A: The pathogenesis of pulmonary and miliary tuberculosis. *Arch Intern Med* 139:1381-1383, 1979.

Gunnels JJ, Bates JH, Swindell H: Infectivity of sputum positive tuberculous patients on chemotherapy. *Am Rev Respir Dis* 109:323-330, 1974.

Stead WW, Bates JH: Epidemiology and prevention of tuberculosis. In *Pulmonary Diseases and Disorders*. Edited by Fishman AP, New York, McGraw-Hill, 1980, pp 1234-1254.

Dannenberg emphasizes pathology, whereas Geppert focuses on natural history. Gunnels provides evidence that transmission occurs before therapy begins. Stead presents an excellent summary of epidemiology.

III. Clinical presentation

Khan MA, Kovnat DM, Bachus B, et al: Clinical and roentgenographic spectrum of pulmonary tuberculosis in the adult. *Am J Med* 62:31-38, 1977.

McClement JH, Christianson LC: Clinical forms of tuberculosis. In *Pulmonary Diseases and Disorders*. Edited by Fishman AP, New York, McGraw-Hill, 1980, pp 1288-1304.

Table 10-5
Characteristics of Pulmonary Mycoses

Organism	Areas in U.S.	Symptoms and Signs	CXR	Diagnosis
Coccidioides immitis	Southwestern U.S.	Cough, chest pain, headache; toxic erythema, erythema nodosum	Hazy infiltrate; cavities, nodules	Skin tests; latex agglutination; complement fixation
Histoplasma capsulatum	Mississippi, Ohio river basins	Malaise, fever, cough	Scattered infiltrate; cavities, nodules	Complement fixation; (skin tests alter serologies)
Blastomyces dermatitidis	South central U.S.	Malaise, fever, cough	Patchy infiltrate	Sputum culture

Sahn SA, Neff TA: Miliary tuberculosis. *Am J Med* 56:395-404, 1974.

Khan describes a series of adults, emphasizing the frequency of "atypical" presentations. McClement reviews various forms, especially "reactivation." Sahn presents a broad summary of miliary tuberculosis and its treatment.

IV. Diagnosis

American Thoracic Society: The tuberculin skin test. *Am Rev Respir Dis* 124:356-363, 1981.

Bates JH: Diagnosis of tuberculosis. *Chest* 76(suppl):757-763, 1979.

Boyd JC, Marr JJ: Decreasing reliability of acid-fast smear techniques for detection of tuberculosis. *Ann Intern Med* 82:489-492, 1975.

Reichman LB: Tuberculin skin testing: the state of the art. *Chest* 76(suppl): 764-770, 1979.

Sharer L, McClement JH: Isolation of tubercle bacilli from needle biopsy specimens of parietal pleura. *Am Rev Respir Dis* 97:466-468, 1968.

Thompson NJ: The booster phenomenon in serial tuberculin testing. *Am Rev Respir Dis* 119:587-597, 1979.

The ATS statement is a concise summary of use and interpretation of skin tests. Bates summarizes information on the diagnosis of tuberculosis; Reichman discusses diagnosis of tuberculous infection. Boyd presents the controversial view that smear techniques are nonspecific. Sharer documents the high yield of pleural biopsies in tuberculous effusions. Thompson presents a series characterizing the booster effect.

V. Treatment

Addington WW: The treatment of pulmonary tuberculosis. *Arch Intern Med* 139:1391-1395, 1979.

Byrd RB, Horn BR, Solomon DA, et al: Toxic effects of isoniazid in tuberculosis chemoprophylaxis. Role of biochemical monitoring in 1,000 patients. *JAMA* 241:1239-1241, 1979.

Comstock GW: Evaluating isoniazid preventive therapy: the need for more data. *Ann Intern Med* 94:817-819, 1981.

Dutt AK, Jones L, Stead WW: Short course chemotherapy for tuberculosis with largely twice-weekly isoniazid-rifampin. *Chest* 75:441-447, 1979.

Fox W: The chemotherapy of pulmonary tuberculosis: a review. *Chest* 79: 785-796, 1979.

Reichman LB: Tuberculosis care: when and where? *Ann Intern Med* 80: 402-406, 1974.

Singapore Tuberculosis Service: Clinical trial of 6-month and 4-month regimens of chemotherapy in the treatment of pulmonary tuberculosis. *Am Rev Respir Dis* 119:579-585, 1979.

Snider DE: Treatment of tuberculosis during pregnancy. *Am Rev Respir Dis* 122:65-79, 1980.

Taylor WC, Aronson MD, Delbanco TL: Should young adults with a positive tuberculin test take isoniazid? *Ann Intern Med* 94:808-813, 1981.

Addington and Fox summarize recent regimens, with Fox concentrating on short-course and intermittent therapy. Dutt's piece and the Singapore Service article report on representative studies of these regimens. Byrd presents a large series using SGOT monitoring to reduce INH toxicity, and Snider discusses safety of drugs in pregnancy. Reichman summarizes evidence allowing treatment of tuberculosis in the home. Taylor and Fox present contrasting views on INH prophylaxis. Taylor develops a model questioning its efficacy; Comstock in turn questions the adequacy of the model.

VI. Nontuberculous Mycobacteria

Dutt AK, Stead WW: Long-term results of medical treatment in *M. intracellulare* infection. *Am J Med* 67:449-453, 1979.

Wolinsky E: Nontuberculous mycobacteria and associated diseases. *Am Rev Respir Dis* 119:107-159, 1979.

Wolinsky exhaustively reviews the field, especially the microbiology. Dutt presents results in 90 cases of *M. intracellulare* infection.

VII. Fungal diseases

Drutz DJ, Catanzaro A: Coccidioidomycosis. *Am Rev Respir Dis* 117: 559-586, 727-772, 1978.

Goodwin RA, Jr, DesPrez RM: Histoplasmosis. *Am Rev Respir Dis* 117: 929-956, 1978.

Goodwin RA, Jr, Owens FT, Snell JD, et al: Chronic pulmonary histoplasmosis. *Medicine* 55:413-452, 1976.

Sarosi GA, Davies SF: Blastomycosis. *Am Rev Respir Dis* 120:911-938, 1979.

All are comprehensive reviews of studies of fungal diseases, with numerous references to primary studies.

11
Interstitial Lung Disease

I. DEFINITION

Interstitial lung diseases (ILD) are a heterogeneous group of disorders affecting the lung parenchyma. Although etiologies and effects vary widely, these diseases share two pathologic features: the accumulation of inflammatory cells around and within functional lung units, designated alveolitis; and subsequent fibrosis in the interstitium. Thus, ILD involve not only the interstitium, the area between epithelial and endothelial cells, but also airways and vasculature. This may occur primarily, as in the vasculitides, or secondarily, as in diffuse diseases.

Despite shared pathologic characteristics, the etiology of these disorders is varied or unknown. Major etiologic categories are presented in *table 11-1*.

II. PATHOGENESIS

Common pathologic findings suggest that these disorders represent a stereotyped response of lung cells to various stimuli. A general natural history of ILD has five major phases: initial injury, alveolitis, maintenance, derangement of alveolar structures, and end-stage fibrosis.

A. Initial injury. As noted above, a variety of agents and processes can initiate an inflammatory reaction in and around the lung interstitium.

B. Alveolitis. Release of mediators subsequent to initial injury causes accumulation of inflammatory cells, especially PMN and lymphocytes. These cells, in turn, re-

Table 11-1
Causes of Interstitial Lung Disease

Category	Example
Collagen-vascular diseases	Rheumatoid arthritis
Pulmonary vasculitides	Wegener's granulomatosis
Eosinophilic lung disease	Löffler's syndrome
Hypersensitivity pneumonitis	Farmer's lung
Pulmonary hemorrhage	Goodpasture's syndrome
Radiation	Radiation pneumonitis
Drugs	Nitrofurantoin
Inorganic dusts or gases	Silicosis
Toxins	Paraquat
Inherited disorder	Neurofibromatosis
Chronic systemic disease	Pulmonary edema; uremia
Idiopathic	Chronic interstitial pneumonitis Sarcoidosis Histiocytosis

lease mediators, enzymes, and cytotoxic substances, magnifying the reaction.

C. **Maintenance.** Acute alveolitis may either continue or resolve. Chronic alveolitis is characterized by continued inflammatory cell infiltration, and by damage to type I pneumocytes and proliferation of type II cells.

D. **Derangement of alveolar structures.** Basement membranes and overall alveolar architecture are eventually disrupted. Destroyed collagen is resynthesized, but type of collagen and arrangement are abnormal. Fibrosis results, but overall lung architecture is preserved at this stage.

E. **End-stage fibrosis.** With sufficient alveolar destruction, marked fibrosis occurs. Overall connective tissue patterns are altered by cystic spaces and fibrous bands. Alveolar structures are unrecognizable, and gas exchange is limited due to destruction of pulmonary capillaries.

Thus, the fibrotic, "honeycomb" lung, seen in patients with longstanding ILD, represents the final stage in a pathway with various origins. The character of the intermediate alveolitis or early lung destruction may vary, but outcome is remarkably similar.

III. CLINICAL MANIFESTATIONS AND DIAGNOSIS

   A. **Symptoms and signs.** Although varying etiologies of ILD produce differing clinical findings, several features are characteristic regardless of etiology. Onset of symptoms is usually insidious. Dyspnea is the most common presenting symptom, accompanied by dry cough. Physical exam may be unremarkable, or may reveal fine end-expiratory dry rales. Clubbing occurs in some patients.

   B. **Laboratory findings.** Chest x-ray findings vary, and may be normal in up to 10 percent of patients, despite abnormal histologic and physiologic findings. A common appearance is a diffuse reticulonodular infiltrate, involving all lung fields. Other laboratory findings vary with etiology and severity of disease.

   C. **Diagnosis.** Diagnosis of ILD is based on associated serologic findings or systemic abnormalities. A careful search should be made for organ system involvement outside the lung. Signs of vasculitis, for example, may provide a diagnosis without extensive lung evaluation.

   D. **Biopsy.** If diagnosis of ILD cannot be made otherwise, lung biopsy may be required. Techniques include needle biopsy, transbronchial biopsy, or open lung biopsy. Cutting or trephine needle biopsy has an unacceptable complication rate; aspiration biopsy is safer, but nonspecific. Transbronchial biopsy is more accurate, but may be normal or nonspecific in a substantial proportion of cases. In addition, heterogeneity of the alveolitis in the early stages of disease may render transbronchial biopsy unreliable. Open lung biopsy remains the definitive procedure, although it entails the risk of thoracotomy. Even then, the procedure yields no specific diagnosis in 10 percent of patients. A reasonable approach at present is to perform transbronchial biopsy, followed by open lung biopsy if results of the former are negative or nonspecific.

   E. **Staging.** Biopsies usually establish an initial diagnosis in ILD, but they are impractical for assessing disease activity and response to therapy. A variety of techniques exists for staging and follow-up, including, chest x-ray, pulmonary function tests, bronchoalveolar lavage, and serologic and radionuclide studies.

   1. **Serologic studies.** Erythrocyte sedimentation rate (ESR) appears nonspecific in most disorders. More

specific assays are useful in some diseases, such as complement in systemic lupus erythematosus (SLE) and angiotension-converting enzyme in sarcoidosis.

2. **Chest x-ray.** Although staging systems have been suggested for various interstitial diseases, radiographic findings generally correlate poorly with histologic studies. Correlation is better in severe, end-stage disease, although in this situation therapeutic options are limited. Even then, a "honeycomb" pattern may mask areas of active alveolitis.

3. **Pulmonary function tests.** Specific pulmonary function abnormalities are described below. Although decreased lung volumes and impaired gas exchange reflect the presence of interstitial disease, correlation of these measurements with disease activity is limited. Where careful studies are available, pulmonary function abnormalities define a wide spectrum of disease activity.

4. **Radionuclide studies.** Of available isotopic techniques, gallium 67 has been studied most extensively. In sarcoidosis, scans are nonspecific in making the diagnosis. However, some studies show correlation between scans and extent and activity of the disease. Data in other diseases are limited.

5. **Bronchoalveolar lavage.** This method involves instillation and removal of fluid through the fiberoptic bronchoscope. Fluid is then analyzed for protein and cell type. Although still a research technique, bronchoalveolar lavage results have been shown to correlate with biopsy findings in several diseases. In sarcoidosis, an increased percentage of lymphocytes, especially "helper" T lymphocytes, suggests active disease. Results are less clear with idiopathic pulmonary fibrosis, but an increased percentage of PMN may indicate active disease.

In summary, no single measurement appears useful in all ILD. In most cases, several parameters should be followed serially to assess disease activity.

IV. **EFFECTS ON LUNG FUNCTION**

A. **Mechanics.** Airways resistance is normal in most ILD. Compliance is usually decreased, correlating with degree of fibrosis. Airflow rates are decreased in proportion to decrease in lung volumes. Peak flow is characteristically well preserved. Tests of small airways function are commonly abnormal in early interstitial disease. In later stages of some diseases, such as sarcoidosis, berylliosis, eosinophilic granuloma, and hypersensitivity pneumonitis, obstruction to airflow may be prominent.

B. **Volumes.** In early ILD, volumes may be normal. As disease progresses, decreased lung volumes become the functional hallmark of ILD. Although most volumes are proportionately decreased, TLC often falls more than RV. The RV/TLC ratio is thus increased. Decreased volumes result from destruction of lung units and increased fibrous tissue in the remaining lung.

C. **Gas exchange.** Hypoxemia is common in ILD, primarily due to increased V/Q inequalities. Shunting may contribute in advanced disease. Diffusion limitation probably accounts for little of the resting hypoxemia; however, the characteristic fall in Pa_{O_2} with exercise is due to both diffusion limitation and increased V/Q inequalities. During exercise, alveolar-capillary transit time for erythrocytes is decreased. When coupled with alteration of the alveolar-capillary membrane, diffusion limitation may result. A-aDO_2 at rest and with exercise is increased by the same mechanisms. Pa_{CO_2} is usually normal or decreased, because ventilation remains adequate until extremely late in the course of ILD.

D. **Pulmonary vasculature.** In specific ILD, such as progressive systemic sclerosis (PSS), pulmonary vasculature may be primarily affected, with resulting pulmonary hypertension. More commonly, pulmonary hypertension is due to chronic hypoxemia.

E. **Respiratory control and respiratory musculature.** Central regulation of respiration appears normal in most patients with ILD. Work of breathing is often increased, due to decreased lung compliance. A characteristic breathing pattern results, with low tidal volumes and rapid respiratory rate. Respiratory muscles appear normal.

Pulmonary function in ILD is summarized in *table 11-2*.

V. **TREATMENT**

Two major classes of agents are used in these disorders: corticosteroids and cytotoxic agents.

A. **Corticosteroids.** Corticosteroids remain the mainstay of therapy for ILD. Mechanisms of action include de-

Table 11-2
Pulmonary Function in Interstitial Lung Disease

Measurement	Early	Late
Volumes	Normal or mild ↓	TLC, VC ↓↓ RV ↓
Flows	Normal	FEV_1, FVC ↓ (proportional to volumes) PEFR Nl or slight ↓
Pressures	Compliance Nl or slight ↓	Compliance ↓↓
Gas exchange	DL_{co} ↓* Pa_{O_2} Nl or Exercise Pa_{O_2} ↓	DL_{co} ↓↓ Pa_{O_2} ↓ Exercise Pa_{O_2} ↓↓
Vasculature	P_A† normal	P_A normal or ↑

*DL_{co} = carbon monoxide diffusing capacity
†P_A = mean pulmonary artery pressure

creased PMN chemotaxis and enzyme release, and decreased lymphocyte proliferation and mediator release. Choice of patient, dose, and duration of therapy remains uncertain. Evidence of efficacy is most compelling for interstitial pulmonary fibrosis, especially in patients with increased cellularity and mild fibrosis, which are indicative of active alveolitis. Steroids also appear useful for at least some patients with sarcoidosis. Although steroids are widely used for pulmonary manifestations of collagen-vascular disease, there is little rigorous evidence to support this practice. Steroids appear to be of little value in diseases in which alveolitis is mild, such as PSS, or apparently resistant, such as histiocytosis X.

Although duration and dose of steroid therapy are uncertain, present practice is to begin with high daily doses, about 1 mg/kg, for weeks to months. Some physicians favor rapid tapering with improvement; others proceed to long-term therapy, with alternate-day steroids. Use of higher doses, or pulse therapy, remains experimental. Side effects of high doses are very common, but most patients tolerate these agents.

B. **Cytotoxic agents.** Specific drugs used in interstitial lung disease include azathioprine, cyclophosphamide, and chlorambucil. Evidence concerning azathioprine is limited. Small series show both improvement and little effect in patients with interstitial pulmonary fibrosis. Although dramatic improvement in Wegener's granulomatosis has been demonstrated with cyclophosphamide, similar responses appear uncommon in other diseases. Success has been reported with cyclophosphamide and chlorambucil in a variety of other interstitial lung diseases.

C. **Other agents.** Penicillamine and vincristine sulfate have been used in a few cases, but evidence of efficacy is limited.

D. **Other forms of treatment.** General supportive therapy remains important, especially in advanced disease. Bronchodilators should be used if obstruction is present. Supplementary oxygen may be given according to the criteria discussed in Chapter 7. Infections should be treated vigorously with antibiotics and physiotherapy, as necessary.

VI. **IDIOPATHIC INTERSTITIAL PNEUMONITIS AND FIBROSIS**

A. **Definition.** This category of ILD is defined by exclusion of known causes; the classification is, therefore, imprecise. Nevertheless, a group of pathologically distinct disorders is recognized. Diagnostic terms include diffuse interstitial fibrosis, interstitial pulmonary fibrosis, and cryptogenic fibrosing alveolitis. The classification below follows Liebow in using the general term interstitial pneumonitis.

B. **Pathogenesis.** Pathogenesis of these disorders remains uncertain. The initial alveolitis may have one of the specific etiologies noted in *table 11-1*, but clinical and histological findings may be nonspecific. Advanced disease, regardless of etiology, is often placed in this category. Immune complexes or inhalants have been implicated in some cases, but evidence is limited. A rare familial form occurs, and patients with neurofibromatosis (von Recklinghausen's disease) often develop interstitial pneumonitis.

C. **Usual interstitial pneumonitis (UIP) and desquamative interstitial pneumonitis (DIP):** These entities are the most common of the interstitial pneumonitides. In some

series, almost half of patients with ILD are diagnosed as UIP. Although controversy exists over whether UIP and DIP are distinct entities or stages of the same disease, preliminary evidence favors the latter hypothesis.
   1. **Clinical findings.** Both DIP and UIP are characterized by progressive dyspnea, dry cough, and weight loss. Arthralgias occur in some patients, and clubbing appears common in progressive disease. Chest x-ray in DIP or in early stages of UIP may be normal. Films early in the course typically show fine reticular infiltrates in the lower lung zones. In DIP, these progress to irregular opacities at the bases. In UIP, a coarser pattern evolves, with eventual honeycombing. Pulmonary function is similar to that described in other ILD: gas exchange abnormalities are followed by restriction of lung volumes. Obstruction to flow is unusual.
   2. **Diagnosis.** Diagnosis is difficult, owing to the uncertainty of the clinical and radiographic natural history of both entities. Histologic studies are required to establish the diagnosis, and even then some cases have features of both diseases. In DIP, biopsy reveals mononuclear cells in distal airspaces; in UIP, the infiltrate is predominantly interstitial.
   3. **Treatment.** Patients with DIP often respond to steroids with improvement in symptoms, pulmonary function, and chest x-ray. Response is less common and less dramatic in UIP. Some evidence indicates that patients with an increased percentage of PMN in bronchoalveolar lavage fluid are more likely to respond to steroids. Survival is variable but clearly decreased in UIP. Cytotoxic agents have shown benefit in some cases, but evidence is limited.
D. **Other interstitial pneumonitides**
   1. **Bronchiolitic interstitial pneumonitis (BIP).** As the name implies, this entity includes an obliterative bronchiolitis as well as interstitial pneumonitis. The disease is rapidly progressive.
   2. **Lymphocytic interstitial pneumonitis (LIP).** This disease is recognizable histologically by the presence of lymphoid infiltrates. Clinical and radiographic findings are similar to those of other interstitial diseases.
   3. **Giant cell interstitial pneumonitis (GIP).** A rare

form, GIP is similar to other syndromes except for its histologic patterns. Bizarre giant cells, in addition to a lymphoid infiltrate, are characteristic.

In summary, types of interstitial pneumonitis and fibrosis are clinically similar, despite histologic variability. For all types, the ultimate outcome appears to be diffuse fibrosis. Treatment is most successful in DIP.

VII. COLLAGEN-VASCULAR DISEASE

Collagen-vascular diseases, or connective tissue diseases, are a diverse group of idiopathic disorders recognizable by clinical findings and by serologic and histologic studies. Inflammation occurs in connective tissue, especially in joints, serosal membranes, and vessels. Pulmonary involvement can occur in any of these diseases; postmortem, the lungs are found to be abnormal in the majority of patients.

A. Systemic lupus erythematosus (SLE). This is a chronic inflammatory disorder occurring primarily in females. SLE is characterized by a group of clinical manifestations, and by the LE cell phenomenon, antinuclear antibodies, and antibodies to native DNA. Pulmonary involvement occurs in 50 to 70 percent of patients. Clinical syndromes in SLE include:

1. Infection. This is probably the most common cause of pulmonary infiltrates in patients with SLE. Immunologic abnormalities contribute to the increased incidence of infection.
2. Pleuritis. This occurs in the majority of patients during the course of their disease. Effusions, if present, usually are small and bilateral.
3. Decreased lung volumes. This may be due to:
   a. Atelectasis: usually basilar, due to pain and splinting
   b. Diaphragmatic dysfunction: probably due to a generalized myopathy
4. Acute pneumonitis. This syndrome is uncommon but severe, with fever, dry cough, and bilateral alveolar or ill-defined infiltrates. Most patients respond to steroid therapy.
5. Diffuse interstitial disease. Chronic ILD is uncommon, and unreported in some series. Interstitial fibrosis is rarely seen. Other manifestations include pulmonary edema due to uremia or cardiomyopathy.

B. **Rheumatoid arthritis (RA).** This disease consists of a characteristic arteritis with prominent joint involvement. Incidence of pulmonary complications varies widely, ranging from 5 to 50 percent. Four major clinical syndromes occur:
  1. **Pleuritis and effusion.** Pleuritis is probably the most common manifestation of RA, although effusion is uncommon. When present, effusions are unilateral and chronic. They are notable for low complement and glucose.
  2. **Pulmonary nodules.** Analogous to subcutaneous nodules, these are uncommon. Most nodules occur in patients with advanced disease. Size and natural history are variable.
  3. **Interstitial fibrosis.** This occurs in 10 percent or fewer patients with RA, usually following joint disease. Most patients are dyspneic. Chest x-ray shows bilateral, asymmetric reticular infiltrates, similar to other interstitial processes. Pulmonary function tests reveal a restrictive defect and impaired gas exchange.
  4. **Pneumoconiosis (Caplan's syndrome).** This syndrome occurs in workers with RA exposed to a variety of inhaled agents, including coal dust, silica, and aluminum. There is little correlation with severity of disease or presence of active arthritis. Chest film shows single or multiple rapidly developing nodules. Most lesions persist, but a few cavitate and resolve.

  Pulmonary hypertension, with histologic evidence of vasculitis, has been reported with RA. These patients often have Raynaud's phenomenon, and their disorder may represent a variant of PSS, SLE, or an "overlap" syndrome, rather than RA.

C. **Progressive systemic sclerosis (PSS).** This is a progressive disease causing atrophy and fibrosis of connective tissue in multiple systems. Postmortem, over 90 percent of patients exhibit pulmonary involvement. Pulmonary complications appear equally common in the CRST variant of the disease. Two major pulmonary syndromes occur with this disease:
  1. **Diffuse interstitial disease.** Dyspnea and mild cough usually occur late in the disease. Chest x-ray shows bilateral lower lung field reticulonodular infiltrates, with relative sparing of upper lung zones. Honeycombing may occur in advanced disease. Pulmonary

function tests show abnormal results in most patients; such results often precede respiratory symptoms or radiographic abnormalities. Diffusing capacity is abnormal early in the course of the disease, followed by a decrease in lung volumes. Biopsy reveals nonspecific interstitial fibrosis. No form of therapy is clearly effective.

2. **Pulmonary vascular disease.** This syndrome may occur in the absence of fibrosis. There is loss of some pulmonary capillaries and thickening of walls in others. Involvement of pulmonary arterioles leads to pulmonary hypertension, with subsequent right heart dysfunction. One subgroup of patients develops rapidly progressive pulmonary hypertension, with a poor prognosis. Treatment is uncertain.

Other pulmonary complications of PSS include aspiration pneumonia due to esophageal dysfunction, and an increased incidence of carcinoma, especially the alveolar cell form.

D. **Dermatomyositis and polymyositis.** These are inflammatory diseases of striated muscle, leading to proximal weakness or pain. Pulmonary involvement occurs in about 5 percent of patients, usually in the form of a basilar interstitial pneumonitis, progressing to fibrosis. Pulmonary function test results resemble those of PSS. Steroids may benefit patients with active alveolitis.

E. **Sjögren's syndrome.** This chronic inflammatory disease is characterized by keratoconjunctivitis sicca and xerostomia. The majority of patients have another, associated, collagen-vascular disease. About 10 percent of patients develop an interstitial lymphocytic pneumonitis leading to fibrosis. Airways may also be involved, resulting in bronchiectasis.

F. **Ankylosing spondylitis.** This chronic inflammatory disease is notable for sacroiliac and vertebral joint involvement. Up to 8 percent of affected individuals have pulmonary disease. Apical infiltrates appear first, followed by diffuse fibrosis with cavitation. Treatment appears ineffective. Chest wall restriction occurs as a result of vertebral disease.

G. **Other.** Many patients with essential mixed cryoglobulinemia develop interstitial changes on chest x-ray. Behçet's disease may include transient infiltrates and hemoptysis. Pulmonary manifestations of major collagen-vascular diseases are summarized in table 11-3.

VIII. PULMONARY VASCULITIDES

Vasculitis of any origin may involve the lung, as in collagen-vascular diseases; however, another group of vasculitides affects the lung primarily. Classification of these disorders is difficult, even when based on histologic results. Nonetheless, six major syndromes are generally recognized: allergic granulomatosis, Wegener's granulomatosis, limited Wegener's, lymphomatoid granulomatosis, necrotizing sarcoidosis, and bronchocentric granulomatosis.

A. **Allergic granulomatosis and angiitis (Churg-Strauss syndrome).** This syndrome is characterized by asthma, eosinophilia, and multisystem involvement. Pathology reveals a necrotizing arteritis with eosinophilic infiltrates.
  1. Clinical findings. Asthma usually predates other symptoms, followed by fever and leukocytosis with eosinophilia. Recurrent pneumonia is common. Other manifestations include abdominal pain, lymphadenopathy, variable skin lesions, and asymptomatic cardiac involvement. Renal involvement is unusual. Chest x-ray is often normal. Bilateral infiltrates may be transitory or persistent.
  2. Diagnosis. Presence of asthma, eosinophilia, and other systemic involvement may suggest this diagnosis. Biopsy is required for confirmation. Differential diagnosis includes periarteritis nodosa, allergic bronchopulmonary aspergillosis, and eosinophilic pneumonia. Presence of persistent asthma and positive biopsy findings distinguishes allergic granulomatosis from these disorders.
  3. Treatment. In several small series, steroids were beneficial. Mean survival is about 5 years after diagnosis.

B. **Wegener's granulomatosis.** This is a necrotizing vasculitis involving lung, upper airway, and kidney. Pathology shows granulomas with an accompanying vasculitis.
  1. Clinical findings. Males are more often affected than females. Onset is usually insidious. Initial symptoms are associated with lung involvement, such as cough,

Table 11-3
Pulmonary Manifestations of Collagen-Vascular Disease

Disorder	Pneumonitis	Parenchymal Fibrosis	Nodules	Pleuritis	Pleural Thickening	Effusion	Vascular Hypertension
SLE	Common	Uncommon	— —	Frequent	Common	Frequent	Uncommon
RA	— —	Common	Uncommon	— —	Common	Uncommon	— —
PSS	— —	Common	— —	— —	Uncommon	— —	Common
D/P	Uncommon	Uncommon	— —	— —	— —	— —	— —

SLE = systemic lupus erythematosus
RA = rheumatoid arthritis
PSS = progressive systemic sclerosis
D/P = dermatomyositis/polymyositis

— — = Rarely occurs

or with sinus involvement, such as fever and headache. Glomerulonephritis, and in some cases, renal failure, also may produce symptoms. Joint and skin involvement occur in about half of patients, and neurologic findings in about 20 percent. Chest x-ray shows multiple large nodular infiltrates, often with cavitation. Mediastinal lymph nodes are rarely involved. Sinus films often reveal chronic sinusitis. In most patients, pulmonary function tests show airflow obstruction, with decreased volumes in diffuse disease.

2. **Diagnosis.** The triad of upper and lower respiratory involvement and glomerulonephritis suggests Wegener's, although biopsy is required to confirm the diagnosis. Differential diagnosis includes antiglomerular basement membrane disease, other granulomatous vasculitides, and infections such as tuberculosis.

3. **Treatment.** Corticosteroid therapy is beneficial in only a small proportion of patients. However, cyclophosphamide has revolutionized the treatment of this disease. Cures are attained in the majority of cases, with improvement or remission in most others. Renal failure in some cases has been treated by transplantation.

C. **Limited Wegener's granulomatosis.** This syndrome is characterized by the pulmonary manifestations of Wegener's, but with limited systemic involvement.

1. **Clinical findings.** Lung lesions often lead to cough, pleuritic pain, and dyspnea. Glomerulonephritis does not occur, although renal lesions may be present, with histologic pattern similar to that of lung lesions. Upper airways are not involved. Chest x-ray reveals multiple bilateral infiltrates, primarily in lower lung fields.

2. **Diagnosis.** Differential diagnosis is that of Wegener's and lymphomatoid granulomatosis. Distinction from Wegener's depends upon lack of systemic involvement. Lymphomatoid granulomatosis is distinguished by lymphocytic infiltrate on biopsy.

3. **Treatment.** Prognosis appears to be better than that associated with Wegener's. Steroids may provide some benefit. Cytotoxic agents, such as cyclophosphamide and chlorambucil, have been effective in occasional patients.

D. **Lymphomatoid granulomatosis.** This disorder is similar to limited Wegener's, but a lymphocytic infiltrate is distinctive.
   1. **Clinical findings.** Symptoms are similar to those in Wegener's. Upper airways are rarely involved, and glomerulonephritis does not occur. A nodular angiitis may be present on renal biopsy. Skin lesions of various types are common, and chest x-ray reveals nodular infiltrates.
   2. **Diagnosis.** As noted above, lymphocytic and plasma cell infiltrates separate this entity from limited Wegener's.
   3. **Treatment.** Both cytotoxic agents and steroids are reported to be effective in this disease, but comparative evidence is limited. The disorder may evolve into lymphoma.

E. **Necrotizing sarcoidosis.** Sarcoidosis is considered on p. 234. This rare variant includes angiitis as well as noncaseating granulomatous disease. Chest x-ray shows multiple nodular or fluffy opacities. Treatment with steroids is similar to that in other forms of sarcoidosis.

F. **Bronchocentric granulomatosis.** This disorder is defined histologically by involvement of small bronchi and bronchioles, with incidental vascular involvement. About half the affected patients have asthma. It is clinically related to allergic bronchopulmonary aspergillosis (ABPA) and mucoid impaction. Chest x-ray abnormalities in bronchocentric granulomatosis are similar to those found in ABPA and mucoid impaction, including lobar and segmental consolidation, atelectasis, and irregular masses.

Major characteristics of the pulmonary vasculitides are summarized in *table 11-4*.

IX. **EOSINOPHILIC LUNG DISEASES**

Eosinophilic lung diseases are a varied group of disorders characterized by pulmonary involvement and tissue or blood eosinophilia. Various classification systems have been based on etiology, pathology, and clinical manifestations. A representative classification system is presented in *table 11-5*.

A. **"Simple": Löffler's syndrome.** This entity is defined, clinically, by the presence of nonsegmental parenchymal infiltrates with peripheral eosinophilia.

Table 11-4
Pulmonary Vasculitides

Vasculitis	Clinical Findings	Chest X-ray	Other Findings
Allergic granulomatosis and angiitis	Asthma, fever, eosinophilia	Normal or bilateral infiltrates	Biopsy: eosinophilic infiltrate
Wegener's granulomatosis	Upper and lower respiratory lesions and glomerulonephritis	Multiple large nodular infiltrates	Biopsy: necrotizing vasculitis with granulomas
Limited Wegener's	Lower respiratory lesions	Multiple large nodular infiltrates	Better prognosis than Wegener's
Lymphomatoid granulomatosis	Lung and skin lesions	Multiple nodular infiltrates	Biopsy: lymphoid and plasma cell infiltrate
Necrotizing sarcoidosis	Lower respiratory lesions, systemic involvement	Multiple nodular or fluffy infiltrates	Biopsy: noncaseating granulomas and angiitis
Bronchocentric granulomatosis	Lower respiratory lesions	Infiltrates, mucoid impaction, atelectasis	May be similar to ABPA

Table 11-5
Classification of Eosinophilic Lung Disease

Type	Etiology
Simple (Loffler's syndrome)	Parasites Drugs (e.g., penicillin, sulfonamides) Idiopathy
Complex (other manifestations)	Drugs (e.g., nitrofurantoin) Parasites (e.g., filariasis) Fungi (e.g., *Aspergillus*, as in ABPA*)
Vasculitis-associated	Allergic granulomatosis and angiitis Wegener's granulomatosis (occasional)
Idiopathic	Chronic eosinophilic pneumonia Hypereosinophilic syndrome

*ABPA: allergic bronchopulmonary aspergillosis

1. Clinical findings. Patients often are asymptomatic, although high fever and severe dyspnea may occur. Leukocytosis—primarily due to eosinophilia—is common. Extensive disease results in decreased lung volumes and impaired gas exchange. Chest film reveals single or multiple transient infiltrates, usually nonsegmental and peripheral.
2. Diagnosis. A variety of etiologic factors is recognized, including parasites, asthma, ABPA, and drugs. Most cases remain idiopathic. Diagnosis is based on chest x-ray pattern, eosinophilia, and the benign course of the disease. Biopsy is rarely necessary.
3. Treatment. This syndrome often remits spontaneously, or when the precipitant is removed. When necessary, severe symptoms respond to corticosteroids.

B. Idiopathic
1. Chronic eosinophilic pneumonia. This is an uncommon disorder, characterized by peripheral infiltrates and evidence of eosinophilic infiltration on biopsy. Patients usually are female. Symptoms include cough, fever, dyspnea, weight loss, and night sweats. Peripheral eosinophilia occurs in two-thirds of cases. Chest x-ray may lead to diagnosis by revealing nonsegmental peripheral lung infiltrates similar to those of Löffler's syndrome, but more persistent. Most such infiltrates occur in apical and axillary regions. A

dramatic response to steroids is seen in most cases, but the disease may recur.
   2. **Hypereosinophilic syndrome.** This rare syndrome involves marked circulating eosinophilia with infiltration of various organs, including the lung.
C. **Parasitic.** As noted above, Löffler's syndrome may occur after parasitic infestation. Organisms implicated include *Strongyloides stercoralis*, and species of *Ascaris*, *Ancylostoma*, *Toxocara*, and *Schistosoma*.
   Disease associated with filariasis is often designated tropical eosinophilia. Findings include bronchospasm and severe leukocytosis with eosinophilia. Diffuse reticulonodular infiltrates are seen in about half of patients. Hilar node enlargement may occur.

D. **Allergic bronchopulmonary aspergillosis (ABPA).** This syndrome consists of asthma, transient pulmonary infiltrates, blood and sputum eosinophilia, and reactivity to *Aspergillus fumigatus*.
   1. **Clinical findings.** Patients have asthma, and most have productive cough. Mucous plugs or casts are produced in up to one half of patients. Fever occurs during exacerbations. Chest x-ray shows transient infiltrates, and in some cases, mucoid impaction and dilated bronchi.
   2. **Diagnosis.** Clinical and chest x-ray findings are confirmed by:
      a. Positive skin test for *A. fumigatus*
      b. Delayed hypersensitivity skin reaction to *A. fumigatus* or serum IgG precipitins against *Aspergillus*
      c. Elevated serum IgE levels
   3. **Treatment.** IgE levels appear to correlate with disease activity. Steroids usually suppress acute episodes, but chronic steroid use is of uncertain benefit.

E. **Drug-induced.** Various drugs and toxins have been implicated in eosinophilic pulmonary disease. Many, such as sulfonamides, penicillins, and nickel carbonyl compounds, produce Löffler's syndrome. Nitrofurantoin causes a diffuse reticular infiltrate with eosinophilia. This usually resolves after withdrawal of the drug, but chronic therapy may lead to fibrosis.

F. **Other types.** Uncomplicated asthma occasionally is associated with eosinophilic lung disease, even in the absence of evidence for ABPA.

X. **HYPERSENSITIVITY PNEUMONITIS**

Hypersensitivity pneumonitis, or extrinsic allergic alveolitis, is an immunologically mediated inflammation of the lung parenchyma caused by inhalation of organic dusts. A variety of antigens is associated with alveolitis, as presented in *table 11-6*.

Despite marked differences in antigen composition, the clinical syndromes produced by these agents are remarkably similar. Pathogenesis remains uncertain. Exposure to antigens capable of reaching distal airspaces is required. Host factors also are important, since most exposed subjects do not develop hypersensitivity. Both type III (Arthus) and type IV (delayed hypersensitivity) reactions appear to be involved in the disease process.

A. Clinical findings. Three syndromes of hypersensitivity pneumonitis are distinguished, based on symptoms and course: acute, subacute, and chronic.

1. Acute. Fever and cough begin 6 to 8 hours after exposure. Chest x-ray may be normal, or it may reveal poorly defined, mid-lung zone nodularity. Symptoms and radiographic changes resolve over days.

2. Subacute. Cough and dyspnea begin insidiously, over a period of several weeks. Chest x-ray may be similar to that of acute disease, or it may show patchy interstitial infiltrates. This form may resolve over weeks, or progress with continued exposure.

3. Chronic. Chronic mild exposure produces a slowly progressive syndrome in susceptible patients. Constitutional symptoms, such as fatigue and weight loss, may overshadow pulmonary symptoms. Progressive dyspnea becomes the predominant symptom, and respiratory failure may occur. Eventually, pulmonary fibrosis occurs, with associated radiographic, pulmonary function, and biopsy findings.

B. Laboratory. Laboratory studies in hypersensitivity pneumonitis show a mild leukocytosis without eosinophilia, and negative collagen-vascular serologic results. Chest x-ray findings are noted above. Pleural effusion, hilar adenopathy, and cavitation are very rare. Acutely, pulmonary function tests may reveal small airways disease, and prominent reductions in Pa_{O_2} and diffusing capac-

Table 11-6
Hypersensitivity Pneumonitis: Known Causes

Disease	Source	Antigen
Farmer's lung[1]	Moldy hay, grain	Thermophilic actinomyces
Humidifier lung[2]	Air conditioning systems	Thermophilic actinomyces
Mushroom worker's lung[3]	Mushroom compost	Thermophilic actinomyces
Bagassosis[4]	Moldy sugar cane	Thermophilic actinomyces
Mill worker's lung[5]	Wheat flour	*Aspergillus fumigatus*
Malt worker's lung[6]	Moldy barley	*Aspergillus clavatus*
"Doghouse disease"[7]	Moldy straw	*Aspergillus versicolor*
Maple bark disease[8]	Maple bark	*Cryptostroma corticale*
Sequoiosis[9]	Redwood dust	*Graphium, Pullularia*
Woodpulp worker's[10] disease	Woodpulp, sawdust	*Alternaria*
Cheesewasher's lung[11]	Moldy cheese	*Penicillium casei*
Bird fancier's lung[12]	Pigeon, parrot, and other bird droppings	Bird sera, protein, droppings
Suberosis[13]	Cork dust	Cork dust
Coffee worker's lung[14]	Coffee bean	Coffee bean dust
Fishmeal worker's lung[15]	Fishmeal	Fishmeal

Pituitary snuff lung[16]	Pituitary snuff	Pituitary snuff
Sauna lung[17]	Sauna water	Unkown
Furrier's lung[18]	Animal pelts	Animal fur dust

1. Emanuel DA, et al: *Am J Med* 37:392, 1964.
2. Banazak EJ, et al: *N Engl J Med* 283:271, 1970.
3. Bringhurst LS, et al: *JAMA* 171:15, 1959.
4. Weill H, et al: *Ann Intern Med* 64:737, 1966.
5. Lunn JA, Hughes DTD: *Br J Ind Med* 24:158, 1967.
6. Riddle HFV, et al: *Thorax* 23:271, 1968.
7. Rhudy J, et al: *Scand J Respir Dis* 52:177, 1971.
8. Emanuel DA, et al: *N Engl J Med* 274:1413, 1966.
9. Cohen HI, et al: *Am J Med* 43:785, 1967.
10. Schlueter DP, et al: *Ann Intern Med* 77:907, 1972.
11. Schlueter DP: *Ann Intern Med* 78:606, 1973.
12. Fink J, et al: *Ann Intern Med* 68:1205, 1968.
13. Avila R, Villar TG: *Lancet* 1:620, 1968.
14. Van Toorn DW: *Thorax* 25:399, 1970.
15. Avila R, et al: *Clin All* 1:343, 1971.
16. Harper LO, et al: *Ann Intern Med* 73:581, 1970.
17. Metzger L, et al: *JAMA* 236:2009, 1976.
18. Pimental J: *Thorax* 25:387, 1970.

Modified with permission of JB Lippincott Company from *Pulmonary Medicine* (p 545) by Guenter CA, Welch MH, © 1977.

ity. Later, restrictive disease develops, similar to other interstitial lung disease.

C. **Diagnosis.** History of occupational and environmental exposure is critical to the diagnosis. The presence of thermophilic actinomycetes in ventilation systems should be considered as a source of nonoccupational exposure. If a particular antigen is suspected, specific serum precipitins should be sought. Precipitin tests are hampered by insufficient purification and standardization. Nonetheless, sensitivity approaches 90 percent, but specificity is limited. Precipitins will be present in up to 40 percent of subjects exposed to the antigen, but without a hypersensitivity response. Antigen challenge may be useful under carefully controlled circumstances.

Differential diagnosis includes viral and other nonbacterial pneumonias, histoplasmosis, sarcoidosis, and idiopathic interstitial pneumonitis. Biopsy may be required to exclude these diagnoses. Presence of a granulomatous interstitial pneumonitis supports the diagnosis of hypersensitivity.

D. **Treatment.** Avoidance of antigen inhalation is the hallmark of therapy. Once the disease begins, steroids aid in resolution of symptoms and functional abnormalities. Steroids may be of limited benefit in advanced disease.

XI. **SARCOIDOSIS**

Sarcoidosis is a multisystemic granulomatous disease of unknown etiology. It is characterized by the presence of noncaseating granulomas in many organ systems. Prevalence varies with race and locale, but a reasonable estimate is 10/100,000. Among black Americans, incidence is higher.

A. **Etiology.** Mycobacteria and several inhaled agents have been studied as possible causes of sarcoidosis, but the evidence is unconvincing. Similarity to disease caused by beryllium inhalation suggests that inhaled agents are important in some cases. Increased lymphocytic infiltrate in association with active disease supports a role for cell-mediated immunity in maintaining the alveolitis. Sarcoidosis probably is a syndrome with multiple etiologic factors, and perhaps, varied natural histories.

B. **Clinical findings.** Although presentation varies, sarcoidosis is usually subacute or chronic. Up to one-half of patients are asymptomatic, with disease discovered on chest x-ray. During the course of the disease, pulmonary symptoms develop in 70 to 80 percent of patients. Dyspnea and dry cough are common; chest pain and hemoptysis are uncommon. Systemic manifestations are widespread, as summarized in *table 11-7*.

C. **Laboratory and pulmonary function tests.** Anemia occurs in a minority of patients, but leukopenia is more common. Eosinophilia is present in up to one-third of patients. Calcium metabolism is abnormal in many patients, but hypercalcemia is uncommon. Most patients with sarcoidosis have abnormal pulmonary function, even with isolated hilar adenopathy on chest x-ray. The pattern of findings is similar to that in other interstitial lung disease: early gas exchange abnormalities (e.g., diffusing capacity), followed by restriction of lung volumes as fibrosis develops.

D. **Radiography.** Radiographic stages of sarcoidosis are noted in *table 11-7*. These stages describe general appearance, but more specific patterns are recognized.
   1. **Hilar adenopathy.** Adenopathy is almost always bilateral. Paratracheal nodes are commonly involved, usually symmetrically. Nodes often appear lobulated, with calcification in about 5 percent.
   2. **Reticulonodular infiltrate.** This is the most common parenchymal pattern, ranging from a very fine to coarse network.
   3. **Acinar infiltrate.** These are large, ill-defined opacities, often appearing along with reticulonodular infiltrates.
   4. **Nodules.** Large nodules simulating neoplasms occur in occasional patients.
   5. Other, less common findings include atelectasis, pleural effusion, and rarely, cavitation.

E. **Diagnosis.** Owing to a lack of pathognomonic findings, sarcoidosis must be diagnosed on the basis of clinical findings, course of the disease, and biopsy material. Asymptomatic bilateral hilar adenopathy almost always represents sarcoidosis. In one large series, almost all such patients were found to have sarcoidosis. In contrast, several patients with symptoms and similar chest x-ray findings had lymphoma.

Biopsy site depends upon clinical evidence. Skin, subcutaneous nodules, extrathoracic lymph nodes, and liver may yield noncaseating granulomas if involved. If no extrathoracic abnormalities are noted and hilar ade-

Table 11-7
Systemic Manifestations of Sarcoidosis

System	Incidence	Comments
Pulmonary	60% at presentation 90% during course	
Parenchymal (at presentation)	50% Stage I 30% Stage II 20% Stage III	BHL with or without paratracheal adenopathy BHL with infiltrate Infiltrate without BHL
Endobronchial	Up to 75%	Usually asymptomatic
Pleural	Uncommon	
Ocular	5% at presentation 20% during course	Usually uveitis
Skin	30% during course	Maculopapular, nodular, plaques, erythema nodosum
Lymph nodes	14% at presentation 40% during course	
Gastrointestinal	20% during course	Hepatosplenomegaly
Neurologic	5% during course	Hypothalamus or cranial nerves, esp. CN 2,7
Cardiac	5% during course	Heart block, tachyarrhythmias
Exocrine glands	4% during course	Salivary enlargement, occasional lacrimal enlargement
Joint and musculoskeletal	15% at presentation	Acute polyarthritis
Bone	3% during course	Cystic or lytic in small bones of hands, feet
Renal	Unusual	
Endocrine	?	Hypercalcemia, hypercalciuria
Immunologic	Common	Increased Igs; decreased delayed hypersensitivity

nopathy is present, scalene node biopsy yields adequate tissue in up to 80 percent of cases. Mediastinoscopy is more invasive but positive in 90 to 100 percent. If lung parenchyma is involved, transbronchial biopsy is highly sensitive. If other procedures fail, open lung biopsy will provide adequate tissue to substantiate or reject the diagnosis.
Yield of mediastinoscopy if hilar nodes are not present is uncertain. Transbronchial biopsy in the absence of parenchymal infiltrate is probably sensitive. Labial gland biopsy appears to be relatively insensitive.

F. **Treatment.** Because of the varied natural history of sarcoidosis, effects of treatment are difficult to assess. Presentation with erythema nodosum and diffuse adenopathy suggests a good prognosis. Bilateral hilar adenopathy alone usually presages a benign course. Natural history with parenchymal involvement varies. Overall mortality from sarcoidosis is 5 to 10 percent.
Determination of disease activity may help to guide therapy. Theoretically, patients with an active alveolitis would benefit most from treatment. Some evidence supports the use of angiotensin-converting enzyme (ACE) levels, gallium scans, and bronchoalveolar lavage to identify active alveolitis. Recent evidence indicates that an increased percentage of T lymphocytes, especially "helper" T cells, in bronchoalveolar lavage identifies patients with active alveolitis.
Conflicting evidence surrounds the use of corticosteroids in sarcoidosis. If treatment is begun, consensus appears to favor daily high-dose therapy followed by tapering or alternate-day therapy. Immunosuppressive and cytotoxic agents are of uncertain benefit.

XII. **PULMONARY HEMORRHAGE SYNDROMES**

Diffuse pulmonary hemorrhage may occur in four major syndromes: systemic vasculitis, coagulation disorders, Goodpasture's syndrome, and idiopathic pulmonary hemosiderosis (IPH). Vasculitides occasionally lead to lung hemorrhage, especially SLE, Wegener's, mixed cryoglobulinemia, and periarteritis nodosa. Coagulation disorders include: clotting factor abnormalities, such as therapeutic anticoagulation; platelet disorders, such as thrombocytopenia due to leukemia; and combined disorders, such as disseminated intravascular coagulation. Goodpasture's syndrome and IPH are more specific to the lung, as discussed below.

A. **Goodpasture's syndrome.** This is an autoimmune disorder characterized by hemoptysis, glomerulonephritis, and antibasement membrane antibody production.
   1. **Clinical findings.** The disease is most common in young adults, especially males. Glomerulonephritis may occur alone, but lung involvement without renal disease is uncommon. When both systems are involved, hemoptysis usually precedes renal disease. Other symptoms include dyspnea, cough, and weakness. Hematuria and anemia are characteristic. Acutely, the chest x-ray shows patchy alveolar densities bilaterally, simulating pulmonary edema. After several days, consolidation clears and is replaced by a reticular infiltrate. This in turn resolves over a period of weeks to months.
   2. **Diagnosis.** Intra-alveolar hemorrhage can be detected by labeled carbon monoxide scan or labeled erythrocyte injection. Specific diagnosis usually requires biopsy. Light microscopy demonstrates intra-alveolar hemorrhage, and occasionally, vasculitis. Immunofluorescence in the kidney, and often, the lung, reveals linear deposits of IgG long basement membranes. Circulating antibasement membrane antibody can be measured in 80 to 90 percent of patients.
   3. **Treatment.** The disease is notable for spontaneous remissions and relapses, but overall prognosis is poor. Uncontrolled studies suggest benefit with steroids, cytotoxic agents, plasmapheresis, or bilateral nephrectomy.

B. **Idiopathic pulmonary hemosiderosis.** This is a syndrome of hemoptysis and diffuse pulmonary hemorrhage without known etiology.
   1. **Clinical findings.** This disorder occurs primarily in children, but may also be seen in young adults. Most patients have episodic hemoptysis, fever, and dyspnea, with spontaneous resolution. Repeated episodes lead to pulmonary fibrosis. Anemia is common, and about 20 percent of cases have lymphadenopathy and hepatosplenomegaly. Chest x-ray results are similar to those described for Goodpasture's syndrome.
   2. **Diagnosis.** Exclusion of other causes of diffuse hemorrhage, especially vasculitides and Goodpasture's syndrome, forms the basis for diagnosis. If hemoptysis is no longer present, sputum may reveal hemo-

siderin-laden macrophages. Light microscopy findings are similar to those of Goodpasture's, but immunofluorescence for antibasement membrane antibody is negative in IPH. Radionuclide techniques in active disease confirm the presence of pulmonary hemorrhage.
3. **Treatment.** Prognosis is poor, but occasionally the disease resolves spontaneously. Improvement has been reported in isolated cases treated with steroids and cyclophosphamide.

XIII. RADIATION PNEUMONITIS

A. **Incidence.** Pulmonary parenchyma is often included in the radiation portal for hematologic, mediastinal, breast, and primary lung neoplasms. Approximately 40 percent of patients irradiated for breast carcinoma develop evidence of radiation pneumonitis, but only 8 percent are symptomatic. Patients with lung neoplasms and lymphomas have a variable incidence of radiation effects. Only 5 to 15 percent have clinical findings referable to radiation pneumonitis. Some patients appear to be "hyper-reactive" to radiation, developing pneumonitis at relatively low doses. Risk factors for development of radiation pneumonitis are presented in *table 11-8*.

B. **Clinical findings.** Clinical presentation of radiation pneumonitis depends upon factors listed above. Parenchymal disease without symptoms often develops in patients receiving radiation to small lung volumes and apical regions, and those receiving total doses less than 200 rads.

Table 11-8
Risk Factors for Radiation Pneumonitis

Increasing volume of lung irradiated

Location in lower lung fields

Total dose: unusual, less than 3000 rads; usual, greater than 3500; invariable, greater than 4000

Increasing rate of dosage

Steroid withdrawal

Concurrent drug therapy: actinomycin D, vincristine sulfate, cyclophosphamide (not hydroxyureas, CNU, bleomycin)

Prior radiation

Possibly hyperreactivity

Regardless of dose, symptoms rarely appear until 8 weeks after radiation. Early symptoms are mild, consisting of cough and slight fever. Chest x-ray may show diffuse haziness within the radiation portal. Dyspnea soon becomes the predominant symptom. The chest x-ray shows progression to diffuse opacification, and eventually, to streaking and volume loss consistent with fibrosis. Effusions occur in less than 10 percent of patients. Infiltrates outside the radiation portal are rarely, if ever, a "reaction" to radiation. More likely, extraportal infiltrates are the result of scatter and inaccurate delivery technique in patients who are sensitive to radiation.

Pulmonary function changes in radiation pneumonitis are consistent with progressive fibrosis decrease in lung volumes and decreased compliance. Hypoxemia and decreased diffusing capacity occur early in the course of radiation pneumonitis. These findings may improve later in the disease if only a small portion of lung is involved. Clinical and pathologic progression of radiation pneumonitis is summarized in *table 11-9*.

C. **Treatment.** Anecdotal evidence supports the use of corticosteroids in acute radiation pneumonitis. However, once fibrosis occurs, steroids have little effect. Use of steroid prophylaxis before patient begins irradiation therapy has been advocated, but it is probably of little value. Consensus appears to favor steroid therapy for acute disease with symptoms.

XIV. **OXYGEN- AND DRUG-INDUCED PNEUMONITIS**

Administration of oxygen or drugs has multiple effects on the lung, including respiratory depression, bronchospasm, and pulmonary edema. In addition, several types of drugs are associated with ILD.

A. **Oxygen.** This is probably the agent most commonly associated with pulmonary infiltrates, as described in Chapter 7.

B. **Antineoplastics.** Most commonly implicated are busulfan and bleomycin. Both cause a diffuse interstitial pneumonitis, progressing to alveolar consolidation, and eventually, to fibrosis. Chest x-ray shows a diffuse reticular pattern. Busulfan pneumonitis begins 3 months to 4 years after initiation of therapy, and relation to total dose is uncertain. Bleomycin toxicity occurs in 3 to 10 percent of patients receiving the drug, and in about 30

Table 11-9
Natural History of Radiation Pneumonitis

	1 mo	2 mo	3 mo	6 mo	12 mo	24 mo
Symptoms		Mild cough, fever		Mild dyspnea		Dyspnea
Chest x-ray		Haziness	Interstitial infiltrate			Fibrosis
Pulmonary function	Decreased vascular flow		Decreased compliance, DL_{CO}	Decreased volumes		Decreased volumes; DL_{CO} near normal
Pathology		Exudative: increased vascular permeability; decreased type II cells		Pneumonitic: mast cell, fibroblast infiltration; atypical type II cells	Reparative: regression of infiltrating cells; thickening of septa, capillary walls	

percent of patients receiving 150 mg/m² total dose. Prior radiation therapy increases incidence of disease. Methotrexate is less commonly involved in pneumonitis. It may cause a diffuse reticular infiltrate progressing to patchy consolidation. Changes begin 10 days to 4 months after initiation of therapy and resolve after withdrawal of the drug. Other agents reported to cause interstitial lung disease include cyclophosphamide, azathioprine, chlorambucil, melphalan, and carmustine (BCNU).

C. **Antibiotics.** Penicillin and sulfonamides produce pulmonary edema but not interstitial infiltrates. Nitrofurantoin may cause interstitial infiltrates, usually with eosinophilia. Chronic administration of the drug in susceptible patients may lead to interstitial fibrosis.

D. **Lupus-like syndrome.** Pulmonary infiltrates may occur in idiopathic SLE, and also in drug-induced lupus-like syndromes. Infiltrates usually assume patchy, interstitial patterns. Drugs most commonly associated with this syndrome are procainamide, phenytoin, hydralazine and isoniazid.

REFERENCES

I. General

Crystal RG, Gadek JE, Ferrans VJ, et al: Interstitial lung disease: current concepts of pathogenesis, staging, and therapy. *Am J Med* 70:542-568, 1981.

Epler GR, McLoud TC, Gaensler EA, et al: Normal chest roentgenograms in chronic diffuse infiltrative lung disease. *N Engl J Med* 298:934-939, 1978.

Turino GM: The assessment of functional impairment in pulmonary interstitial fibrosis. In *Pulmonary Diseases and Disorders.* Edited by Fishman AP, New York, McGraw-Hill, 1980, pp 725-732.

Turner-Warwick M: Widespread pulmonary fibrosis. In *Pulmonary Diseases and Disorders.* Edited by Fishman AP, New York, McGraw-Hill, 1980, pp 675-684.

Crystal presents an exhaustive review of interstitial disease, emphasizing staging and the role of bronchoalveolar lavage. Epler finds almost 10 percent of patients have normal chest x-rays. Turino discusses pulmonary function tests in these disorders, and Turner-Warwick concentrates on pathogenesis.

II. Idiopathic Interstitial Pneumonitides

Carrington CB, Gaensler EA, Coutu RE, et al: Natural history and treated course of usual and desquamative interstitial pneumonia. *N Engl J Med* 298:801-809, 1978.

Turner-Warwick M, Burrows B, Johnson A: Cryptogenic fibrosing alveolitis: clinical features and their influence on survival. *Thorax* 35:171-180, 1980.

Wall CP, Gaensler EA, Carrington CB, et al: Comparison of transbronchial and open biopsies in chronic infiltrative lung disease. *Am Rev Respir Dis* 123:280-285, 1981.

Winterbauer RH, Hammar SP, Hallman KO, et al: Diffuse interstitial pneumonitis. Clinicopathologic correlations in 20 patients treated with prednisone/azathioprine. *Am J Med* 65:661-672, 1978.

These authors use somewhat different classifications for idiopathic pneumonitides. Carrington distinguishes DIP and VIP, noting increased response to steroids and survival in the latter. Turner-Warwick and Winterbauer do not make this distinction. Both papers note increased survival in the presence of prominent cellular infiltrates. Wall finds that transbronchial biopsies are useful in some cases, but open biopsies are often necessary.

III. Collagen-Vascular Diseases

Hunninghake GW, Fauci AS: Pulmonary involvement in the collagen vascular diseases. *Am Rev Respir Dis* 119:471-503, 1979.

Matthay RA, Schwartz MI, Petty TL, et al: Pulmonary manifestations of systemic lupus erythematosus. *Medicine* 54:397-409, 1974.

Schwartz MI, Matthay RA, Sahn SA, et al: Interstitial lung disease in polymyositis and dermatomyositis: analysis of six cases and review of the literature. *Medicine* 55:89-104, 1976.

Walker WC, Wright V: Pulmonary lesions and rheumatoid arthritis. *Medicine* 47:501-502, 1968.

Young RH, Mark GJ: Pulmonary vascular changes in scleroderma. *Am J Med* 64:998-1003, 1978.

Hunninghake presents an exhaustive review of collagen vascular diseases. The other authors discuss specific entities. Walker compares patients with rheumatoid arthritis to those with osteoarthritis, confirming increases in lung disease in the former. Young discusses pathologic material, finding one group of patients with accelerated vascular disease.

IV. Pulmonary Vasculitides

Chumbley LC, Harrison RA, DeRemee RA: Allergic granulomatosis and angiitis. *Mayo Clin Proc* 52:477-484, 1977.

Fauci AS, Haynes B, Katz P, et al: The spectrum of vasculitis: clinical, pathologic, immunologic and therapeutic considerations. *Ann Intern Med* 89: 660-676, 1978.

Liebow AA: Pulmonary angiitis and granulomatosis. *Am Rev Respir Dis* 108:1-17, 1973.

Wolff SM, Fauci AS, Horn RG, et al: Wegener's granulomatosis. *Ann Intern Med* 81:513-525, 1974.

Definitions of these syndromes are variable. Chumbley refers to the Churg-Strauss syndrome, describing a retrospective series. Liebow uses the same title to refer to all pulmonary vasculitides, presenting a classification for these disorders. Fauci discusses vasculitides in general, with brief consideration of pulmonary diseases. Wolff reviews Wegener's disease, emphasizing the benefits of cyclophosphamide.

V. Eosinophilic Lung Disease

Gaensler EA, Carrington CB: Peripheral opacities in chronic eosinophilic pneumonia: the photographic negative of pulmonary edema. *AJR* 128:1-13, 1977.

Mayock RL, Saldana MJ: Eosinophilic pneumonia. In *Pulmonary Diseases and Disorders*. Edited by Fishman AP, New York, McGraw-Hill, 1980, pp 926-939.

Pearson DJ, Rosenow EC: Chronic eosinophilic pneumonia (Carrington's). *Mayo Clin Proc* 53:73-78, 1978.

Gaensler argues that radiographic findings in chronic disease are pathognomonic. Mayock presents a concise review of eosinophilic syndromes. Pearson describes clinical features in this syndrome.

VI. Pulmonary Hemorrhage Syndromes

Finley TN, Aronow A, Cosentino AM, et al: Occult pulmonary hemorrhage in anticoagulated patients. *Am Rev Respir Dis* 112:23-29, 1975.

Thomas HM, Irwin RS: Classification of diffuse intrapulmonary hemorrhage. *Chest* 68:483-484, 1975.

Wilson CB: Immunologic diseases of the lung and kidney. In *Pulmonary Diseases and Disorders*. Edited by Fishman AP, New York, McGraw-Hill, 1980, pp 699-706.

Finley describes hemorrhage due to anticoagulation. Thomas briefly discusses the distinction between Goodpasture's syndrome and other hemorrhage syndromes, especially IPH. Wilson reviews Goodpasture's syndrome, and also, evidence for immune complex-mediated disease.

VII. Hypersensitivity Pneumonitis

Ganier M, Lieberman P, Fink J, et al: Humidifier lung: an outbreak in office workers. *Chest* 77:183-188, 1980.

Richerson HB: Hypersensitivity pneumonitis. In *Pulmonary Diseases and Disorders*. Edited by Fishman AP, New York, McGraw-Hill, 1980, pp 691-697.

Salvaggio JE, Karr RM: Hypersensitivity pneumonitis: state of the art. *Chest* 75(suppl):270-274, 1979.

Ganier describes an "occupational" outbreak due to thermophilic actinomyces. Richerson and Salvaggio review the topic extensively.

VIII. Sarcoidosis

Colp C: Sarcoidosis: course and treatment. *Med Clin North Am* 61:1267-1278, 1977.

Daniele RP, Dauber JH, Rossman MD: Immunologic abnormalities in sarcoidosis. *Ann Intern Med* 92:406-416, 1980.

Mitchell DN, Scadding JG: Sarcoidosis. *Am Rev Respir Dis* 111:774-802, 1974.

Winterbauer RH, Belic N, Moores KD: A clinical interpretation of bilateral hilar adenopathy. *Ann Intern Med* 78:65-71, 1973.

Mitchell concentrates on pathogenesis, whereas Daniele presents more recent immunologic data. Winterbauer finds that adenopathy alone almost always represents sarcoidosis. Colp discusses neural history and effects of therapy.

IX. Radiation Pneumonitis

Gross NJ: Pulmonary effects of radiation therapy. *Ann Intern Med* 86:81-92, 1977.

Phillips JC, Wyatt JP: Radiation fibrosis. In *Pulmonary Diseases and Disorders*. Edited by Fishman AP, New York, McGraw-Hill, 1980, pp 658-674.

Both are excellent reviews of the subject, including pathogenesis and clinical manifestations.

X. Drug-induced Interstitial Disease

Kilburn KH: Pulmonary disease induced by drugs. In *Pulmonary Diseases and Disorders*. Edited by Fishman AP, New York, McGraw-Hill, 1980, pp 707-724.

Weiss RB, Muggia FM: Cytotoxic drug-induced pulmonary disease: update 1980. *Am J Med* 68:259-266, 1980.

Kilburn reviews drug-induced lung disease, including interstitial disease, with an excellent table of drug effects. Weiss focuses on cytotoxic agents and their effects.

12
Lung Neoplasms

I. DEFINITION AND INCIDENCE

Lung neoplasms include tumors arising from bronchial wall, lung parenchyma, and pleura. The first group, tumors arising from the bronchial wall, is designated bronchogenic carcinoma. This is by far the most common type, constituting about 90 percent of all lung neoplasms. Incidence of this tumor in the United States has increased rapidly in the last few decades; currently there are approximately 100,000 new cases per year. In men, bronchogenic carcinoma is the most common malignant neoplasm. There is a 3- or 4-to-1 male predominance, but incidence in women is now increasing more rapidly than in males. Bronchogenic carcinoma usually occurs in the fifth or sixth decade of life; the disease is much less common before the age of 35.

Tumors of the lung parenchyma and pleura are uncommon, comprising only 2 to 3 percent of lung neoplasms. Benign tumors account for the remaining 5 to 8 percent.

II. ETIOLOGY AND PATHOGENESIS

A. Etiology

1. Smoking. Although the etiology of lung carcinoma is not clearly understood, epidemiologic and experimental evidence have established the causative role of cigarette smoke, and to a lesser extent, other inhaled toxins. A list of substances associated with development of lung cancer follows:

a. Cigarette smoke
b. Asbestos

c. Arsenic
   d. Hematite
   e. Radioactive material (e.g., uranium)
   f. Bichromates
   g. Bischloromethyl ether
   h. Possibly nickel
   i. Possibly coal dust
   Although the association with smoking is especially strong for squamous and small cell carcinomas, adenocarcinoma is also associated with smoking. The relative risk of bronchogenic carcinoma for all smokers is 4 to 10 times that for nonsmokers—for heavy smokers, the risk is increased 15 to 30 times. Risk remains unchanged for 3 or more years after smoking is discontinued, and then gradually decreases, until after 10 to 13 years the risk returns to that of nonsmokers.
2. **Industrial exposure.** Asbestos is an especially important toxin, owing to its widespread use and to the heavy industrial exposure of certain groups of individuals to asbestos in recent decades. Asbestos exposure is common among shipyard workers and pipe fitters. Asbestos-related disease may develop, not only in persons having direct contact with the agent, but also in some persons whose exposure is relatively indirect. Exposure is associated with mesothelioma, and to a lesser extent, squamous cell carcinoma. Smoke and asbestos appear to be synergistic, so that smokers exposed to asbestos are at extreme risk for lung cancer.
3. Other risk factors
   a. **Genetic predisposition.** A rare abnormality—elevated levels of the enzyme aryl hydrocarbon hydroxylase—appears to increase susceptibility to lung carcinoma by an unknown mechanism.
   b. **Associated disease.** Pathologic evidence supports an association of lung carcinoma with tuberculous scars. An association also has been reported with scleroderma and other interstitial lung diseases, which produce "honeycombing" fibrosis.
   c. **Immune defects.** Immune deficiency predisposes to neoplasia, including lung cancer, through an unknown mechanism.

B. **Pathogenesis.** Pathogenesis of lung carcinoma is inferred from pathologic data in humans and animal models. Exposure to a carcinogen such as cigarette smoke leads to basal cell hyperplasia in the airway mucosa. Continued exposure causes stratification of mucosal cells, followed by squamous metaplasia. Eventually, carcinoma in situ develops, with subsequent progression to invasion and metastasis. Most carcinomas arise in segmental bronchi. Cancers in the major bronchi are uncommon, and in the trachea, rare. Although the time lapse between initial insult and development of carcinoma is uncertain, epidemiologic data indicate an interval of at least a decade. Once a carcinoma is present, pathologic evidence suggests that 20 to 40 doublings, requiring 8 to 14 years, are required for the tumor to reach 1 cm in diameter, the minimum size detectable on chest x-ray.

C. **Pathology.** Bronchogenic carcinoma shows four common histologic patterns, with a fifth, bronchioalveolar carcinoma, as a possible variant. Each cell type shows unique growth and metastatic characteristics, as summarized in *table 12-1*.

III. **CLINICAL PRESENTATION AND DIAGNOSIS**

A. **Symptoms.** The clinical presentation of lung carcinoma is nonspecific. In one large screening program, most patients developing neoplasms had little change in chronic cough. This study found hemoptysis and increased cough to be uncommon preludes to cancer. Other series—usually retrospective—have noted an increase in cough or the onset of hemoptysis in 20 to 40 percent of patients in whom the diagnosis of carcinoma was subsequently made. Other pulmonary symptoms include dyspnea and chest pain. Wheezing is a rare manifestation of lung cancer. Constitutional symptoms of fever and weight loss each occur in 20 to 30 percent of affected patients.

B. **Signs.** Pulmonary signs are uncommon. Unless a mass is huge or an effusion is present, lung examination is usually unrevealing. Except in rare cases, signs of hypoxia or hypercapnia are related to lung disease other than carcinoma. Clubbing occurs in 20 to 30 percent of patients with carcinoma, although its presence in other lung disorders renders it nonspecific.

C. **Systemic effects.** Paraneoplastic syndromes, especially endocrinopathies and neuromuscular disorders, are commonly associated with bronchogenic carcinoma.
   1. **Endocrinopathies.** Clinical evidence of endocrine

Table 12-1
Growth Characteristics of Bronchogenic Carcinomas

Type of Carcinoma	Prevalence (% of lung cancer cases)	Predisposition	Location (% peripheral)	Growth Rate	Metastases
Squamous cell or epidermoid	30-40	Smoking	30	Slow to moderate	30-40% at presentation; to hilar and mediastinal nodes, soft tissue, then liver, adrenals, kidney, bone, brain
Small-cell or oat cell	25	Smoking	20	Rapid, early metastasis	Almost all at presentation; to adjacent nodes, then liver, adrenals, bone, pancreas, brain
Adenocarcinoma	25	Smoking, asbestos	75	Moderate; increasing with poor differentiation	Frequent at presentation; to adrenals, liver, bone, brain
Large-cell	15	?	Usually	Slow	Occurs late; similar pattern to adenocarcinoma
Bronchoalveolar cell (may be variant of adenocarcinoma)	<10	?	Usually	Variable	About 50% at presentation; to nodes, pancreas, colon, breast, stomach, kidney

dysfunction occurs in 10 to 12 percent of patients with bronchogenic carcinoma. Recent improved assays detected an elevated hormone in 65 percent of patients in one series. Endocrine abnormalities include hypercalcemia, syndrome of inappropriate antidiuretic hormone (SIADH), Cushing's syndrome, gynecomastia, and hyperpigmentation.
  a. **Hypercalcemia.** Elevated serum calcium is present in 7 to 8 percent of bronchogenic carcinoma cases, usually those with the squamous cell type. Only a minority of such patients appear to have osseous metastases. The majority produce a parathyroid hormone-like substance responsible for hypercalcemia. Parathyroid hormone levels are often elevated in the absence of hypercalcemia, occurring in 32 percent of squamous cell carcinoma in one series.
  b. **Syndrome of inappropriate antidiuretic hormone (SIADH).** One to 2 percent of patients with bronchogenic carcinoma—usually small-cell—develop hyponatremia and inappropriate urine concentration. In one series of patients with small-cell carcinoma, 68 percent had an abnormal response to water loading, suggesting antidiuretic hormone (ADH) dysfunction.
  c. **Cushing's syndrome.** Presentation is more acute but otherwise similar to that caused by hypophyseal adenomas, with edema, hypertension, weakness, and hypokalemic alkalosis. Although the syndrome itself is uncommon, occurring in 0.5 percent of patients with bronchogenic carcinoma, a majority of such patients have elevated ACTH levels. Most patients have elevations of pro-ACTH ("big ACTH"), a relatively inactive precursor.
  d. **Gynecomastia.** This is an uncommon syndrome that presumably is due to gonadotropins and placental hormone production. Although the presence of clinical manifestations is unusual, elevated hormone production is not. In one series, elevated human chorionic gonadotropin (hCG) was present in 32 percent of small-cell, 26 percent of large-cell, and 19 percent of squamous cell carcinomas. Human placental lactogen (hPL) was also found in some patients.
  e. **Hyperpigmentation.** This rare syndrome is pre-

sumably due to elevated melanocyte-stimulating hormone (MSH) levels.

Increased hormone levels without corresponding clinical syndromes are common. Calcitonin was elevated in 48 percent of patients with small-cell carcinoma, in one series, although no effects were evident. Increased insulin-like activity, growth hormone, and prolactin also have been reported.

2. **Neuromuscular disorders.** Neuromuscular syndromes are common in bronchogenic carcinoma, occurring in 4 to 16 percent of patients. Cell types associated with these syndromes include **small-cell** in 52 percent, **squamous cell** in 22 percent, **large-cell** in 16 percent, and **adenocarcinoma** in 5 percent. In one-third of such cases, the chest x-ray was normal at the onset of neurologic symptoms. Uncommonly, symptoms may precede evidence for malignancy by months, or rarely, years. Syndromes include myopathies and neuropathies.
   a. **Myopathies.** Eaton-Lambert syndrome, a myasthenia-like disorder, occurs primarily in small-cell carcinoma. The resulting motor weakness is distinguished from myasthenia gravis by proximal extremity distribution, ocular and bulbar sparing, and increased response to repetitive stimulation on electromyography. Polymyositis may also cause proximal motor weakness, often with muscle wasting and tenderness.
   b. **Neuropathies.** Peripheral neuropathies usually involve both sensory and motor components. Central syndromes include subacute cerebellar degeneration, and rarely, necrotizing myelopathy and encephalomyelopathy.
3. **Connective tissue and dermatologic disorders**
   a. **Hypertrophic pulmonary osteoarthropathy.** Bronchogenic carcinoma is the most common cause of this syndrome, which occurs in 1 to 3 percent of affected patients, usually those with squamous cell carcinoma. Excess growth hormone has been suggested, but not confirmed, as the causal agent.
   b. **Acanthosis nigricans.** This uncommon syndrome consists of bilateral, symmetric hyperkeratosis and hyperpigmentation, usually in intertriginous or flexor areas.
   c. **Scleroderma.** An association between sclero-

derma and lung cancer has been suggested, but causality is uncertain.
4. **Vascular and hematologic disorders**
   a. **Thrombophlebitis** was noted in 3 percent of patients in one series. Episodes were often of the "migratory" type, occurring repeatedly and in unusual sites.
   b. **Anemia** occurs in about 8 percent of patients. The majority of cases are due to bone marrow hypoproliferation, the "anemia of chronic disease."
   c. **Coagulation disorders.** Thrombocythemia is common, perhaps predisposing to embolic episodes. Thrombocytopenia is rare.

   Extrapulmonary manifestations of bronchogenic carcinoma are summarized in *table 12-2*.

D. Diagnosis. In dealing with suspected bronchogenic carcinoma, two major issues must be addressed: identifying the cell type, and determining the extent of systemic involvement. The diagnosis is usually suggested by one of three presentations: **mass or infiltrate on chest x-ray; positive sputum cytologic studies;** or **biopsy of an extrapulmonary** lesion suggesting the presence of a primary bronchogenic tumor. The first presentation, a radiographic abnormality, is the most common presentation of bronchogenic carcinoma.

Evaluation of the solitary pulmonary nodule (less than 4 cm) is discussed on p. 268. In the case of positive cytologic evidence but negative chest x-ray, aggressive search must be made for a primary lesion, using tomography, and probably, bronchoscopy with segmental washings. Such patients may have early tumors accessible to surgical cure. If no lesion is found, chest x-ray should be repeated monthly and bronchoscopy every 3 months in an attempt to detect an early tumor. In the third presentation, if biopsy of a metastasis suggests bronchogenic origin, frequently no further evaluation is required.

Radiographic characteristics of various types of bronchogenic carcinoma are presented in *table 12-3*. Diagnostic methods in patients first diagnosed by chest x-ray abnormality include evaluation of sputum and pleural fluid, serologic studies, and biopsy.
1. **Sputum.** Cytologic studies of expectorated sputum are 60 to 70 percent sensitive for carcinoma; sensitivity is higher with central lesions and in squamous

Table 12-2
Extrapulmonary Manifestations of Bronchogenic Carcinoma

Syndrome	Agent*	Tumor	Incidence
Constitutional			
Weight loss	?	Varied	30%
Fever	?	Varied	20%
Endocrine			
Hypercalcemia	PTH	Squamous, then small-cell	PTH up in 30%; calcium up in 8%
SIADH	ADH	Small-cell	Clinical 1-2%; water load abnormal 50%+
Cushing's syndrome	ACTH	Small-cell, then large-cell	ACTH up in 20-30%; clinical in 1%
Gynecomastia	hCG Possibly, hPL	Varied	hCG up in 20-30%; clinical 0.5%
Hyperpigmentation	MSH	Small-cell, squamous	Common
Carcinoid syndrome	Serotonin, kinins	Bronchial adenoma	Rare
No clinical effect	Calcitonin	Small-cell	50%
Connective tissue			
Clubbing	?	Varied	20-30%
HPO	Possibly hGH	Squamous, then adenocarcinoma	3%

Neuromuscular			
Myasthenia-like (Eaton-Lambert)	Possibly autoimmune	Small-cell	Rare
Polymyositis	?	Varied	Uncommon
Peripheral neuropathy	?	Varied	Uncommon
Vascular-hematologic			
Thrombophlebitis	?	Varied	3%
Anemia	?	Varied	8%

*PTH: parathyroid hormone
ADH: antidiuretic hormone
ACTH: adrenocorticotropic hormone
hCG: human chorionic gonadotropin
hPL: human placental lactogen
MSH: melanocyte-stimulating hormone
hGH: human growth hormone

Table 12-3
Radiographic Characteristics of Bronchogenic Carcinoma

Size: less than 4 cm — adenocarcinoma
   greater than 4 cm — small-cell or other carcinoma
Location: apical with no other findings — squamous-cell carcinoma
   hilar — small-cell, rare in adenocarcinoma
Atelectasis: squamous cell
Pneumonitis (no other findings): squamous cell
   (other findings): small-cell or large-cell
Cavitation: squamous cell, not small-cell
Multiple masses: uncommon in all types
Mediastinal widening: small-cell, then large-cell

Data taken from *Mayo Clin Proc* 43:327, 1968.

cell carcinoma. In patients unable to expectorate spontaneously, aerosol inhalation may be used to stimulate cough. Sensitivity increases with two or three specimens when sputum is induced, although the number required to maximize diagnostic yield is uncertain. Specificity is very high; false positive cytologic results are occasionally reported in a variety of conditions, notably pulmonary infarction and chronic infection.

2. **Pleural fluid.** If pleural fluid is present, cytologic studies may also yield a diagnosis. Sensitivity appears greatest for metastatic carcinoma, especially breast, and for small-cell carcinoma. Overall sensitivity is about 50 to 60 percent. Specificity is high, although occasional false positives are reported. If fluid cytologic result is negative, pleural biopsy should be performed. When multiple samples are obtained, diagnostic yield increases up to 70 percent.

3. **Serodiagnosis.** The discovery of hormones and other peptides produced by bronchogenic tumors led to attempts at serologic diagnosis. Unfortunately, no marker appears sufficiently sensitive or specific to replace tissue identification. Among the most carefully studied markers are pro-ACTH and carcinoembryonic antigen (CEA). While pro-ACTH is increased in the majority of patients with lung cancer, it is also increased in a substantial percentage of patients with obstructive lung disease and with exacerbations of granulomatous lung disease. CEA is likewise increased in a large proportion of cancers, but

is nonspecific due to elevations with age and smoking. Of other peptides, one pathologic study found variable levels of histamine, L-dopa decarboxylase, and calcitonin among cells from primary lesions, hilar metastases, and distant metastases. This confirmed an overall lack of correlation between marker levels and extent of disease.

4. **Biopsy.** The desirability of searching for metastatic disease before biopsy of the primary lesion is uncertain. In general, if cytologic or pleural fluid studies are negative, biopsy should be considered. Two major biopsy techniques are used: bronchoscopy with washings, brushings, and biopsy; and needle biopsy. Technical aspects and complications of both procedures are discussed in Chapter 9. Of the needle biopsy techniques, aspiration has been most extensively studied and appears to be the safest. Tumor implantation along the path of the needle, a possible complication of needle biopsy, has been reported rarely.

Reported diagnostic yields for both biopsy procedures vary with patient selection and technique. The methods appear somewhat complementary: comparison studies show some lesions diagnosed by one technique but not the other. Despite problems in comparing data, several general conclusions can be drawn:

a. Needle aspiration appears most useful for smaller, **peripheral** lesions and in suspected metastatic disease.
b. Bronchoscopy is most useful in larger, **central** lesions, which are primary lung neoplasms.
c. Both appear less accurate for adenocarcinoma than for other cell types.

Evidence concerning biopsy techniques is summarized in *table 12-4*.

Specificity is high; nevertheless, a few false positives are reported with both techniques. Limited sensitivity of both procedures renders negative biopsy results nondiagnostic.

E. **Staging.** Staging of bronchogenic carcinoma usually follows identification of the primary lesion. Extent of disease, independent of cell type, is commonly reported according to the World Health Organization Tumor-Node-Metastasis (TNM) classification system, as presented in *table 12-5*.

Table 12-4
Comparison of Biopsy Techniques for Lung Carcinoma

Factor	Needle Aspiration	Bronchoscopy
Sensitivity	About 80%	About 50%
Specificity	95 + %	95 + %
Yield increased with:	Smaller lesions, peripheral lesions, mass lesion	Large lesions, central lesions, diffuse infiltrate
Yield decreased with:	Adenocarcinoma; possibly diffuse infiltrate	Smaller lesions, peripheral lesions, metastatic disease, adenocarcinoma
Complications	About 20% pneumothorax, about 10% require chest tube	10-20% pneumothorax; 5-10% require chest tube

In some cases, such as high risk for biopsy, or obvious extrapulmonary abnormality on routine investigation, biopsy of a metastatic lesion establishes cell type and stage without the risk of pulmonary diagnostic procedure. In most cases, staging is performed to determine potential for surgery, since resection offers the major hope for cure. Small-cell carcinoma is now presumed to be metastatic when diagnosed, and routine staging appears unnecessary.

At the time of diagnosis, about 50 percent of bronchogenic carcinomas have metastasized to the mediastinum or to distant organs. Preliminary evaluation often suggests the presence of metastases. Symptoms or signs, such as severe low back pain, depression of sensorium, or hepatomegaly, may indicate the need for further investigation. Routine laboratory studies, especially liver enzymes and bone alkaline phosphatase, also suggest specific organ involvement. Liver alkaline phosphatase appears to be sensitive but nonspecific for hepatic involvement by tumor. As previously noted, hypercalcemia should suggest bone metastases, but many patients with squamous cell carcinoma have hypercalcemia on a humoral basis.

Other techniques involved in the detection of metastases are controversial. The most common sites of metastasis for lung cancer are liver, bone, and brain. Radionuclide scans of these organs have been extensively

Table 12-5
TNM Classification and Lung Cancer Staging

I. TNM Classification

T(primary tumors)

- T0: No evidence of primary tumor
- TX: Tumor diagnosed by cytology but not visualized by other means
- TIS: Carcinoma in situ
- T1: Tumor 3.0 cm or less in greatest diameter, distal to lobar bronchus at bronchoscopy
- T2: Tumor 3.0 cm or greater in greatest diameter, or tumor of any size invading visceral pleura, or tumor with atelectasis or obstructive pneumonitis extending to hilar region
- T3: Tumor of any size extending into adjacent structures: e.g., parietal pleura, diaphragm, chest wall, or mediastinum; or tumor involving bronchus less than 2.0 cm distal to carina; or tumor associated with atelectasis or obstructive pneumonitis of entire lobe or pleural effusion

N(regional lymph nodes)

- N0: No metastasis to regional lymph nodes
- N1: Metastasis to ipsilateral peribronchial or perihilar nodes
- N2: Metastasis to mediastinal lymph nodes

M(distant metastasis)

- M0: No distant metastasis
- M1: Distant metastasis to other organs or contralateral lung or lymph nodes

II. Staging

Occult carcinoma: TX N0 M0

Stage I: T1S N0 M0
T1S N0 M0
T1 N0 M0
T1 N1 M0
T2 N0 M0

Stage II: T2 N1 M0

Stage III: T3 with any N or M
N2 with any N or M
M1 with any T or N

studied. In the absence of clinical or laboratory abnormalities, several series report low diagnostic yields for scanning; however, other studies show significant detection of "silent" metastases. Yields are much increased in the presence of symptoms or positive laboratory findings. Both false positive and false negative scans occur, false positives more frequently in asymptomatic patients. Interpretation of scans may be difficult; further confirmation is often required, especially in the case of solitary lesions on bone scan. Computed tomography is probably superior in sensitivity and specificity to brain scanning for brain metastases.

One series suggests the superiority of gallium scanning over other scans, although evidence is limited. On the basis of present evidence, symptoms or laboratory abnormalities should lead to scans of specific organs; scanning of asymptomatic patients is of uncertain value.

Staging also includes further examination of the involved lung and the contralateral lung. Bronchogenic carcinoma rarely presents as multiple masses; this presentation is more common in cancer metastatic to the lung. If metastatic disease is suspected or chest x-ray suggests several lesions, further evaluation should be performed by whole lung tomography, computed tomography, or gallium scanning. Whole lung tomography appears to be sensitive for multiple lesions, although computed tomography may increase sensitivity in patients at risk for metastatic disease to the lung. Evidence concerning gallium scanning is limited.

If no metastases are evident, resectability should be demonstrated by evaluation of the mediastinum. Chest x-ray alone is insufficiently sensitive to show mediastinal involvement, detecting only 70 percent of metastases in one series. Other methods include tomography, computed tomography, gallium scanning, and mediastinoscopy or mediastinotomy. Tomography appears specific but less sensitive; in one series, sensitivity was 76 percent, and specificity, 95 percent. Computed tomography had similar sensitivity and specificity results, with inaccuracy most often occurring in the middle mediastinum. Gallium scans in one series appeared specific if the primary lesion took up gallium. Direct visualization and biopsy by mediastinoscopy (for right-sided lesions and left lower lobe lesions), and mediastinotomy (for left upper lobe lesions), are the standard techniques for evaluation of the mediastinum. Morbidity is less than 2 percent. At present, tomography should be performed to identify and localize mediastinal involvement. If positive, mediastinoscopy may still be necessary if resection appears possible; if negative, mediastinoscopy should be performed prior to resection.

An approach to the diagnosis and preliminary staging of suspected bronchogenic carcinoma is presented in figure 12-1.

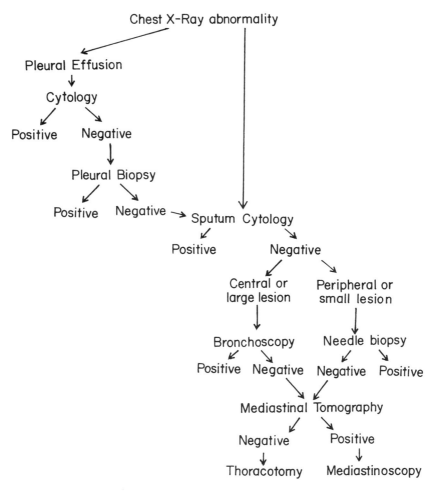

Figure 12-1. An approach to suspected bronchogenic carcinoma.

IV. ALTERATIONS IN LUNG FUNCTION

Unless they are massive or diffuse, neoplasms seldom contribute to lung dysfunction. Most patients with neoplasms have underlying lung disease secondary to chronic bronchitis or emphysema, both the result of smoking. Lung volumes may be decreased due to partial or complete obstruction and atelectasis from an endobronchial lesion. Gas exchange is occasionally hindered by widespread lymphangitic lesions.

V. THERAPY AND PROGNOSIS

Therapy for bronchogenic carcinoma is determined by cell type, extent of involvement of disease, and clinical status. Major therapeutic modalities are surgery, radiotherapy, and chemotherapy.

A. Surgery

1. **Staging and surgical procedure.** Resection offers a chance for cure in all tumors except small-cell carcinoma, which should be treated medically. Resectability is only partially predicted by stage and TNM classification. In general, all patients with Stage I disease should have resections if able to tolerate surgery, and all patients with distant metastases (M_1) or invasion of adjacent structures (T_3) should be considered unresectable (see discussion of superior sulcus tumors below). Decisions concerning Stage II patients and some Stage III patients with mediastinal node involvement (T_1 N_2 M_0 or T_2 N_2 M_0) are more difficult, and results vary among series. A contraindication to surgery is involvement of other mediastinal structures, such as proximal pulmonary artery, pulmonary veins, or heart. Also contraindicating resection are extranodal extension in any cell type and nodal involvement in adenocarcinoma. Involvement of inferior ipsilateral nodes (N_1 in squamous cell or large-cell carcinoma), and perhaps, superior nodes (N_2 in squamous cell carcinoma), may allow resection.

    If resection is undertaken, success of the operative procedure depends upon tumor involvement and upon the patient's ventilatory status. Small peripheral masses may be removed by wedge or segmental resection with relatively little loss of function. Larger lesions require lobectomy, and extensive Stage I and almost all Stage II or III lesions require pneumonectomy.

2. **Prediction of postoperative pulmonary function.** If staging and overall clinical status are amenable to surgery, level of preoperative pulmonary function determines ability to survive resection. Hypercapnia and FEV_1 less than 1.0 L are contraindications to surgery, except in very limited resections. Techniques for evaluation of postoperative function are discussed in Chapter 14.

3. **Adjuvant therapy.** Adjuvant irradiation or chemo-

therapy has not significantly altered morbidity and mortality in surgical patients. Superior sulcus tumors are an exception, as they appear best treated by irradiation, followed by resection.
4. **Surgery for complications.** Surgery generally is not used to control metastases from primary lung lesions. Rarely, pleural decortication is performed to control malignant pleural effusions.
5. **Monitoring of therapy.** Response to therapy is monitored by chest x-ray and attention to symptoms. At present, peptide hormones and other markers do not correlate sufficiently with disease recurrence or progression.

B. **Radiation therapy.** Radiation therapy is generally reserved for inoperable lesions or patients unable to tolerate surgery. Although various cell types are differentially radiosensitive, radiation to the primary lesion appears useful in bronchogenic carcinoma other than small-cell carcinoma. Radiation clearly should be employed in patients with obstruction, recurrent infection, hemoptysis, or other severe symptoms referable to an unresectable lung lesion. Treatment of asymptomatic patients remains controversial: studies differ concerning reduction of morbidity and mortality in treated versus untreated patients. If radiotherapy is begun, usual doses are 5000 to 6000 rads given in fractions (180-200 rads/d) over 5 to 6 weeks. Complications include **constitutional symptoms**, usually resolving after completion of therapy; **esophagitis**, occurring 7 to 10 days after initiation of therapy and resolving after completion; and **pneumonitis and fibrosis** (see Chapter 11.) If the spinal cord is included in the field, **myelitis** may occur with doses greater than 4500 rads.

Radiation therapy for metastatic disease is discussed below. Several recent studies found decreased morbidity from brain metastases in small-cell carcinoma and adenocarcinoma with administration of prophylactic brain irradiation.

C. **Medical therapy**
1. **Small-cell carcinoma.** Among the most important recent developments in treatment of lung cancer is the use of combination chemotherapy in small-cell carcinoma, previously the most resistant of bronchogenic neoplasms. Combination regimens produce a

response in up to 70 percent of patients, with complete regression in 15 to 40 percent of patients. Up to 30 percent of patients remain in remission at one year, and most of these survive 2 years. Regimens include cyclophosphamide, doxorubicin, and vincristine. The value of adjunctive radiation is uncertain, except for prophylaxis of brain metastases.

At present, patients with small-cell carcinoma should undergo limited staging, in view of the dismal results of surgery. Complications of chemotherapy include neutropenia in virtually all patients, with subsequent risk of infection. Patients with small-cell carcinoma may be at particular risk for herpes zoster infection. Mild thrombocytopenia also occurs.

Therapy is monitored by chest x-ray and attention to symptoms. Markers do not appear to correlate with relapse. One study indicates that serial bronchoscopy may be more sensitive than radiography.

2. Non-small-cell carcinomas. Similar chemotherapeutic regimens in other bronchogenic carcinomas have been less successful. Only mild improvement in survival was demonstrated in squamous cell carcinoma, and no clear benefit has been achieved with adenocarcinoma. Large-cell carcinoma appears more responsive, but experience is limited.

3. Immunotherapy. Evidence for a depressed immune response in patients with lung neoplasms has led to efforts to stimulate immune mechanisms. Experience with nonspecific adjuvants, such as BCG or thymosin fraction 5, has thus far shown no increase in survival.

Therapy and prognosis of bronchogenic carcinoma are summarized in *table 12-6*.

D. Complications
  1. Due to primary lung lesion
     a. **Hemoptysis.** This occurs due to erosion into bronchial or pulmonary vessels with airway communication. Therapy consists of radiation to the primary lesion.
     b. **Superior vena cava obstruction.** This is due to direct compression either by a mass lesion or by mediastinal nodes. High-dose radiation is used (400 rads/d for 3 d), followed by conventional radiotherapy. Chemotherapy may be useful in small-cell carcinoma.

Table 12-6
Suggested Primary Therapy and Prognosis in Bronchogenic Carcinoma

Cell Type	Stage	Therapy	Prognosis
Small-cell	All presumed III	Combination chemotherapy	20% 2-yr
Squamous cell	I	Surgery	40-50% 5-yr
	II	Surgery or radiation	20% 5-yr
	III (T_1 or $_2$; N_2, M_0)	Surgery or radiation	
	Other III	Possibly chemotherapy	8-10% 5-yr
Large-cell	I	Surgery	30% 5-yr
	II	Surgery or radiation	5-7% 5-yr
	III	Chemotherapy	4-5% 5-yr
Adenocarcinoma	I	Surgery	30-40% 5-yr
	II	Radiation	8% 5-yr
	III (limited, M_0)	Radiation	
	Other III	Chemotherapy	2-4% 5-yr

  c. **Recurrent infection.** Infection distal to an obstructing lesion should be treated with antibiotics, and with irradiation of the lesion in an attempt to restore airway patency.
2. Due to metastases or systemic effects
  a. **Spinal cord compression.** Metastases usually are extradural, and symptoms are an indication for myelography. If a neurologic deficit is found, decompression laminectomy should be performed. If symptoms but no signs are present, radiotherapy alone is used.
  b. **Brain metastases.** Prophylactic brain irradiation is discussed above. If metastasis occurs, steroids should be administered acutely and whole brain irradiation given (up to 4000 rads).
  c. **Bone metastasis.** Relief of pain often can be accomplished with local irradiation, usually up to 3000 rads over 2 weeks. Occasionally, surgical fixation is required to prevent pathologic fractures.
  d. **Pleural effusion.** Recurrent effusion may occur even in the absence of positive fluid cytologic

studies or positive pleural biopsy. If infection occurs, or respiratory status is compromised, sclerosis should be performed with an agent such as tetracycline. Rarely is surgical decortication required.
    e. **Paraneoplastic syndromes.** Characteristics are discussed above. Therapy is directed toward restoring metabolic balance and treating the underlying disease. Many case reports exist of paraneoplastic syndromes resolving with control of the primary lesion.

VI. **OTHER LUNG NEOPLASMS**

  A. **Bronchial adenoma.** These comprise 1 to 5 percent of primary lung neoplasms. Often presenting in the fourth decade of life, they are indolent, locally invasive tumors. The usual symptoms are cough, hemoptysis, and recurrent infection. Chest x-ray may show a nodule or distal infiltrate. About 80 percent of adenomas are bronchial carcinoids. The carcinoid syndrome, with flushing, tachycardia, diaphoresis, and tremulousness, is uncommon, occurring in 2 percent of patients with bronchial adenomas in one series. Mediators involved are kinins, and serotonin and its precursors. Other cell types among adenomas are adenoid cystic and mucoepidermoid carcinomas. Treatment consists of resection, if possible.

  B. Unusual neoplasms
    1. **Giant cell carcinoma.** A histologic variant of adenocarcinoma, it usually presents as a large peripheral mass with pleural involvement.
    2. **Clear cell carcinoma.** A large-cell variant, this usually presents as a peripheral nodule.
    3. **Endobronchial metastases.** These occurred in 2 percent of patients in a series of patients with mixed neoplasms, and were especially prevalent in those with renal and gastric carcinomas. Presentation is similar to that of primary endobronchial lesions.
    4. **Primary sarcoma.** These very rare neoplasms are of mesenchymal origin.
    5. **Mixed tumors** ("blastoma"). These are tumors of mixed cell types, including poorly differentiated precursors.
    6. **Plasmacytoma.** A rare tumor, this presents as a lobulated mass.

7. **Hematologic neoplasms.** Hodgkin's disease most often presents as mediastinal adenopathy. Extension to the lung occurs in about 30 percent of patients, appearing either as consolidation or nodules. Other lymphomas have variable presentation. Leukemia usually presents as a diffuse infiltrate.

C. **Benign neoplasms: hamartomas.** These tumors are of connective tissue origin, and constitute about 7 percent of surgically resected solitary nodules.

VII. **APPROACH IN SPECIAL SITUATIONS**

A. **Metastases to the lung.** Common metastatic lesions are summarized in *table 12-7*.

In several series, 30 to 60 percent of lung nodules in patients with other cancers were found to be primary in origin. Evaluation of lung nodules should therefore depend upon the patient's overall status and the control of the other neoplasm. If these are adequate, then a diagnosis should be sought.

Opinions differ concerning therapy of metastatic lesions. Resection may be considered for a nodule if

1. The primary tumor is controlled.
2. No other metastases are present.
3. The patient is a good operative risk.
4. No other treatment is effective.

Results of resection of metastases vary widely. Good

Table 12-7
Metastases to the Lung

Parenchymal nodules
  Solitary: Carcinomas — colon, breast, kidney, female genital tract, skin, testis
    Sarcomas — bone
  Multiple: any carcinoma or sarcoma
Endobronchial metastases
  Carcinomas: kidney, colon
  Sarcomas: fibrosarcomas
  Melanomas
Lymphangitic metastases
  Carcinomas: lung, stomach, breast, colon, pancreas

results have been reported with sarcomas, testicular tumors, and occasionally, melanoma and renal cell carcinoma.

B. **Superior sulcus tumors.** Bronchogenic carcinoma occurring in the superior sulcus of the lung may invade adjacent nerves, causing two distinct syndromes or a combination, such as the following:
   1. Shoulder and ulnar distribution pain with subsequent motor weakness
   2. Horner's syndrome with ipsilateral miosis, ptosis, and facial anhidrosis.

   As lesions may be difficult to detect on routine chest x-ray, apical lordotic films or tomography should be performed if a lesion is suspected. Peripheral location makes cytologic studies and bronchoscopy insensitive; diagnosis should be sought by needle biopsy. About two-thirds of tumors are squamous cell carcinomas, and most of the remainder, large-cell. Therapy consists of irradiation followed by en bloc resection.

C. **Solitary pulmonary nodule.** The suspicion of lung carcinoma is commonly raised by the appearance of a solitary pulmonary nodule on chest x-ray. Although the approach generally resembles that for other suspicious radiographic findings, extensive study allows further conclusions about nodules:
   1. A significant proportion are malignant, the extent depending on the population studied; for example, the majority of lesions in patients over 40 years of age with smoking histories are malignant.
   2. Prognosis with resection is much better than for other carcinomas of similar cell type.
   3. As clinical differentiation of benign from malignant disease is difficult, all nodules should be evaluated for resection on the assumption that malignancy is present. Useful differential features for benign lesions include
      a. Age under 35
      b. Symptoms or signs of pneumonia
      c. Smoking history or other predisposition
      d. No change on chest x-ray in 2 years
      e. Concentric or stippled calcification on tomography

      Consensus appears to be against observation and calculation of doubling time. Needle aspiration biopsy is specific and moderately sensitive, although a negative biopsy requires further evaluation in a patient at risk.

An approach to the diagnosis of the solitary pulmonary nodule is present in figure 12-2.

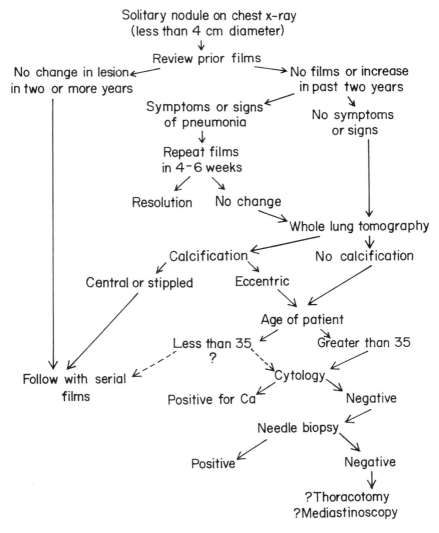

Figure 12-2. Diagnosis of the solitary pulmonary nodule.

REFERENCES

I. General

Greco FA, Oldham RK: Current concepts in cancer: small-cell lung cancer. *N Engl J Med* 301:355-358, 1979.

Rodescu D: Lung cancer. *Med Clin North Am* 61:1205-1218, 1977.

Straus MJ (ed): *Lung Cancer.* New York, Grune and Stratton, 1977.

Weiss L, Gilbert HA (eds): *Pulmonary Metastasis.* Boston, GK Hall, 1978.

Greco succinctly reviews small-cell carcinoma. Rodescu offers a brief review of lung neoplasms in general. Straus's book is a good collection, covering most aspects of lung carcinoma; Weiss deals exclusively with metastases to the lung.

II. Etiology and Pathogenesis

Auerbach O: Natural history of carcinoma of the lung. In *Pulmonary Diseases and Disorders.* Edited by Fishman AP, New York, McGraw-Hill, 1980, pp 1388-1396.

Hassan FM, Nash G, Kazemi H: Asbestos exposure and related neoplasia. *Am J Med* 65:649-654, 1978.

Matthews MJ: Morphologic aspects of malignant tumors of the lung. In *Pulmonary Disease and Disorders.* Edited by Fishman AP, New York, McGraw-Hill, 1980, pp 1383-1387.

Auerbach describes progression of carcinoma and association with smoking, whereas Matthews discusses pathology and growth characteristics. Hassan presents a series of asbestos-related carcinomas.

III. Clinical

Gropp C, Havemann K, Scheuer A: Ectopic hormones in lung cancer patients at diagnosis and during therapy. *Cancer* 46:347-354, 1980.

Ross EJ: Extrapulmonary syndromes associated with cancer of the lung. In *Pulmonary Diseases and Disorders.* Edited by Fishman AP, New York, McGraw-Hill, 1980, pp 1404-1406.

Weiss W, Seidman H, Boucot KR: The Philadelphia pulmonary neoplasm research project: symptoms in occult lung cancer. *Chest* 73:57-61, 1978.

Gropp and Ross describe hormonal and other systemic manifestations of bronchogenic carcinoma. Weiss demonstrates that there are few changes in symptoms in prospectively screened high-risk patients.

IV. Diagnosis and Staging

Carr DT: The staging of lung cancer. *Am Rev Respir Dis* 117:819-823, 1978.

Coombes RC, Ellison ML, Neville AM: Biochemical markers in bronchogenic carcinoma. *Br J Dis Chest* 72:263-287, 1978.

Herman PG, Hessel SJ: The diagnostic accuracy and complications of closed lung biopsies. *Radiology* 125:11-14, 1977.

Hooper RG, Beechler CR, Johnson MC: Radioisotope scanning in the initial staging of bronchogenic carcinoma. *Am Rev Respir Dis* 118:274-286, 1978.

James EC, Ellwood RA: Mediastinoscopy and mediastinal roentgenology. *Ann Thorac Surg* 18:531-538, 1974.

Kelly RJ, Cavan RJ, Ferree CB, et al: Efficacy of radionuclide scanning in patients with lung cancer. *JAMA* 242:2855-2857, 1979.

Rosa VW, Prolla JC, Gastal, ES: Cytology in diagnosis of cancer affecting the lung. Results in 1,000 consecutive patients. *Chest* 63:203-207, 1973.

Sindelar WF, Bagley DH, Felix EL, et al: Lung tomography in cancer patients. Full-lung tomograms in screening for pulmonary metastases. *JAMA* 240: 2060-2063, 1978.

Sinner WN: Pulmonary neoplasms diagnosed with transthoracic needle biopsy. *Cancer* 43:1533-1540, 1979.

Underwood GH, Hooper RG, Axelbaum SP, et al: Computed tomographic scanning of the thorax in the staging of bronchogenic carcinoma. *N Engl J Med* 300:777-778, 1979.

Wolfsen AR, Odell WD: Pro-ACTH: use in early detection of lung cancer. *Am J Med* 66:765-772, 1979.

With regard to diagnosis, Rosa presents a large cytology series; Herman and Sinner compile extensive experience with needle biopsy. Coombes summarizes evidence on the lack of specificity of markers, corroborated by Wolfsen in a more detailed study of pro-ACTH. Hooper and Kelly present conflicting evidence concerning scanning as a means of staging. James notes good correlation between tomography and mediastinoscopy, and Sindelar reports sensitivity of tomography in the lung parenchyma. Underwood presents an early study noting limited value of computed tomography. Carr briefly summarizes the TNM staging classification.

V. Therapy

Ali MK, Mountain CF, Ewer MS, et al: Predicting loss of pulmonary function after pulmonary resection for bronchogenic carcinoma. *Chest* 77:337-342, 1980.

Bitran JD, Desser RK, DeMeester T, et al: Metastatic non-oat cell bronchogenic carcinoma. Therapy with cyclophosphamide, doxorubicin, methotrexate, and procarbazine. *JAMA* 240:2743-2746, 1978.

Cox JD, Yesner RA: Adenocarcinoma of the lung: recent results from the Veterans Administration lung group. *Am Rev Respir Dis* 120:1025-1029, 1979.

Durrant KR, Berry RJ, Ellis F, et al: Comparison of treatment policies in inoperable bronchial carcinoma. *Lancet* 1:715-719, 1971.

Mountain CF: Surgical therapy. In *Pulmonary Diseases and Disorders.* Edited by Fishman AP, New York, McGraw-Hill, 1980, pp 1422-1429.

Perez CA, Stanley K, Rubin P, et al: A prospective randomized study of various irradiation doses and fractionation schedules in the treatment of inoperable non-oat cell cancer of the lung. Preliminary report by the Radiation Therapy Oncology Group. *Cancer* 45:2744-2753, 1980.

Straus MJ: New developments in the treatment of advanced lung cancer. *Am Rev Respir Dis* 120:967-971, 1979.

Walkup RH, Vossel LE, Griffin JP, et al: Prediction of postoperative pulmonary function with the lateral position test. *Chest* 77:24-27, 1980.

The papers by Ali and Walkup are representative of the literature on evaluating patients for lung resection. Mountain summarizes surgical approaches and survival statistics; Bitran, Cox, and Perez present evidence concerning irradiation for non-small-cell neoplasms. Durant offers evidence against irradiation in asymptomatic patients, whereas Straus discusses chemotherapy in small-cell carcinoma.

VI. Other Topics

Cahan WG, Castro EB, Hadjo SI: The significance of a solitary lung shadow in patients with colon cancer. *Cancer* 33:414-421, 1974.

Greene RE, McCloud TC, Stark P: Other malignant tumors of the lung. *Semin Roentgen* 12:225-237, 1977.

Lillington GA: The solitary pulmonary nodule-1974. *Am Rev Respir Dis* 110:699-707, 1974.

Nathan MH: Management of solitary pulmonary nodules. *JAMA* 227:1141-1144, 1974.

Cahan points out the frequency of lung primaries in patients with colon cancer. Lillington provides a balanced discussion of nodules; Nathan extends the doubling time hypothesis to the extreme. Greene provides a clear presentation of nonbronchogenic neoplasms.

13
Thromboembolic Disease

I. DEFINITION AND INCIDENCE

The term thromboembolic disease encompasses a series of events leading to deposition of embolized material in the lungs. Generally, two major pathologic processes occur in sequence: deep venous thrombosis, and pulmonary embolism. In this progression, emboli consist of clots originating from the lower extremities, although other substances and sources occasionally are involved.

Thromboembolic disease is common, although actual incidence is uncertain. Deep venous thrombosis is found in 7 to 9 percent of necropsies; in carefully conducted necropsies, however, the prevalence of pulmonary embolism is as high as 60 percent. Estimated incidence of thromboembolic disease in the United States is 500,000 per year, with a mortality rate of about 1 percent.

II. ETIOLOGY AND PATHOGENESIS

Thromboembolic disease usually begins in lower extremity veins and progresses according to the sequence outlined in figure 13-1. Each of these steps will be discussed in more detail below.

Virchow's triad—stasis, endothelial damage, and hypercoagulability—remains the theoretical basis for considering pathogenesis of deep venous thrombosis (DVT). The specific contribution of each factor in the triad is uncertain. For example, thrombosis does not occur in animals with experimental venous stasis alone. Similarly, deep venous thrombosis occasionally occurs in patients without obvious predisposition. Nonetheless, risk factors based on this triad are

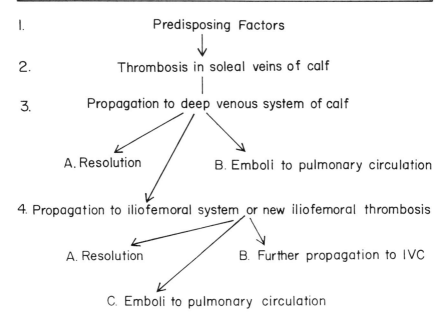

Figure 13-1. Natural history of thromboembolic disease.

associated with development of DVT. These are presented in *table 13-1*.

The increased risk posed by an individual risk factor is difficult to determine. Epidemiologic studies of relative risk for pulmonary embolus indicate highest risk associated with prior pulmonary embolus, inactivity, and lower extremity surgery. Rarely, patients with DVT have intrinsic coagulation abnormalities, notably antithrombin III deficiency. This should be suspected if there is a family history of such deficiency or if recurrent episodes of thromboembolic disease occur without clear predisposition.

Pathologic and labeling studies indicate that most thrombi (80 to 90 percent) begin in the soleal veins of the calf muscles. Origin of thrombi appears to be at sites of decreased flow, such as valve cusps or bifurcations. Thrombi may then propagate to the deep venous system of the calf, usually remaining fixed distally to the site of formation. Most calf thrombi, 70 to 80 percent, remain confined to the calf or resolve spontaneously. Some may undergo embolization to the lung, although the frequency and consequences are uncertain. Consensus appears to be that such emboli are silent clinically, although chronic embolization may lead to pulmonary hypertension.

Table 13-1
Risk Factors for Deep Venous Thrombosis

Age
Oral contraceptives or estrogens
Obesity
Congestive heart failure
Malignancy, especially GI, GU, lung
Prior history of DVT
Postoperative, especially lower half of body
Bed rest or immobility
Ulcerative colitis
Systemic lupus erythematosus
Pregnancy
Thrombocythemia
Possibly trauma
Possibly varicose veins

About 20 to 30 percent of calf thrombi propagate above the knee to the iliofemoral venous system. In addition, approximately 10 to 20 percent of DVT cases are thought to originate in this system without prior calf involvement. These thromboses may resolve spontaneously, undergo embolization to the lungs, or propagate further to the vena cava. Iliofemoral thromboses are thought to be the source of most clinically apparent pulmonary emboli. Pelvic veins, especially in parous women, also serve as sources for emboli, with an incidence as yet uncertain.

Once in the pulmonary circulation, large clots can lodge at the bifurcation of the pulmonary or lobar arteries, causing hemodynamic compromise. Smaller clots continue distally to arterioles and capillaries. Lower lobes are more often involved than upper lobes, and emboli are usually multiple. Only about 10 percent of emboli cause infarction, probably because of collateral flow from both bronchial and pulmonary circulations. Infarction is more common in patients with pre-existing cardiopulmonary disease.

III. DIAGNOSIS

   A. **Deep venous thrombosis.** Clinical presentation of deep venous thrombosis (DVT) is notoriously variable. Indeed, prospective fibrinogen scanning in high-risk patients indicates that the majority of DVT patients have no signs or symptoms referable to the disease. Symptoms, when present, include calf pain, pain on weight bearing, and swelling of ankle. Signs are similarly unhelpful; sensitivity and specificity of clinical signs of DVT are presented in *table 13-2*.

Differential diagnosis includes: **superficial venous thrombosis**, which does not appear to cause embolic complications; **cellulitis**; **trauma**; **venous insufficiency**; and **popliteal (Baker's) cyst**.

Clinical evaluation of DVT is both insensitive and nonspecific. Lack of sensitivity will be addressed in the discussion of prophylaxis. Lack of specificity can be approached with further diagnostic maneuvers.

The standard method for diagnosing DVT is ascending venography. Contrast medium is injected into distal leg veins and roentgenograms are taken of the deep venous system up to the inferior vena cava. Sensitivity and specificity are difficult to define. Careful venography probably will reveal all DVT except very small thrombi in calf veins; false positives are rare. Interpretation may be difficult, however, in the presence of past DVT or venous insufficiency. Risks include contrast reactions in

Table 13-2
Clinical Signs of Deep Venous Thrombosis

Sign	Sensitivity (%)	Specificity (%)
Autopsy confirmation		
Unilateral ankle swelling (left)	83	94
Increased skin temperature	50	100
Local tenderness	41	89
Homans's sign	8	94
Venous dilatation	25	89
Clinical confirmation		
Leg tenderness	62	71
Homans's sign	42	84
Edema	40	52
Moses's sign (AP tenderness)	38	88
Lowenberg's sign (cuff 180 torr)	37	81
Increased calf circumference	35	89
Local hyperthermia	33	87
Pratt's sign (pretibial veins)	27	91
Peabody's sign (calf spasm)	17	98
Ramirez's sign (cuff 45 torr)	15	97

susceptible patients, and induction of thrombophlebitis in 1 to 2 percent of normal venous systems. Occasionally, noninvasive tests may obviate the need for venography. Techniques include:

1. Radiolabeled fibrinogen
   a. Risk. Hepatitis (rare)
   b. Technique. Injection of labeled fibrinogen after suppression of thyroid uptake; scan at 24 hours to determine localization
   c. Advantage. Extremely sensitive below knee
   d. Disadvantages. Less sensitive above knee, nonspecific above mid-thigh; requires 24 hours for results
   e. Sensitivity/specificity. 90%/90%
2. Impedance plethysmography
   a. Risk. None
   b. Technique. Compression by inflatable cuff while measuring electrical resistance along leg; resistance inversely proportional to blood remaining in leg.
   c. Advantages. Sensitive above knee; standardized interpretation.
   d. Disadvantage. Insensitive below knee
   e. Sensitivity/specificity. 90%/90%
3. Doppler ultrasonography
   a. Risk. None
   b. Technique. Ultrasonic amplification above venous channels to determine turbulence
   c. Advantage. Sensitive above knee
   d. Disadvantage. Observer variation; insensitive below knee
   e. Sensitivity/specificity. 90%/90%
4. Thermography. Insufficient experience at present
5. Radioisotope venography. Insufficient experience at present

Recent studies have employed combination of these techniques, either impedance plethysmography and Doppler scanning, or plethysmography and fibrinogen scanning. Although evidence is limited, it appears that both combinations are sufficiently sensitive and specific to diagnose suspected DVT above the knee. One study used venography to confirm the results of the noninvasive tests. The few patients with false negative noninvasive test results remained untreated and developed no apparent progression of calf DVT. Coupled with the small (<2 percent) risk of DVT from venography, these data suggest that venography is unnecessary if noninvasive tests are used to diagnose iliofemoral thrombosis. Suspected calf or popliteal DVT may require venographic confirmation. A proposed scheme for evaluating DVT is presented in figure 13-2.

B. **Pulmonary embolism.** Clinical evaluation of pulmonary embolism (PE) is difficult, because, as necropsy studies attest, most pulmonary emboli are clinically "silent." When present, symptoms and signs are often nonspecific. Common symptoms include dyspnea, chest pain, cough, and hemoptysis; however, massive PE may be heralded by syncope or cardiac arrest. Signs include tachypnea and tachycardia, both present in the majority of patients with PE. Fever or pleural rub may occur in patients with infarction. In massive PE, hypotension accompanied by signs of right heart failure may occur, including increased right ventricular impulse, loud P_2, narrow splitting of S_2, right ventricular S_3, and tricuspid regurgitation murmur.

Laboratory evaluation may be helpful in suggesting, but not confirming, the diagnosis. Nonspecific findings include leukocytosis, elevated ESR, and increased fibrin degradation products. The triad of increased lactic de-

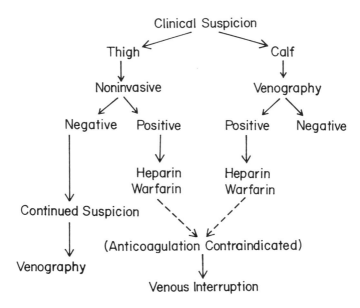

Figure 13-2. Diagnosis of deep venous thrombosis (DVT).

hydrogenase and bilirubin, but normal SGOT, is uncommon. ECG abnormalities occur in about 40 percent of patients, especially those with submassive or massive PE. The chest film also is abnormal in 40 to 70 percent, especially in the presence of infarction. Pleural effusion, if present, is usually hemorrhagic. ECG and chest film findings are summarized in *table 13-3*.

Arterial blood gases usually reveal hypoxemia, hypocapnia, and alkalosis. Massive PE with hypotension and respiratory collapse may lead to hypercapnia and acidosis. Normal oxygenation does not exclude the possibility of PE, although PE is uncommon in patients

Table 13-3
Radiographic and Electrocardiographic
Findings in Pulmonary Embolism

Finding	Frequency (%)
1. Chest x-ray	
Embolism without infarction	90
Normal	7-32
Elevated hemidiaphragm	30-40
Linear shadows	20
Atelectasis	
Thrombosed vessels	
Pleural markings	
Oligemia	80 (massive)
Contralateral hilar enlargement	?
Infarction	10
Infiltrate	90 + (↑with time)
"Hampton's Hump"	<10
Elevated hemidiaphragm	40
Effusion	30-50
2. Electrocardiogram	
Normal	
Massive	6
Submassive	23
Nonspecific T-wave changes	42
Nonspecific ST-segment changes	41
Left-axis deviation	7
Right-axis deviation	7
$S_1Q_3T_3$	<10
Incomplete right bundle-branch block	<10
Atrial arrhythmias	?

with Pa_{O_2} greater than 80 torr, and rare with Pa_{O_2} greater than 90 torr.

In summary, clinical and laboratory evaluation of suspected PE is often nonspecific. Further diagnostic measures include ventilation/perfusion (V/Q) scanning and pulmonary angiography. These techniques are often complementary rather than redundant. Pulmonary angiography is the standard procedure in diagnosing PE; it appears to be extremely sensitive, except possibly in detecting emboli in small distal vessels. A positive result consists of a filling defect in a large vessel or a sharp cutoff in a smaller vessel. Carefully performed, angiography is specific for PE. Risks include contrast reactions, exacerbation of pulmonary hypertension, and local trauma at the catheter site. Mortality is rare—in most series, well below 0.5 percent. Morbidity is 2 to 5 percent.

V/Q scanning involves two scintigraphic procedures: inhalation of radioactive xenon to assess distribution of ventilation, and injection of labeled microspheres or albumin macroaggregates (50 to 100 microns in diameter) to assess pulmonary perfusion. Perfusion scans alone are extremely sensitive for PE; a normal perfusion scan virtually excludes PE. Unfortunately, perfusion scans are nonspecific, especially in patients with pre-existing lung disease. Ventilation scans may increase specificity: corresponding defects in both scans suggest intrinsic lung disease, whereas isolated perfusion defects suggest PE. Recent experience substantiates the utility of both scans:

1. Multiple segmental or lobar perfusion defects with normal ventilation make the diagnosis of PE likely.
2. Nonsegmental or subsegmental perfusion defects with abnormal ventilation make the diagnosis of PE unlikely. Even if nonspecific, perfusion scans may indicate areas of suspicion, allowing for selective angiography, and thereby increasing overall diagnostic yield.

V/Q scans are interpreted as normal, or showing low, medium, or high probability of PE, depending on size and distribution of defects. A normal perfusion scan is considered to exclude PE. However, whether a high probability perfusion scan confirms the clinical diagnosis, or a low probability scan is sufficient to exclude it, is uncertain. Many clinicians prefer to perform angiography in these situations. Strong clinical suspicion should lead to angiography, regardless of nonconfirmatory scan results.

Serial scanning, especially if a premorbid scan is available, may increase scintigraphic detection of PE. However, increased yield is uncertain, and routine scanning of patients with DVT to establish baseline scans is of doubtful benefit. Rarely, if scanning is nonspecific and angiography is unavailable or deemed risky, venography may be used to diagnose DVT, and indirectly, PE. This approach is limited by the need for bilateral venograms if clinical signs are absent, and by the occurrence of negative venograms even in the presence of PE.

Another type of radionuclide scan, using oxygen-labeled carbon dioxide, may have promise in the diagnosis of PE. Because a cyclotron is required to generate the isotope, however, this procedure is not generally available.

In summary, clinical and laboratory evaluation must be supplemented by scanning and angiography to diagnose PE. A scheme for evaluating suspected PE is presented in figure 13-3.

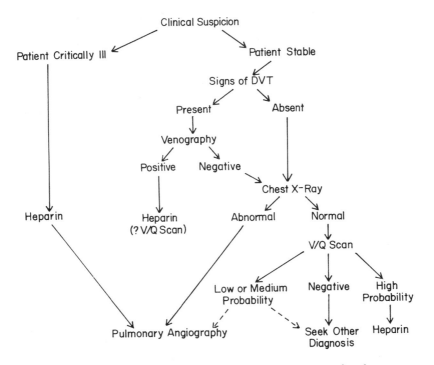

Figure 13-3. Flow chart showing steps to diagnosis of pulmonary embolism (PE).

IV. ALTERATIONS IN LUNG FUNCTION

A. **Volumes.** Acutely, PE usually leads to a reduction in FRC, presumably due to "pneumoconstriction." By 24 to 48 hours, surfactant production decreases in the area of hypoperfusion. This results in atelectasis and further decrease in volumes.

B. **Mechanics.** Airway pressures are usually increased due to constriction of small bronchi and bronchioles. This may be caused by hypocapnia, vasoactive substances released by emboli, or vagal reflexes. Flow rates are usually reduced, due to increased airway resistance.

C. **Gas exchange.** Hypoxemia almost invariably results from PE, primarily due to V/Q inequalities. Animal experiments indicate an increase in units with high V/Q, but few units with complete loss of flow. Shunt is probably a minor contributor to hypoxemia.

D. **Vasculature.** Decreased vascular capacity leads to increased pulmonary vascular resistance. Mechanical obstruction of vessels by emboli may not be sufficient to account for increased pulmonary vascular resistance. Reflex and humoral factors may also contribute through vasoconstriction. Given the high capacitance of the pulmonary circulation, marked obstruction is required before pressures increase. In patients with previously normal cardiopulmonary function, effects of obstruction based on total pulmonary vascular bed occluded are:

1. **Obstruction less than 25%.** Little effect or mild increase in pulmonary artery pressure
2. **Obstruction greater than 25%.** Pulmonary artery pressure increased, usually less than 40 torr
3. **Obstruction greater than 30%.** Increased right atrial pressure
4. **Obstruction greater than 40 to 50%.** Decreased cardiac index

V. TREATMENT

Therapeutic objectives in thromboembolic disease are primarily the prevention of clot formation and propagation, so that pulmonary emboli do not occur. Once emboli are diagnosed, therapy is supportive, seeking to limit complications and prevent further embolic episodes.

A. **Predisposing factors.** As previously noted, the majority of patients with DVT are not recognized clinically. Therefore, recognition of risk factors and prophylaxis for high-risk patients offer the best hope for early intervention. Five types of agents have been used in prophylaxis against thromboembolic disease:

1. **Warfarin.** Warfarin anticoagulation, using prothrombin time as an index of efficacy, is clearly effective in preventing thrombosis. This agent may be contraindicated in several patient groups because of hemorrhagic complications.
2. **Low-dose heparin** ("miniheparin"). This method has been used primarily in postoperative patients. Although standard clotting parameters (PT, PTT, or bleeding time) are unaffected, several large studies demonstrate the efficacy of low-dose heparin in reducing thrombosis and embolism. Exceptions include patients who have undergone hip surgery, neurosurgery, and open prostatectomy. Efficacy in medical patients is less certain. Dose is 5000 units subcutaneously every 8 to 12 hours.
3. **Antiplatelet agents.** Aspirin and sulfinpyrazone have been used to interfere with platelet function, perhaps decreasing the tendency to thrombosis. Evidence of efficacy is meager; with regard to hip surgery, evidence is conflicting.
4. **Dextran.** This high molecular weight compound acts by an unknown mechanism, perhaps by increasing intravascular volume, preventing endothelial damage, or diminishing platelet aggregation. Its efficacy is unknown.
5. **Mechanical compression.** Support stockings are not effective in preventing thrombosis. Intermittent pneumatic compression by calf boots yielded good results in neurosurgical and urologic studies, but experience is limited, and tolerance by patients may be poor.

Despite persistent controversy, low-dose heparin is probably indicated in hospitalized patients judged at risk for PE, if no contraindications are present. Patients who have had several episodes of DVT or PE should be chronically anticoagulated if no contraindication exists.

B. **Heparin.** The mainstay of therapy in thromboembolic disease is heparin. A wealth of clinical experience, but surprisingly little experimental evidence, supports its efficacy. Heparin does not directly lead to clot lysis, but rather halts clot propagation, enabling endogenous fibrinolytic mechanisms to remove clot. Heparin may be given by continuous infusion or intermittent injection; the former method may reduce hemorrhagic complications. Heparin should be administered immediately after the diagnosis of DVT or PE, or before if there is a strong suspicion that either disorder is present. Usual doses are 5000 to 10,000 units loading dose (bolus), followed by 800 to 1500 units/hr infusion, maintaining PTT at 1.5 to 2.5 times control. Although the optimal duration of heparin therapy is uncertain, treatment for 5 to 7 days with DVT, and 7 to 10 days with PE, followed by warfarin anticoagulation is recommended. Warfarin may be begun concurrently, and is usually continued for several weeks to 3 months in DVT, and for 6 months in PE. Subcutaneous heparin may also be used for anticoagulation after intravenous heparin therapy is complete. A recent study found fewer bleeding complications with heparin than with warfarin.

Heparin is among the drugs most commonly associated with morbidity and mortality in hospitalized patients. Complications are primarily hemorrhagic; hypersensitivity is rare. Thrombocytopenia, which occurs in 10 to 15 percent of patients, appears to be more common in patients treated with bovine-lung heparin.

C. **Fibrinolytic agents.** Fibrinolytic therapy has been advocated as superior to heparin for both DVT and PE. Fibrinolytic agents, urokinase and streptokinase, act by accelerating endogenous fibrinolytic activity. Their effect is to prevent clot propagation and promote clot lysis. In DVT, fibrinolytic agents have been shown in small series to hasten venographic improvement, and possibly, to decrease late venous insufficiency.

Fibrinolytic agents have been studied extensively in PE. The largest study, the Urokinase Pulmonary Embolism Trial, was divided into two phases. The first phase demonstrated more rapid angiographic and hemodynamic improvement with urokinase, compared with heparin, especially in cases of massive emboli. The second phase showed little difference between 12 and 24 hours of urokinase, and demonstrated the superiority of urokinase to streptokinase only in massive embolism. Both thrombolytic agents were judged better than heparin as referred to controls for the first phase of the study. Other smaller studies subsequently compared heparin to streptokinase in massive embolism and found streptokinase superior. A recent study indicated improved diffusion and perfusion parameters with streptokinase compared to heparin, at 1-year follow-up. None of these studies was sufficiently large to demonstrate a reduction in mortality with thrombolytic agents.

Disadvantages of fibrinolytic agents include increased cost of urokinase and, with streptokinase, increased antigenicity leading to fever and rash. Hemorrhagic complications may be no worse than with heparin. Both urokinase and streptokinase are contraindicated postoperatively for 10 days. These agents are recommended for treating PE that is accompanied by systemic hypotension or marked clinical deterioration. In these patients, rapid reduction in pulmonary vascular pressures may be particularly important. Heparin and warfarin should then follow in the doses described above. Clinical use of anticoagulants and fibrinolytic agents is summarized in *table 13-4*.

D. Surgery. Surgical therapy of thromboembolic disease is infrequently indicated. Experience in the United States with thrombectomy for DVT is limited, and indications for embolectomy in PE are controversial. If performed, surgical embolectomy, which requires cardiopulmonary bypass, should be limited to hypotensive or critically ill patients because of the high risk of mortality. No comparison between surgery and thrombolytic agents is available. Catheter embolectomy via an angiographic approach may be less risky than open surgery, but few data are available.

E. Vena caval interruption. Occasionally, PE is suspected in patients previously anticoagulated, or in patients in whom anticoagulation is contraindicated. An approach to this situation is presented in figure 13-4.

Of methods available for surgical interruption of the venous system, those involving the inferior vena cava are preferable to bilateral femoral vein ligation. Risk of recurrence and stasis is increased with femoral vein procedures. Inferior vena cava ligation poses a serious risk of mortality, and should be reserved for patients with septic emboli or recurrent emboli causing pulmonary hypertension.

Fenestrated clips are used for the other indications noted above. These devices have an early patency rate of about 85 percent, with surgical mortality ranging

Table 13-4
Anticoagulant and Fibrinolytic Therapy of Thromboembolic Disease

Drug	Dose	Monitor*	Duration
Heparin	5000 to 10,000 U bolus; 800 to 1500 U/hour (usual)	PTT	DVT: 5-7 days; PE: 7-10 days
Warfarin	5-10 mg/day (usual)	PT	DVT: 6 weeks-3 months; PE: 6 months
Urokinase	4400 U/kg over 10 minutes; 4400 U/kg/hour	TT or PTT after 2 hours	12-24 hours
Streptokinase	250,000 U over 20 minutes; 100,000 U/hour	TT or PTT after 2 hours	24 hours

*PTT = partial thromboplastin time
PT = prothrombin time
TT = thrombin time

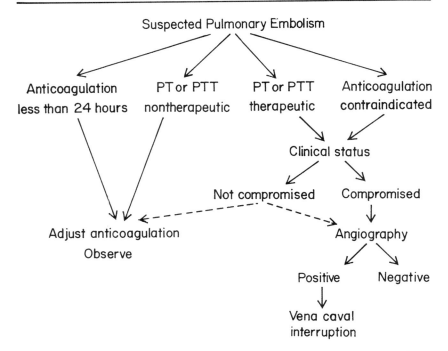

Figure 13-4. Therapy for pulmonary embolism (PE) in patients who have been anticoagulated, or for whom anticoagulants have been contraindicated.

from 0 to 40 percent. Embolism recurs in 0 to 30 percent—and fatal embolism in 0 to 20 percent—of patients subjected to this procedure. Transvenous filter placement is usually reserved for patients in whom an open procedure is contraindicated. Several types of filter are available: the Mobin-Uddin umbrella is most widely used, although several studies report decreased recurrence with the Kimray-Greenfield device. If possible, anticoagulation treatment should be continued after the interruption procedure.

VI. NATURAL HISTORY AND PROGNOSIS

Venographic resolution of DVT may begin several days after the event, although changes often persist for weeks. Most patients with DVT suffer few long-term effects, although they remain at increased risk for additional thromboembolic episodes. A minority develops chronic venous insufficiency, with pedal edema and stasis dermatitis. Patients with recurrent DVT should be evaluated for predisposing factors, and treated with anticoagulants if possible.

Resolution of pulmonary emboli begins rapidly—in animal models as early as 2 to 3 days. Resolution appears to be hastened by heparin, and especially, by fibrinolytic agents. Complete resolution may occur as early as 10 to 15 days, although angiographic defects usually persist for weeks. Follow-up perfusion scans generally show complete resolution of defects by 6 to 12 months.

Most patients with massive emboli die within 1 hour. In patients with smaller emboli, death is due to coexistent chronic disease rather than to embolism. Physiologic abnormalities related to capillary bed volume (e.g., D_{LCO}) persist after PE, according to some studies. Eventual resolution is uncertain. Chronic cor pulmonale appears uncommon in recognized and treated PE patients, but it may occur in cases of "silent" or undiagnosed recurrent PE. Patients with vena caval interruption often have leg pain, swelling, and dermatitis. However, one series found no greater incidence than in other patients with thromboembolic disease. Patients with PE remain at increased risk of recurrent thromboembolic disease.

VII. OTHER TYPES OF THROMBOEMBOLIC DISEASE

A. **Upper extremity venous thrombosis.** This syndrome, which occurs primarily in hospitalized patients, is due to cannulation of upper extremity veins. The infrequent occurrence of arm, compared to leg, thrombosis may be a consequence of fewer valves, greater motion, and higher blood temperature in the upper extremity. Clinical characteristics of upper extremity thrombosis resemble those of lower extremity thrombosis, and venography and heparin therapy appear to be indicated.

B. **Septic embolism.** Septic emboli usually occur in patients with endocarditis (e.g., tricuspid, or left-sided, with VSD) or septic thrombophlebitis. A less common source is staphylococcal osteomyelitis. A cardiac origin of embolism is highly likely in patients with rheumatic or congenital heart disease, drug addiction, or alcoholism. Septic thrombophlebitis most often occurs in intravenous drug abusers, or in patients with pelvic infection, pharyngeal infection, or indwelling venous catheters. Staphylococci and streptococci are the organisms commonly cultured, although mixed infections also occur.

Diagnosis is based on chest x-ray evidence of multiple ill-defined peripheral infiltrates, apparently migratory. Cavitation occurs frequently, but pleural effusion is uncommon. Clinical findings are nonspecific: fever, rigors, and tachycardia. Careful cardiac and peripheral examination may disclose a source for emboli. Treatment consists of antibiotics and removal of foreign material or septic veins.

C. **Fat embolism.** The characteristics of the fat embolism syndrome remain controversial, and its incidence is uncertain. It appears that fat embolism most often follows lower extremity trauma, usually fractures. Necropsy series disclose emboli in the majority of post-traumatic or postfracture deaths, whereas the incidence in clinical studies is less than 10 percent. Pathogenesis is thought to depend on fat entering torn veins near a fracture site. Triglycerides are then carried to the lungs, and converted by lipase to chemically active fatty acids. These, in turn, damage vascular endothelium. Other conditions associated with fat embolism are pancreatitis, burns, diabetes mellitus, corticosteroid therapy, and extracorporeal circulation.

Clinical manifestations appear 1 to 2 days after injury, and consist of cough, dyspnea, fever, and tachypnea. The fully expressed syndrome evolves into ARDS, as described in Chapter 6. Central nervous system and skin changes are common, chiefly depression of sensorium and petechiae, respectively. While no specific diagnostic test exists, the fat embolism syndrome is defined by presence of petechial rash, depression of sensorium, and pulmonary findings of ARDS several days after trauma. Therapy is that of ARDS. Evidence supporting steroid therapy is inconclusive.

D. **Amniotic fluid embolism.** Infusion of amniotic fluid into endocervical veins, placental site, or myometrium leads to a life-threatening postpartum syndrome. Fluid is transported to the lung, leading to

   1. Vascular obstruction by fetal squames
   2. Possible anaphylactoid reaction to meconium
   3. Disseminated intravascular coagulation (DIC), due to amniotic fluid proteins

   Older, multiparous women are predisposed to amniotic fluid embolism, which is associated with fetal death, difficult labor, and meconium-stained amniotic fluid. Clinical presentation is similar to that of other episodes of PE, except that hypotension is common and prognosis is dismal. Most patients die within hours of the event. Therapy is supportive.

REFERENCES

I. Deep Venous Thrombosis

A. Reviews

Madden JL, Hume M: *Venous Thromboembolism: Prevention and Treatment.* New York, Appleton-Century-Crofts, 1976.

Nicolaides AN (ed): *Thromboembolism: Etiology, Advances in Prevention and Management.* Baltimore, University Park Press, 1975.

Sasahara AA, Sharma GVRK, Parisi AF: New developments in the detection and prevention of venous thromboembolism. *Am J Cardiol* 43:1214-1224, 1979.

Madden and Nicolaides are detailed but somewhat dated collections; Sasahara offers a brief recent review.

B. Natural history

Coon WS: Epidemiology of venous thromboembolism. *Ann Surg* 186:149-164, 1977.

Mudge M, Hughes LE: The long term sequelae of deep venous thrombosis. *Br J Surg* 65:672-674, 1978.

Sevitt S, Gallagher N: Venous thrombosis and pulmonary embolism. *Br J Surg* 48:475-489, 1961.

Coon discusses risk factors; Mudge considers the occurrence of late venous insufficiency. Sevitt presents an early study establishing DVT as a precursor of PE.

C. Diagnosis

Flanigan DP, Goodreau JJ, Burnham SJ, et al: Vascular laboratory diagnosis of clinically suspected acute deep venous thrombosis. *Lancet* 2:331-334, 1978.

McLachlin J, Richards T, Paterson JC: An evaluation of clinical signs in the diagnosis of venous thrombosis. *Arch Surg* 85:738-744, 1962.

Richards KL, Armstrong JD Jr, Tikoff D, et al: Noninvasive diagnosis of deep venous thrombosis. *Arch Intern Med* 136:1091-1096, 1976.

Hull R, Hirsh J, Sackett DL, et al: Replacement of venography in suspected venous thrombosis by impedance plethysmography and 125 I-fibrinogen leg scanning: a less invasive approach. *Ann Intern Med* 94:12-15, 1981.

Flanigan, McLachlin, and Richards document the inaccuracy of clinical evaluation; Flanigan and Richards also consider accuracy of noninvasive diagnostic methods. Hull compares noninvasive tests with venography, indicating adequacy of these methods.

D. Therapy

Harris WH, Salzman EW, Athanasoulis CA, et al: Aspirin prophylaxis of venous thromboembolism after total hip replacement. *N Engl J Med* 297: 1246-1249, 1977.

Kiil J, Kiil J, Axelsen F, et al: Prophylaxis against postoperative pulmonary embolism and deep venous thrombosis by low-dose heparin. *Lancet* 1: 1114-1116, 1978.

Marder VT: Guidelines for thrombolytic therapy of deep venous thrombosis. *Prog Cardiovasc Dis* 21:327-332, 1979.

Skillman JJ, Collins RE, Coe NP, et al: Prevention of deep venous thrombosis in neurosurgical patients: a controlled randomized trial of external pneumatic compression boots. *Surgery* 83:354-358, 1978.

Strandness DE: The case against low-dose heparin. In *Current Controversies in Cardiovascular Disease*. Edited by Rapoport E, Philadelphia, WB Saunders, 1980, 483-487.

Wessler S: Low-dose heparin significantly reduces the incidence of postoperative pulmonary emboli and should be used routinely in general abdominal and thoracic surgery. In *Current Controversies in Cardiovascular Disease*. Edited by Rapoport E, Philadelphia, WB Saunders, 1980, pp 488-496.

All but Marder discuss methods of prophylaxis; Strandness and Wessler summarize data on low-dose heparin. Marder considers thrombolytic agents in DVT.

II. Pulmonary Embolism

A. Reviews

Fishman AP: Pulmonary thromboembolism. In *Pulmonary Diseases and Disorders*. Edited by Fishman AP, New York, McGraw-Hill, 1980, pp 809-816.

Moser KM: Pulmonary embolism. *Am Rev Respir Dis* 115:829-852, 1977.

Robin ED: Overdiagnosis and overtreatment of pulmonary embolism: the emperor may have no clothes. *Ann Intern Med* 87:775-781, 1977.

Sharma GVRK, Sasahara AA: Diagnosis and treatment of pulmonary embolism. *Med Clin North Am* 63:239-250, 1979.

Fishman, Moser, and Sharma provide good general discussions. Robin questions the accuracy of noninvasive diagnosis.

B. Natural history

Dalen JE, Alpert JS: Natural history of pulmonary embolism. *Prog Cardiovasc Dis* 17:259-270, 1975.

Dalen JE, Banas IS, Brooks HL, et al: Resolution rate of acute pulmonary embolism in man. *N Engl J Med* 280:194-199, 1969.

Sharma GVRK, Burleson V, Sasahara AA: Effect of thrombolytic therapy on pulmonary-capillary blood volume. *N Engl J Med* 303:842-845, 1980.

Both articles by Dalen provide evidence that resolution of pulmonary embolism occurs over weeks to months. Sharma finds improvement in vascular patency with thrombolytic therapy.

C. Diagnosis

Bell WR, Simon TL, DeMets DL: The clinical features of submassive and massive pulmonary embolism. *Am J Med* 62:355-360, 1977.

Cheely R, McCartney WH, Perry JR, et al: The role of noninvasive tests versus pulmonary angiography in the diagnosis of pulmonary embolism. *Am J Med* 70:17-22, 1981.

Szucs MM: Diagnostic sensitivity of laboratory findings in acute pulmonary embolism. *Ann Intern Med* 74:61-66, 1971.

Bell analyzes the UPET data (see below), indicating nonspecificity of clinical evaluation and utility of perfusion scans. Cheely provides evidence that ventilation/perfusion scanning may supplant angiography in some cases. Szucs finds that other laboratory evidence is nonspecific.

D. Treatment

Genton E: Thrombolytic therapy of pulmonary thromboembolism. *Prog Cardiovasc Dis* 21:333-341, 1979.

UPET Study Group: Urokinase pulmonary embolism trial: phase I results. *JAMA* 214:2163-2172, 1970.

UPET Study Group: Urokinase-streptokinase embolism trial. *JAMA* 22:606-613, 1974.

Weissler S, Gitel GN: Heparin: new concepts relevant to clinical use. *Blood* 53:525-544, 1979.

Genton summarizes evidence concerning thrombolytic therapy. Results from both UPET studies establish the utility of these agents. Weissler reviews use and side effects of heparin.

14
Preoperative Evaluation and Postoperative Management

Pulmonary problems are among the most common complications of surgery. Pulmonary morbidity is approximately 3 to 6 percent, and mortality about 1 percent, for surgical patients over the age of 40. Four major issues to be addressed regarding pulmonary care of surgical patients are: effects of anesthesia and surgery; assessment of surgical risk; prevention of postoperative complications; and specific problems associated with pulmonary resection.

I. EFFECTS OF ANESTHESIA AND SURGERY ON LUNG FUNCTION

Effects upon lung function vary with the proximity of the incision to the diaphragm. Loss of function is greatest in upper abdominal and thoracic surgery and decreases with lower abdominal and extremity surgery.

A. **Volumes.** Static lung volumes decrease 25 to 50 percent after an abdominal operation. In particular, vital capacity decreases 45 percent (55 percent for upper abdominal, 40 percent for lower abdominal procedures) for 1 to 2 days postoperatively, returning to preoperative levels over 1 to 2 weeks. RV and FRC decrease 10 to 20 percent, with the nadir on the fourth postoperative day. Mechanisms responsible for these changes in lung function include recumbency, splinting, and analgesia.

B. **Mechanics.** Compliance is usually decreased after abdominal surgery, perhaps due to atelectasis with alveolar collapse (see below).

C. **Gas exchange.** Hypoxemia is common intraoperatively and postoperatively, due to increases in V/Q inequalities. Causes of hypoxemia include recumbency, immobilization, and maldistribution of ventilation due to splinting. Pa_{O_2} usually returns to normal within 1 week postoperatively.

D. **Ventilatory pattern.** After laparotomy, tidal volume decreases about 20 percent and respiratory rate increases about 26 percent, leading to preservation of minute ventilation. These changes occur in the first 24 hours postoperatively, usually as a result of splinting and recumbency, and improve in the second postoperative week.

Other effects of surgery include interference with defense mechanisms such as cough, ciliary function, mucus composition, and mucus clearance.

II. **ASSESSMENT OF SURGICAL RISK**

A. **Risk factors for surgical procedures.** Beyond type of surgery, risk relates to underlying disease and duration of procedure. Risk factors for postoperative complications are summarized in *table 14-1*.

Spirometry appears more sensitive than static lung volumes in assessing specific pulmonary risks of surgery. Spirometric values help differentiate patients at low or high risk, but patients at moderate risk are not further distinguished. Measurement of arterial blood gases (ABG) is a valuable adjunct, as hypercapnia constitutes high risk. Hypoxemia, however, is less reliable as a risk factor. This is especially true in pulmonary surgery, where the affected area may contribute little to gas exchange. Patients undergoing thoracic or abdominal surgery, and those with the risk factors delineated above, should undergo spirometry. Those judged at higher risk should also have ABG evaluation. Pulmonary indicators of high risk are summarized in *table 14-2*.

B. **Preoperative assessment for lung resection.** If staging and overall clinical status show a patient to be a good surgical risk, the level of preoperative pulmonary function determines ability to survive lung resection. Contraindications to surgery, except perhaps for very limited resections, are an FEV_1 less than 1.0 L and a Pa_{CO_2} greater than 45 torr. Patients with FEV_1 greater than 2.0 L probably can tolerate procedures including pneumonectomy, while those with FEV_1 between 1.0 and 2.0 L require further evaluation. Methods include per-

Table 14-1
Risk Factors For Surgery

	Relative Risk
1. Pre-operative	
a. General	
Age greater than 60	3-4x
Obesity (30% over ideal weight)	2x
Smoking (more than 10 cigarettes/d)	2-7x
Alcoholism	
Coma	
b. Specific	
Acute or chronic pulmonary disease	3-4x
Sepsis	3x
Hematologic disorder	
Acid-base imbalance	
Electrolyte abnormality	
2. Intraoperative	
Proximity of incision to diaphragm	
Emergency procedure	
Shock	
Anesthesia longer than 3 hours	
3. Specific Risks	
a. Pulmonary embolus (See Chapter 13)	
b. Bleeding	
Trauma	
Anticoagulants	
Shock	
Cardiac or vascular surgery	
c. Aspiration	
Emergency procedure	
Full stomach	
Coma	
Narcotics	
Swallowing disorders	

fusion scans, lateral position pulmonary function tests, and balloon occlusion of the pulmonary artery.

1. **Quantitative perfusion lung scanning.** This is similar to the procedure used in diagnosing pulmonary emboli. Postoperative function is predicted from pre-

Table 14-2
Pulmonary Risk Factors for Surgery

Spirometry
  Maximal breathing capacity (MBC) less than 50% of predicted
  FVC less than 1.85 L
  FEV_1 less than 1.2 L

Arterial blood gases
  Pa_{CO_2} greater than 45
  Possibly level of oxygenation

---

operative pulmonary function and perfusion estimates. Thus, percent perfusion of the area to be resected is measured; the decrement in FEV_1 following resection will correspond to the perfusion loss measured preoperatively. Correlation with postoperative function is good in resections involving four or more segments, and less accurate for limited resections. The addition of ventilation scans and V/Q correlation permits more sophisticated calculations and may increase accuracy. Risk associated with pneumonectomy appears moderate (15 percent or less) if the predicted postoperative FEV_1 is greater than 800 ml. One study, however, noted a disproportionate loss of function in the early postoperative period, indicating that risks must be carefully weighed in patients with marginal function.

2. **Lateral position test.** If scanning is unavailable, this procedure may be used. Spirometry performed with the diseased lung in the dependent position correlates adequately with scans and outcome. Guidelines for pneumonectomy are similar to those mentioned above for perfusion lung scanning.

3. **Balloon occlusion of the pulmonary artery.** This procedure evaluates pulmonary artery pressures. Pulmonary hypertension in the lung that is to remain is a contraindication to pneumonectomy; if mean Pa pressure during unilateral occlusion is greater than 30 torr, the risk associated with pneumonectomy is high. This test is rarely indicated, except perhaps in patients with primary vascular disease who are being considered for pneumonectomy.

III. POSTOPERATIVE COMPLICATIONS
  A. Types of complications
    1. Atelectasis. This is defined as the collapse of lung units. Clinically, atelectasis is manifested by increased work of breathing and low-grade fever, and occasionally by radiographic abnormalities. Functionally, atelectasis leads to decreased ventilation and hypoxemia, due to V/Q inequalities and increased shunt. Causes of atelectasis include retained secretions, decreased FRC due to splinting and recumbency, and perhaps, lack of periodic hyperinflations. The most important factor appears to be decreased FRC. Because of the alveolar pressure gradient down the lung, dependent lung units collapse at low lung volumes. If the FRC is depressed below this "closing volume," atelectasis may occur during tidal breathing.
    2. Infection. Atelectasis predisposes to infection, as does decreased cough resulting from splinting and analgesia.
    3. Respiratory failure. This postoperative complication is discussed in Chapter 5.
    4. Pulmonary embolus. This occurs in 1 percent of patients over the age of 40 who have major surgery. Fat embolism may occur after orthopedic procedures. For discussion, see Chapter 13.
    5. Pulmonary edema. This often results from volume overload in patients with impaired cardiac function.
    6. Aspiration. This tends to occur in patients with altered mental status or depressed gag reflex.
    Other complications, such as pneumothorax and subcutaneous emphysema, relate to specific procedures.
  B. Prevention of postoperative complications. Careful attention to care and education of patients, both before and after surgery, has been shown to decrease the incidence of postoperative pulmonary complications.
    1. Preoperative measures. Careful assessment of surgical risk, with appropriate choice of anesthetic and procedure, is mandatory, as described above. Other measures include education of the patient, physiotherapy, and medications.
      a. Patient education. Careful description of the

procedure, the effects of anesthesia, and the expected postoperative course, can decrease analgesic requirements and encourage patient cooperation with respiratory maneuvers.
   b. **Physiotherapy.** Although preoperative chest physiotherapy has not been rigorously examined, it appears to be justified in patients with chronic bronchitis who produce large volumes of sputum. Use of this measure in other patients is of uncertain benefit.
   c. **Medications.** Patients with reversible pulmonary disease, such as bronchospasm, should have medications adjusted preoperatively in an attempt to maximize pulmonary function.
2. **Intraoperative.** Surgeon and anesthesiologist both should attempt to decrease the duration of anesthesia and avoid hypoxemia and hypotension, which may, in turn, contribute to postoperative respiratory failure. Commonly used agents in "balanced" anesthetic technique act to depress respiration, an effect that can be rectified by careful postoperative observation.
3. **Postoperative.** Use of recovery areas is now a routine procedure to allow for resolution of anesthetic effect. Other postoperative measures include:
   a. **Analgesia.** Care should be taken to avoid oversedation, because of its concomitant respiratory and cough depression.
   b. **Early mobilization.** Assumption of the erect position increases FRC, thereby preventing atelectasis. Mobilization also increases respiratory effort and reduces the risk of thromboembolic events.
   c. **Physiotherapy.** As noted previously, chest physiotherapy is probably useful in patients who are unable to clear copious secretions. In some patients, intermittent suctioning may suffice.
   d. **Respiratory maneuvers.** These are designed to reverse the deleterious effects of surgery, primarily by increasing FRC and preventing atelectasis. FRC is increased by augmenting alveolar pressure, which, in turn, is accomplished by increasing inhaled volume. Various techniques have been employed, including expiratory maneuvers, positive pressure breathing, and inhalation maneuvers.

(1) **Expiratory maneuvers** (e.g., blow bottles). In forced expiration, pleural pressure exceeds airway pressure, and alveoli deflate. By diminishing, instead of augmenting, alveolar pressure, this maneuver may counteract the desired effect on FRC.

(2) **Positive pressure breathing** (e.g., IPPB). This technique may increase alveolar pressure, but the volume of gas delivered (and thus the effect on alveolar pressure) is dependent upon peak airways pressure. When atelectasis reduces FRC, the volume required to achieve peak airway pressure decreases, diminishing the effect of positive pressure breathing. In addition, positive pressure breathing may lead to barotrauma and circulatory depression.

(3) **Inhalation maneuvers** (e.g., incentive spirometry). Stimulating voluntary inhalation increases inhaled volume and therefore alveolar pressure, without incurring the complications of positive pressure. It is thus the ideal method for increasing FRC. Patient cooperation is required in order to achieve adequate inspirations. Currently, incentive spirometry is considered the most effective means of encouraging deep inspiration and preventing atelectasis.

Other postoperative measures include careful attention to volume status to avoid pulmonary edema, and prevention of aspiration by careful sedation and selective nasogastric suction.

IV. EFFECTS OF PULMONARY RESECTION

A. **Physiologic adaptations.** Removal of one lung leads to the expansion of the remaining lung as pleural pressure decreases. Static volumes decrease, although RV is relatively less affected. Expansion reduces compliance of the remaining lung. Gas exchange may be preserved at rest if the remaining lung is normal, but reserve is limited. Similarly, vasculature may be little affected at rest. In the absence of other disease, mean PA pressure remains normal until cardiac output is doubled. Physiologic changes following pneumonectomy are summarized in *table 14-3*.

Table 14-3
Functional Effects of Pneumonectomy

1. Volumes
   Vital capacity decreased
   Residual volume (relatively less) decreased
   RV/TLC increased

2. Pressures
   Pleural pressure decreased
   Compliance decreased

Gas exchange
   ABG may be normal (if remaining lung is normal)
   Diffusing capacity decreased

Vasculature
   PA pressure little changed (unless remaining lung is abnormal)

B. **Early postoperative problems.** Common problems after pneumonectomy include empyemas, residual intrapleural spaces, and bronchopleural fistulas. Empyemas, which occur in less than 5 percent of pneumonectomies, usually arise in the early postoperative period as a result of infection of residual serous fluid. Common organisms include staphylococci, *Pseudomonas*, streptococci, and *Aerobacter*. Treatment consists of antibiotics and drainage. Residual intrapleural spaces may become infected, leading to late empyema. However, these spaces usually resolve spontaneously over several months without infection, regardless of the presence of fluid.

Bronchopleural fistulas develop in less than 3 percent of pneumonectomy patients, especially in those with tuberculosis. Fever, cough, air leak, or drainage, occurring 7 to 14 days postoperatively, suggest the presence of a fistula. Many fistulas will resolve with chest tube drainage, but the majority require further surgery.

C. **Late postoperative problems.** Expansion of the remaining lung causes the mediastinum to shift toward the lateral chest wall on the resected side. This is not functionally harmful, and requires no therapy. The postpneumonectomy space remains gas-filled postoperatively. Over the ensuing 1 to 7 months, gas is resorbed and serosanguineous fluid fills the space. A fall in the fluid level should raise the possibility of bronchopleural fistula. If a fistula is demonstrated, antibiotics and drainage should be instituted for presumed infection, followed by fistula closure.

REFERENCES

I. General

Bendixen HH: Pulmonary problems in the postoperative patient. In *Pulmonary Diseases and Disorders*. Edited by Fishman AP, New York, McGraw-Hill, 1980, pp 1711-1727.

Rehder K, Sessler AD, Marsh HM: General anesthesia and the lung. *Am Rev Respir Dis* 112:541-563, 1975.

Tisi GM: Preoperative evaluation of pulmonary function. *Am Rev Respir Dis* 119:293-310, 1979.

In their reviews of pulmonary dysfunction due to surgery, Bendixen concentrates on postoperative problems, whereas Tisi discusses preoperative evaluation. Rehder reviews animal and human evidence concerning the effects of anesthesia.

II. Prevention of Postoperative Problems

Bartlett RH, Gazzinga AB, Geraghty TR: Respiratory maneuvers to prevent postoperative complications. *JAMA* 124:1017-1021, 1973.

Dohi S, Gold MI; Comparison of two methods of postoperative respiratory care. *Chest* 73:592-595, 1978.

Hedley-Whyte J, et al: Critical analysis of preventive measures. In *Applied Physiology of Respiratory Care*. Edited by Hedley-Whyte J, et al, Boston, Little, Brown, 1976, pp 119-132.

Bartlett presents a clear discussion of the physiology of postoperative maneuvers, favoring incentive spirometry. Dohi, in a comparative study of spirometry and IPPB, shows the results to be comparable, with IPPB causing complications. Hedley-Whyte discusses alteration of risk factors, and recommends the use of incentive spirometry.

III. Pneumonectomy

Ali MK, Mountain CF, Ewer MS, et al: Predicting loss of pulmonary function after pulmonary resection for bronchogenic carcinoma. *Chest* 77:337-342, 1980.

Epstein PE: Effects of pulmonary resection. In *Pulmonary Diseases and Disorders*. Edited by Fishman, AP, New York, McGraw-Hill, 1980, pp 1701-1708.

Kirsh MM, Rotman H, Behrendt DM, et al: Complications of pulmonary resection. *Ann Thorac Surg* 20:215-216, 1975.

Walkup RH, Vossel LE, Griffin JP, et al: Prediction of postoperative pulmonary function with the lateral position test. *Chest* 77:24-27, 1980.

Ali and Walkup document the use of scanning and the lateral position test, respectively, in assessing patients for pneumonectomy. Kirsh discusses operative complications of pneumonectomy, whereas Epstein summarizes physiologic and natural history data.

15
Disorders of Respiratory Control

I. **DEFINITION**

Disorders of respiratory control are manifested by changes in alveolar ventilation. Alveolar ventilation is defined and measured with reference to carbon dioxide excretion:

$$\dot{V}_A = \dot{V}_{CO_2} / Pa_{CO_2}$$

where $\dot{V}_{CO_2}$ is carbon dioxide production. Alveolar ventilation and Pa_{CO_2} are tightly controlled in normal subjects, with little fluctuation, despite hemodynamic and metabolic changes. Abnormalities in respiratory control, therefore, lead to hyperventilation or hypoventilation, reflected in decreased Pa_{CO_2} or increased Pa_{CO_2}, respectively.

Hyperventilation usually is an episodic complication of systemic disorders, such as encephalopathy or, occasionally, severe hypoxemia. Hypoventilation more often is chronic, occurring in both systemic disorders and primary lung disease. Most disorders of respiratory control result in alveolar hypoventilation.

Two major types of alveolar hypoventilation syndromes may be distinguished: **disorders in which intrinsic lung function is relatively well preserved; and disorders in which lung function is abnormal.** Examples of the latter group are emphysema and chronic bronchitis; mechanisms of hypoventilation in these disorders are discussed in Chapter 4. Diseases in which the airways and lung parenchyma are intact will be discussed here.

Normal respiratory pathways are described in Chapter 1. Dysfunction may occur at various points in the sequence, as shown in figure 15-1. Alveolar hypoventilation syndromes

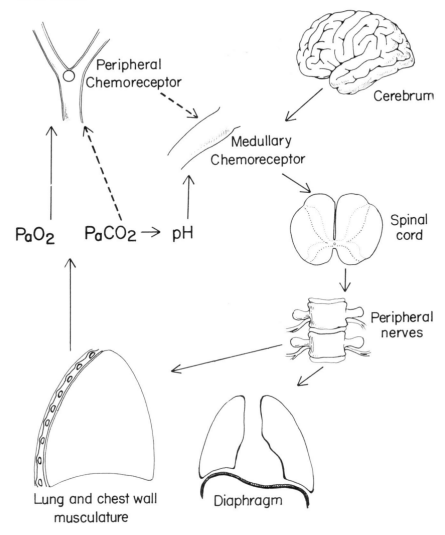

Figure 15-1. Pathways of respiratory control.

correspond to these anatomic deficits, as presented in *table 15-1*.

II. PRIMARY ALVEOLAR HYPOVENTILATION

A. **Automatic ventilatory dysfunction.** This syndrome is best known as Ondine's curse, from the title of a play by Jean Giraudoux. Patients have adequate ventilation while awake, but profound apnea occurs with sleep.

Table 15-1
Alveolar Hypoventilation Syndromes

Anatomic Source	Syndrome

1. Disorders of Ventilatory Control

Cerebral	Functional
	  Sleep
	  Metabolic alkalosis
	  Drugs
	  Hypercapnia
	Structural
	  Neurologic: status epilepticus, Parkinson's disease
	  Infection: encephalitis, tetanus
	  Vascular: bilateral infarction

Brain stem	Functional
	  Myxedema
	  Metabolic alkalosis
	Structural
	  Infarction
	  Poliomyelitis
	Idiopathic
	  Primary alveolar hypoventilation
	  Obesity-hypoventilation
	  Sleep apnea

Spinal cord pathways	Cervical cord trauma or cordotomy Transverse myelitis Multiple sclerosis Parkinson's disease
Peripheral receptor	Carotid body destruction or resection Familial dysautonomia Diabetes mellitus

2. Disorders of Respiratory Pump

Spinal cord (anterior horn cells)	Poliomyelitis Amyotrophic lateral sclerosis
Peripheral nerves	Landry-Guillain-Barre Paralytic shellfish poisoning Acute intermittent porphyria Phrenic nerve paralysis
Myoneural junction	Myasthenia gravis (and related syndromes) Botulism Fish poisoning (ciguatera)

(Table 15-1 continued)

Anatomic source	Syndrome

Respiratory muscles	Dystrophic
	  Myotonia
	  Duchenne's
	Collagen-vascular
	  Polymyositis
	  Systemic lupus erythematosus
	Metabolic
	  Hypokalemia
	  Hypophosphatemia
	  Pompe's disease

Disorders of Chest Wall	Kyphoscoliosis Flail chest Thoracoplasty

Modified with permission of WB Saunders Company from *Diagnosis of Diseases of the Chest*, 2nd ed. (p 1920) by Fraser RG, Pare JAP, © 1979.

In one series of 30 cases, 15 individuals had prior or coexisting central nervous system disease, but lungs and chest wall were substantially normal. The syndrome apparently results from a deficient central chemoreceptor response to carbon dioxide. Symptoms include headache, somnolence, confusion, and irritability; dyspnea does not occur.

Functional tests in some patients reveal the ability to increase ventilation while awake, but a decreased response to increasing carbon dioxide concentrations. In a few patients in whom pathologic data were available, bilateral tegmental medullary infarcts were found. Pharmacologic agents show little benefit in these patients. Diaphragmatic pacing (see below) may be useful in some cases.

B. **Other primary hypoventilation syndromes.** Decreased ventilatory responses to both hypoxia and hypercapnia, with occasional respiratory failure on this basis, have been reported in isolated cases and in a few families. Abnormalities are often exacerbated during sleep and may contribute to the sudden infant death syndrome (SIDS). Patients who have undergone bilateral glomectomy (carotid body resection) as therapy for asthma have normal ventilation at rest, but response to hypoxemia and hypercapnia is blunted.

C. **Secondary hypoventilation.** Defects in ventilatory drive or response may occur at any of the steps noted in figure 15-1.
  1. Central nervous system
     a. **Decreased central respiratory drive** may be due to cerebral or brain stem dysfunction. Causes include encephalitis and infarction and drugs such as barbiturates and opiates. Drugs depressing central respiratory drive are listed in *table 15-2*. Diagnosis is based on careful history, neurologic exam, and a search for drug effects.
     b. **Dyskinesias** may affect the respiratory center in occasional patients, usually those with neuroleptic-induced tardive dyskinesia. Dyspnea with adequate ventilation often results, but hypoventilation may occur. Monitoring of breathing pattern may establish this diagnosis.
     c. **Respiratory muscle spasm** may occur due to status epilepticus, tetanus, or parkinsonism. Associated findings confirm these diagnoses.
  2. Peripheral nervous system
     a. **Cervical cord lesions** cause hypoventilation by interrupting neuronal supply of respiratory muscles.
     b. **Autonomic dysfunction,** such as familial dysautonomia (Riley-Day syndrome), or perhaps,

Table 15-2
Drugs Depressing Respiratory Drive

Opiates (e.g., morphine, heroin, meperidine, codeine, propoxyphene)
Barbiturates
Benzodiazepines (e.g., chlordiazepoxide, diazepam, oxazepam)
Phenothiazines
Tricyclic antidepressants
Meprobamate
Ethchlorvynol
Diphenhydramine hydrochloride

diabetes mellitus, occasionally leads to hypoventilation due to unknown mechanisms.
  c. **Peripheral neuropathies** may affect respiratory muscles, leading to hypoventilation.

Diagnosis is based on associated findings and history, or in the case of phrenic nerve damage, by the sniff test (see below).

3. **Myoneural junction.** Botulism and myasthenia gravis, which prevent myoneural transmission, result in decreased respiratory muscle response. A myasthenia-like syndrome is associated with a variety of neoplasms and also is attributable to the effects of aminoglycosides, penicillamine, and organophosphates.
4. **Respiratory muscles**

  a. **Muscular dystrophies,** both of the myotonic variety and the Duchenne type, lead to decreased total lung capacity, and eventually, decreased ventilation. Carbon dioxide response remains normal.

  b. **Inflammatory diseases,** especially polymyositis, may cause respiratory muscle weakness and hypoventilation.

  c. **Metabolic disorders,** such as severe hypokalemia, hypophosphatemia, and steroid withdrawal cause muscular dysfunction. Rare metabolic disorders, such as Pompe's disease, lead to similar syndromes.

D. **Diagnosis.** As noted above, diagnosis is usually based on accompanying clinical information. In addition, several types of pulmonary function tests allow detection and discrimination of alveolar hypoventilation syndromes.

1. **Observation.** Simple assessment of respiratory rate and rhythm, tidal volume, and inspiratory and expiratory time may reveal disordered breathing patterns, such as those due to central dyskinesias. If rate and tidal volume are markedly abnormal, muscle dysfunction may be present.
2. **Spirometry and lung volumes.** Spirometry may reveal decreased airflow, suggesting neurologic or muscular dysfunction. Restrictive defects, due to chest wall or muscular disease, can be recognized by lung volume measurements. However, sensitivity of

these indices is limited, and central disturbances may go unrecognized.
3. **Maximal inspiratory and expiratory pressures.** These tests, which are simple to perform, may be more sensitive than spirometry in detecting neuromuscular dysfunction. Increased airways resistance or decreased elastic recoil alter these results.
4. **Mouth occlusion pressure.** This measurement provides an index of central respiratory stimulus. Measured at zero air flow, mouth occlusion pressure is independent of lung and chest wall compliance and airway resistance. Results are dependent upon **efficiency of respiratory muscles**, which are sensitive to metabolic alterations, and **structural changes**, such as alterations in functional residual capacity.
5. **Carbon dioxide and oxygen response.** Sensitivity of central and peripheral chemoreceptors is measured using different inspired gas concentrations. Characteristic curves are generated for both carbon dioxide and oxygen, individually, while the other gas is held constant.
6. **Radiologic.** Diaphragmatic function is evaluated by the sniff test, in which the diaphragm is observed under fluoroscopy while the patient sniffs. This test appears to be more sensitive than fluoroscopy alone in detecting diaphragmatic paralysis.
7. **Other tests.** Ventilation against elastic or resistive loads and ventilation during exercise are primarily research tests, although both may be useful in individual patients. The diaphragmatic electromyogram (EMG) is also used in research. A characteristic pattern allows recognition of muscle fatigue.

E. **Complications.** Complications of hypoventilation include acute respiratory failure, cardiac arrhythmias and pulmonary hypertension due to hypoxemia and acidosis, and perhaps, sudden death.

F. **Treatment.** Three general modes of therapy are available for hypoventilation:
1. **Pharmacologic.** Most respiratory stimulants result in little improvement in these patients. Doxapram increased ventilation in one series during intravenous infusion, but efficacy of chronic administration is

uncertain. Results of progesterone therapy are variable, but some patients appear to respond to medroxyprogesterone acetate, in doses of 20 to 40 mg tid. If gas exchange abnormalities are mild, low-flow oxygen may suffice to prevent hypoxemic complications.

2. **Mechanical.** If hypoventilation is due to upper airway obstruction, as in some cases of sleep apnea, tracheostomy bypasses obstruction. Muscle weakness may be treated on an acute basis by mechanical ventilation. Therapy for chronic muscle weakness includes rocking beds and the cuirass, used especially at night, to supplement ventilation. Some patients require portable mechanical ventilators.

3. **Electrical.** Diaphragmatic pacing, or "electrophrenic respiration," involves artificial stimulation of the phrenic nerve to induce diaphragmatic contraction. This procedure may be effective if phrenic nerve, diaphragm, and chest wall are intact, but central drive is abnormal. An electrode is implanted adjacent to the phrenic nerve and connected, in turn, to a subcutaneously implanted radio-receiver. A programmed external transmitter then triggers the receiver, leading to diaphragmatic contraction. This technique has achieved long-term success in small groups of patients, although widespread utility is uncertain.

III. OBESITY-HYPOVENTILATION SYNDROME

The obesity-hypoventilation (or Pickwickian) syndrome is a collection of disorders involving obesity and ventilatory impairment. Mild hypoventilation occurs in about 10 percent of markedly obese patients; symptoms are prominent only in those with more severe defects. Degree of hypoventilation correlates poorly with degree of obesity.

A. **Pulmonary function in obesity.** Abnormalities in obese patients are summarized in *table 15-3*. The combination of decreased chest wall compliance and inspiratory muscle weakness predisposes to hypoventilation. In some patients, these defects are compounded by decreased response to hypercapnia and hypoxemia and by upper airway obstruction during sleep. Rarely, hypothalamic lesions lead to both obesity and hypoventilation.

B. **Clinical findings and diagnosis.** Symptoms are similar to

Table 15-3
Respiratory Complications of Obesity

Function	Complication
Mechanics	Decreased chest wall compliance Decreased lung compliance
Volumes	Decreased functional residual capacity Decreased expiratory reserve volume Elevated closing volume
Gas exchange	V/Q inequalities, due to basal airway closure
Respiratory muscles	Decreased efficiency
Metabolic	Increased work of breathing Increased oxygen consumption Increased carbon dioxide production
Circulatory	Increased systemic and pulmonary blood volume

those in other hypoventilation syndromes, including lethargy, headaches, and somnolence. Signs are those of impaired oxygenation and pulmonary hypertension. Complications are common, including sudden death, arrhythmias, pulmonary embolism, respiratory failure, and cor pulmonale. Diagnosis is based on evidence of hypoventilation as above and is often confirmed by abnormal oxygen and carbon dioxide response curves, or by sleep studies.

C. Treatment. Treatment depends upon mechanism of hypoventilation. In some patients, weight reduction reverses both mechanical and chemosensitivity abnormalities. Ketotic diet alone may increase chemosensitivity. In others, chronic progesterone therapy ameliorates hypoxemia and hypercapnia by increasing respiratory drive. Patients with upper airway obstruction during sleep benefit from tracheostomy.

IV. SLEEP APNEA SYNDROMES

Sleep apnea syndromes, as commonly defined, include hypersomnia and intermittent nocturnal apnea. More precise definition of these syndromes must await further studies on the physiology of sleep and especially of upper airway responses.

A. **Respiration during sleep.** Sleep is defined as a temporary state of unconsciousness that can be interrupted by external stimuli. Three general stages of sleep are recognized:
 1. **Relaxed wakefulness**
 2. **Non-rapid eye movement (NREM) sleep.** With increasing depth (stage of sleep), decreases in temperature, heart rate, and respiratory rate occur. Breathing is regular and responds to the usual chemical stimuli.
 3. **Rapid eye movement (REM) sleep.** This stage is defined by conjugate eye movements. Breathing becomes irregular and is unresponsive to the usual chemical stimuli.
  In young or middle-aged subjects, respiratory disturbances during sleep are uncommon. In normal elderly subjects, brief interruptions of respiratory effort during sleep are common, in both REM and non-REM phases.
  Sleep apnea syndromes are characterized by multiple periods of apnea, defined as cessation of airflow at the nose and mouth for 10 to 15 seconds. These patients have at least 30 to 40 such episodes during 7 hours of sleep, primarily during REM sleep, but also during non-REM sleep.
B. **Mechanisms of sleep apnea.** Two major defects lead to sleep apnea:
 1. **Central.** Cessation of airflow with concurrent cessation of thoracic and abdominal respiratory movements.
 2. **Obstructive (peripheral).** Cessation of airflow due to mechanical obstruction, despite normal or increased thoracic and abdominal respiratory efforts.
 Mixed disturbances, combining both mechanisms, are probably the most common type. Site and nature of central hypoventilation are uncertain. Obstructive apnea occurs at the level of the pharynx, often from malfunction of the genioglossus muscle. Coordinated contraction of this muscle and the diaphragm suggests that some cases of obstructive apnea are mediated centrally. Hormonal influences upon apnea are implicated by the increased frequency of disordered breathing in postmenopausal women.

C. **Clinical findings.** Sleep apnea is more common in men than women, correlating with age and obesity. It is also more common in patients with jaw abnormalities (such as micrognathia or acromegaly), tonsillar hypertrophy, hypothyroidism, and Down's syndrome. Symptoms and signs of sleep apnea are presented in *table 15-4*.

Snoring indicates mild upper airway obstruction, which should be carefully sought if the syndrome is suspected. Daytime hypersomnolence is common, but not universal, occurring in 50 to 90 percent of patients. Complications of sleep apnea include cardiac arrhythmias and, perhaps, sudden death. If hypoxemia is chronic, pulmonary hypertension and, perhaps, systemic hypertension result.

D. **Diagnosis.** Sleep apnea is often suspected from a history of snoring or sleep abnormalities or from the development of systemic complications, as noted above.

Table 15-4
Clinical Findings in Sleep Apnea Syndromes

1. Symptoms
   A. Sleep
      Snoring
      Abnormal motor activity
      Enuresis

   B. Waking
      Hypersomnolence
      Morning headaches
      Hypnagogic hallucinations
      Personality disturbances
      Disorientation on awakening
      Decreased intellectual function
      Impotence

2. Signs
   A. Systemic
      Obesity
      Pulmonary hypertension with right ventricular dysfunction

   B. Upper airway
      Jaw abnormality, e.g., micrognathia, retrognathia
      Tonsillar hypertrophy
      Large tongue

The diagnosis should be sought in patients with unexplained hypoxemia, hypercapnia, erythrocytosis, or right ventricular dysfunction. Several studies found characteristic expiratory fluttering or awake flow-volume loops or decreased FIF_{50}/FEF_{50} (<1) in most affected patients. Diagnosis is confirmed by sleep evaluation. A full sleep study includes measurement of

1. Sleep stage, by electroencephalography and electrooculography
2. Mouth airflow, by thermistor or pneumotachygraph
3. Oxygenation, by arterial cannula or ear oximeter
4. Respiratory effort, by esophageal balloon or chest wall magnetometer
5. Upper airway muscle function, by genioglossal EMG

If such a study discloses sleep apnea, pulmonary function testing and laryngoscopy should be performed to exclude obvious structural defects, and thyroid function should be evaluated to exclude metabolic causes.

E. **Treatment.** Treatment of sleep apnea syndromes prevents development of complications and reverses existing abnormalities. Several modes of therapy are used, corresponding to those used in other hypoventilation syndromes:

1. **Pharmacologic.** Patients with centrally mediated apnea may benefit from theophylline or medroxyprogesterone acetate (MPG). A recent study indicated that a subgroup of patients with waking hypoxemia is more likely to respond to MPG than patients who do not have waking hypoxemia.
2. **Mechanical.** Patients with obstructive sleep apnea are unlikely to respond to pharmacologic agents and require tracheostomy to facilitate sleep-breathing below the obstructed area. In small groups, tracheostomy has been shown to decrease symptoms and complications, such as cardiac arrhythmias and pulmonary hypertension.
3. **Electrical.** If the above therapies are ineffective, diaphragmatic pacing, as previously described, may be useful in some patients.

REFERENCES

I. Alveolar Hypoventilation

Ahman M, Cressman M, Tomashefski J: Central alveolar hypoventilation syndromes. *Arch Intern Med* 140:29-30, 1980.

Farmer WC, Glenn WWL, Gee JBL: Alveolar hypoventilation syndromes. *Am J Med* 64:39-49, 1978.

Lourenco RV: Assessment of respiratory control in humans. *Am Rev Respir Dis* 115:1-5, 1977.

Mellins RB, Baltour HH, Turino GM, et al: Failure of automatic control of ventilation. *Medicine* 49:487-504, 1970.

Ahman offers a brief guide to various syndromes, including sleep apnea and obesity-hypoventilation. Mellins presents a series of patients with automatic respiratory failure; Farmer describes a series of patients with varying diagnoses, including data on electrophrenic pacing. Lourenco briefly reviews diagnostic methods in these disorders.

II. Obesity-Hypoventilation

Luce JM: Respiratory complications of obesity. *Chest* 78:626-631, 1980.

Sutton FD Jr, Zwillich CW, Creagh CE, et al: Progesterone for outpatient treatment of Pickwickian syndrome. *Ann Intern Med* 83:476-479, 1975.

Zwillich CW, Sutton FD, Pierson DJ, et al: Decreased hypoxic ventilatory drive in the obesity-hypoventilation syndrome. *Am J Med* 59:343-348, 1975.

Luce summarizes effects of obesity on respiration, including pathogenesis of obesity-hypoventilation syndromes. Zwillich presents evidence in favor of central dysfunction, and Sutton finds progesterone useful in some patients.

III. Sleep Apnea

Cherniack NS: Respiratory dysrhythmias during sleep. *N Engl J Med* 305: 325-330, 1981.

Guilleminault C, Dement WC (eds): *Sleep Apnea Syndromes.* New York, Liss, 1978.

Guilleminault C, Simmons FB, Motta J, et al: Obstructive sleep apnea syndrome and tracheostomy. *Arch Intern Med* 141:985-988, 1981.

Phillipson EA: Control of breathing during sleep. *Am Rev Respir Dis* 118: 909-939, 1978.

Sanders MH, Martin RJ, Pennock BE, et al: The detection of sleep apnea in the awake patient. *JAMA* 245:2414-2418, 1981.

Strohl KP, Hensley MJ, Saunders NA, et al: Progesterone administration and progressive sleep apneas. *JAMA* 245:1230-1232, 1981.

Phillipson reviews breathing during sleep in normal persons, whereas Cherniack concentrates on abnormal patterns. The monograph by Guilleminault and Dement is an exhaustive review of the subject. Sanders describes flow-volume loop abnormalities in a small series of patients. Guilleminault and Strohl present results of different modes of therapy.

16
Pleural Diseases

PART 1
PLEURAL EFFUSIONS

I. DEFINITION AND PATHOPHYSIOLOGY

A pleural effusion is formed when excess fluid accumulates in the pleural space. Type and extent of fluid formation depend upon the characteristics of the normal pleural space. The visceral and parietal pleura form a continuous serosal surface of the lung and chest wall. Normally, only a potential space separates these surfaces, and most healthy subjects have less than 10 ml of fluid per hemithorax. However, fluid continually moves across this space, with amount and rate determined by three factors: **Starling forces, lymphatic drainage,** and **surface area of membrane.** Starling forces are summarized in figure 16-1.

The balance of hydrostatic pressure and colloid osmotic pressure (COP) leads to net movement of transudated fluid from systemic capillaries in the parietal pleura to pulmonary capillaries and lymphatics in the visceral pleura. A small amount of protein also leaks into the pleural space, so that normal protein concentration is 1.5 g/100 ml or less. Lymphatic drainage normally is sufficient to remove protein, maintaining stable pleural COP, and therefore, constant flow across the pleural space.

An alteration in any of the above factors can lead to formation of an effusion. Inflammation, for example, increases capillary permeability, allowing exudation of fluid and protein into the pleural space. A pleural protein concentration of 4 g/100 ml equalizes pleural COP and hydrostatic forces, obligating all drainage through lymphatics. Obstruction to lymph flow may also upset fluid homeostasis, allowing fluid to accumulate. Loss of fluid-exchanging surface by

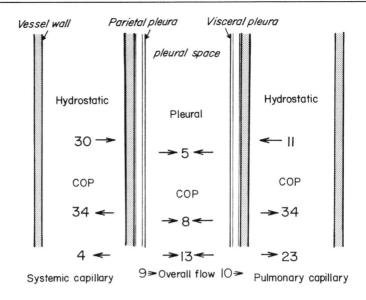

(COP = colloid osmotic pressure)

Figure 16-1. Pleural fluid dynamics.

fibrosis or necrosis diminishes area for fluid exchange and may disrupt fluid balance.

This scheme for pleural fluid accumulation allows changes in character of effusions. Because fluid absorption is more effective than protein removal, a low protein "transudative" effusion may, with time or diuresis, develop increased protein concentration. The reverse process does not occur, however, because elevated COP in exudative effusions prevents absorption of fluid unaccompanied by protein.

II. CLINICAL MANIFESTATIONS

A. **Symptoms.** Symptoms associated with fluid in the pleural space are variable. Pleuritic pain may accompany an effusion, or it may occur with pleural inflammation, resolving when fluid accumulates. The parietal pleura has sensory innervation, primarily via the intercostal nerves. Pain usually is well localized, but may occasionally be referred to the abdomen, which is supplied by the lower intercostals. Owing to phrenic innervation of the pleural surface along the central diaphragm, pain may be referred to the ipsilateral shoulder. Dyspnea may occur in patients with effusions, due to restriction of lung expansion, and to splinting, if pain is present. Cough is variable; it may result from compression of bronchi or alveoli by adjacent fluid. Fever is unlikely to be caused by the presence of uninfected fluid; fever and other symptoms are more likely to be a result of underlying disease than of the effusion per se.

B. **Signs.** Physical examination often discloses the presence of an effusion. Except in massive effusions, which may cause bulging of the intercostal spaces and diminished chest wall motion during respiration, inspection is seldom useful. Dullness to percussion, shifting with position, is the hallmark of an effusion. Breath sounds are decreased on auscultation. Egophony may be heard just above the effusion, due to compression of adjacent lung parenchyma.

C. **Radiography.** Diagnosis is confirmed by chest x-ray. Effusions typically are located at the bases if the patient is upright. A moderate amount of fluid (probably 250 ml or more) must be present to be seen on upright PA or lateral x-ray. The earliest finding is obliteration of the costophrenic angle. Occasionally, there is shifting of the angle medially by a fluid margin adjacent to the ribs. Additional fluid forms a wedge-shaped posterior density, and more fluid forms an upward concavity. A supine film shows diffuse haziness, but no distinct density. Lateral decubitus films cause free effusions to shift with gravity, allowing vastly improved sensitivity: as little as 5 to 10 ml can be detected.

A less common, and perhaps less recognized, configuration is an infrapulmonary effusion. Fluid is present under the lung, but does not track posteriorly. Findings include elevation of the hemidiaphragm, flattening of the diaphragmatic surface, and widening of the space between diaphragm and gastric air bubble (2 cm or less is normal). Other atypical presentations may occur. Interlobar tracking is common, especially on the right. Fluid dissects into the major or minor fissures, especially in the presence of congestive heart failure. The resulting loculated densities disappear with resolution of the effusion--hence the terms "vanishing tumors" or "pseudotumors."

Effusions may also be loculated peripherally, with a broad base and convexity toward the mediastinum, or in an inferior paramediastinal location. Very large effusions may obliterate the hemithorax, simulating lung collapse. Distinction between effusion and collapse is based on shift of the mediastinum away from the effusion, but toward lung collapse. Loculated or atypical effusions may be diagnosed reliably by ultrasonography, which distinguishes density of infiltrates. Computerized tomography is especially useful for pleural plaques, and probably is also sensitive for pleural effusions.

III. DIAGNOSIS

A wide variety of conditions causes accumulation of fluid in the pleural space. These are summarized in *table 16-1*.

Determination of the etiology of an effusion is based on presence of other signs of disease, other radiographic abnormalities, and examination of a pleural fluid sample. Other evidence of disease might include signs of congestive heart failure, ascites, or malignancy. Associated findings on chest x-ray include masses suggesting neoplasm, cardiomegaly accompanying congestive heart failure, or rib fractures indicating trauma. Pleural fluid sample for examination is obtained by thoracentesis.

A. **Thoracentesis.** Examination of pleural fluid may reveal a specific etiological factor, or may suggest a diagnostic category. Not all cases of pleural effusion require fluid examination. The decision to perform thoracentesis depends upon suspected diagnosis and clinical course. If infection or malignancy is suspected, thoracentesis will help to confirm or reject these diagnoses. Effusions thought to be due to congestive heart failure or ascites may respond to treatment of the underlying disease, without fluid examination. Effusions in patients with bacteremia may become seeded and should be tapped if infection is suspected.

Technique of thoracentesis will not be discussed in detail here. Before the procedure, amount of fluid and distribution should be assessed with lateral decubitus films. Contraindications to thoracentesis include uncorrected bleeding diatheses and inability of the patient to cooperate; extensive bullous disease and blebs are relative contraindications. Complications of the procedure include pneumothorax, usually due to nicking of the visceral pleura, and rarely, bleeding or infection. Seeding of tumor along the needle track is extremely rare.

B. **Fluid examination.** Once pleural fluid is obtained, a variety of tests may be performed:

Table 16-1
Effusions: Etiology

I. Transudate
  A. Increased hydrostatic pressure: congestive heart failure
  B. Decreased oncotic pressure: nephrotic syndrome
  C. Lymphatic drainage
    1. Ascites, including cirrhosis, Meigs's tumor
    2. Peritoneal dialysis
    3. Pancreatitis

II. Exudate
  A. Pleural inflammation due to:
    1. Infection: bacterial, tuberculous, mycoplasmal, fungal
    2. Pulmonary infarction
    3. Neoplasia
    4. Connective tissue disease, i.e., rheumatoid arthritis, SLE
    5. Autoimmune disease: Dressler's syndrome, familial Mediterranean fever
    6. Subphrenic inflammation: pancreatitis, subphrenic abscess, postoperative, dialysis
    7. Endometrial implants
    8. Drugs: nitrofurantoin, methysergide
  B. Lymphatic obstruction: malignancy

III. Empyema: pyogenic, mycobacterial, or fungal

IV. Hemorrhagic
    1. Trauma
    2. Neoplasia
    3. Pulmonary infarction
    4. Tuberculosis

V. Lipidic
    1. Chylous due to rupture or obstruction of thoracic duct
    2. Cholesterol due to tuberculosis, rheumatoid arthritis

---

1. Appearance. Most effusions are yellow, and often clear, if transudative. Presence of chyle, blood, or pus suggests specific etiologies, as noted in *table 16-1*. However, other causes may mimic these gross characteristics. For example, cholesterol may appear similar to chyle, but etiology is markedly different (see below). A blood-tinged effusion usually has 5000 or more red blood cells/mm^3, but must be distinguished from a traumatic tap. A true sanguin-

eous effusion is characterized by lack of clearing during the tap, presence of hemoglobin pigment in a spun specimen, or hemoglobin in macrophages on a Wright stain of sediment. Effusions due to rheumatoid arthritis (RA) may be dark yellow or green, mimicking pus.

2. **Transudate versus exudate.** These categories suggest pathophysiologic origin of fluid, whether due to enhanced filtration into the pleural space or increased vascular permeability. Originally distinguished by specific gravity, distinction between transudate and exudate is now based on the presence of protein and lactate dehydrogenase (LDH), as summarized in *table 16-2*.

    Although not specific, these categories are useful in suggesting a diagnosis. Causes of exudates, such as malignancy, pneumonia, infection, or tuberculosis, rarely produce transudates. Conversely, it is unusual to find exudates resulting from diseases such as congestive heart failure, ascites, or nephrotic syndrome.

3. **Blood cell counts.** Red blood cell count or hematocrit may be useful in assessing the amount of blood in a sanguinous effusion. Absolute level of white blood cell count, if markedly elevated, suggests empyema or infected effusion. The lymphocyte is the predominant cell in pleural fluid, accounting for

Table 16-2
Transudale versus Exudate

Measurement	Transudate	Exudate
Total protein	<3.0 mg/dl	>3.0 mg/dl
$\left(\dfrac{\text{Pleural total protein}}{\text{Serum total protein}}\right)$	<0.5	>0.5
Lactic dehydrogenase (LDH)	<200 U/dl	>200 U/dl
$\left(\dfrac{\text{Pleural LDH}}{\text{Serum LDH}}\right)$	<0.6	>0.6
Specific gravity	<1.016	>1.016

Used with permission of Light RW, et al; Pleural effusions: the diagnostic separation of transudates and exudates. *Ann Intern Med* 17:507-513, 1972.

greater than 50 percent of cells in most exudates. Diagnostic significance of white blood cell types is presented in *table 16-3*.

4. **Chemistries.** Protein and LDH are discussed above. Amylase levels, which appear to be elevated in most cases of effusions due to pancreatitis, often exceed serum amylase concentration. Amylase levels also may be elevated in esophageal rupture, due to the salivary enzyme, and in some nonpancreatic neoplasms, due to an unknown source. Glucose levels in pleural fluid may be decreased relative to serum in bacterial infection or tuberculosis, but the levels vary widely. Glucose concentration is markedly decreased in effusions due to rheumatoid arthritis—usually to below 20 mg/100 ml—due apparently to a block in serum uptake, and perhaps to increased utilization by mesothelial cells. Pleural fluid glucose concentration is normal in systemic lupus erythematosus (SLE).

5. **Fats.** Owing to the presence of chylomicrons, triglyceride levels are high in chylous effusions, whereas cholesterol is low. The converse occurs in cholesterol effusions, which are usually due to tuberculosis or rheumatoid arthritis. The two types may be distinguished by refrigerating fluid overnight to observe chylomicrons, or by measuring triglyceride and cholesterol levels.

6. **pH.** A pH less than 6.0 suggests esophageal rupture.

Table 16-3
Differential White Blood Cell Count in Pleural Fluid

Factor	Typical Finding
Polymorphonuclear leukocytes	Inflammation; predominant in infection
Lymphocytes	Predominant in most exudates, especially tuberculosis, neoplasia
Macrophages	Nonspecific
Plasma cells	Nonspecific
Eosinophils	Commonly elevated, especially in trauma; nonspecific
Basophils	Nonspecific
Mesothelial cells	Nonspecific, except more than 5 percent excludes tuberculosis

Empyemas are usually somewhat less acidic, with a pH between 6.0 and 7.0. A pH less than 7.2 in a nonpurulent effusion may suggest early infection, although specificity is uncertain. Most malignant effusions, and those due to pulmonary emboli, have a pH greater than 7.30.

7. **Microscopic analysis.** Fluid should be examined for bacteria if infection is suspected.
8. **Cultures.** Cultures are highly sensitive in the diagnosis of bacterial infection. Sensitivity is limited for tuberculosis, about 30 percent, but it may increase with volume of fluid cultured. Sensitivity in fungal, viral, and mycoplasmal infections, although probably low, has not been adequately studied.
9. **Cytologic study.** In effusions due to neoplastic involvement of the pleura, cytologic study is positive in about 50 percent of cases. Yield increases with multiple specimens, although further increase after five specimens is uncertain.
10. **Other.** Use of other tests depends upon suspected diagnosis. If Legionnaire's disease is considered, antibody titers, and perhaps, immunofluorescence, are indicated. Cryptococcal antigen may be present in effusions caused by *C. neoformans*. Some data support the use of carcinoembryonic antigen (CEA) in identifying malignant effusions. Rheumatoid factor is nonspecific, but low complement levels occur in rheumatoid arthritis and SLE. LE cells may appear in pleural fluid in the presence of SLE.

In summary, a variety of tests may be performed on pleural fluid. Routine analysis should include protein and LDH levels, cultures, and microscopic examination. Cytologic study should be added if malignancy is considered. Performance of other tests depends upon suspected etiology and associated clinical findings.

Pleural biopsy may increase diagnostic yield in several types of pleural effusions. This is especially true of tuberculosis, in which fluid cultures are insensitive. Tissue histology and culture of parietal pleura are positive in over 80 percent of cases. In malignant effusions, cytology and biopsy appear complementary, with the combination positive in 70 to 90 percent of cases. Complications of pleural biopsy are similar to those of thoracentesis, although pneumothorax may be more common with the biopsy needle. Yield is improved if multiple specimens are obtained.

IV. ETIOLOGY

Characteristics of pleural effusions vary with etiology; these are summarized for common diseases in *table 16-4*. Further details are presented below.

A. **Congestive heart failure (CHF).** About 10 percent of patients with CHF have effusions, usually transudates. Brisk diuresis or prolonged failure may lead to exudate formation.

B. **Cirrhosis.** About 10 to 15 percent of patients with cirrhosis have effusions, almost always those with ascites. Fluid accumulates as a result of lymphatic drainage across the diaphragm.

C. **Malignancy.** About 40 percent of neoplastic effusions are due to bronchogenic carcinoma, and another 20 to 25 percent occur with breast carcinoma. Other common causes include lymphoma and leukemia (8 percent), ovarian carcinoma (8 percent), and gastric carcinoma (6 percent). In most cases, there is neoplastic involvement of the ipsilateral lung. Several mechanisms lead to effusion formation in malignancy:

1. **Vascular and lymphatic obstruction.** Fluid may have low cell counts.
2. **Serosal implants.** Probably the most common cause; cell counts range from 500 to 2000/mm^3.
3. **Parenchymal tumor eroding into the pleural space.** These are uncommon, and cell counts are high.

D. **Pneumonia.** Pneumonia may be complicated by several types of effusions:

1. **Empyema.** Purulent material in the pleural space
2. **Infected effusion.** Organisms present, but without purulence
3. **Parapneumonic.** Sterile fluid, presumably due to adjacent inflammation

When carefully sought, effusions were found in about 50 percent of one series of patients with pneumococcal pneumonia. Pleural fluid formation is more likely with prolonged fever or symptoms or bacteremia. Small effusions occur in about 20 percent of viral or mycoplasmal pneumonias.

E. **Tuberculosis.** Effusions in tuberculosis are usually part

Table 16-4
Characteristics of Effusions by Etiology

Etiology	Trans/Ex*	Gross	Cell Ct/mm³	Diff	Chem	Other	Chest film
Congestive heart failure	Trans, except chronic	Serous	<500	Lymphs			Bilateral with cardiomegaly in 75%; right more than left
Cirrhosis	Trans	Serous	Variable	Variable			Right more than left
Nephrotic syndrome	Trans	Serous	Variable	Variable			Often bilateral
Meigs's tumor	Trans	Serous	Variable	Lymphs			Right in 70%
Tuberculosis	Ex	Serous/bloody	500-2000	Lymphs >80%; mesos <5%	Glu† down mildly	Culture + in 30%	Moderate, unilateral
Pneumonia	Ex	Serous	>1000	Polys	pH down if infected		Ipsilateral with pneumonia
Fungus	Ex	Serous	Variable	Variable	Crypto Ag may be +	*Actinomyces*, *Nocardia* common	
Neoplasia	Ex	Serous/bloody	Variable	Lymphs	pH may be down	Cytologic + 40-60%	Unilateral, if lung primary; bilateral in 25% of metastatic; 25% loculated

Condition	Trans/Ex*	Appearance		Cells	Other	Notes
Pulmonary embolism	Ex	Often bloody	Variable	Polys up in 70%		Infiltrate in 60%
Rheumatoid arthritis	Ex	Turbid/yellow	Variable	Lymphs	Glu† less than 30	Complement decreased	Bilateral in 30%; right more than left
SLE	Ex	Serous	>1000	Lymphs	Glu† Nl	Complement decreased	Small; unilateral, or bilateral
Subphrenic abscess	Ex	Serous	Variable	Polys			Right in 70%
Pancreatitis	Variable	Serous	Variable	Variable	Amylase up >serum		Left in 70%

*Trans: transudate
Ex: exudate
†Glucose level (mg/100ml)

of the syndrome of tuberculous pleurisy, consisting of effusion, chest pain, and fever. Cough and sputum production are characteristically mild. Effusions are moderate, unilateral, and spontaneously resolving. The mechanism appears to be an immunologic response to a small number of organisms, so that cultures of effusion samples are often negative.

F. Parasites. Although uncommon in the United States, *Entamoeba histolytica* may cause a right pleural effusion by extension from hepatic abscess. Fluid is thick and dark, and serum ameba titers are positive.

G. Pulmonary embolism. Effusions are usually bloody, and almost always accompanied by infarction.

H. Collagen-vascular disease. Effusions are unusual in diseases other than RA or SLE. Differential glucose values are noted above.

I. Autoimmune disease. Effusions occur in 60 to 90 percent of patients with Dressler's syndrome, and are usually small and unilateral. Effusions in familial Mediterranean fever are due to generalized polyserositis.

J. Drugs. Effusions are uncommon in drug reactions, although methysergide may lead to a polyserositis, and nitrofurantoin may cause effusion and lung infiltrates.

K. Mesothelioma. Effusions often are bloody, and increased viscosity is due to fibrin production.

L. Meigs's syndrome. This describes predominantly right-sided, transudative effusions associated with ovarian fibromas, and less frequently, other pelvic neoplasms. Fluid appears due to lymphatic drainage of ascites.

M. Chylous effusions. Causes include congenital absence or atresia of the thoracic or other major lymphatic ducts; surgery or trauma to the duct; or obstruction, due to tumor or granulomatous mediastinal disease.

N. Idiopathic. Even after initial investigation, 10 to 20 percent of effusions exhibit no clear etiology. Further study reveals that transudates are often due to CHF, whereas exudates are often caused by neoplasms. Open pleural biopsy should be considered if percutaneous pleural biopsy and other studies are negative. The value of systemic search for malignancy is uncertain.

V. EFFECTS ON PULMONARY FUNCTION

The presence of pleural fluid, without other symptoms, may lead to decreases in lung volumes, and hypoxemia. Small amounts of fluid have little effect, merely displacing the adjacent lung. As fluid volume increases, displacement leads to decreased lung volumes. Concomitant collapse of lung units exacerbates this change. Presence of cough and dyspnea may be due to restriction of lung expansion, bronchial compression, or stimulation of parenchymal receptors. In one study, thoracentesis produced rapid subjective improvement, but little change in volumes or hypoxemia.

VI. TREATMENT

Treatment of pleural effusions depends upon etiology and clinical consequences.

A. **Therapeutic drainage.** Regardless of etiology, thoracentesis should be performed if restriction of lung volumes leads to marked dyspnea or hypoxemia. Otherwise, treatment is usually directed to the underlying disease. For effusions due to systemic hypervolemia, such as CHF, cirrhosis, or nephrotic syndrome, efforts should be made to restore normal volume. Effusions will reaccumulate after drainage if the disease process is not altered.

B. **Infection.** If infection is suspected, treatment depends upon fluid examination and clinical course. Purulent effusions (empyemas) should be treated by chest tube drainage. This should also be performed in nonpurulent effusions if organisms are seen on gram stain or culture, unless effusions are very small and can be removed by needle aspiration. Several studies indicate that significant acidity (pH < 7.20) signals the presence of organisms. Acidic pH might therefore indicate the need for early drainage, regardless of microscopic examination, and before results of culture are known. In other series, this degree of acidity was found in some effusions associated with neoplasia, tuberculosis, or hemothorax, and was thus nonspecific. The benefits of early drainage remain uncertain.

C. **Hemothorax.** The problem posed by large, bloody effusions, usually due to trauma or subclavian cannulation, is that organization of blood may lead to fibrothorax. Although evidence is limited, it appears that only 10 to 20 percent of moderate-to-large hemothoraces progress to organization. Routine drainage may, therefore, be unnecessary.

D. **Chylothorax.** Chylous effusions, if large, should be drained by aspiration or chest tube. Many effusions, especially postoperative, will resolve. Recurrence may be treated with a medium-chain triglyceride diet (directly absorbed) to decrease chyle flow. If this fails, thoracic duct ligation should be performed for benign cases, and radiation given for malignancies.

E. **Malignancy.** Malignant effusions often recur after drainage, causing discomfort and respiratory compromise. If accumulation is slow, intermittent thoracenteses may suffice. Rapid reaccumulation of fluid necessitates a procedure to obliterate the pleural space. Methods include:

1. **Chest tube drainage.** Drainage alone is successful in less than half of cases.

2. **Chemical pleurodesis.** This is the preferred method, and tetracycline is the drug of choice. After chest tube drainage, 500 mg tetracycline in 30 to 50 ml saline is infused through the tube, the tube is clamped, and over the next 1-2 hours patient position is changed to ensure distribution of fluid. Chest tube is then returned to suction and removed after drainage ceases for 24 hours. If tetracycline fails, talc, 100 g in 250 ml saline, may be used. Of other agents, quinacrine hydrochloride causes pain, fever, and occasional hypotension. Nitrogen mustard is less effective.

3. **Pleurectomy.** If chemical pleurodesis fails, surgical pleurectomy should be considered, although this entails the risks associated with open thoracotomy.

PART 2
PNEUMOTHORAX

I. **DEFINITION AND ETIOLOGY**

Pneumothorax is defined as the presence of gas in the pleural space. Causes include trauma, such as blunt or penetrating injuries to the chest, and surgery. Spontaneous pneumothorax occurs without obvious antecedent. Causes of pneumothorax are presented in *table 16-5*.

Primary spontaneous pneumothorax occurs in young adults, in males more than females. It appears to be due to alveolar rupture in apical regions, followed by gas entering the interstitium, dissecting distally, and eventually rupturing into the pleural space. Primary pneumothorax is uncommon over 40 years of age. Most older patients with pneumothorax have associated diseases, as noted in *table 16-5*. Pneumothorax associated with mechanical ventilation is discussed in Chapter 5.

II. **CLINICAL PRESENTATION AND DIAGNOSIS**

Clinical presentation of pneumothorax depends upon its extent and on the presence of other disease. Almost all affected patients have chest pain and dyspnea. Cough, hemoptysis, or syncope may also occur. If pneumothorax is

Table 16-5
Causes of Pneumothorax

Category	Specific Disease or Condition
Trauma	Penetrating or blunt injury
Surgery	Thoracotomy, thoracentesis
Spontaneous	
Primary	
Secondary	Emphysema and chronic bronchitis
	Asthma
	Tuberculosis (extensive)
	Necrotizing pneumonia
	Interstitial fibrosis
	Catamenial (menses-related)
	Esophageal rupture
	Positive pressure ventilation

sufficiently large, breath sounds are decreased or absent, and percussion is hyperresonant. Arterial blood gases reveal hypoxemia, which often improves with time as hypoxic vasoconstriction occurs. Chest x-ray demonstrates the outward margin of the lung, although adhesions may mask this finding by allowing only partial collapse. About 53 percent of spontaneous pneumothoraces occur on the right, 45 percent on the left, and 2 percent bilaterally. Up to 20 percent may exhibit air-fluid levels.

Diagnosis is based on symptoms and chest x-ray; expiratory films may enhance visualization as a consequence of decreased parenchymal volume and shift of gas to the apex.

III. COMPLICATIONS

A. **Tension pneumothorax.** A "ball-valve" effect produces positive pressure in the affected pleural space, leading to lung collapse and impedance of venous return. Patients are severely dyspneic and often hypotensive. Examination may show tracheal deviation, and chest x-ray confirms mediastinal shift.

B. **Pyopneumothorax.** This is associated with necrotizing pneumonias.

C. **Hemopneumothorax.** This is usually a result of trauma; continued bleeding may necessitate thoracotomy and ligation of the bleeding vessel.

D. **Chronic pneumothorax.** This occurs if bronchopleural fistula exists, either postoperatively or due to bullae or parenchymal disease. Thoracotomy and fistula closure may be required.

E. **Pneumomediastinum and subcutaneous emphysema.** These occur in a manner similar to primary spontaneous pneumothorax, except that air dissects from the interstitium into the mediastinum. Rarely, compression of the great vessels must be relieved. Subcutaneous emphysema may occur through further extension of air or by tracking into a chest tube wound site. Clinical consequences are rare.

IV. TREATMENT

Tension pneumothorax is life-threatening and should be treated by rapid decompression via needle or chest tube. Other pneumothoraces may be treated according to size and clinical compromise. Small amounts of gas will resolve spontaneously if the bronchopleural fistula closes. Larger collections may require chest tube evacuation. Most primary spontaneous pneumothoraces do not recur; recurrences may necessitate pleurectomy.

Persistent bronchopleural fistula may be evident from chest tube drainage apparatus, but diagnosis is occasionally difficult. Open fistulas are characterized by either intrapleural pressure similar to atmospheric, or pleural gas Pa_{O_2} less than 40 torr, and Pa_{CO_2} greater than 45 torr.

PART 3
MESOTHELIOMA

Mesotheliomas arise from mesothelial lining cells of the pleura or peritoneum. Both benign and malignant pleural tumors are recognized, and histologic findings are variable. Localized fibrous mesothelioma is rare, presenting as a mass arising from the visceral pleura. Symptoms include dull persistent chest pain and a high incidence of arthralgias. Clubbing and hypertrophic pulmonary osteoarthropathy (HPO) are common. Diagnosis is suggested by chest x-ray findings. Resection of the tumor and histologic study establishes benign cell type, resulting in cure.

Diffuse malignant mesothelioma may arise from visceral or parietal pleura. The disease is rare, but incidence is markedly increased in workers exposed to asbestos. Pathogenesis is uncertain. Most patients are men in their sixth decade. Symptoms include dull chest pain, cough, and dyspnea. Pleural effusion is common, but clubbing and HPO are uncommon. Chest film reveals a lobulated density adjacent to the chest wall, usually with accompanying effusion, or diffuse thickening encasing the entire lung. The rest of the lungs and pleura are normal. Distinguishing this tumor from neoplasms metastatic to the pleura is difficult. Cytologic study of the effusion, or pleural biopsy, may establish malignancy, but site of origin is often uncertain. Some patients appear to respond to radiation, but variable natural history makes the results of therapy difficult to interpret. Prognosis is dismal, with few patients surviving 2 years.

REFERENCES

I. Pleural Effusions

A. General

Johnston RF, Dovnorsky JH: Pleural diseases. In *Pulmonary Diseases and Disorders.* Edited by Fishman AP, New York, McGraw-Hill, 1980, pp 1357-1380.

Light RW: Pleural effusions. *Med Clin North Am* 61:1339-1352, 1977.

Lowell JR: *Pleural Effusions: A Comprehensive Review.* Baltimore, University Park Press, 1977.

Johnston and Light offer succinct reviews. Lowell presents an exhaustive monograph covering findings up to 1977, with a wealth of clinical observations.

B. Pathophysiology

Black LF: The pleural space and pleural fluid. *Mayo Clin Proc* 47:491-506, 1972.

An excellent and still current review of normal pleural function and formation of effusions.

C. Diagnosis

Good JJ, Taryle DA, Mavlitz RM, et al: The diagnostic value of pleural fluid pH. *Chest* 78:55-59, 1980.

Hirsch A, et al: Pleural effusion: laboratory tests in 300 cases. *Thorax* 106-112, 1979.

Hirsch A, Ruffie P, Nebut M, et al: Pleural effusion: laboratory tests in 300 cases. *Thorax* 106-112, 1979.

Light RW, MacGregor I, Wohsinger PC: Pleural effusions: the diagnostic separation of transudates and exudates. *Ann Intern Med* 17:507-513, 1972.

Light RW, Erozan YS, Ball WC Jr: Cells in pleural fluid. Their value in differential diagnosis. *Arch Intern Med* 132:854-860, 1973.

Vix VA: Roentgenographic manifestations of pleural disease. *Semin Roentgenol* 12:277-286, 1977.

Good argues that pH is nonspecific. Hirsch presents a large group of effusions, showing little diagnostic benefit from most lab tests. Light and MacGregor establish the value of total protein and LDH measurements; Light and Erozan find cell counts to be of little use.

D. Etiology

Berger HW, Mejia E: Tuberculous pleurisy. *Chest* 63:88-92, 1973.

Bynum LJ, Wilson JE: Characteristics of pleural effusions associated with pulmonary embolism. *Arch Intern Med* 136:59-62, 1976.

Chernow B, Sahn SA: Carcinomatous involvement of the pleura. *Am J Med* 63:695-702, 1977.

Sahn SA, Kaplan RL, Mavlitz RM, et al: Rheumatoid pleurisy. *Arch Intern Med* 140:1237-1238, 1980.

Storey DD, Dines DE, Coles DT: Pleural effusion: a diagnostic dilemma. *JAMA* 236:2183-2186, 1976.

Berger, Bynum, Chernow, and Sahn all describe characteristics of effusions, as described in the titles. Storey presents a series of effusions, including patients in whom no etiology could be found despite thorough evaluation.

E. Treatment

Austin EH, Flye MW: The treatment of recurrent malignant pleural effusion. *Ann Thorac Surg* 28:190-203, 1979.

Light RW: Management of parapneumonic pleural effusions. *Chest* 70:325-326, 1976.

Austin describes chemical pleurodesis and surgical pleurectomy. Light advocates drainage of acidic effusions in the absence of organisms.

II. Pneumothorax

Greene R, McCloud TC, Stark P: Pneumothorax. *Semin Roentgenol* 12:313-320, 1977.

Lichter I, Gwynne JF: Spontaneous pneumothorax in young adults. *Thorax* 26:409-417, 1971.

 Greene reviews radiologic manifestations; Lichter presents a clinical series with some pathological material. See also the article by Johnston and Dovnorsky, cited in the section on Pleural Effusions, above.

Abbreviations

A-aD$_{O_2}$	alveolar-arterial oxygen difference
ABPA	allergic bronchopulmonary aspergillosis
Abscess	an area of parenchymal necrosis in the lung
Acanthosis nigricans	bilateral symmetric hyperkeratotic and hyperpigmented lesions, associated with a variety of neoplasms
ACE	angiotensin converting enzyme
Acidosis	a process tending to lower systemic pH
ACTH/pro-ACTH	adrenocorticotrophic hormone and its precursor, the latter associated with bronchogenic carcinoma
Alkalosis	a process tending to raise systemic pH
Alpha-1-antitrypsin	protease inhibitor normally found in the circulation; absence is associated with emphysema
Antithrombin	circulating substance that inhibits thrombin and other activated mediators of coagulation
ARDS	adult respiratory distress syndrome
Aryl hydrocarbon hydroxylase	increased circulating levels of this enzyme are associated with heightened susceptibility to lung cancer
Atelectasis	collapse of lung units
Atypical mycobacteria	pathogenic mycobacteria other than *M. tuberculosis*

Atypical pneumonia	pneumonia due to nonbacterial organisms, or unusual bacteria, usually with little sputum production
Barotrauma	pressure-induced trauma due to positive-pressure ventilation
BCG	Bacille Calmette-Guérin, an attenuated strain of *M. tuberculosis* used as a vaccine or immunologic adjuvant
BIP	bronchiolitic interstitial pneumonitis
Bronchogenic carcinoma	neoplasm originating in the bronchial wall
Bronchopleural fistula	communication between the bronchial tree and the pleural space
Bronchopneumonia	pneumonia with multiple bronchiolar foci, often caused by gram-negative organisms
Carcinoma in situ	carcinoma localized to within the epithelial surface
CEA	carcinoembryonic antigen, associated with various neoplasms
CHF	congestive heart failure
Clubbing	bulbous enlargement of distal digits associated with chronic pulmonary diseases
CMV	continuous mandatory ventilation (also used for cytomegalovirus)
CNS	central nervous system
CO	cardiac output
COP	colloid osmotic pressure
COPD	chronic obstructive pulmonary disease
CPAP	continuous positive airway pressure
CRST	a variant of progressive systemic sclerosis comprising calcinosis, Raynaud's phenomenon, sclerodactyly, and telangiectasias
Dead space	physiologic—areas of the lung not participating in gas exchange; anatomic—trachea and conducting airways
DIC	disseminated intravascular coagulation
DIP	desquamative interstitial pneumonitis
2,3 DPG	2,3 diphosphoglycerate, present in erythrocytes in equimolar quantities as hemoglobin

Droplet nuclei	minute particles transmitted between humans by sneezing or cough, containing virus particles or tuberculous organisms
DVT	deep venous thrombosis
Eaton-Lambert syndrome	myasthenia-like syndrome primarily associated with small-cell carcinoma
Ecthyma gangrenosum	necrotic skin lesions associated with *Pseudomonas* bacteremia
Elastance	restorative forces tending to move lung and chest wall toward the resting position
EMG	electromyogram, electromyography
Empyema	presence of pus in the pleural space
Eosinophilia	increase in number of circulating eosinophils, with total eosinophil count usually greater than $400/mm^3$
Erythema nodosum	subcutaneous nodules, often on the anterior tibial surface, associated with tuberculosis, sarcoidosis, and fungal infections
FEF_{50}/FIF_{50}	flow at 50% VC during a forced expiratory maneuver or forced inspiratory maneuver
Ghon lesion	calcified nodule in the lower lobes appearing on chest x-ray, presumably the primary site of tuberculous infection
GIP	giant-cell interstitial pneumonitis
Glomectomy	carotid body resection, formerly performed for asthma
Hb	hemoglobin
hCG	human chorionic gonadotropin, occasionally associated with bronchogenic carcinoma
Helium dilution	method for determining lung volumes, in which the subject breathes a fixed quantity of helium in a closed circuit
Hering-Breuer reflex	decreased frequency of respiratory efforts caused by continuous distention of the lungs in animals (inhibito-inspiratory reflex)
hPL	human placental lactogen, occasionally associated with bronchogenic carcinoma

HPOA	hypertrophic pulmonary osteoarthropathy, subperiosteal new bone formation in distal portions of long bones associated with carcinoma and other chronic diseases
Hysteresis	variation in forces across the lung depending upon volume history—e.g., inspiration or expiration
ILD	interstitial lung disease
IMV	intermittent mandatory ventilation
Inertance	opposition to gas flow caused by inertia of the gas
INH	isoniazid
IPH	idiopathic pulmonary hemosiderosis
IPPB	intermittent positive-pressure breathing
Lateral position test	assessment of pulmonary function, with the diseased lung dependent, to determine suitability for resection
LDH	lactic dehydrogenase
LIP	lymphocytic interstitial pneumonitis
Lobar pneumonia	pneumonia with an airspace focus, usually gram-positive
Löeffler's syndrome	nonsegmental parenchymal infiltrate and peripheral eosinophilia
Mantoux	method for intradermal injection for skin testing
Mesothelioma	asbestos-associated neoplasm of pleura or peritoneum
Miliary tuberculosis	disseminated tuberculosis, often appearing as multiple tiny nodules on chest x-ray
MSH	melanocyte-stimulating hormone
Nosocomial infection	hospital-acquired infection
Oncotic pressure	colloid osmotic pressure
Ondine's curse	automatic ventilatory dysfunction, with apnea during sleep but not during waking
OT	old tuberculin
P_{50}	partial pressure of oxygen at which hemoglobin is 50% saturated
PCWP	pulmonary capillary wedge pressure
PE	pulmonary embolism

PEEP	positive end-expiratory pressure
Pickwickian syndrome	syndrome of obesity and hypoventilation
Plethysmography	method for determining FRC, in which the subject breathes in a sealed chamber and pressure or volume changes are measured
Pleurodesis	instillation of an irritant agent to eradicate the pleural space
PMN	polymorphonuclear leukocyte
Pneumonia/pneumonitis	inflammatory process involving the lung parenchyma
PPD	purified protein derivative
PSS	progressive systemic sclerosis
$P{v_{O_2}}$	partial pressure of mixed venous oxygen
RA	rheumatoid arthritis
Ranke complex	unilateral hilar adenopathy accompanied by a Ghon lesion
REM/NREM	rapid eye movement/non-rapid eye movement sleep
Respiratory exchange ratio(R)	the ratio of V_{CO_2} exhaled to V_{O_2} taken up; at steady state equivalent to RQ, respiratory quotient
Resistance	opposition to flow, defined as driving pressure divided by volume flow rate
Reynolds number(Re)	dimensionless number describing flow in a rigid tube as laminar or turbulent
Riley-Day syndrome	familial dysautonomia, possibly associated with hypoventilation
Runyon class	classification of non-tuberculous mycobacteria
SGOT	serum glutamic oxaloacetic transaminase (also alanine aminotransferase)
Shunt	blood transported from right to left heart without undergoing gas exchange
SIADH	syndrome of inappropriate antidiuretic hormone, associated with bronchogenic carcinoma
SIDS	sudden infant death syndrome
Simon's focus	apical calcified lesion, presumably the focus of tuberculous infection

SLE	systemic lupus erythematosus
$S_{O_2}T$	systemic oxygen transport
Spirometry	measurement of airflow in terms of volume per unit time
Surfactant	phospholipid lining on the alveolar surface that reduces surface tension
Sympathomimetics	drugs with actions similar to sympathetic nervous system stimulation—e.g., tachycardia
Thrombolysis	therapy for thromboembolic disease utilizing streptokinase or urokinase
Tine test	multiple puncture technique for tuberculosis skin testing
TNM	tumor-node-metastasis system for cancer staging
Toxic erythema	macular exanthem associated with coccidioidomycosis
Type I cell	squamous lining cell of alveoli similar to capillary endothelial cells
Type II cell	cuboidal lining cell of alveoli secreting surfactant
UIP	usual interstitial pneumonitis
V/Q inequalities	suboptimal matching of ventilation and perfusion in the lung
V/Q scan	ventilation/perfusion scan, an isotopic technique incorporating a xenon inhalation scan and a perfusion scan obtained by injection of labeled microspheres or albumin macroaggregates
VSD	ventricular septal defect

Index

Note: Page numbers followed by the letter "*t*" refer to tables.

ABG. See Arterial blood gases.
ABPA. See Allergic bronchopulmonary aspergillosis.
"Absorption atelectasis," causes of, 97
Acanthosis nigricans, 252
ACE. See Angiotensin-converting enzyme.
Acid-base equilibrium
 alteration of, 28
 approaching disorders of, 30-31
 maintenance of, 27-28
 mechanisms affecting, 30-31
Acidemia
 defined, 28
 and resistance, 23
Acidosis, respiratory
 in chronic bronchitis, 71
 defined, 28
 in emphysema, 71
 treating, 93
Acids
 elimination of, 28
 production of, 28
Acinar infiltrate, and sarcoidosis, 235
Acinetobacter species, 170
Adenocarcinoma
 growth characteristics of, 250*t*
 and neuromuscular disorders, 252
 radiographic characteristics of, 256*t*
 and smoking, 248
 treatment of, 264, 265*t*
Adhesion, 166
Adult respiratory distress syndrome (ARDS)
 alterations in lung function caused by, 114-16
 causes of, 111-12
 defined, 111
 diagnosis of, 114
 effects of PEEP in, 122*t*, 123
 fluid management in, 121-23
 hypoxemia in, 90
 pathogenesis of, 111-14
 pathophysiologic subgroups in, 116*t*
 and pneumonia, 152, 158
 prognosis for, 123-24
 treatment of, 116-23
Airflow, in ILD, 218*t*
Airway morphometry, and resistance, 9
Airways. See also Chronic airways obstruction; Small airways dysfunction.

Airways (Cont.):
  identifying abnormalities in, 36
  resistance in, 38
Albuterol, use of, in treating asthma, 53, 55, 59
Alcoholism, and pneumonia, 140, 150, 157
Alkalemia
  and asthma, 48
  and chronic bronchitis, 79
  defined, 28
  and emphysema, 79
Alkalosis
  and ARDS, 114
  and chronic bronchitis, 79
  defined, 28
  and emphysema, 79
  and mechanical ventilation, 101
Allergic bronchopulmonary aspergillosis (ABPA), 56
  clinical findings in, 230
  diagnosis of, 230
  treatment of, 230
Allergic granulomatosis. *See also* Churg-Strauss syndrome.
  characteristics of, 224, 228*t*
  diagnosis of, 224
  treatment of, 224
Alpha$_1$-antitrypsin deficiency, and emphysema, 65, 66
Altered chest wall configuration, respiratory failure and, 104
Alveolar-arterial oxygen difference test, 38
Alveolar gas composition test, 38
Alveolar hypoventilation, 303, 304, 305-06*t*. *See also* Chronic bronchitis; Emphysema.
  complications of, 309
  diagnosis of, 308-09
  treatment of, 309-10
Alveolar ventilation, 3, 4, 13; defined, 303
Alveoli, 1, 6
Alveolitis
  acute, 214
  chronic, 214
  and idiopathic interstitial pneumonitis, 219
  and ILD, 213-14
Aminophylline. *See* theophylline preparations.
Amniotic fluid embolism, 289-90
Ampicillin, use of, in treating pneumonia, 150, 153*t*
Anaerobes, role of, in pneumonia, 151
Analgesia, postoperative use of, 298
Anemia, and lung cancer, 253, 255*t*
Anesthesia, surgical use of, 298
Angiitis. *See* Allergic granulomatosis.
Angiotensin-converting enzyme (ACE), use of, in treating sarcoidosis, 237
Ankylosing spondylitis, and pulmonary involvement, 223
Antibiotics
  role of, in pulmonary disease, 242
  use of, in treating ARDS, 116
  use of, in treating bullous disease, 83
  use of, in treating chronic bronchitis and emphysema, 78, 79
  use of, in treating empyema, 161
  use of, in immunocompromised patients, 180
  use of, in treating ILD, 219
  use of, in treating pneumonia, 152, 153-54*t*, 160
Anticoagulants, use of, in treating ARDS, 123
  thromboembolic disease, 286*t*
Antigens, and asthma, 44, 45
Antimicrobial therapy, effect of, on pneumonia, 138, 160
Antineoplastics, and ILD, 240, 242
Antiplatelet agents, use of, in treating thrombosis, 283
Apnea, causes of, 27, 75
ARDS. *See* Adult respiratory disease syndrome.
Arsenic, and lung cancer, 248

Arterial blood gases (ABG)
  effect of mechanical ventilation on, 99, 105
  role of, in diagnosing respiratory failure, 92, 92t
  use of, in oxygenation, 132
Asbestos, and lung cancer, 247, 248
Aspergillus species, role of, in fungal pneumonias, 172
Aspiration. *See also* biopsy.
  gastric, 193, 194
  needle, 142, 143, 180, 257, 258t, 269
  role of, in ARDS, 112
  role of, in pneumonia, 151
  postoperative, 297
  transtracheal, 142, 143, 151, 160
Aspiration pneumonia, 158-59
Asthma
  and ABPA, 230, 231
  and allergic granulomatosis, 224
  and alterations in lung function, 47-49
  causes of, 43, 44, 45, 56t
  characteristics of, 36
  chronic, 55, 56, 57, 59
  compared to COPD, 63
  complications of, 55
  defined, 43
  diagnosis of, 43, 46-47, 46t
  emergency therapy for, 52
  etiology of, 45-46
  extrinsic and intrinsic, 45t
  high-risk, 54
  and hospitalization, 52, 53
  use of mechanical ventilation for, 103-04
  natural history of, 59
  pathophysiology of, 43-45
  prognosis for, 59
  symptoms of, 46
  treatment of, 45, 49-59, 58t
Atelectasis
  in ARDS, 113, 115
  in bronchogenic carcinoma, 256t
  characteristics of, 299
  in patients with altered chest wall configuration, 104
  prevention of, in postoperative patients, 298
  in sarcoidosis, 235
  and SLE, 221
Atropine, use of, in treating asthma, 53
Auramine-rhodamine fluorochrome stain, 193

Bacille Calmette-Guérin (BCG), 190, 196
Bacteremia, 166, 170
Bacteria. *See also* Bacterial infection.
  and chronic bronchitis, 78-79
  and pneumonia, 137, 138, 146-47, 150, 158
  role of, in chronic intracellular infection, 166
  in the upper respiratory tract, 137
Bacterial infection, 166, 169-71
Bagassosis, 232t
Balloon occlusion of pulmonary artery, 296
Barotrauma
  and mechanical ventilation, 100
  and PEEP, 121
"base excess," concept of, 30
BCG. *See* Bacille Calmette-Guérin.
Beclomethasone dipropionate, 57, 59
Berylliosis, 217
Beta-thalassemia, 167
Bichromates, 248
Biopsy. *See also* Aspiration.
  needle, 215, 257, 268
  open lung, 142-43, 215, 237
  transbronchial, 215, 237
  use of, in diagnosing bronchogenic carcinoma, 253, 257, 258, 259t, 268
  use of, in diagnosing ILD, 215
  use of, in diagnosing pleural effusions, 324

Biopsy (Cont.):
　use of, in diagnosing sarcoidosis, 235, 237
　use of, in immunocompromised patients, 179-80
BIP. See Broncholitic interstitial pneumonitis.
Bird fancier's lung, 232t
Bischloromethyl ether, 248
Blastoma. See mixed tumors.
Blastomyces dermatitidis, 207
Blastomycosis
　causes of, 207
　diagnosis of, 208
　natural history of, 208
　treatment of, 208
Bleomycin, 240
Blood pH, normal, 28
"Booster effect," defined, 190
Botulism, 308
Boyle's law, and plethysmography, 34, 35
Bradykinin, 24
Bronchial adenoma, 266
Bronchial vessels, 24
Bronchial wall, 11
Bronchiolitic interstitial pneumonitis (BIP), 220
Bronchitis, 36. See also Chronic bronchitis
Bronchoalveolar lavage, use of, in diagnosing
　ILD, 216
　sarcoidosis, 237
　UIP, 220
Bronchocentric granulomatosis, 227, 228t
Bronchodilators, use of, 36-38, 49, 73, 74, 219
Bronchogenic carcinoma. See also Cancer, lung; Neoplasms.
　complications of, 264-65
　defined, 247
　diagnosis of, 259-60
　extrapulmonary manifestations of, 254-55t, 268
　incidence of, 247

　growth characteristics of, 250t
　histologic patterns of, 249
　and smoking, 248
　systemic effects of, 249-53
Bronchoscopy, use of,
　in diagnosing bronchogenic carcinoma, 253, 257, 258t
　in diagnosing tuberculosis, 193-94
　in immunocompromised patients, 180
Bronchospasm, and asthma, compared, 43
Buffers, role of, in acid-base metabolism, 28
Bullous disease, 82
Busulfan, 240

Cancer, lung. See also Bronchogenic carcinoma; Neoplasms.
　and pneumonia, 157
　risk factors in, 247-48
Candida species, role of, in fungal pneumonia, 173
Caplan's syndrome. See Pneumoconiosis.
Carbon dioxide. See also Gas exchange; Hypercapnia.
　effect of diffusion limitation on, 20
　generation of, 20
　and Haldane effect, 21-22
　transport of, 21
Carbonic acid, formation of, 28
Carbon monoxide, uses of, in measuring diffusion capacity, 39
Carbon monoxide poisoning
　oxygenation for, 133
　respiratory failure in, 103
Carcinoembryonic antigen (CEA), 256
Cardiac dysfunction, and pulmonary edema, 177. See also Congestive heart failure.
Cardiac output, effect of stress on, 130

CEA. *See* carcinoembryonic antigen.
Central nervous system, and respiratory failure, 90. *See also* nervous control.
Cephalosporins, use of, in treating pneumonia, 149, 150, 151
Cheesewasher's lung, 232*t*
Chemical pleurodesis, use of, for pleural effusions, 330
Chemotaxis, 166
Chemotherapy. *See also* Drugs.
  use of, in treating lung cancer, 263-64
  use of, in treating tuberculosis, 194, 201*t* 202
Chest tube drainage, use of, for pleural effusions, 330
CHF. *See* Congestive heart failure.
Chlamydiae, and pneumonia, 137
Chronic airways obstruction. *See also* Chronic bronchitis; Emphysema.
  causes and treatment of, 76-77, 83
  cor pulmonale and, 80
Chronic bronchitis. *See also* Bronchitis.
  clinical manifestations of, 67
  complications of, 78-83
  and cor pulmonale, 80-81
  defined, 63
  diagnosis of, 63, 67, 69
  effect of, on cardiac function, 71
  effect of, on lung function, 70-72
  and emphysema, compared, 67, 69, 70*t*
  etiology of, 64-65
  functional abnormalities of, 73*t*
  mortality in, 84-85
  natural history of, 83, 84*t*
  pathogenesis of, 65, 66
  and pneumonia, 140*t*, 157
  prognosis for, 83, 84
  respiratory failure in, 79-80
  treatment of, 72-77, 83

Chronic eosinophilic pneumonia, 229-30
Chronic obstructive pulmonary disease (COPD). *See also* Chronic airways obstruction; Chronic bronchitis; Emphysema.
  diagnosis of, 43
  types of, 63
Churg-Strauss syndrome, and asthma, 46. *See also* Allergic granulomatosis; Angiitis.
Chylothorax, and pleural effusions, 330
Chylous effusions, 328
Cirrhosis, and pleural effusions, 325, 329
Clear cell carcinoma, 266
Clinical syndromes, use of, in diagnosing pneumonia, 144
Clubbing
  and lung cancer, 249, 254*t*
  and mesothelioma, 335
Coal dust, and lung cancer, 248
Coccidioides immitis, 205
Coccidioidomycosis
  clinical findings of, 205-06
  diagnosis of, 206
  epidemiology of, 205
  treatment of, 206
Coffee worker's lung, 232*t*
Collagen
  and compliance, 5
  and ILD, 214
Collagen-vascular disease
  defined, 221
  and pleural effusion, 328
  pulmonary manifestations of, 225*t*
  types of, 221-24
Colloid osmotic pressure (COP), and pleural effusions, 317
Compliance, lung
  effects of anesthesia and surgery on, 293
  effect of ARDS on, 115, 116

Compliance, lung *(Cont.)*:
  effect of asthma on, 48
  effect of diffuse infiltrates on, 179
  effect of PEEP on, 119, 120
  in emphysema, 70
  forces determining, 5
  structural basis for, 5
Computed tomography, 260. *See also* Tomography.
Continuous positive airways pressure (CPAP)
  defined, 117
  effects of, 117
COPD. *See* Chronic obstructive pulmonary disease.
Cor pulmonale
  causes of, 80, 81
  described, 80, 81
  pathogenesis of, 80, 81
  treatment of, 81, 83
Corticosteroids
  and emphysema, 74, 83
  side effects of, 57
  use of, in treating ARDS, 123
  use of, in treating asthma, 49, 50, 53, 55, 56, 59
  use of, in treating chronic bronchitis, 74, 83
  use of, in treating ILD, 217-18
  use of, in treating sarcoidosis, 237
  use of, in treating tuberculosis, 203
Cough. *See also* Sputum.
  role of, in host defense, 137
  as symptom of pulmonary disease, 167, 169, 172
  in tuberculosis, 192
CPAP. *See* Continuous positive airways pressure.
Cromolyn sodium, 50
  side effects of, 59
  use of, in treating asthma, 57
Cryoglobulinemia, essential mixed, and pulmonary involvement, 223, 224, 237

Cryptococcus neoformans, role of, in fungal pneumonias, 172-73
Cushing's syndrome, and bronchogenic carcinoma, 251, 254*t*
Cyanosis, and ARDS, 114
Cystic fibrosis
  characteristics of, 36, 167
  and pneumonia, 140*t*
Cytomegalovirus, role of, in viral influenza, 174

Deep venous thrombosis (DVT)
  incidence of, 273
  risk factors of, 274, 275*t*
Dermatomyositis, pulmonary involvement in, 223, 225*t*
Desquamative interstitial pneumonitis (DIP), 219, 220, 221
Dextran, 283
Diabetes mellitus
  and hypoventilation, 308
  and miliary tuberculosis, 195
  and pneumonia, 149, 150, 157
  role of, in tuberculosis reactivation, 187, 192
Diaphragm, 2
Diaphragmatic dysfunction, and SLE, 221
Diaphragmatic electromyogram, diagnostic use of, 309
Diffusing capacity test, 39, 40*t*
Diffusion
  factors in, 15
  in ILD, 217
Digitalis, 81
DIP. *See* Desquamative interstitial pneumonitis.
Disulfiram, 135
Diuretic therapy
  and ARDS, 122
  in immunocompromised patients, 180
  in chronic airways obstruction, 83

in cor pulmonale, 81
in hypercapnia and metabolic alkalosis, 79
Doghouse disease, 232t
Doppler ultrasonography, 277
Drug overdose
 and ARDS, 112
 and pneumonia, 149
Drugs. See also Chemotherapy; individual drugs.
 effect of, on immunocompromised patient, 167, 176, 177t
 and pleural effusions, 328
 role of, in eosinophilic pulmonary disease, 230
 role of, in treating tuberculosis, 197, 198-99t, 200
 use of, in treating ILD, 218
 use of, in treating nontuberculous micobacterial disease, 204
DVT. See Deep venous thrombosis.
Dynamic compression, 9-10
Dyskinesias, 307
Dyspnea
 in ARDS, 114
 in ILD, 215
 role of, in diagnosis of emphysema, 69

Eaton-Lambert syndrome, 252, 254t
ECMO. See Extracorporeal membrane oxygenation.
Edema, pulmonary
 and ARDS, 112, 115, 123
 in immunocompromised patient, 167, 177
 and SLE, 221
Elastance, 1, 2, 4, 6
Elastic recoil
 effect of asthma on, 48
 effect of emphysema on, 65, 66
 process of, 9-10, 11
Elastin, and compliance, 5
Electroencephalography, and sleep study, 314

Electrolyte imbalance, 101
Electrooculography, and sleep study, 314
Emphysema
 characteristics of, 36
 and chronic bronchitis, compared, 67, 69, 70t
 clinical manifestations of, 67
 compliance in, 5
 complications of, 78-83
 and cor pulmonale, 80-81
 defined, 63
 diagnosis of, 63, 67, 69
 effect of, on cardiac function, 71
 effect of, on lung function, 70-72
 etiology of, 64-65
 functional abnormalities of, 73t
 and histoplasmosis, 207
 mortality in, 84-85
 natural history of, 83, 84t
 pathogenesis of, 65, 66
 and pneumonia, 140t, 157
 prognosis for, 83, 84
 respiratory failure in, 79-80
 treatment of, 72-77, 83
 types of, 66
Empyema
 defined, 160
 diagnosis of, 159, 160
Endobronchial metastases, 266
Endotoxin, 135
Eosinophilia
 peripheral, 43, 73
 sputum, 73
 tropical, 230
Eosinophilic granuloma, airflow in, 217; See also Eosinophilic lung diseases.
Eosinophilic lung diseases, 217, 227, 229t, 229-31
Epidermoid carcinoma. See Squamous carcinoma.
Epinephrine, use of, in asthma, 49, 50, 51t, 52, 57
Erythrocytes
 effect of increased capillary permeability on, 113

Erythrocytes *(Cont.)*:
role of, in carbon dioxide transport, 21
Erythrocyte sedimentation rate (ESR), use of, in diagnosing ILD, 215
Erythrocytosis, 76
Erythromycin, use of, in treating pneumonia, 147, 148, 149, 154*t*
ESR. *See* Erythrocyte sedimentation rate.
Ethambutol, 203, 204
Exercise, role of, in treating chronic bronchitis, 72, 77
emphysema, 72, 77
Exercise testing, 39, 41, 217
Expiration, 1, 2
Expiratory flow limitation, 11
Extracorporeal membrane oxygenation (ECMO), 103
Exudates, 322, 322*t*

Face tent, 131, 132
Familial dysautonomia, 307
Farmer's lung, 232*t*
Fat embolism, 289
Fever, diagnostic role of, 178
Fiberoptic bronchoscopy, 142, 143. *See also* Bronchoscopy.
Fibrinolytic therapy, 284-85, 286*t*
Fibrosis. *See* pulmonary fibrosis.
Fick principle, and pulmonary circulation flow, 23
Fluid exchange, pulmonary, process of, 24, 25
Fishmeal worker's lung, 232*t*
Forced Vital Capacity (FVC), measuring, 35
FRC. *See* Functional residual capacity.
Functional residual capacity (FRC)
in ARDS, 115, 116
defined, 2, 4*t*
Fungal infections. *See also* Fungal pneumonias; Fungi.
in immunocompetent hosts, 205-08
in immunocompromised patients, 166, 179
Fungal pneumonias
in immunocompromised patients, 172-73
in normal persons, 172
Fungi, 137, 139
FVC. *See* Forced vital capacity.

Gallium scanning, 237, 260
Gas exchange. *See also* diffusion; Shunt; Ventilation/perfusion (V/Q).
effect of anesthesia and surgery on, 294, 300*t*
effect of ARDS on, 115
effect of asthma on, 48
effect of chronic bronchitis on, 73*t*
effect of DIP and UIP on, 220
effect of emphysema on, 73*t*
effect of ILD on, 214, 216, 217, 218*t*
effect of mechanical ventilation on, 100
effect of neoplasms on, 261
effect of obesity on, 311*t*
effect of PEEP on, 118
effect of pneumonia on, 152
effect of stress on, 130
evaluation of, 38-39
models of, 19
normal, 13
process of, 1, 3, 12-13
and respiratory failure, 92-93
Gas pressure, pulmonary, 14*t*
Gastrectomy, and tuberculous reactivation, 187
Gastrointestinal bleeding, and respiratory failure, 102
Genetic predisposition, and chronic bronchitis and emphysema, 64
Genioglossal EMG, use of, in sleep study, 314

Ghon lesion, 186
Giant cell carcinoma, 266
Giant cell interstitial pneumonitis (GIP), 220-21
Giardiasis, 166
GIP. See Giant cell interstitial pneumonitis.
Glomerulonephritis
 and Goodpasture's syndrome, 238
 and Wegener's granulomatosis, 226
Goodpasture's syndrome, 237
 clinical findings of, 238
 defined, 238
 diagnosis of, 238
 treatment of, 238
Gram stain. See also Sputum.
 use of, in diagnosing bacterial pulmonary infection, 170, 171
 use of, in diagnosing pneumonia, 141, 143, 151
 use of, in immunocompromised patient, 179
Granulocyte function
 defects in, 168t
 in immunocompromised patient, 165-66
Gynecomastia, 251, 254t

Haldane effect, 21, 22
Hamartomas, 267
Heart failure. See Congestive heart failure (CHF)
Helium dilution, use of, in measuring volume, 33-34
Hematite, 248
Hematologic disease, 112
Hemopneumothorax, 332
Hemoptysis, and bronchogenic carcinoma, 264
Hemorrhage, in immunocompromised patient, 167, 177
Hemothorax, and pleural effusions, 330
Henderson-Hasselbalch equation, 28, 30

Heparin,
 low-dose ("miniheparin"), 283
 studies regarding use of, 284-85
 use of, in treating ARDS, 123
 use of, in treating thromboembolic disease, 283-84, 286t, 288
Hepatitis, and antituberculous drugs, 200
Hering-Breuer reflex, 25
Herpes simplex, role of, in viral pneumonia, 74
Herpes varicella-zoster, role of, in influenza, 174
Hilar adenopathy, 235
Histamines
 effect of, on bronchial vessels, 24
 use of, in diagnosing asthma, 47
Histoplasmosis, 205
 clinical findings for, 206-10
 diagnosis of, 207
 epidemiology of, 206
 pathogenesis of, 206
 treatment of, 207
Hodgkin's disease
 and lung neoplasms, 267
 and pneumonia, 155, 172, 175
Horner's syndrome, 268
Host defenses, 167
 and pneumonia, 137-38
 and tuberculosis, 185
HPO. See Hypertrophic pulmonary osteoarthropathy.
Humidifier lung, 232t
Hydration
 in asthma treatment, 52
 in diagnosing pneumonia, 143-44
Hypercalcemia, and bronchogenic carcinoma, 254t
Hypercapnia
 and apnea, 27
 and asthma, 52, 54
 causes of, 20, 92, 99
 and chronic bronchitis, 71, 72, 75, 79
 and cor pulmonale, 80

Hypercapnia *(Cont.)*:
and emphysema, 71, 72, 75, 79
and respiratory failure, 89
use of oxygen in treating, 97, 133
Hypereosinophilic syndrome, 230
Hyperpigmentation, and bronchogenic carcinoma, 251-52, 254*t*
Hypersensitivity pneumonitis (extrinsic allergic alveolitis)
clinical findings of, 231
defined, 231
known causes of, 232-33*t*
laboratory studies in, 231, 234
treatment of, 234
Hypersomnia, 311, 313*t*
Hypertension, pulmonary
causes of, 217, 223
and RA, 222
Hypertrophic pulmonary osteoarthropathy (HPO), 252, 335
Hyperventilation, 303
Hypervolemia
causes of, 99
and PEEP, 119, 122
and pleural effusions, 329
Hypocapnia
and ARDS, 114
treating, 93
Hypocarbia, and asthma, 48
Hypogammaglobulinemia, 166; and pneumonia, 147
Hypokalemia, 308
Hypophosphatemia, 308
Hypoventilation. *See also* Alveolar hypoventilation.
causes of, 306-08
and hypercapnia, 20
Hypoxemia
abnormalities caused by, 75*t*
amelioration of, 20
and ARDS, 114, 115, 116
and asthma, 48, 49, 52
causes of, 18, 92-93, 99
and chronic bronchitis, 71, 75, 83

and cor pulmonale, 83
effects of increased oxygen concentration on, 18, 19
and emphysema, 71, 75, 83
and ILD, 217
and pleural effusions, 329
and pneumothorax, 332
and respiratory failure, 89
and surgery, 294
use of oxygen in treating, 75, 76, 93
Hypoxic constriction of pulmonary vessels, 17-18
Hysteresis, 5

Idiopathic interstitial pneumonitis
defined, 219
pathogenesis of, 219
treatment of, 220, 221
types of 220, 221
Idiopathic pulmonary hemosiderosis (IPH). 237
clinical findings of, 238
diagnosis of, 238-39
treatment of, 239
ILD. *See* Interstitial lung disease.
Immunocompromised patient
effects of drugs on, 177*t*
etiology of pulmonary infiltrates in, 169*t*
and histoplasmosis, 207
immune defects in, 168*t*
infection in, 166-67
leukoagglutinin reaction in, 176
pulmonary disease in, 165-82
Immunosuppression, role of, in tuberculosis reactivation, 187, 192
Immunotherapy, use of, for lung neoplasms, 264
Impedance plethysmography, 277
IMV. *See* Intermittent mandatory ventilation.
Incentive spirometry, postoperative use of, 299. *See also* Spirometry.
Inertance, 1

Infection
  fungal, 205-08
  in immunocompromised patient, 165-67
  and mechanical ventilation, 101
  role of, in ARDS, 111, 123
  role of, in chronic bronchitis and emphysema, 77, 78-79, 82, 83
  role of, in pneumonia, 137-139
  subclinical mycobacterial, 186
Inflammatory diseases, effect of, on ventilation, 308
Influenza, 138, 140t, 141, 146; in immunocompromised patients, 173-74, 178
Infrapulmonary effusion, 319
INH. See Isoniazid.
Innvervation, structures of, 25
Inspiratory vital capacity, 4t
Intercostals, 2
Interferon, 174
Intermittent mandatory ventilation (IMV), 98, 99
Intermittent nocturnal apnea, 311
Intermittent positive pressure breathing (IPPB)
  in emphysema, 75
  postoperative, 299
Interstitial lung disease (ILD). See also Idiopathic interstitial pneumonitis; Pulmonary fibrosis
  causes of, 214t
  clinical manifestations of, 215
  defined, 213
  diagnosis of, 215-16
  effects on lung function of, 216-17, 218t
  and lung cancer, 248
  pathogenesis of, 213-14
  treatment of, 217-19
Intubation, use of,
  in oxygen transport, 131
  in treating ARDS, 117
  in treating astyma, 54, 55
  in treating respiratory failure, 93, 94

IPH. See Idiopathic pulmonary hemosiderosis.
IPPB. See Intermittent positive pressure breathing.
Irritant receptors, pulmonary, 25, 26t
Isoetharine, use of, in treating asthma, 50, 51t, 53, 55, 59
Isoniazid (INH)
  and hepatitis, 200
  use of, during pregnancy, 203
  use of, in treating tuberculosis, 195, 196, 197, 198-99t, 200
Isoproterenol, use of, in treating asthma, 50, 51t, 53, 55

Jejunoileal bypass, role of, in tuberculosis reactivation, 187
Juxtacapillary ("J") receptors, 25, 26t

Kidneys, role of, in acid-base metabolism, 28
Kyphoscoliosis, 36

Laminar flow, 9
Laplace relationship, 6
Large-cell carcinoma
  and neuromuscular disorders, 252
  treatment of, 264, 265t
Larynx, 7
Lateral position test, 296
Legionnaire's disease, 324
Leukemia
  functional antibodies in, 166
  and lung parenchyma, 175-76
  and pulmonary hemorrhage, 177
  treatment of, 178
Leukoagglutinin reactions, in immunocompromised patients, 167
Limited Wegener's granulomatosis. See also Lymphomatoid granulomatosis; Wegener's granulomatosis.

Limited Wegener's granulomatosis (*Cont.*):
  clinical findings of, 226, 228*t*
  diagnosis of, 226, 228*t*
  treatment of, 226
LIP. *See* Lymphocytic interstitial pneumonitis.
Listeria monocytogenes, 171
Löffler's syndrome
  clinical findings of, 229
  definition of, 227
  diagnosis of, 229
  etiology of, 229*t*
  role of drugs in, 230
  treatment of, 229
Lung abscess, 159-60
Lung capacity, defined, 2, 4*t*
Lung collapse, causes of, 6
Lungs, role of, in acid-base metabolism, 28
Lupus-like syndrome, drug-induced, 242
Lymphatic network, role of, in fluid exchange, 24
Lymphocytic interstitial pneumonitis (LIP), 220
Lymphomatoid granulomatosis
  clinical findings of, 227, 228*t*
  diagnosis of, 227, 228*t*
  treatment of, 227

M. africanum, 185
Malt worker's lung, 232*t*
Mantoux administration, 189, 190
Maple bark disease, 232*t*
M. avium-intracellulare, 203, 204
M. avivum, 185
Maximal expiratory flow-volume (MEFV) curves, uses of, 35-36
Maximal voluntary ventilation (MVV), 38
M. bovis, 185
Mediastinoscopy, 260
Medulla, role of, in regulating respiration, 27

MEFV curves. *See* Maximal expiratory flow-volume curves.
Meigs's syndrome, 328
Mesothelioma, 328, 335
Metacholine, 47
Metaproterenol sulfate, use of, in treating asthma, 50, 51*t*, 53, 57, 59
Metastatic lesions,
  therapy for, 267-68
  types of, 267*t*
Methotrexate, 242
Miliary tuberculosis
  clinical presentation of, 195
  defined, 194
  diagnosis of, 195
  laboratory findings of, 195
  predisposing factors in, 195
  signs of, 195
  symptoms of, 195
  treatment of, 195
Mill worker's lung, 232*t*
M. intracellulare, 185
Mixed tumors ("blastoma"), 266
M. kansasii, 203, 204
Monocyte-macrophage system, 167
Mouth occlusion pressure, 309
M. tuberculosis, 185, 187, 189, 196
Mucocutaneous barriers, 168*t*
Multiple myeloma
  functional antibodies in, 166
  and pulmonary involvement, 176
Muscular dystrophies, effect of, on ventilation, 308
Mushroom worker's lung, 232*t*
Myasthenia gravis, effect of, on respiratory muscle response, 308
Mycobacteria. *See also* Mycobacterial diseases.
  described, 185
  infection by, 186
  and sarcoidosis, 234
Mycobacterial diseases. *See also* Fungal diseases; Mycobacteria; Mycobacterial infection; Tuberculosis.

characteristics of, 209t
definition of, 185
diagnosis of, 187, 189-95
etiology of, 185-86
fungal, 205-08
incidence of, 185
nontubercular, 190, 203-04
pathology of, 185-87, 188t
treatment of, 195-97, 198-99t, 200, 201t, 202-03
Mycobacterial infection, in immunocompromised patient, 171-72
Myopathies, 252
Mycoplasmas
and chronic bronchitis, 78
and pneumonia, 137, 138, 140
treatment of, 152

Nasal cannula, 131, 132
Neoplasia. *See also* Neoplasms.
and immunocompromised patient, 167, 176, 179
and miliary tuberculosis, 195
Neoplasms, lung. *See also* Neoplasia.
benign, 247, 267
and bronchial adenoma, 266
clinical presentation of, 249, 251-53
complications of, 264-66
defined, 247
diagnosis of, 253, 256t, 256-58, 258t, 259t, 259-60
effect of, on lung function, 261
etiology of, 247-48
incidence of, 247
and metastatic lesions, 267-69, 267t
pathogenesis of, 248-49
prognosis for, 262-64, 265t
therapy for, 262-64, 265t
unusual forms of, 266-67
Nephrotic syndrome, and pleural effusions, 329
Nervous control
of pulmonary muscle arteries, 23
of respiration, 27, 90

Neurofibromatosis (von Recklinghausen's disease), 219
Neuromuscular disorders, and bronchogenic carcinoma, 252
Neuropathies, 252
Neutrophils, 165-66
Nickel, and lung cancer, 248
Nocardia species, 171
Nodules, pulmonary, and lung carcinoma, 268
Non-rapid eye movement (NREM) sleep, 312
Nutrition, role of, in immunocompromised patient, 167, 181

Obesity, and respiratory failure, 104
Obesity-hypoventilation (Pickwickian) syndrome,
clinical findings and diagnosis in, 310
pulmonary function in, 310
respiratory complications of, 311t
treatment of, 311
Old tuberculin (OT), 189
Ondine's curse, 304, 306
Oropharynx, and resistance, 7
OT. *See* Old tuberculin.
Oxygen. *See also* Oxygen diffusion; Oxygen transport; Oxygen therapy.
apparatus for delivery of, 131-32, 132t
and hypoxemia, 18
interaction of drugs with, 135
procedures for use of, 96-97
toxicity of, 133-35, 135t
use of, in sleep study, 314
Oxygen therapy
apparatus used in 131-32, 132t
goals for, 134t
and hypoxia, 93, 130
monitoring, 132-33
physiologic processes of, 127
and stress, 130

Oxygen therapy (Cont.):
  in treating acidosis, 93
  in treating ARDS, 117
  in treating asthma, 52
  in treating bronchitis, 75, 85
  in treating carbon monoxide poisoning, 103
  in treating ILD, 219, 240
  use of, with mechanical ventilators, 102
Oxygen diffusion, 39
Oxygen transport, 127-30

Paraneoplastic syndromes, and bronchogenic carcinoma, 249-53, 266
Parasites, and pleural effusions, 328
Parasitic pneumonias, in immunocompromised patient, 174-75
Parenchyma, lung
  and ILD, 213
  in immunocompromised patient, 175, 176
  mycobacterial infection in, 187
  and pneumonia, 137
Parenteral aminophylline dosage, for asthma, 50t
PCWP. See Pulmonary capillary wedge pressure.
PE. See Pulmonary embolism.
Peak expiratory flow rate (PEFR), 35
PEEP. See Positive end-expiratory pressure.
Penicillin. See also Semi-synthetic penicillin.
  and pulmonary edema, 242
  use of, in treating pneumonia, 147-48, 149, 150, 152, 153t, 159
Periarteritis nodosa, and pulmonary hemorrhage syndrome, 237
Phagocytosis, 166
Phycomycetes, role of, in fungal pneumonias, 173

Physiologic dead space test, 38, 93, 99, 100
Physiotherapy
  postoperative, 298
  preoperative, 298
  use of, in chronic bronchitis and emphysema, 74, 75, 77
  use of, in ILD, 219
  use of, in pneumonia, 152, 155
Pickwickian syndrome. See Obesity-hypoventilation syndrome.
Plasmacytoma, 266
Plethysmography, 34-35
Pleural biopsy, 194
Pleural effusion
  clinical manifestations of, 318-20
  definition and pathophysiology of, 317-18
  diagnosis of, 319, 320-24
  effects of, on pulmonary function, 329
  etiology of, 321t, 325-29, 326-27t
  in sarcoidosis, 235
  treatment of, 329-30
Pleural fluid
  in empyema, 160
  in pneumonia, 143
  in tuberculosis, 194
  white blood cell count in, 323t
Pleurectomy, use of, for pleural effusions, 330, 333
Pleuritis
  and RA, 222
  and SLE, 221
Pneumoconiosis (Caplan's syndrome), 222
Pneumocystis infections, in immunocompromised patient, 174, 182
Pneumonectomy
  functional effects of, 299, 300t
  postoperative problems of, 300-01
Pneumomediastinum, 332
Pneumonia. See also Immuno-

compromised patient;
Pulmonary disease.
alterations in lung function
caused by, 152
aspiration, 158-59
causes of, 137
clinical categorizations of, 144
complications of, 147, 148, 151
and coccidioidomycosis, 205
defined, 137
diagnosis of, 140-52
and empyema, 152, 160-61
extrapulmonary manifestations
of, 145t
and lung abscess, 159-60
mortality from, 156
natural history of, 155
nosocomial, 138, 139, 178
pathogenesis of, 137-40
and pleural effusions, 325
predisposition to, 166
prevention of, 155
prognosis for, 155-56
radiographic patterns of, 144t
recovery from, 156
recurrent, 156-57
and right middle lobe syndrome,
157-58
signs of, 141
symptoms of, 140, 146, 148t
treatment of, 145, 147, 150,
151, 152-55, 159
Pneumonitides, noninfectious, 137
Penumonitis. See also Hypersensitivity pneumonitis;
Radiation pneumonitis.
acute, 221
airflow in, 217
and bronchogenic carcinoma,
256t
Pneumotachygraph, use of, in sleep
study, 314
Pneumothorax
causes of, 331t
chronic, 332
clinical presentation of, 331
complications of, 332

definition and etiology of, 331
diagnosis of, 331-32
treatment of, 332-33
use of mechanical ventilation for,
104-05
Pollution, and chronic bronchitis
and emphysema, 64
Polymyositis, 252, 255t, 308;
pulmonary involvement in,
223, 255t
Positive end-expiratory pressure
(PEEP)
and chest x-ray, 121
defined, 117
effects of, 117-19, 123
monitoring, 119-20
volume status and, 120
weaning from, 121, 122
Positive pressure breathing, 299
Positive pressure ventilators, 95-
96, 117
Postoperative complications, 297-
99
PPD. See Purified protein derivative.
Preventive therapy, in immunocompromised patients, 181
Pro-ACTH, and lung cancer, 256
Progressive systemic sclerosis (PSS)
clinical syndromes in, 222-23
complications of, 223
pulmonary manifestations of,
217, 225t
Prostaglandin receptors, 44
Protein-calorie malnutrition, 167
Pseudomonas infections, 170, 182
PSS. See Progressive systemic
sclerosis.
Pulmonary alveolar proteinosis,
140t
Pulmonary angiography, 280
Pulmonary artery catheter, 41
Pulmonary capillary wedge pressure
(PCWP)
and PEEP, 120-21, 122
role of, in mechanical ventilation, 102, 105

Pulmonary capillary wedge pressure (*Cont.*):
    use of, in diagnosing ARDS, 114, 116
Pulmonary disease
    in immunocompromised patient, 165-82
    infectious, 165-67
    signs of, 167
    symptoms of, 167
Pulmonary embolism (PE)
    diagnosing, 179, 278-81
    effect of, on lung function, 282
    electrocardiographic findings in, 279t
    in immunocompromised patients, 167, 176
    and pleural effusions, 328
    radiographic findings in, 279t
    resolution of, 288
    treatment of, 283
Pulmonary fibrosis
    and ARDS, 123
    characteristics of, 36
    compliance in, 5
    diagnosis of, 216
    and hypocapnia, 90
    and hypoxemia, 140
    and idiopathic pulmonary hemosiderosis, 238
    and ILD, 213, 214, 219
    and interstitial pneumonitis, 221
    and pneumonia, 140
    and RA, 222
Pulmonary function tests
    types of, 33-40
    uses of, 33-35, 73, 215, 216, 222, 226, 231, 234, 314
Pulmonary hemorrhage syndromes, 237-39
Pulmonary infiltrates
    causes of, 169-75
    diagnosis of, in immunocompromised patients, 178-80
    etiologies of, 167, 169t
Pulmonary mycosis
    characteristics of, 209t
    types of, 205
Purified protein derivative (PPD), 189, 190, 191, 194, 196
Pyopneumothorax, 332

RA. *See* Rheumatoid arthritis.
Radiation pneumonitis. *See also* Pneumonitis.
    clinical findings of, 239-40
    in immunocompromised patients, 176
    incidents of, 239
    natural history of, 241t
    risk factors for, 239t
    treatment of, 240
Radiation therapy, use of,
    for bronchogenic carcinoma, 263
    for immunocompromised patient, 167
Radioactive material, and lung cancer, 248
Radiography, diagnostic use of
    for lung abscess, 159
    for lung cancer, 253, 256t
    for nontuberculous mycobacterial disease, 203
    for pleural effusions, 319
    for pulmonary infiltrates, 169, 175, 178
    for sarcoidosis, 192
Radioisotope venography, 277
Radiolabeled fibrinogen, 277
Radionuclide studies, use of, in diagnosing ILD, 216
Ranke complex, 186
Rapid eye movement (REM) sleep, 312
Raynaud's phenomenon, 222
REM. *See* Rapid eye movement sleep.
Resistance, 1, 2, 6-7, 11. *See also* Resistance equation.
    in bullous disease, 82
    effect on ARDS on, 116
    effect of ILD on, 216-17
    in pulmonary vasculature, 22-23
    in respiratory failure, 92
Resistance equations, 7, 8t
Respiration, 27
Respiratory drive, drugs affecting, 307t

Respiratory dysfunction. *See also* Respiratory failure.
  in asthma, 54
  detecting, 36-38
  patterns of, 36
Respiratory failure
  alterations in lung function caused by, 92-93
  in asthma, 103-04
  in carbon monoxide poisoning, 103
  in chronic airways obstruction, 104
  defined, 89
  diagnosis of, 90-92
  mortality of, 105
  natural history of, 105
  in obesity, 104
  pathophysiology of, 89-90, 91t
  in patients receiving mechanical ventilation, 105, 106t
  in patients with altered chest wall configuration, 104
  in pneumothorax, 104
  postoperative, 104
  prognosis for, 105
  role of nutrition in, 102-03
  signs and symptoms of, 90
  treatment of, 93-103
Respiratory muscles, 2
Reticuloendothelial function, 167, 168t
Reticulonodular infiltrate, in sarcoidosis, 235
Reynolds number, 9
Rheumatoid arthritis (RA), 222, 225t
Rickettsiae, 137
Rifampin, 200, 203
Right middle lobe (RML) syndrome, 157-58
Riley-Day syndrome, 307
RML. *See* Right middle lobe syndrome.

Sarcoidosis
  airflow in, 217
  clinical findings of, 234-35
  diagnosis of, 216, 235, 237
  etiology of, 234
  incidence of, 234
  laboratory and pulmonary function tests of, 235
  necrotizing, 227, 228t
  radiographic stages of, 235
  systemic manifestations of, 236t
  treatment of, 218, 237
Sarcoma, primary, 266
Scalenes, 2
Scanning, ventilation
  radionuclide, 281
  serial, 281
  use of, in diagnosing PE, 280, 281
Scleroderma, 252-53
Sedation, use of, in treating asthma, 54
  respiratory failure, 97
Semi-synthetic penicillin, use of, in treating pneumonia, 150, 152, 153t, 159
Septic embolism, 288-89
Sequoiosis, 232t
Serologic diagnosis, use of, for bronchogenic tumors, 256
  ILD, 215-16
Serratia marcescens, 170
Serum, 165
Shock, and ARDS, 111
Shunt
  and ARDS, 115, 117
  characteristics of, 15
  in chronic bronchitis and emphysema, 71
  and hypercapnia, 20
  and hypoxemia, 90, 93
  in ILD, 217
  and PEEP, 120
  in pneumonia, 152
SIADH. *See* Syndrome of inappropriate antidiuretic hormone.
Sickle cell anemia
  effect of, on reticuloendothelial system, 167
  and pneumonia, 147
SIDS. *See* Sudden infant death syndrome.

Silicosis, and tuberculosis, 187, 192, 203
Simon's foci, 187
Sinusitis, 166
Sjögren's syndrome, 223
Skin testing
   for fungal diseases, 205, 206, 207
   for nontuberculous mycobacterial disease, 203-04
   for tuberculosis, 194
SLE. See Systemic lupus erythematosus.
Sleep. See also sleep apnea syndromes.
   defined, 312
   study of, 314
Sleep apnea syndromes
   characteristics of, 312
   clinical findings of, 313t
   complications of, 313
   defined, 311
   diagnosis of, 313-14
   mechanisms of, 312
   treatment of, 314
Small airways dysfunction, in respiratory disease, 38, 216
Small-cell carcinoma
   growth characteristics of, 250t
   and neuromuscular disorders, 252
   radiographic characteristics of, 256t
   treatment of, 263-64, 265t
Smoking
   and chronic bronchitis, 64, 72, 83
   and emphysema, 64, 65, 72, 83
   and lung carcinoma, 247, 248, 261, 268
Sniff test, 308
Snoring, 313
Solute exchange, pulmonary, 24, 25
Spirometry
   measurements in, 35
   use of, in diagnosing alveolar hypoventilation, 308
   use of, in diagnosing emphysema and chronic bronchitis, 69
   use of, in measuring volume, 35
Splenectomy, 147, 167
Sputum. See also Gram stain; Sputum culture.
   in fungal disease, 206, 207
   in immunocompromised patient, 165, 170, 179
   in pneumonia, 141, 143, 145, 146, 147, 151, 159
   in tuberculosis, 192, 193
Sputum culture, use of, in diagnosing
   bronchogenic carcinoma, 253, 256
   fungal disease, 206, 207, 208
   tuberculosis, 193
Squamous cell carcinoma
   growth characteristics of, 250t
   and hypercalcemia, 258
   and neuromuscular disorders, 252
   radiographic characteristics of, 256t
   treatment of, 264, 265t
"Standard bicarbonate," 30
Starling equation, 25
Starling forces, 317
Starling resistor, 16
Static lung volumes. See Volumes, lung.
Sternocleidomastoids, 2
Steroids, use of, in treating
   ABPA, 230
   allergic granulomatosis, 224
   asthma, 56, 57
   dermatomyositis, 223
   DIP, 220
   ILD, 218
   limited Wegener's granulomatosis, 226
   necrotizing sarcoidosis, 227
   polymyositis, 223
   UIP, 220
Streptokinase, 286t
Stress, and oxygen transport, 130
Stretch receptors, 25, 26t
Subclinical infection, 186, 187
Suberosis, 232t

Sudden infant death syndrome (SIDS), 306
Sulfonamides, and pulmonary edema, 242
Superoxide, 135
Surgery, 297-99
Sympathomimetics, use of, in treating
  asthma, 49, 51t, 53, 56, 57, 59
  chronic bronchitis and emphysema, 74, 83
Syndrome of inappropriate antidiuretic hormone (SIADH), 251, 254t
Systemic lupus erythematosus (SLE), 216
  clinical syndromes in, 221
  and pulmonary hemorrhage syndromes, 237
  pulmonary manifestations of, 225t
Systemic vasculitis, 237

Tachypnea, 25, 114
T-cell defects, 166
Tension pneumothorax, 332, 333
Terbutaline sulfate, use of, in asthma, 49, 50, 53, 55, 57, 59
Theophylline preparations, use of, in treating
  asthma, 49, 53, 56, 57, 58t, 59
  chronic bronchitis and emphysema, 74, 83
Thermistor, 314
Thermography, 277
Thoracentesis, 160, 320
Thrombocythemia, 253
Thrombocytopenia, 253, 284
Thromboembolic disease. *See also* Pulmonary embolism.
  clinical signs of, 276t
  defined, 273
  diagnosis, of 275-81
  effect of, on lung function, 282
  etiology of, 273
  incidence of, 273
  natural history of, 287
  pathogenesis of, 274-75
  prognosis for, 288
  treatment of, 282-85, 286t, 287
  types of, 288-90
Thrombophlebitis, 253, 255t
Tidal volume
  defined, 2
  in ILD, 217
  monitoring, during mechanical ventilation, 105
Tine testing, 189, 194
T lymphocytes, 166
TNM. *See* Tumor-node-metastasis.
Tomography, 260, 268. *See also* Computed tomography.
Toxoplasma gondii, 175
Tracheostomy, 310
Transfusion, in ARDS, 122
Transudates, 322, 322t
Trauma, in ARDS, 111
Tuberculin, 187, 189
Tuberculosis
  causes of, 171, 185
  diagnosis of, 178, 187, 191, 192, 193, 194
  diseases associated with, 171, 248
  effect of drugs on, 197, 198-99t
  incidence of, 185
  miliary, 194-95
  natural history of, 188t
  and pleural effusions, 325, 328
  prevention of, 195
  primary, 191-92
  reactivation of, 187
  secondary, 192, 193
  transmission of, 186
  treatment failure in, 200, 201t, 202
  treatment of, 172, 195-203
Tumor-node-metastasis (TNM), 257, 259t
Turbulent flow, 9

UIP. *See* Usual interstitial pneumonitis.

Ultrasound, 160. *See also* Doppler ultrasonography.
Upper extremity venous thrombosis, 288
Urokinase Pulmonary Embolism Trial, 284
Usual interstitial pneumonitis (UIP), 219, 220

Vancomycin, 150
Vasculature, pulmonary
  and bronchial circulation
  chemical effects on, 24t
  dynamic properties of, 22-23
  effect of ARDS on, 114, 116, 119
  effect of asthma on, 49
  effect of chronic bronchitis and emphysema on, 73t
  effect of ILD on, 217, 218t
  effect of obesity on, 311t
  effect of pneumonectomy on, 300t
  effect of respiratory failure on, 93
  hemodynamic effects on, 24t
  humoral effects on, 24t
  nervous control of, 23
  neurological effects on, 24t
  nonrespiratory functions of, 22
Vasculitides, pulmonary, 224-27
Vasculitis, and ILD, 215
Venography, 276, 277
Ventilation. *See also* Alveolar ventilation.
  and air volume, 23
  collateral, 12
  control of, 27
  distribution of, 11
  effects of disease on, 17, 48, 71, 73t
  interdependent mechanisms of, 12
  pleural pressure, 11
  process of, 1
  regional compliance and resistance, 11
  tracheobronchial asymmetry, 11

Ventilation, mechanical
  complications of, 100-02
  contamination of, 170
  diagnosis and therapy for patients receiving, 106t
  effects of, 99-100
  indications for use of, 94t
  procedure of, 94-96
  respiratory distress during, 105
  use of, in respiratory failure, 93, 94
  use of, in ARDS, 117
  weaning from, 97-99
Ventilation/perfusion (V/Q)
  and ARDS, 115
  effect of chronic bronchitis and emphysema on, 71
  effects of oxygen concentration on, 19, 97
  effect of pneumonia on, 152
  effect of surgery on, 294
  and gas exchange, 16
  and hypercapnia, 20
  and hypoxemia, 90, 93
  and ILD, 217
  measurement of, 18
  mechanisms limiting, 17-18
  use of, in diagnosing PE, 280
Venturi mask, 131, 132
Viral infection, 166
Viral pneumonia, 173-74
Virchow's triad, 273
Viruses
  and chronic bronchitis, 78
  and pneumonia, 137, 138, 139, 140, 146
Volumes, lung
  ascertaining, 33-35
  defined, 2, 4t
  effect of anesthesia on, 293, 300t
  effect of ARDS on, 114-15
  effect of asthma on, 48
  effect of chronic bronchitis and emphysema on, 69, 70, 73t
  effect of diffuse infiltrates on, 179

effects of interstitial disease on, 216, 217, 218*t*
effect of mechanical ventilation on, 99
effect of neoplasms on, 261
effect of obesity on, 311*t*
effect of pleural effusions on, 329
effect of pneumonia on, 152, 158
effect of respiratory failure on, 92
effect of SLE on, 221
effect of resistance on, 9, 23
von Recklinghausen's disease. *See* Neurofibromatosis.
V/Q. *See* Ventilation/perfusion

Warfarin, 283, 286*t*
Wegener's granulomatosis
    clinical findings of, 224-25, 228*t*
    diagnosis of, 226, 228*t*
    pathology of, 224
    and pulmonary hemorrhage syndromes, 237
    treatment of, 219, 226
Woodpulp worker's disease, 232*t*

X-rays, chest
    and PEEP, 121
    use of, in diagnosing ARDS, 114
    use of, in diagnosing DIP and UIP, 220
    use of, in diagnosing fungal diseases, 205, 207, 208
    use of, in diagnosing ILD, 215, 216
    use of, in immunocompromised patients, 179
    use of, in diagnosing lung cancer, 249, 253, 260
    use of, in diagnosing nontuberculous mycobacterial disease, 203
    use of, in diagnosing pleural effusions, 319
    use of, in diagnosing pneumonia, 140, 141, 143, 144, 145, 146, 147, 149, 150, 151, 157, 169, 170
    use of, in diagnosing respiratory failure, 92
    use of, in diagnosing tuberculosis, 192-93

Ziehl-Neelsen strain, 193